LAND USE POLICY

LAND USE POLICY

ALEXANDER C. DENMAN
AND
OLIVER M. PENROD
EDITORS

Nova Science Publishers, Inc.
New York

For permission to use material from this book please contact us:
Telephone 631-231-7269; Fax 631-231-8175
Web Site: http://www.novapublishers.com

LIBRARY OF CONGRESS CATALOGING-IN-PUBLICATION DATA
Available upo nrequest

ISBN: 978-1-60741-435-3

Published by Nova Science Publishers, Inc. ✢ New York

CONTENTS

PREFACE

Land use is the human modification of natural environment or wilderness into built environment such as fields, pastures, and settlements. More recent significant effects of land use include urban sprawl, soil erosion, soil degradation, salinization, and desertification. Land use and land management practices have a major impact on natural resources including water, soil, nutrients, plants and animals. This new book presents a global perspective on this issue and provides research on scientific databases developed using remote sensing and geospatial analysis of retrospective and prospective scenarios that have facilitated the development of land use planning and policies towards sustainable development. Research is also presented on how agricultural land use change has led to a lowering of the diurnal temperature range.

Chapter 1 - California has long been a leader in both its attempts to preserve land devoted to agricultural production and in its approach to funding its state and local governments. Recently it has become the leader in crafting a statewide policy to reduce the amount of greenhouse gases generated within its border.

California's Williamson Act of 1965 allows the payment of lower local property taxes by farmers and ranchers for a 10 year renewable term in exchange for agreeing to keep their land in agricultural production or open space. The Open Space Subvention Act of 1972 provides for the state to partially reimburse county governments directly for the property taxes foregone under this program, and indirectly reimburse school districts. The California Farmland Conservancy Program (CFCP) of 1996 uses grant funding to permanently protect farmland in exchange for conservation easements that compensate the landowner based upon the appraised value of lost development rights and other restrictions. Started in 1998, the Williamson Act Easement Exchange Program allows the release of agricultural land from a previous Williamson Act contract if it enters into an agricultural conservation easement through the CFCP or through other state agencies that also engage in the purchase of agricultural conservation easements. Furthermore, the "Super Williamson Act" of 1998 allows agricultural property to enroll for a 20 year term in exchange for property tax payments that are 35 percent less than under the Williamson Act.

Chapter 2 - The population growth, rapid industrialization and changing life styles in India have made the development of land use policies very critical. The social, economic and ecological imperatives have become the interwoven driving forces of land use planning to meet resources requirements, developmental activities and global change .The challenges of land use policy in India today is to meet the food security for 46 M people living below poverty line through integrated land use management practices, development of scientific planning and mechanisms to resolve conflicting land use systems and conservation of natural habitats, biodiversity and carbon sequestration to sustain ecosystem services and goods.

The paper presents how scientific databases developed using remote sensing and geospatial analysis of retrospective and prospective scenarios using prognostic and diagnostic methods have facilitated the development of land use planning and policies towards sustainable development. These efforts include development of geospatial databases and integrated analysis of natural resources, socioeconomics, infrastructure and environmental data to facilitate natural resources planning, suitability assessment, visualization for alternatives; smart growth planning, impact analysis and land use decision support systems.

Integrated Mission for Sustainable development, watershed development, comparative evaluation and prioritization of tribal areas, urban growth planning studies under taken in India using multi thematic remote sensing based information in conjunction with ancillary information provides how land use planning efforts are facilitated at local and regional level to meet food and water security. Coastal zone regulation, protected area development and monitoring, development of Special Economic Zones and delineation of eco-sensitive areas are a few other examples where land use planning has been effectively facilitated to address environmental security. Studies on river basin ecology, carbon sequestration and biodiversity being conducted at decadal scales for the entire nation using satellite remote sensing and agent based change models are aimed to provide various scenarios of impact of land use planning and policies.

Chapter 3 - During the last century, a deep discontinuity occurred in urban growth patterns: a break between the pre-existent urban development model, where building growth was led by the planning rules typical of compact cities, and the following model characterizing the contemporary town where growth has exponential speed, and incoherent and chaotic forms. This phenomenon, commonly called urban sprawl, interests almost all the main urbanized areas of the world, even if its evolution has had different origins and paths in the diverse geographic areas. Studies that until now have examined the history of contemporary urbanization appear varied and composite in relation to the different cultural and social settlement situations in which urbanization took hold. Each context seems to be the result of a different creative process, of several heterogeneous stories describing diverse events, knowledge and habits. It is important to highlight, as this chapter observes, how territories of deeply different cultural, economic, and social points of view, through different evolutionary trajectories, have produced spaces with similar characteristics. The homologation of the results seems to be in contrast with the multiplicity of trajectories that produced them, but different stories could have common threads that can be tied again to build one single story. This chapter rewrites the fragmentary history of urban sprawl in the light shed by those who can be considered the homogenizing factors helping to define the domain of any trajectory of urban evolution. To reconstruct a single story from all different urban histories is needed to define action systems and strategies aiming at imposing an organizing structure on the spaces of the urban sprawl. Current strategies are discussed and some new ones are proposed for the existing suburbs. The thesis intervention in diffused urbanization can't be reduced to the identification of spaces to be transformed and activities to be introduced. It is a more complex work requesting active involvement of the community to define spaces able to give rise to new identities.

The main results include a new approach to urban sprawl study, the identifying and the role of the forces underlying urban sprawl, and the identifying of a system of actions on different levels to intervene in urban sprawl.

Chapter 4 - During the last decades Mediterranean systems are being affected by important land use changes which are transforming the entire landscape. Traditional irrigated lands have constituted one of the most characteristic agro-landscapes in the Mediterranean and have played a relevant socio-economic, ecological and environmental role. However, these valuable agro-landscapes are progressively decaying due to recent socio-economic changes which, at the same time, are promoting new irrigated lands outside the river valleys. These new irrigated lands have a major effect on land, water resources, landscape and the biodiversity value of extensive tracts of the Mediterranean area. At the same time, Mediterranean drylands are quickly disappearing due to land abandonment. In addition, Mediterranean areas are suffering a quick urbanisation process affecting both natural and agricultural areas. These trends may be considered as a reduction of the most characteristically rural Mediterranean landscape to favour ecologically extreme landscapes: on one side the natural areas and on the other side the new irrigated lands and urban areas. It is necessary, therefore, to understand the factors driving the land use changes in the Mediterranean, to analyse their ecological effects and to explore the potential implications of several policies regarding land use and natural resources.

To this aim, we have analysed the land use changes and their socio-economic and environmental context in three study cases in Southeastern Spain, an arid Mediterranean area where the four above-mentioned land use changes are taking place. These study cases are the traditional irrigated land of Murcia, the agricultural system of Mazarron-Aguilas and the land use changes in the Mar Menor watershed. The ancient Murcia irrigated lands constitutes a paradigmatic example of the loss of this valuable agro-landscape and its highly fertile soils due to the urbanisation process and spread of infrastructures. The Mazarron-Aguilas new irrigated lands may be considered as representative of the most intensive agricultural systems in the Mediterranean area, which are quickly spreading at the expense of drylands and natural areas. The Mar Menor watershed have suffered important agricultural and urban-tourist land use changes affecting the hydrological and nutrient dynamics and the biological communities of the coastal lagoon and associated wetlands. An integrated approach has been applied combining GIS, Remote Sensing, spatial and environmental modelling and dynamic system models to analyse the sustainability of these three case studies, the spatial and temporal patterns of land use, the main socio-economic and environmental driving factors and their ecological implications.

Chapter 5 - In this chapter we develop a spatially explicit economic land-use model that gives insights into the determinants of land-use patterns and how these patterns are affected by policy changes. The model explicitly takes into account the decision-making process as to why and where farmers convert the use of forest land. This is different from previous spatially disaggregated models – such as simulation models – where the underlying decision-making process is imposed. The micro-economic focus in this paper is crucial for understanding the ongoing human-induced land-use change process and is essential in the land-use change literature – that is dominated by natural scientists focusing on geophysical and agro-climatic processes. Our model is extremely valuable to inform land-use policy as it specifies how individual decision makers will react to policy and other exogenous changes in their environment and how this response will alter the landscape.

The model is derived from the von Thunen-Ricardo land rent model that describes land-use patterns as a result of variability in geophysical land attributes and differences in location and transport costs. However, this model is valid only under certain assumptions and is less suited to describe land-use patterns in forest frontier areas characterized by semi-subsistence agriculture and imperfect markets. We refine the model to account for the fact that agricultural prices and wages might be endogenously determined and households cannot be considered as profit maximizing agents.

We empirically estimate the model for a forest-frontier area in Indonesia using a combination of data from satellite image interpretation, GIS data and a socio-economic survey data. The results demonstrate that differences in Ricardian land rent are important in determining spatial land-use patterns. However, we do not find evidence in support of the von Thunen idea that land-use patterns are determined by differences in transport costs. Rather the labor intensity of land-use systems, population levels, the access to technology and household characteristics matter. This has important implications for forest conservation and land-use policy. In addition, the refinement of the von Thunen-Ricardo land rent model – which incorporates more realistic descriptions of economic behavior – is justified by the empirical results.

Chapter 6 - Studies around the world have shown that there is a significant correlation between children's personal development and the neighbourhood environment in which they are brought up. While the neighbourhood environment is a master set of a vast number of interdependent and intermingled variables, one particular factor, the urban land use environment, sometimes tends to be overlooked. In fact, all other neighbourhood variables work inside the framework of land use settings as all human activities take place on and above land and certainly within some form of physical structure. On the other hand, land use settings are constantly shaped and reformed by the urban land policies devised by the public sector through different channels. This chapter attempts to provide some insights into this particular aspect through a qualitative analysis. A major youth survey is carried out, and the views of young people on two major aspects of land use settings are collated. In the micro-system, the extent to which young people enjoy the urban land use environment is examined through an urban experience analysis. In the macro level, their views on whether and how the physical land use environment affects them are tallied. We find that urban land use environment in the neighbourhood does impose important impacts on young people, and young people do recognise this. However, they seem to be unable to capitalize the benefits of "routine activities" due to various reasons, and the management of public space is a major reason. In general, there is inadequate government effort in trying to stimulate young people's interest in contributing to the debate of urban land use policy, making most young children rather indifferent on a number of socio-economic land use issues.

Chapter 7 - Spatiotemporal analysis of land use/land cover is crucial in formulating an appropriate set of actions in landscape management and in developing appropriate land use policies. On the other hand, understanding the interaction between landscape pattern and land use policy is important to reveal the detrimental consequences of land use change on soil and water quality, biodiversity, and climatic systems. This study focuses on the spatial and temporal pattern analysis of land use/land cover change in the Sarıyer Forest Planning Unit surrounding the district of Sarıyer in a megacity of Istanbul, Turkey. The spatio-temporal pattern of the study area was evaluated with Geographical Information System and FRAGSTATS to assess the change over 31 years. As a result of population increase and urbanization, the Sarıyer district expanded very fast and many changes in land use/land covers between 1971 and 2002 were realized. As an overall change, there was a net decrease of 1243 ha in total forested areas compared to a net increase of 1331 ha in settlement areas. However, both forest areas with full crown closure and regenerated or young forest areas increased due mainly to reforestation of degraded forests and agricultural areas and the conversion of coppice forests to high forests. In terms of spatial configuration, analysis of the metrics revealed that landscape structure in Sarıyer forest planning unit changed substantially over the 31-year study period, resulting in fragmentation of the landscape as indicated by the higher number of large patches and the smaller mean patch sizes. In conclusion, understanding of the factors affecting the land use/land cover is increasingly important for the design and planning of urban areas and the sustainable management of natural resources.

Chapter 8 - Land is the scarcest resource in Bangladesh economy. The average land-person ratio is only 0.12 ha which is inadequate to sustain livelihood of an average farm household. The present chapter paper provides a detailed analysis of the agricultural land use changes at the national level in Bangladesh over a 34 year period (1973-2006) and examines the trends in productivity, crop diversity and its link towards achieving self-sufficiency in food production. Results revealed that agricultural land use in Bangladesh became intense reflected by an increase in cropping intensity from only 142.9% in 1973 to 176.9% in 2005 facilitated by an increased provision of irrigation infrastructure to diffuse a rice-based Green Revolution technology package throughout the country. Although total cereal production (dominated by rice) has increased substantially, productivity of crops per unit of key inputs (i.e., land area, fertilizers, and pesticides) has been declining consistently over the years, thereby, raising doubt on the sustainability of the agricultural sector. Contrary to expectation, crop diversity seems to have increased over the years. Also, Bangladesh seems to have achieved the goal of self-sufficiency in food production, mainly contributed by a boost in foodgrain production. However, concentration of energy availability from cereals as opposed to non-cereals raises concern on the dietary health of the Bangladeshi population. Bangladesh needs to widen its technology base and go beyond the diffusion of a single crop of HYV rice and should diversify its land use towards producing non-cereals, which are more profitable and could enhance farmers' earnings and livelihoods as well as generate valuable foreign exchange for the economy through exports.

Chapter 9 - Land use change has been an inevitable consequence of human activities throughout the centuries. One of the most prominent impacts of human activities can be found in agricultural expansion and resultant modification of the natural landscape. Numerous observed data- and model-based studies have shown that agricultural land use change has modified meteorological, seasonal, and climate-scale root zone soil moisture distribution, energy partitioning, near surface energy balance, and temperature. The most typical spatial scales include local and regional. Studies along a similar theme even suggest that these changes affect meteorological events (e. g., convective activities). In addition, widespread adoption and application of irrigation further enhances these impacts.

Based on the results from several of our own and numerous studies completed by others, the objective of this paper is to propose the concept of '*Agricultural Cool Island' (ACI)*. It is overwhelmingly evident that agricultural land use change has lowered mean maximum and extreme maximum temperatures. This, in turn, has led to a lowering of the diurnal temperature range. This temperature decrease occurred primarily due to changes in energy partitioning which are associated with changes in bio-physical characteristics of the landscape. In many cases the changes are related to changes in root zone soil moisture and its role in energy partitioning. Since this cooling is clearly evident and the most notable of all impacts, we coined the concept ACI.

As suggested above, lowering of temperature (which is an important aspect) is not the only impact of agricultural land use change. There are many other impacts of these modifications. The changes associated with the impacts can be dynamic over time and space. We note that ACI is both a self-contained and interactive entity. The feedback loops within this entity itself are non-linear and complex like other components of the earth system. In light of these, like urban heat island (UHI), we suggest that the concept of ACI should allow for more focused and organized scientific investigations. Furthermore, ACI should serve as a platform for well thought-out research activities.

Chapter 10 - There is a broad recognition that sustainable land management (SLM) is crucial for ensuring an adequate, long-term supply of food, raw materials and other services provided by the natural environment to the human society. However, to date, SLM practices are the exception rather than the rule in many parts of the world. Among the causes for unsustainable land management is a general lack of understanding of the economic costs of land degradation and the benefits of sustainable land management. This paper presents a methodological framework for analyzing the benefits of sustainable land management. The framework comprises three complementary types of assessment: partial valuation, total valuation and impact analysis. The first two allow for static assessment of selected respectively all economic benefits from a certain land use. The third approach is dynamic, and allows for analyzing the costs and benefits related to changes in land use. Each approach requires the application of a number of sequential methodological steps, including (i) ecosystem function and services identification; (ii) bio-physical assessment of ecosystem services; (iii) economic valuation; and (iv) ecological-economic modeling. The framework is demonstrated by means of a simple case study in the Guadalentin catchment, SE Spain.

In: Land Use Policy
Editors: A. C. Denman and O. M. Penrod

ISBN: 978-1-60741-435-3

Chapter 1

CALIFORNIA'S FARMLAND PRESERVATION PROGRAMS, TAXES, AND FURTHERING THE APPROPRIATE SAFEGUARDING OF AGRICULTURE AT THE URBAN FRINGE TO REDUCE GREENHOUSE GAS EMISSIONS*

Robert W. Wassmer†
Department of Public Policy and Administration
California State University, Sacramento, CA

1. INTRODUCTION

California has long been a leader in both its attempts to preserve land devoted to agricultural production and in its approach to funding its state and local governments. Recently it has become the leader in crafting a statewide policy to reduce the amount of greenhouse gases generated within its border.

California's Williamson Act of 1965 allows the payment of lower local property taxes by farmers and ranchers for a 10 year renewable term in exchange for agreeing to keep their land in agricultural production or open space. The Open Space Subvention Act of 1972 provides for the state to partially reimburse county governments directly for the property taxes foregone under this program, and indirectly reimburse school districts. The California Farmland Conservancy Program (CFCP) of 1996 uses grant funding to permanently protect

* Commissioned by the California Department of Conservation. Helpful comments were offered by Al Sokolow, Lareelle Burkham-Greydanus, Peter Detwiler, Fielding Greaves, Brian Leahy, Scott Limpach, and Charles Tyson on an earlier draft that made the final product better. Any errors that remain are my own. The opinions expressed here are also only my own and in no way represent the opinions of the California Department of Conservation

† Sacramento, CA 95819-6081; (916) 278-6304; rwassme@csus.edu; www.csus.edu/indiv/w/wassmerr

farmland in exchange for conservation easements that compensate the landowner based upon the appraised value of lost development rights and other restrictions. Started in 1998, the Williamson Act Easement Exchange Program allows the release of agricultural land from a previous Williamson Act contract if it enters into an agricultural conservation easement through the CFCP or through other state agencies that also engage in the purchase of agricultural conservation easements. Furthermore, the "Super Williamson Act" of 1998 allows agricultural property to enroll for a 20 year term in exchange for property tax payments that are 35 percent less than under the Williamson Act.

California's path down an alternative way of funding its state and local governments began with voter approval of Proposition 13 in 1978. As a result, local governments in the state dramatically reduced their reliance on property taxation and instead turned to greater revenue sharing from the state, the collection of fees, and the chasing after local sales tax revenue through local land use decisions that favor big-box retailers and auto malls ("fiscalization of land use"). After Proposition 13, the state garnered the revenue necessary for its greater support of local government through the establishment of statewide personal income and corporate income tax rates that are higher than in most other states.

With a 2005 Executive Order (S-3-05) from Governor Schwarzenegger declaring climate change a reality, California also became the policy leader among the states in efforts to reduce greenhouse gas emissions (GHGs). The Global Warming Solutions Act (AB 32, Nunez, 2006), passed by the California Legislature and signed into state law by Governor Schwarzenegger in 2006, requires the state to reduce its 2010 GHGs to 2000 levels; by 2020 to reduce them to 1990 levels; and by 2050 to reduce GHGs to 80 percent of 1990 levels. By early 2009, AB 32 also requires a specific plan that will achieve the required GHC emission levels through regulation, market mechanisms, and/or other actions. As noted by the Economic and Technology Advancement Advisory Committee (ETAAC, 2008, pp. 1-2) commissioned to advise the California's Air Resources Board on the implementation of AB 32, just over 40 percent of the state's current GHGs are generated in transportation activities. Thus, a reduction in automobile use is necessarily required if California desires to meet the GHG reductions required under AB 32. As described by Ewing *et al.* (2008), such a reduction in automobile use can only come about if Californians choose to live in more compact and mixed-use land use patterns that allow walking, biking, and mass transit as replacements for current automobile trips.

California's policy choices regarding state and local revenue reliance, farmland preservation, and reducing greenhouse gas emissions are interrelated. There is a concern among environmental and agricultural stakeholders that elements of the system of state and local taxation that developed in California after Proposition 13 discourages the retention of land in agriculture and this subsequently generates greater urban sprawl in the state. These same stakeholders point to the presence of the state's three major farmland conservation programs (and other programs and multiple policies throughout different codes) as encouraging the retention of agricultural land and thus resulting in less urban sprawl in the state. The overall purpose of this chapter is to examine these two claims in as unbiased a manner as academically possible and to offer an opinion on their validity. Such an opinion is necessary to offer an informed comment on the desirability of reforming the state's tax system, and/or expanding the state's system of farmland preservation, to reduce the degree of sprawl experienced in California and thus be better poised to achieve the reduction in GHGs mandated by AB 32.

The remainder of this chapter contains five additional sections. Section 2 offers a definition of urban sprawl, and how the presence of sprawl contributes to the generation of GHGs. The battle to reduce sprawl occurs at the urban/rural boundaries or "urban fringe" that surround urban areas. Land use at this fringe is often agricultural and if preserved appropriately, the spread of sprawl can be slowed or even stopped. Section 2 also looks at the available information on the likely effect of sprawl reduction on the generation of fewer GHGs in California.

Section 3 continues with a review of the California state and local taxes that some observers say encourages farmland conversion to non-agricultural uses. This section also examines the likely influence of the federal estate taxes and planned changes. Described are the mechanisms by which this greater farmland conversion could or could not occur due to California's choice of state and local tax instruments and the federal estate tax. Empirical evidence on the effect that these taxes have been shown to have on agricultural conversion is also described. Section 4 provides a description of California's farmland conservation programs and previous empirical studies that have examined the effects of farmland conservation programs in California and the United States.

Section 5 concludes with a summary of the available evidence on the influence that California tax and farmland conservation policies have on the appropriate conservation of agriculture land to reduce sprawl. Where the conclusion warrants that a specific tax or farmland conservation policy is likely generating greater sprawl, I suggest potential policy solutions to reduce this effect.

2. Urban Sprawl, Farmland Preservation, and GHGs

What is Urban Sprawl?

To consider the impact that California's system of taxes and farmland preservation programs has on the conversion of agricultural land, the impact this agricultural conversion has on the generation of urban sprawl, and the subsequent greater production of greenhouse gases that comes from urban sprawl, it is first necessary to clarify what is meant by urban sprawl. Urban sprawl is characterized here as low-density residential and "strip-mall" commercial development that is distant from an urban area's employment centers. Such non-contiguous and non-integrated forms of development at the fringe of a urban area concerns planners and policymakers due to the dependence it creates on the automobile for personal transportation and the driving distances necessary for the typical commute to work.

Economists have (see Brueckner, 2000; Mills, 1999; and Wassmer, 2008 as examples) described the following cause and effect occurrences as the primary reasons for urban sprawl. As population rises in an urban area of a fixed land area, it becomes more difficult to locate new residential and business activity in the area's existing employment centers. Land prices increase in these employment centers and new residents increasingly decide to tradeoff a longer commute to work for less expensive housing options at the fringe of the urban area. Even if an urban area experiences no population growth, as the real incomes of some existing residents rise, they often desire to live in larger houses and lots. The inexpensive land to build these on is more likely on the urban/rural fringe that surrounds urban areas. In addition, the "flight from blight" that occurs as residents that are more affluent seek the real and perceived lower crime rates and higher performing public schools outside of a metropolitan area's central places also generates urban sprawl. The construction of state and federally subsidized highways, and the relatively low private cost of using an automobile to get to work, has further facilitated urban sprawl.

Economics help us better understand why a household, where the primary and even secondary wage earner works in a metropolitan area's central place, decides to locate at the urban fringe and thus contribute to sprawl. A household makes a choice of residence by weighing the private benefits of a decentralized location (cheaper land to build a larger house with a larger lot on, perceived "better" public schools, lower crime rates, newer infrastructure, neighbors they would rather associate with, closer to public open space, etc.) against the private costs of this decentralized location (a longer and more expensive commute, greater traffic congestion in the commute, less urban amenities, etc.). If a household chooses to be a contributor to an urban area's sprawl, it has very likely determined that the private benefits of living on the urban/rural fringe of the area greater than the private costs. However, in making this decision it is unlikely that the household has fully considered the social costs (greater air pollution from a longer commute, greater freeway congestion, increased publicly-funded infrastructure costs, the social and economic isolation of the poor and/or racial/ethnic minorities left behind at the core of the metropolitan area, the social loss of prime agricultural land and/or open space valued at greater than its market price, etc.). The immortal words of a Pogo comic strip from Earth Day 1971 still rings true in regard to the primary cause of urban sprawl: "Yep son, we have met the enemy and he is us." But as Levine (1997, p. 280) points out: "What to one person is sprawl, to another is his/her home."

Economists refer to privately ignored social costs as negative externalities. Thus, a policy prescription often given by economists to reduce sprawl is to get housing consumers (or the developers that build houses for them) to consider the external costs of choosing a decentralized location through the payment of fees/charges equivalent to these social costs. As will be discussed later, fees are widely levied on developers and owners of newly built homes in California to help cover the additional cost of infrastructure constructed for them. But due to both the difficulty of determining the appropriate fees to charge and the strong political resistance to implement them, fees are rarely levied on fringe development to specifically cover the social costs just described. Policy activists interested in reducing urban sprawl have instead chosen to conceptualize forms of suburbanization in which they are certain that the total private and social costs of their development are greater than the total benefits.

The Sierra Club (1998) defines sprawl as low-density development beyond the edge of service and employment, which separates where people live from where they work and requiring cars to move between zones. Continuing this theme, the *Planning Commissioners Journal* (2002) describes urban sprawl as dispersed development outside of compact urban and village centers along highways and in the rural countryside. Downs (1998) recognizes urban sprawl by observable traits such as unlimited outward extension of new development, low density developments in new-growth areas, leapfrog development, and strip commercial development. Ewing (1994 and 1997) takes a very deliberate approach to conceptualizing urban sprawl. Surveying 15 academic articles on the subject, he found that the terms low-density, strip or ribbon, scattered, or leapfrog development are most often used by urban planners to characterize sprawl. Ewing lumps these characteristics under the term "non-compact development."

In California, where demographers at the State's Department of Finance anticipate that population will grow from 32.5 million in 2000 to near 50 million in 2025, the question of how to accommodate a greater than 50 percent increase in population in 25 years is widely asked.[1] How environmentally and fiscally feasible will it be to live and work in a state if a majority of its population growth continues to occur at low density at the fringe of its current urban areas?

How Sprawl Contributes to GHG Emissions

Urban sprawl is low density residential development far removed from the major employment centers in a urban area. As discussed in Frumkin, Frank, and Jackson (2004), such lower density (or less compact development) forces residents on more frequent trips, limits their transportation options, and greatly increases the necessity of owning an automobile. Residents must travel outside of their neighborhood to work, and to consume office, retail, entertainment, and other service activities because there is very little mixing of the non-residential land uses with housing subdivisions.

As noted in Frumkin (2002, pp. 202-203), carbon dioxide emissions (CO_2) account for about 80 percent of the green house gases emitted in the United States. Transportation activities result in about one-third of all of CO_2 emissions in the country. Noteworthy is the fact that transportation activities generated as much as 60 percent of all CO_2 emissions in California (see www.smartgrowthamerica.org/documents/State_Emissions_by_Sector). As described in Ewing *et al.* (2008), a policy to reduce CO_2 emissions in California (and thus achieve the ambitious GHG reductions mandated by AB 32) must stand on a "three-legged stool." One leg rests on improving fuel economy, a second on reducing the carbon content of fuels, and a third on reducing vehicle miles traveled (VMT). The necessity of improvements in the first two legs of this stool are widely discussed and being encouraged through public policy. The same cannot be said about the third.

VMT in the United States since 1980 has risen three times faster than the country's population. Observers attribute this to the increase in urban sprawl that occurred over the same period. This has led many to conclude (for an example see Steinbach, 2007) that technological advancements in fuel efficiency and the carbon content of fuel will not be enough to meet the ambitious goals for GHG reduction set by AB 32. VMT will need to come down, and this is only possible if Californians chose more compact and mixed-use forms of residential development.

California's Economic and Technology Advancement Advisory Committee (2008, p. 3-12), charged with coming up with a plan to reach the GHG goals laid out in AB 32, calls for the need to shift demand for VMT through greater smart growth planning:

---

[1] This paper takes this assumption as a given. An alternative approach could also look at ways to attack sprawl through policies designed to reduce California's future population growth.

> Planning measures can shift investments in housing and transportation infrastructure in a way that would reduce GHG emissions over the long term by providing desirable and low-GHG transportation options, largely by replacing automobile trips. Partnerships between the state government and regional and local agencies are critical to achieving these goals.

Furthermore, this same report notes the possibility of revising California's current farmland preservation policy to better meet the GHG reductions required by AB 32 (p. 3-14):

> The current Williamson Act mechanism, used to keep farmland in agricultural use and delay housing or commercial development may not provide sufficient incentives for farmland owners to prevent urban sprawl and halt the growth of VMT. A large share of Williamson Act land in San Joaquin County is in non-renewal status, for example..

Estimates of the Contribution of Sprawl Reduction to GHG Reduction

In a review of over 50 empirical studies on the relationship between compact development and automobile use, Ewing and Cervero (2001) report the consensus finding that the built environment one lives in as the most important determinant of vehicle miles traveled (VMT). Ewing, Pendall, and Chen (2003) specifically found, after accounting for income and socio-economic differences in 83 of the United State's largest metropolitan areas, that VMT was 25 percent less in compact metropolitan areas. After reviewing previous empirical literature on the topic, Ewing *et al.* (2008) report that it is reasonable to assume that individuals in a household located in an area with twice the prevalence of density, diversity of uses, accessible destinations, and interconnected street grids end up driving about one-third less. Studies such as these are the basis for the CalTrans estimate offered in the ETAAC (2008. p. 3-12) report that a family living in a compact transit village could reduce its household's VMT by 20 to 30 percent.

Ewing *et al.* (2008) also concur that residence in a compact, non-sprawled neighborhood results in a 30 percent reduction in VMT. This study uses an elaborate simulation model to predict that by 2050 total transportation related CO_2 emissions could fall by seven to 10 percent from current trends if a feasible percent of future development is steered toward mixed-use and high-density neighborhoods. They point out that by shifting just 60 percent of new development to a more compact form by 2030 would be equivalent to a 28 percent increase in federal vehicle efficiency standards (or the same as the new development being sprawl and all residents in the new sprawl driving a hybrid automobile). Of course, GHG emissions fall even further if instead new development is compact and residents of it drive a hybrid and used an automobile fuel with lower carbon content (or relied more upon mass transit, walking, or biking). Thus, the conclusion that reducing sprawl is an all important leg on the three legged policy stool absolutely necessary to meet the ambitious GHG mandates set by AB 32 for California.

The Appropriate Preservation of Agricultural Land to Reduce Sprawl

As noted by Daniels and Lapping (2005), there are two types of land preservation associated with the discouragement of urban sprawl and the encouragement of a form of compact development that most people would likely desire to live in. These include (1) the preservation of lands for parks, recreation, and green spaces within built-up areas and (2) the preservation of rural land for agriculture, to maintain valuable natural areas, and to channel development into more compact and mixed uses. If applied appropriately – and within an appropriate use of regulatory programs, general plans, consistent zoning, and subdivision ordinances – California's state-level farmland conservation programs are potential policy instruments that could achieve both of these desirable forms of land preservation. However, appropriateness requires preserving enough farmland to constitute a greenbelt that surrounds an urban area and effectively becomes a growth boundary for it.

California's farmland preservation programs can be a powerful policy tool in helping to defeat the state's urban sprawl if applied in a well coordinated and contiguous manner around the entire fringe of the state's growing urban areas. Such a greenbelt arises if the vast majority of agricultural lands within the greenbelt enroll in current farmland preservation programs. This greenbelt can effectively become a growth boundary for an urban area if it is wide enough, and/or if other methods are used discourage development beyond the greenbelt. Such a greenbelt would act steer future development into the existing urban area. This would very likely result in the desired mixed-use and compact development that, as described, yields the lower statewide average household VMT necessary to reduce GHG emissions as required by AB 32.

Later I examine the extent to which California's farmland preservation programs have achieved these desirable anti-sprawl goals. But before doing this, I examine the current system of state and local taxation in the California and explore the arguments given for it encouraging agricultural conversion and possibly greater sprawl.

3. California Taxes and Agricultural Land Conversion

Proposition 13 changed the state and local government revenue structure in California into one that is different from that observed in most of the rest of the United States. The passage of this proposition placed in California's Constitution the requirement that the *ad valorem* rate of property taxation anywhere in the state not exceed one percent of a property's acquisition value. Acquisition value begins as market value at the time of the most recent sale that occurred after 1975, and increases annually from the time of sale at a rate that cannot exceed the higher of either two percent or the rate of inflation.

Proposition 13 resulted in a nearly 60 percent cut in the property tax revenue collected by the state's local governments. An equivalent fall in state and local spending never occurred. Instead, lost local property tax revenue was made up by increasingly larger grants from the state, and local governments relying on increasingly higher fees and chasing after the point-of-sale tax revenue they keep if it is generated within their borders. Next I examine arguments on how California's post-Proposition 13 revenue structure influences the amount of land converted from agriculture in the state.

Lower Reliance on Property Taxation

The higher the rate of traditional property taxation in a state, the greater the pressure put upon farmers at the boundary between rural and urban uses to remove land from agricultural uses. This pressure arises because the traditional value which property taxation is levied upon is not its value in current use, but its market value in "best" use. At the urban fringe, due to residential demand for reasonably priced large homes on larger lots, the higher market value land use is very often not in agriculture. Farmers at the urban fringe, under a traditional system of property taxation, face the additional pressure to convert their land to non-agriculture uses to obtain the higher revenue stream they are required to pay taxes on.

However, as a result of Proposition 13, the pressure on agriculture land conversion in California due to *only* property tax reasons is not as great in other states. The two reasons for this are acquisition based property assessment and the mandated one-percent rate of property taxation. Under acquisition based assessment a property's value for tax purposes is only allowed to increase a maximum of the lower of two percent per year or the rate of inflation, and only jumps to market value when it is sold. Thus a piece of agricultural property that was acquired by the present owner when agricultural production was its best use and the market price it sold for reflected this, retains it agricultural-based property tax assessment until sold. This does not occur in states where market-based assessment is the rule. In such states, assessment rises to best-use by appraisal even if the farm's ownership does not change hands.

As compiled by Moody's (http://www.nytimes.com/2007/04/10/business/11leonhardt-avgproptaxrates.html), California's average property tax rate of 0.68 – calculated as the average percentage of a property's market value paid in property taxes in a year – is only bested at the low end by Hawaii's rate of 0.40. In comparison there are nine states with rates above 2.00, with Texas topping the list at 2.57. California's extremely low rate of property taxation further reduces the incentive for farmland conversion in the state. Facing a lower penalty (in the form of higher property taxes) for non-conversion, there is less incentive to do it. Finally, California's Williamson Act or its "Super" variant allows farmers to permanently lock in an agricultural assessment value or an assessment value 35 percent below it. This points to the likelihood that when considering only the influence of California's system of property taxation, it alone is much less of a direct determinant of the amount of agricultural conversion occurring in California than in other states with a much high rate of property taxation. Though if the state were to eliminate property taxation entirely (as no other state has), it is fair to say that the there would be less conversion of agricultural land at California's urban-rural boundaries.

Regarding the overall theoretical influence of local property taxation on urban sprawl – and not just on farmland conversion – Brueckner and Kim (2003) demonstrate that the expected influence on land use in an urban area whose jurisdictions rely on property taxation to a lesser degree could be an increase in the intensity of land development (because the physical property placed on it is taxed less), a subsequent increase in population density, and a reduction in sprawl in the urban area. However, a lower rate of property taxation in a metropolitan area also results in a higher quantity of housing capital demanded by the typical resident in the metropolitan area. Holding population and improvements per acre constant, if typical lot size increases in response to the increase in demand for housing capital, population density decreases and the land required to house a fixed population increases (more sprawl). The theoretical effect of local property taxation on the size of an urban area is therefore theoretically ambiguous under general assumptions and requires an empirical investigation. Using a specific form of an individual preference function, Song and Zenou (2006) derive the theoretical effect that a lower reliance on local property taxation should result in more urban sprawl. They confirm this prediction with an appropriate empirical investigation of the size of United State's urban areas and find that a one percent decrease in the overall effective rate of property taxation in a metropolitan area is expected to increase the land area of the metropolitan area by about 0.4 percent (or more sprawl).

In comparison to property taxation in other states, California's system of property taxation relies on acquisition value assessment and a low rate of property taxation. For the reasons just discussed, this makes it less likely to be a direct driver of farmland conversion in California than in other states with higher property taxes. But it has also been shown that an overall lower rate of property taxation in a state increases the amount of sprawl experienced in the state's metropolitan areas by encouraging people to purchase larger homes and lots. These homes are more likely to be built on the urban fringe and require greater farmland conversion to produce them.

Higher Reliance on Local Sales Taxation

Sales taxation can play a role in the rate of farmland conversion in a state, not based upon the overall rate of taxation, but upon how the receipts of the tax are subdivided between the state and the local jurisdiction where a taxable sales tax transaction occurs. In California, the municipality or unincorporated portion of a county in which retail sales are generated gets to keep at least one percent of their value as pure discretionary revenue. In the revenue-constrained environment that California's local governments now find themselves, this is an attractive revenue stream to go after.

Economic theory predicts that a retail firm chooses a location in a metropolitan area based upon the location of its customers, transportation costs, other retailers, and degree of economies of scale in retail production. In an urban area with dominant central places, these factors push retailers that exhibit high and even moderate-scale economies in production to primarily locate in the central places. But between 1950 and 1990, the percentage of the United States metropolitan population living in these central places fell from 64 to 38 percent. A reflection of this decline is more retail activity moving to the urban fringe because larger percentages of metropolitan residents chose to live there, and falling automobile transportation costs reduced even the ties of central place residents to a central place shopping location.

Greater sprawl also reflects the result of citizen desires to form and fund more homogenous communities. To fund such communities, land use controls and subsidies are used by the new communities to attract residents and businesses that offer a net fiscal gain. Retail activity that, in most instances, requires relatively few local-government services and generates relatively little environmental damage offers a good choice of self-generated funding for local treasuries. If suburban communities actively seek retail activity for the purpose of the fiscal gain it generates, their actions may be a factor in the generation of further sprawl. The concept does not mean that the choices made in the raising of local government revenue can induce more or less retail activity in an urban area, but such choices may induce changes in where the fixed amount of urban area retail locates. A smaller percentage of the overall retail activity in an urban area necessary to support a given population is going to existing central places and more is going to new communities forming at the urban fringe.

Misczynski (1986) coined the term "fiscalization of land use" to describe what he increasingly expected to happen after California's post-Proposition 13 abandonment of property taxation as a discretionary source of local revenue. Innes and Booher (1999) continue with Misczynki's theme and point to the complex and fragmented system of local finance in California, with its heavy reliance on sales taxation as a source of local discretionary revenue, as the single most important factor driving local land-use decisions in the state. Atkinson and Oleson (1996) believe the automobile to be the major culprit of sprawl, but maintain that this would not have been possible without complimentary local finance policies. Though in a monograph-length study of sales taxation in California, Lewis and Barbour (1999, p. 126) conclude that local sales-tax reliance motives local land-use decisions in the state, "...although [such reliance is] unlikely to systematically alter broad patterns of retail development." They argue that retailers primarily base location on economic factors that are not subject to much control by local government.

Some data-based evidence exists for the theory that if local governments in a metropolitan area rely to a greater extent on sales taxes collected within their borders for revenue, the area is likely to exhibit greater urban sprawl. After surveying land use officials in 471 California cities on what causes them to desire new and redevelopment projects, Lewis (2001) found that "new sales tax revenues generated" ranked first for new development and was tied for first with "city council support for the project" for redevelopment projects. In support of the argument just presented, non-central city officials were more likely to rank sales tax revenue higher than their central city colleagues. Wassmer (2002) also finds that overall and big-box retail sales at the fringe of urban areas in the western United States are positively related to the fraction of statewide own-source municipal revenue gained from sales taxation. For every 10 percent increase in local sales tax reliance in a western urban area, the dollar value of retail sales occurring in non-central places in the urban area (a proxy for greater sprawl), rose by 2.4 percent.

Higher Reliance on Local Fees

Following Proposition 13, local governments in California have been forced to seek new sources of revenue. This is especially the case in providing services and infrastructure to new residential development where it is unlikely that the one percent rate of property taxation on the market value of new development covers the annual cost of provision. To cover these costs, local governments in the state have increasingly turned to development exactions. Exactions require the payment of fees by a developer before they can proceed, and/or the developer's donation of land for public uses, infrastructure construction, and the provision of public services. As noted in Dresch and Sheffrin (1997), California leads the nation in imposing exactions on new housing. Bluffstone *et al.* (2008) finds a current average per-house development fee of just over $15,000 in California's Inland Empire. In their earlier analysis, Dresch and Sheffrin report a 1992 to 1996 range of $20,000 to $30,000 (in current dollars) per-house development fees in the Bay Area's Contra Costa County.

Whether the imposition of these greater exactions in California results in the generation of more or less urban sprawl in the state (and subsequently less or more farmland conversion) depends on the response to two questions. (1) Who ultimately pays for these exactions? (2) Are the exactions imposed on new development likely to be greater at the urban fringe or urban core?

In an economic analysis, a development fee is considered no different than a tax on new development. It can be paid by either the landowner receiving a lower price for their land when purchased by a developer, the developer receiving a lower return on investment from the new development, or the buyer of the new development paying a higher price for it. All of these occurrences discourage new development. The imposition of greater fees can make the (agricultural) landowner less likely to convert the current land use to new development, less likely for the developer to undertake it, and/or less likely for the consumer to purchase it. Crucial to the assessment of the final impact of development fees on urban sprawl is whether they are likely to be larger for new development at the fringe or core of an urban area. Where they are higher is where the greater discouragement of development will occur. If exactions for a new home are expected to be higher for a new home at the fringe of an urban area because the marginal cost of providing services are greater there than at the urban core, then California's greater reliance on fees after Proposition 13 has likely resulted in greater farmland conservation and less sprawl.

Empirical evidence on whether a home built in an established central place in California is likely to pay more or less in development fees than one built on the urban fringe is offered by the California Department of Housing and Community Development (2001). In this study, two statistical studies using 1999 fee data collected from 89 cities in California look at the factors that make it more likely for a new house to pay different types of fees, and the factors that drive the magnitude of per-home fees paid in different categories. The study reports that a city is more likely to charge a school construction based fee and a capital outlay based fee the greater the 1990 to 1997 percentage growth in population experienced in the city. Additionally, the magnitude of the per-home subdivision fees in total, for capital outlay, for school construction, and for transportation and parks is expected to be greater the larger the 1990 to 1997 percentage growth in homes in the city. Since both of these percentage growth rates are greater in cities at the fringe of California's urban areas, the evidence points to fringe cities being more likely to use fees. In another regression analysis, this Housing and Community Development study found that for every 100 percent increase in a city's housing supply rate, the ratio of fees charged to the market price of the home increased by 57 percent. Fee-price ratios were highest in fringe jurisdictions with higher volumes of housing construction activity. Thus it is reasonable to conclude that California's post-Proposition 13 shift to greater fees has likely resulted in less sprawl occurring than would have occurred without it.

Higher Reliance on State Personal Income and Corporate Income Tax

As described in Keating (2008), California currently has the highest state marginal income tax rate levied on individuals in the country. In 2007 it stood at 10.3 percent, of which 9.3 percent applies for any taxable individual income greater than $40,346 and an additional one percent is levied on an taxable individual income earned after one million dollars. This compares to nine states (including Nevada) that levy no personal income tax, and 19 other states whose highest marginal income tax bracket is less than six percent. Regarding the corporate income tax, California's top corporate income tax rate (which is applied equally to all taxable corporate income) is 8.84 percent. This top rate is the eighth highest among all the states. Since approximately 90 percent of the state's farmers pay personal income taxes and not corporate income taxes, but 53 percent of all California's farm income is earned on corporate farms, both of these forms of income taxation are relevant to consider in their potential impact on farmland preservation (derived from Rand California Business and Economic Statistics, http://ca.rand.org/stats/economics/farmincome.html).

Two issues immediately arise in regard to income taxes and farmland preservation. The first being the higher the rate of income taxation, the lower the after-tax return that a landowner receives from farming, and the more likely they are to leave farming by selling all or portion of their agricultural land to a developer. Second, the higher the rate of income taxation, the greater the benefits a farmer receives from enrolling in one of California's farmland preservation programs, the more likely they are to do it, and their land will subsequently not be converted from agricultural use. Thus, California's relatively high rates of personal and corporate income tax exert differential effects on farmland preservation.

California's high rate of state income tax makes it less likely for a farmer to enroll in the Williamson Act. Why? Because the burden of property taxation is less due to their increased value as a deduction toward high state income tax payments. At a six percent rate of income taxation, the farmer pays 94 percent of all deductible property taxes. While at a nine percent rate of property taxation the farmers pays only 91 percent of all deductible property taxes. Alternatively, the same higher rate of state income taxation makes it more lucrative for a farmer to charitably donate a portion of their land to satisfy requirements of the California Farmland Conservancy Program because the value of the charitable tax deduction is worth more when facing a higher rate of marginal income taxation. A search of the literature revealed no empirical studies that would allow a quantification of the impact of a higher rate of income taxation on enrollment in a use value property tax program like the Williamson Act or in a farmland conservation program like the CFCP.

Presence of Federal Estate (Death) Tax

An estate (or death) tax is levied upon the value of all property owned by a decedent at the time of their death or half of a couple's interest in community property; less the value of deductions allowed for debts, charitable bequests, and spousal bequests. Through 2004, the State of California imposed an estate tax separate from the federal government. Now a resident of California only pays the federal estate tax. As detailed in Buckley (2005), a decedent's heirs are only required to file a federal estate tax return if the gross (value less allowed deductions) amount of the estate exceeds $2 million. The federal tax rates applied to an estate are progressive and in 2008 the top rate was 45 percent. In 2009 the exemption rises to $3.5 million. In 2010 the federal estate tax is scheduled to end for one year and will return in 2011 with a lower exemption of $1.3 million and a higher top tax rate of 60 percent. Many expect the planned 2011 implementation to never occur. Instead, the post-2011 federal estate tax situation is likely to remain in hiatus (as supported by a majority of Republicans) or an alternate structure imposed (as supported by a majority of Democrats). Given the politics involved in this decision, this is not likely to be decided until after the November 2008 election.

Along with the California specific taxes described earlier, the influence of federal estate taxation on farmland preservation in California is widely discussed among stakeholders in the state's agricultural community. In an editorial written by the President of the California Farm Bureau Federation, Pauli (2005) summarizes the feelings of many in the farm community regarding the federal death tax. California is the nation's number one agricultural producer and its farmers produce on some of the highest land values in the country. In addition, the assets of a farm (land, machinery, equipment, and buildings) are much less liquid than other business owners. Since the estate value of a California farmer is often beyond the exemption allowed, and with non-liquid assets, heirs are forced to sell the family farm to a developer to pay the federal estate tax. The presence of the federal death tax therefore acts as a significant factor in the conversion of agricultural land in the state. Pauli's argument is legitimate providing that upon death a significant percentage of California's family farmers are subject to the estate tax and pay amounts that are significant enough to require the liquidation of a farm. Nonetheless, an additional cause and effect argument made by the Friends of the Earth (2001) is that the presence of a federal estate tax also acts to encourage more of California's farmers to participate in its Farmland Conservancy Program through a charitable donation of their own land. The market value of such a donation is subtracted off the top of the decedent's estate and can help put them under the exemption level for paying the estate tax. Some empirical evidence on the role that the estate tax plays in the conversion of farmland is offered next.

Burman *et al.* (2005) uses 2003 filing data from the federal estate tax and reports that about 66,000 returns were filed nationwide that year, but less than half of these resulted in taxable estate income. The result being that less than 1.5 percent of all 2003 decedents in the United States owed an estate tax. Over 99 percent of these returns consisted of individuals who earned income greater than 90 percent of all others in the country. Small farms and businesses (defined as valued at less than $5 million) made up less than two percent of all taxable estate returns (or about 660 in number) and only a half percent of estate tax liability. Given the increase in the exemption scheduled for 2009, Buckley (2005, p. 839) estimates that this number will fall to less than 300 small farm and business owing any estate taxes in that year. These are not large numbers and hence do not make a strong case for a huge influence of the federal estate tax on California farmland conversion. Burhman *et al.* (2005, p. 379) also points out that family-owned farms and closely held business subject to an estate tax now receive especially generous treatments that allows them to make interest free tax payments on an estate tax balance for as long as 14 years. As described in Daniels and Bowers (1997, Chapter 12), adequate estate planning greatly increases the likelihood that a family farm can remain as such.

Understanding this, perhaps it is not a surprise that Professor Harl, an Iowa State University estate tax expert is quoted as saying he has heard many horror stories about people having to sell farms to pay estate taxes but has "...not been able to find a single case where estate taxes caused the sale of a family farm" (Johnston, 2000). As noted in a press release by the American Farm Bureau Federation (2007), there is anecdotal evidence of families selling off a portion of their farm after the owner's death, but even here there is no example offered of complete liquidation of a farm to pay the federal estate tax. Even if such an example is found, without the use of advanced statistical techniques (as later described in the Brunetti

(2006) study) it would be hard to directly attribute the cause of liquidation to the death tax alone, as heirs may have just decided to get out of farming for other reasons after the principal operator of the farm passed away.

As further analyzed in Buckley (2005), the 2011 total repeal of the federal estate tax will very likely create more losers than winners among farmers. This is because the cost basis of assets passed on by a decedent to their heirs is now "stepped-up" to the market value of the property at death and this eliminates any separate capital gains tax levied the heirs. The planned repeal of the estate tax in 2011 removes this step-up rule and according to Buckley's analysis (p. 838) the number of farming families facing overall tax increases from this change will increase. He suggests not a repeal of the tax, but leaving intact the exemption and rate structure scheduled for 2009.

Brunetti (2006) offers the only found empirical analysis of the influence of the estate tax on the ongoing viability of family businesses. Using San Francisco probate court date from 1979 to 1982 from 312 estates that included a family farm or small business, he uses advanced statistical methods to examine the combined influence of a then California and federal estate tax on the likelihood that the business was sold after the owner's death. After controlling for differences in financial and owner characteristics of these businesses, he found that the greater the amount of estate tax paid, the greater probability of selling the business after death. For every one percent increase in the amount of tax paid, the probability of sale went up by nearly the same one percent. But there are important caveats, noted by the author, to this finding. First, a measure of the liquidity of the business is found to exert no influence on its sale. This is suspect since lack of liquidity is likely the mechanism that causes the estate tax to force a business sale. Second, since data was only drawn from probate sales, the decedent may have not adequately planned for disposition of his estate and the finding may only apply in such a case. Finally, all factors that could have caused differences between selling a business and not (besides estate taxes) were not adequately controlled for. Because of this, Brunetti cautions that his result of a positive relationship between degree of estate taxation and business liquidation must be considered preliminary until confirmed through further and improved upon research.

4. California's Farmland Preservation Programs and Sprawl

The previous section examined the influences that California's system of state and local taxation and federal estate taxation have on the direct generation of urban sprawl, indirect generation of urban sprawl through the discouragement of farmland preservation. As will be discussed later, just because a specific tax instrument encourages (or discourages) the preservation of California's farmland does not mean that it necessarily results in a reduction (an increase) in urban sprawl and a subsequent reduction in green house gas emissions. A farm preserved in a rural area that is beyond the automobile commuting distance to an urban employment center does little to reduce the sprawl that flows from urban areas.

This section provides an examination of the three main farmland preservation policies in California and asks the same questions directed at taxation in the previous section. What is the structure and intent of these programs, and how well do they work at not only preserving agricultural production in California, but also at saving farms in a manner that reduces urban sprawl and the greater greenhouse gas emissions that can arise from it?

Williamson Act

According to Daniels and Bowers (1997), the statewide movement to encourage the preservation of family farms by allowing farmers to owe property taxes on the use value of their land instead of the development value began during the late 1950s. California's program began in 1965 with the Williamson Act. By the early 1970s, every state had instituted some form of a program that allows farmers, under agreed upon restrictions, to pay lower than normal property taxes. California's program is characterized by a "restrictive agreement" where preferential property tax treatment is only granted for agricultural land (and some grazing land) after the farm owner signs a legally binding agreement to maintain the land as a farm for 10 years (with annual renewal), with a penalty paid of 12.5 percent of the land's market value if conversion occurs before the contract expires (Institute for Self Local Government, 2002, p. 67). Similar programs exist in New Hampshire, Pennsylvania, and Vermont.

California's Williamson Act is a state policy that is voluntarily administered by its city and county governments. If a local government desires the possibility for its farmers to enter into a Williamson contract, it first must set up rules regarding the establishment of agricultural preserves within its boundaries. Some local leeway is granted for determining the extent that nonagricultural uses can qualify, but a designated preserve must be at least 100 acres. The minimum parcel sizes for prime and non-prime agricultural land within a preserve is respectively 10 and 40 acres. A local government's planning department must also describe the consistency of a proposed agricultural preserve with its general plan, and subject the proposal to a public hearing before being approved. As described above, the local government may then offer Williamson contracts to privately owned parcels seeking them within established agricultural preserves.

In 2007, about 17 million of California's 27 million acres of acres used to agricultural purposes were subject to preferential tax treatment due to the Williamson Act. Since 1972 the State of California has partially reimbursed its local governments for the property tax revenue lost due to Williamson contracts. In 2005 these intergovernmental transfers amounted to nearly $39 million dollars (California Department of Conservation, 2006a, p. 18). A 1997 State Board of Equalization study found that in the 27 counties where Williamson contracts were most prevalent, potential property tax revenue lost by counties was $27 million, of which $24.4 million was made up by the state's subvention payments (Governor's Office of Planning and Research, 2003, p. 4). It should be pointed out that these subvention payments have recently come under attack. The Legislative Analyst's Office (2008) recommended that legislation be enacted that prevents the State of California from renewing or entering into new Williamson Act Contracts. They base this recommendation on their assessment that the act is not "cost–effective." In their words: "In many cases, it may subsidize landowners for behavior they would have taken regardless" (p. 1).

If a farm currently under a Williamson contract wishes to end its commitment without penalty, it must undertake a nine-year process in which the assessed value each year increases by formula to its market value. Kovacs (2008) has recently examined the pattern of

Williamson contract non-renewals in California and notes a steady statewide increase in yearly initiations of acres of farmland put up for non-renewal between 2001 and 2007. He attributes this to the housing market boom over most of this period that fueled subdivision developer demand at the urban fringes, especially in the San Joaquin Valley, South Coast, and the Desert regions.

Responding to criticism that the offerings of the Williamson Act did not do enough to encourage farmland preservation in California, Senate Bill 1182 (or the "Super Williamson Act") added a Farmland Security Zone (FSZ) provision. An FSZ was originally created within an existing agricultural preserve at the request of landowners to the appropriate local government, but in 2000 a new FSZ could be formed outside of an earlier created agricultural preserve. A farmland security zone must contain one or more of the following: prime agricultural land, farmland of statewide significance, unique farmland, and/or farmland of local importance. A farmer who finds his land in a FSZ may enroll in a Super Williamson contract that allows a 35 percent reduction in property tax payments below the already reduced Williamson Act amount. The cost to the farmer of obtaining this benefit is a 20 year commitment to maintain the land in agricultural production, required state approval of a cancellation of this commitment, and a penalty for cancellation that is raised to 25 percent of the land's market value. The public benefit of agricultural land enrolled in this program is the increased likelihood it remains in agriculture production for 20 or more years without reverting to the establishment of a permanent farm easement that, as described next, can create long-term lock-in problems. In 2005 there was about 818,000 acres of prime California farmland enrolled in Super Williamson contracts. This represents only five percent of the total farmland enrolled in any Williamson Act program. I now turn to an assessment of how well the traditional and "Super" variants of the Williamson Act work to preserve agricultural production in California and for the specific purpose of this chapter, to saving farms in a manner that reduces urban sprawl.

If the success of the Williamson Act is measured by farmland participation alone, it must be considered triumphant. Over two-thirds of all California acres in agricultural production are currently under a Williamson contract. However, the vast majority of this land has only committed to 10 years or less in agricultural production. Only five percent of the acres under Williamson contract fall under the longer 20 year commitment allowed in a FSZ. Also noteworthy is acres of new enrollment since 2003 have continually fallen behind the cumulative non-renewal of existing acres covered under Williamson contracts (Kovacs, 2008, p. 5).

The protection of California's farmland through the Williamson Acts is occurring within the shorter window than existing policy allows for. There is also evidence that less and less is being protected over time, especially in regions of the state experiencing greater increases in population and the urban sprawl it can generate. Given the low enrollment in the Super Williamson contracts, it reasonable to presume that the vast majority of California's farmers have evaluated the expected cost of putting their property in a FSZ as being higher than the expected benefit. This is perhaps not a surprise given the 20 year commitment that such contract requires, the future potential for high-market value non-agricultural development on much of these lands, and the steep penalties faced if the 20 year commitment is violated.

Figure 1 below offers a map of California in which the state's urban areas (defined as an accumulation of Census blocks in which the population density in each is at least 1,000 people per square mile) are represented in black. Population density varies within these urbanized areas, with higher densities usually occurring in an urban area's employment/shopping/residential hubs and falling as you move away from these hubs of compact development to the urban/rural fringe that surrounds an urban area. In Figure 1, land under a Williamson Act contract of either type is denoted in light gray. Though the scale is large, it is telling to look at this map of California and notice that most of the state's urban areas (denoted in black) are framed by a ring of white. This represents land that is neither urban or protected by Williamson Act contracts. These white rings offer a nice visual representation of the urban/rural fringe discussed earlier. This is where sprawl is occurring and/or will occur in the upcoming decades.

Urban sprawl in California could be slowed if its urban areas were completely surrounded by land falling under either of the two forms of the Williamson Act.[2] If land at the urban fringe was designated farmland security zones, sprawl could be slowed for at least 20 years. If it consisted of agricultural preserves, population growth in an urban area could be contained within an agriculturally-imposed growth boundary for at least 10 years. And as described earlier, a slowing of sprawl will help achieve the mandated AB 32 policy goal of reducing green house gas emissions in the state.

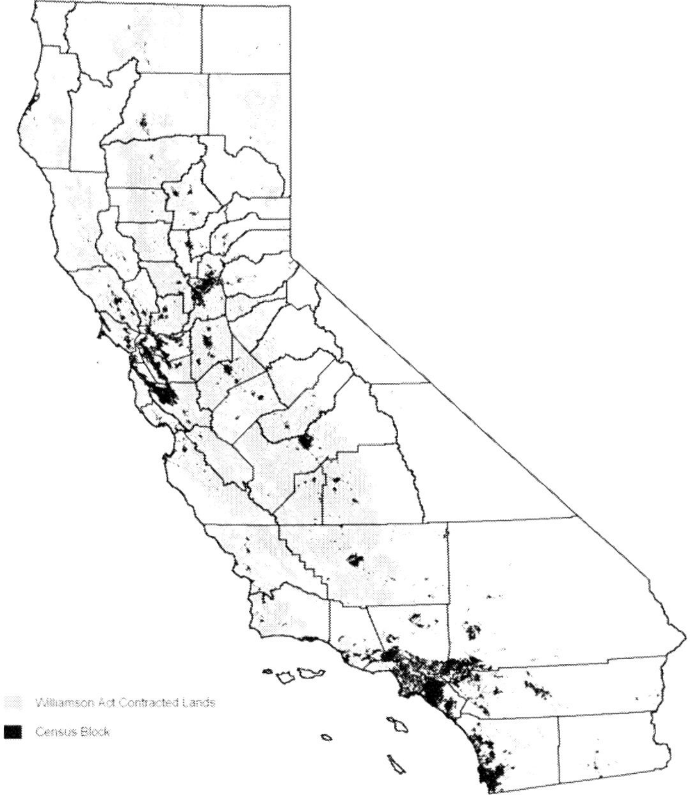

Figure 1. GIS map created by James Nordstrom at California Department of Conservation.

---

[2] To make this truly effective at controlling sprawl, further regional-based land use planning and appropriate zoning would also need to be adopted. This is discussed later in the paper.

What can be immediately seen from Figure 1 is California's current lack of using either of the two forms of the Williamson Act to completely surround its urban areas with a boundary for stopping growth. The best examples of were this is close to occurring is in the Central Valley counties of Yolo, San Joaquin, Stanislaus, Madera, Fresno, Kings, and Tulare. But even in these counties where much of the major urban areas (designated in black) are surrounded by agricultural land under Williamson or Super Williamson contracts (designated in gray), there is a very telling band of white between the black and gray. Also revealing is the fact there is very little to no use of Super Williamson contracts around these rapidly growing Central Valley urban areas, or for that matter, around any of California's urban areas. The vast majority of FSZs in California are in Kings, Kern, and Glen counties. With the exception of the Willows urban area in Glenn County and Corcoran urban area in Kings County, farmland security zones are not adjacent to the state's urban areas. Even in these two urban areas, they are only used to any extent on one side of the urban area.

Williamson Act contracts are being used extensively in the state, but they are fulfilling far less than their full potential at preserving farmland at the urban fringe for the purpose of slowing sprawl and working to curb future GHG emissions. Where a growth boundary in the form of farmland under Williamson Act contracts surround an urban area, it is largely in place for no more than 10 years and there is a ring of unprotected property at the urban fringe waiting to accept sprawling development before protected farmlands are reached. Since protected farmland is only under Williamson contract for 10 years or less, farmers at these existing growth boundaries rescind their commitment when this ring of unprotected land fills with sprawl. In essence, no long-term urban growth boundaries have been established around California's urban areas through the use of Williamson Act contracts.

To examine this depiction in further detail, a similar map is offered in Figure 2 for the Sacramento Region. I define this area by Sacramento, Yolo, Sutter, Placer, and El Dorado Counties. The primary urban area within this region extends from the City of Sacramento north and south along interstate highways five and 99, and east along interstates 50 and 80. West of the City of Sacramento, the urban area jumps the Sacramento River into the City of West Sacramento, but a flood plain and farmland protected by 10 year Williamson contracts offers a buffer between the primary urban development in the Sacramento Area, and the Davis and Woodland urban areas in Yolo County. Important to note is that the County of Sacramento maintains an urban service boundary in its southeast corner that effectively curtails non-agricultural development there without the need for farmland to enter into Williamson contracts.

In Figure 2, the Sacramento Region is offered as a prime example of how the current implementation of the Williamson Act is not working as effectively as it could to slow the area's continuing urban sprawl. First, there are very few Super Williamson contracts used. In the counties of Sacramento, Placer, and Sutter no FSZs exist; while in the counties of El Dorado and Yolo only 185 and 159 acres were respectively under Super Williamson Act contracts in 2008. The reason for the high use of farmland preservation in the western area of the Sacramento Region is Yolo County's explicit planning desire to steer the limited residential development it allows to within the city limits of Davis and Woodland. This creates a form of compact development in these two cities, but even here there is the telling ring of white around the two large black-designated urban areas in Yolo county.

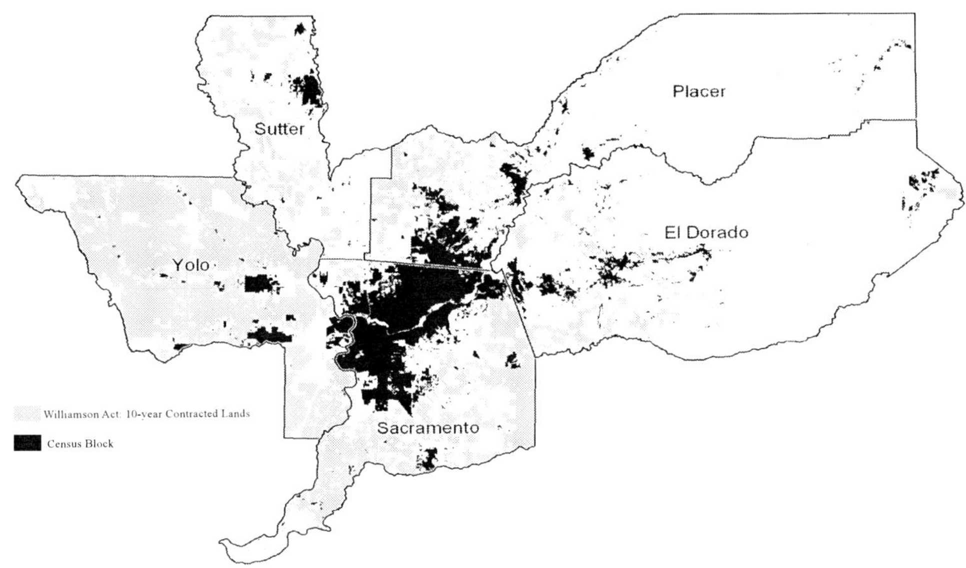

Figure 2. GIS map created by James Nordstrom at California Department of Conservation.

Traditional Williamson contracts only exist haphazardly in the northern portion of the Sacramento Region which includes north Sacramento, south Yuba, and east Placer Counties. As such, this portion of the metropolitan area has seen its share of sprawling development over the last two decades. But the real occurrence of sprawl in the Sacramento Region has occurred along the northeast Interstate 80 corridor extending to Auburn City, and the southeast Interstate 50 corridor extending to Folsom City and beyond to Placerville City. As Figure 2 shows, this sprawl has been facilitated by the nearly non-existent practice of preserving farmland through Williamson Act contracts.

In the conclusion to this chapter I will discuss potential policy alternatives to consider that would strengthen California's Williamson Act in a manner that would render it more effective in controlling the state's sprawl and subsequent emissions of GHGs. But before doing this, I offer descriptions of two other California programs designed to preserve the state's farmland. There effectiveness at doing this, and reducing sprawl are also assessed.

Farmland Conservation Program

The California Farmland Conservancy Program (CFCP) was established in 1996 to offer state assistance, with local government collaboration, in the permanent conservation of economically viable farmland. The CFCP manages state provided dollars and private grant funds to purchase agricultural conservation easements that are typically held and monitored by land trusts or transferred to local governments. As described in Daniels and Bowers (1997, Chapter 11), a land trust is a private, non-profit organization that exists to acquire farmland, natural areas, and open space. The American Farmland Trust (2007) is one example that exposes the dual purpose of stopping the loss of productive farmland and promoting environmentally sustainable farming practices. Daniels and Lapping (2005) describe conservation easements as restricting land in perpetuity from residential, commercial, industrial, or institutional uses, but allowing a farmer to make ongoing agricultural management decisions. A trust acquires such an easement from a private landowner in exchange for usually both a cash payment and the income/estate tax benefits available through the donation of a portion of the value of land to the non-profit trust. The benefit of this technique is the guaranteed long-term protection of farmland. But the cost of achieving this can be large and includes the likelihood of paying a high price to purchase permanent development rights and the likely gaps of unpreserved land from holdout farmers who do not wish to forever remove the potentially lucrative option of future development.

Prior to 2000, CFCP grants were minimal and only funded by yearly appropriations from the state's General, Soil Conservation, and Environmental License Funds. Using an allocated $25 million in bond funds from the passage of Proposition 12 in 2000, the CFCP has since helped fund 39 individual conservation easements on close to 11,000 acres of farmland (California Department of Conservation, 2006b, p. 2). In addition, California voters approved Proposition 40 in 2002 which allocated an additional $45 million in funds to help support the further establishment of conservation easements in the state.

The scale of California farmland subject to conservation easements is miniscule in comparison to the state's 17 million acres of agricultural land currently under Williamson contracts. An obvious budgetary reason for the limited use of the farmland policy tool is the direct and large expenditure that the permanent acquisition of development rights entails. Even California's Department of Conservation (2006a, p. 4) concludes that agricultural conservation easements are not well suited to the preservation of urban fringe farmland for the sole purpose of directing growth back to the urban core. The high level of land speculation occurring at the urban fringe discourages most farmers from making a permanent commitment to agriculture. Instead, agricultural conservation easements are perhaps better used to guarantee the perpetual conservation of prime farmland in rural regions far from where urban development is ever wanted to occur. Here, farmers are much more likely to agree to not developing their land for the far less than infinite commitment of 10 or 20 years as required under a Williamson contract, and the cost to securing this agreement is more obtainable. But as emphasized in Daniel and Lapping (2005), if used appropriately, both Williamson type property tax forgiveness programs and conservation easements can offer an effective combination of policy tools to steer development from the urban fringe. An examination of the 39 CFCP grants offered through Proposition 12 show only a few attempts to preserve farmland in a manner that creates a growth boundary around any of California's urban areas. But these have only been attempts and in no case has a complete growth boundary using the CFCP been established.

Easement Exchange Program

Beginning in 1998, legislation went into effect that allows the cancellation of a Williamson Act contract without the payment of the specified penalties of monetary penalties to California's General Fund if the landowner/local government arranges a conservation easement on other farmland in the jurisdiction. The stated goal of this program is the allowance of potential cancellation fees to work to preserve local agriculture. Requirements for this to happen are that the value of the new easement must be equal or greater in value than the cancellation fee that would have been paid, and the acreage of the new easement must also be equal or greater than the acreage of Williamson contracted land that is cancelled.

The easement exchange process is entirely voluntary and begins with a Williamson Act contract holder submitting a proposal to a locality that must approve it and then pass it on for Department of Conservation approval.

California farmland under Williamson contract at the urban fringe is eligible provided that the termination of a the contract does not result in "discontinuous" patterns of development (California Government Code Section 51256(a)). It is crucial as to how the Department of Conservation interprets this term in determining whether this exchange program contributes to the further generation of urban sprawl. The reason being that farmers most likely interested in facilitating an exchange hold land at the urban fringe. Development pressures there have driven up the market price of land such that the return from selling before the Williamson contract expires exceeds the return from farming even with property tax forgiveness. Furthermore, the conservation easement that can be purchased with the equivalent penalty funds of 12.5 or 25 percent of the market value of this fringe land is necessarily farther removed from development pressure than the farmland being converted. Thus, the presence of this exchange program very likely facilitates the break down of boundaries that have arisen around the urban fringe areas designated in white in Figures 1 and 2. Through an examination of the data offered by the Department of Conservation on the use of this program show that between 2000 and 2005, only 435 acres of farmland in Riverside County took advantage of the Easement Exchange Program. Thus, at the present its existence is exerting no effect on the generation of urban sprawl in California, but it would be wise to monitor its use in the future.

5. Conclusion and Suggested Policy Changes

> Planners and academics, together with land preservationists, need to present more studies on how the acquisition of land and conservation easements can help to clarify where developments should or should not go, and how land preservation can help to achieve the smart growth goals of cutting sprawl and reviving cities and suburbs (Daniels and Lapping, 2005, p. 324)

With AB 32, California set itself on a track to reduce green house gas emissions in the state in 2050 to 80 percent or less of that emitted in 1990. This must be considered a highly ambitious goal given the growth anticipated in both the state's population and vehicle miles traveled (VMT) by the typical Californian. Since over 40 percent of California's current GHG emissions are generated in transportation activities, the achievement of this goal will only come about if public policy tackles all three of the elements that make the automobile currently such a large contributor to climate change: (1) the high carbon content of automobile fuel, (2) the low fuel efficiency of automobiles, and (3) the large VMT generated by the typical automobile owner in the state. As shown in Ewing et al. (2008), VMT can only decrease by the necessitated amount if Californians make future land use decisions that results in more compact and mixed-use development patterns.

With the goal of offering advice to state policymakers on how to reduce sprawl in order to reduce VMT and GHG emissions, this chapter has looked at how California's current system of funding its state and local governments, the federal estate tax, and the state's farmland conservation programs influence the compactness of urban land use choices made in the state. I conclude the chapter with a summary of the earlier reported upon evidence. This evidence is then used as a basis to offer politically feasible policy suggestions that would likely reduce the positive influence that these factors have had on the generation of sprawl. Finally, I provide suggestions on needed further work that would empirically verify the relationship between the presence of Williamson Act contracts and reduced sprawl, and a more detailed examination of other states' practices regarding the use of farmland protection programs to curtail is sprawl.

Summary of Available Evidence

Lower Reliance on Property Taxation

The overall influence of California's lower rate of property taxation on the compactness of land development in its urban areas is theoretically indeterminate. One empirical study shows that the overall influence leans toward the generation of greater sprawl. However, a lower rate of property taxation puts less pressure on owners of agriculture land at the urban fringe to develop farmland and thus the state lower rate of property taxation also works to encourage less sprawl. *Given California's low rate of property taxation and the high rate at which its farmland enjoys additional Williamson Act property tax concessions, it is reasonable to conclude that relative to other states with much higher rates of property taxation, property taxation in California exerts little direct influence on the further generation of the state's urban sprawl.*

Higher Reliance on Local Sales Taxation

Revenue constrained localities in California retain at least one percent of the value of all taxable retail sales generated within their boundaries. *Since jurisdictions at the urban fringe are more likely to seek this discretionary revenue, California's higher reliance on local sales taxation very likely encourages the fiscalization of land use choices toward higher-value retail at the urban fringe and this results in the generation of greater sprawl.*

Higher Reliance on Local Fees

California leads the nation in imposing exaction fees on the construction of new housing. The fees charged in jurisdictions at the fringe of the state's urban areas are on average greater because the marginal cost to provide public services to a new home is greater there. *California's shift to greater fees has resulted in less sprawl in the state because higher fees at the urban fringe drive up the final cost of a home and/or reduce the return on developers or landowners where they are built, and thus less homes are built in the urban fringe.*

Higher Reliance on State Personal and Corporate Income Taxes

The marginal personal and corporate income tax rates levied by the State of California are some of the highest in the country. The expected influence of this on the generation of sprawl through farmland conversion is uncertain because the higher rates makes it less likely for a farmer to seek a property tax reduction through a farmland preservation commitment, and more likely to seek the tax write-off if farmland is donated to a trust to create a conservation easement. *A search through the literature revealed no empirical studies that would quantify whether California's higher state income tax rates are responsible for the generation of more or less sprawl.*

Presence of Federal Estate Tax

A death tax can act as an important deterrent to a family farmer's heirs remaining in the business if: (1) a significant percentage of them are subject to the tax and (2) the payment level of the tax leaves them little choice but to liquidate the farm. Empirical evidence cited earlier shows that this is very likely not the case on both accounts. In fact, the threat of paying an estate tax can actually encourage the greater participation of family farmers in moving to perpetual easements after the owner's death due to the generous deduction they generate toward reducing taxable estate income. Evidence was also offered that the current proposed repeal of this tax in 2011 will hurt more of California's family farmers through regular income tax implications than it helps through reduced estate taxes owed. *The furor over the estate tax as a major cause of the loss of California's family farms is largely political and likely driven by a larger anti-tax/anti-government agenda.*

Williamson Act and Farmland Security Zones

Given the fact that nearly two-thirds of all California's acres in agricultural production are under a Williamson contract, by participation alone the program is a success. However, a geographic representation of the use of the these farmland preservation programs shows that it rarely provides an effective growth boundary around any of the state's urban areas. *The current use of Williamson contracts are not fulfilling their full potential as a policy instrument in the fight to slow the state's sprawl and to help achieve the reduction in GHGs mandated by AB 32 .*

Farmland Conservation Program

California farmland subject to conservation easements is miniscule in comparison to the millions of acres currently enrolled in Williamson contracts. *For this reason, and the observation that there has been little effort in the use of CFCP grants to assist in the generation of a fixed agricultural buffer around any urban area in California, it must be concluded that this program has not achieved the potential they have for effectively slowing the spread of sprawl in the state.*

Easement Exchange Program

This program potentially allows a farmer at the fringe of an urban are to get out of their Williamson commitment to agriculture production if they can find another plot of agricultural land willing to commit to entering into a perpetual easement. *Though the perpetually preserved farmland is likely to be farther removed from the urban fringe than the previous agricultural land lost to development. For this reason the easement exchange program offers the potential of actually facilitating greater sprawl. Though the nearly non-existent use of its application in California makes this currently unlikely.*

Policy Changes to Consider

I now offer a set of suggestions to consider regarding current California policy instruments and conservation of urban fringe farmland. My policy suggestions are based both on the causal relationships described earlier and my own assessment of the political likelihood of implementing these suggestions

Beginning with the low rate of local property taxation and high rates of state income taxation in California, I suggest that no action be taken to try and alter these forms of California revenue instruments for the purpose of farmland conservation at the urban fringe. I offer two reasons for this opinion. First, the theoretical effect they can have on farmland conversion that generates sprawl is ambiguous. Also important is the reality of insufficient political support for altering these taxes. The system of California property taxation established after Proposition 13 is often referred to as the "third rail of California policy," meaning anyone who dares touches it, dies a quick political death. Democrats would perhaps like to see even higher rates of income taxation in the state to cure the state's current budget woes. While even in the face of a massive budget deficit, all Republicans in California's Legislature have taken no new tax pledges and may even support a cut in these rates.

Regarding the federal estate tax, I conclude that the available empirical evidence does not support the often heated rhetoric regarding its importance to driving the California family farm into the hands of subdivision developers. Reasonable reforms to the structure of this tax have already been taken. With some estate planning, a family farm in California can very likely remain as such if that is what the heirs desire. What should concern California's agricultural stakeholders is the planned repeal of the federal estate tax in 2011. Subsequent changes from it could actually raise the overall tax burden imposed upon heirs to a family farm. Efforts should be made to lobby for the continuation of the federal estate tax exemption and rate structure now scheduled to be in place for only 2009.

Two local fiscal variables that very likely exert an influence on the degree of farmland conservation going on in California are its local government's reliance on development fees and locally generated sales tax revenue. The increased reliance on both have exerted opposite influences on farmland preservation at the fringe of California's urban areas. The more prevalent use of higher fees by fringe jurisdictions increased farmland conservation in these areas because they serve to decrease the profitability or increase the price of homes developed there. While fringe jurisdictions chasing after local sales tax revenue has increased the likelihood of locating auto malls, big-box retailers, and regional shopping malls at the urban fringe and not in California's current central places. The two policy courses I suggest are thus the greater use of fees for fringe development and reduced incentives for fringe jurisdiction to fiscalize their land use decisions.

Economic theory offers a justification for charging even greater development fees at the urban fringe if such developments impose social costs that are not being paid for, and hence considered when the development is proposed and built. There is a large volume of literature (for an overview see Burchell *et al.*, 1998) on the existence of these external social costs of sprawl (air pollution, traffic congestion, etc.) and thus higher fees could be theoretically justified. The problem in doing so stems from a current lack of political will at the state level to require that local governments levy these higher fees and even the questionable legality of their use in California. Remember the suggested increase in fees is not for the direct higher costs of a new development to a jurisdiction (which fringe jurisdictions have already demonstrated they are willing to charge), but for social costs that affect the entire metropolitan area and beyond. In the case of greater GHG emissions through the higher VMT that results from fringe development, these higher social costs are currently born by the entire world through climate change.

Local governments at the fringe, and the League of California Cities and California State Association of Counties that represent them, will strongly resist the levying of these additional fees because they would place a direct hit on the affected jurisdiction's land owners and developers in the form of lower returns, and/or a hit on new homeowners in the form of higher prices. Currently a movement exist, that flows from AB 32 and is spearheaded by California Attorney General Jerry Brown, that the development approval process under California's Environmental Quality Act (CEQA) be amended to account for the affect of GHGs produced from new development on global climate change (Latham and Watkins, 2008). If successful, such a CEQA change would impose greater mitigation costs upon fringe developers, or force fringe communities to implement greater mitigation fees. Either way, the result is the equivalent of an increase in fees paid at the urban fringe. Thus the support of this CEQA policy change seems like the most politically expedient way to seek the desired policy change of greater fees at the urban fringe, less development there, and greater farmland conservation there.

Fiscalization of land use in California is driven by the discretionary revenue sought by an urban fringe jurisdiction that receives too little property tax revenue from its non-compact and single-use subdivision development, and subsequently seeks the creation of high revenue-generating retail activities that require large patches of existing farmland to assemble. The policy course necessary to reduce this drive is to decrease the fiscal benefits expected from such land use choices. Assemblyman Steinberg realized this and in 2002 authored California Assembly Bill (AB) 680 that would have created a more rational and equitable distribution of the site-based local sales tax revenue collected throughout the Sacramento Area. In addition, AB 32 had provisions to reward compact growth projects undertaken in the area and to encourage local planning aligned with regional goals (PolicyLink, 2002). Steinberg's bill passed the Assembly, but died in the Senate when the California League of Cities and California Association of Counties both raised strong objections to the curtailment of local revenue choices that it entailed. Organizations that represent California's local governments viewed the sales tax redistribution portion of AB 680 as a zero-sum gain. Some central-place jurisdictions would win additional revenue from it, but only because of the losses experienced by others. Until a local sales tax proposal can be crafted that is perceived as a win-win for all, I do not recommend the further pursuit of this policy course.

To understand my policy suggestions regarding the use of current farmland preservation instruments used in California, I first offer my vision of the "ideal" set of instititutions that would allow for compact and mixed use development to occur in California's current urban regions and simultaneously protect as much of the prime farmland that surrounds these urban regions as possible. For every urban region in the state, this ideal set of institutions begins with a region-wide planning group that consists of all cities and counties in a region that are economically and environmentally connected, or expected to be in the region's future footprint. Based upon the expected population growth in a region over the next 50 years, the region's planning group would need to reach a consensus on where this growth should occur to best achieve the compact and mixed use developments that are necessary to achieve the region's share of reduction in GHGs specified in AB 32. In the short term, much of the population growth could be steered back into the existing urban places within the region in the form of infill development. If long-term population growth is great enough, new land at the fringe of the urban region will need to become urbanized. The choice of these new urbanized places should in part be driven by the desire to preserve the prime farmland that abuts the existing urban places. Through such a consensus-based ideal of regional planning, needed future development can be steered to not so prime farmland at an urban region's fringe.

The difficulty with a California region undertaking the just described ideal for creating compact and mixed-use urban growth that preserve prime farmland, is that there is no metropolitan-wide organization that can bring an area's cities and counties together to make binding regional land use decisions. Currently, the closest things are the 18 Council of Governments (COGs) that were originally formed in California's large regions to facilitate the orderly distribution of federal transportation funds. Among these COGs, the Sacramento Area Council of Governments (SACOG) has garnered national attention in the creation of the beginnings of the ideal institutions just described (Campoy, 2008). Labeled the "Blueprint Project," representatives from the area's local governments, with the assistance of input from citizens, developers, and the agricultural community, reached a consensus on where they would like to see future development occur. The consensus was also that future development be at a higher rate of density and mixed use than was originally projected. Though the implementation of the preferred development plan is voluntary, local officials in the Sacramento Area now have a region-wide blueprint to help guide their own land use decisions by.

Now Senator Steinberg, who represents the Sacramento Area in California's Legislature, and was the earlier architect of AB 680, wants the state to encourage the remaining 17 COGs in California to take a similar consensus approach to region wide land use. He has authored Senate Bill (SB) 375 that would require such a process. Under SB 375, the process must demonstrate how the resulting plan yields measurable green house gas reductions that are in line with those mandated statewide under AB 32 (Planning Report, 2007). SB 375 offers carrots in the form of state funded incentives for regions that achieve this. My strong policy suggestion is that those interested in the preservation of farmland in California's urban fringes need to do everything possible to see that SB 375 ultimately becomes law. In addition, SB 732 also authored by Senator Steinberg in 2007-2008 legislative session, creates the Sustainable Communities Council to coordinate the activities of various state agencies that aim to improve air and water quality, natural resource protection, affordable housing, and transportation. Both SB 375 and 732 are truly the beginnings of a pubic policy course that leads to the ideal set of regional planning institutions described earlier.

Once a region reaches a consensus on a course of future development that helps to satisfy statewide goals regarding GHG reductions, the next policy concern that emerges is how to achieve it. This is where the existing tools of farmland preservation, used in coordination with appropriate local general plans, farmland zoning, and subdivision ordinances, can be put to more effective use. If all the projected development for a metropolitan area over the next 10 years is expected to be accommodated through higher infill development in existing urban areas, then the relevant local communities in the area (most likely the unincorporated portions of counties at the region's fringe) should coordinate a ring of agricultural preserves that surround existing urban areas in the region. All private farms in these preserves need to then be strongly encouraged to take on a traditional Williamson contract. Since it is a landowner's choice to enter into a Williamson contract, stronger encouragement could come through appropriate forms of local zoning, and perhaps additional forms of farmland protection (transferable development rights, formal growth boundaries, etc.) that would heighten the attraction of farmers to enroll in Williamson Act contracts. An appropriately established ring of agricultural preserves would leave no unprotected land (as shown in Figures 1 and 2 with white bands) between current and desired future land in urban use and protected farmland.

If projected development over the next 20 years or more around a metropolitan area can be accommodated through infill development, then this ring of preserved agricultural land around an urban areas should be converted into Farmland Security Zones. Private farms in these FSZs need to be better encouraged to take on a Super Williamson Contract. If there is a part of the current urban fringe in a metropolitan area that will need to developed in 10 to 20 years from now, then this land should only be under traditional Williamson contracts and the land beyond that under Super Williamson contracts.

Under this suggested policy course, Williamson contracts are used to set growth boundaries around California's urban areas that work to steer development back to its central places in urban area to achieve more of the mixed-use and compact development necessary to satisfy AB 32. A permanent easement within a current or projected future urban area should only receive the support of the California Farmland Conservancy Program (CFCP) if it used specifically to establish a permanent stopping point for urban development because of its encroachment on prime agricultural land. The same can be said for setting up the criteria the Department of Conservation should use for the future approval of an easement exchange.

REFERENCES

American Farm Bureau (2007), "Congress Urged to Remedy Federal Death Tax Now," November 15, Washington, D.C.: Author, available at: http://www.idahofb.org/archivej/htmArchive/showPage.aspx?page=15452.htm&id=15452 .

American Farmland Trust (2007), *Paving Paradise: A New Perspective on California Farmland Conversion*, Washington, D.C.: author, available at http://www.farmland.org/programs/states/ca/Feature%20Stories/PavingParadise.asp .

Atkinson, Glen and Ted Oelson (1996), "Urban Sprawl as a Path Dependent Process," *Journal of Economic Issues,* 30(2), 607-09.

Bluffstone, Randy, Matt Braman, Linda Fernandez, Tom Scott And Pei-Yi Lee (2008), "Housing, Sprawl, and the Use Of Development Impact Fees: The Case Of The Inland Empire," *Contemporary Economic Policy.* 26, 433-447.

Brueckner, Jan K. (2000), "Urban Sprawl: Diagnosis and Remedies," *International Regional Science Review. 23,* 16-171.

Brueckner, Jan K. and Hyun-A Kim (2003), "Urban Sprawl and the Property Tax," *International Tax and Public Finance.* 10, 5-23.

Brueckner, Jan. K and D.A. Fansler, "The Economics of Urban Sprawl: Theory and Evidence on the Spatial Sizes of Cities," *Review of Economics and Statistics.* 65, 479–482.

Brunetti, Micheal J. (2006), "The Estate Tax and the Demise of the Family Business," *Journal of Public Economics*, 1975-1993.

Buckley, John (2005), "Estate Tax Repeal: More Losers than Winners," *Tax Notes*, February 14.

Burchell, Robert, Naveed Shad, David Listokin, Hilary Philips, Anthony Downs, Samuel Seskin, Judy davis, Terry Moore, David Helton, and Michele Gall (1998), *The Costs of Sprawl—Revisted*, Transportation Research Board, Washington, D.C.: National Academy Press, available at http://onlinepubs.trb.org/Onlinepubs/tcrp/tcrp_rpt_39-a.pdf .

Burhman, Leonard E., William G. Gale, and Jeffrey Rohaly (2005), "Options for Reforming the Estate Tax," *State Tax Notes*, April 18, 379-385.

California Department of Conservation (2006a), *The California Land Conservation (Williamson) Act: 2006 Status Report*, Sacramento, CA: Author, available at http://www.consrv.ca.gov/dlrp/lca/stats_reports/Pages/2006%20williamson%20act%20status%20report.aspx .

California Department of Conservation (2006b), *California Farmland Conservancy Program Proposition 12 Bond Fund Report*, Sacramento, CA: Author, available at http://www.conservation.ca.gov/dlrp/cfcp/docs/Documents/CFCP%20Prop%2012%20Bond%20Fund%20Report%20-%20print%20quality.pdf .

California Department of Housing and Community Development (2001), *Pay to Play: Residential Development Fees in California Cities and Counties, 1999*; Sacramento, CA: Author, available at http://www.hcd.ca.gov/hpd/pay2play/fee_rpt.pdf .

Campoy, Ana (2008), "With Gas Over $4, Cities Explore Whether It's Smart to Be Dense: Sacramento's 'Blueprint' for Growth Draws National Attention," *Wall Street Journal*, p. A1, available at http://online.wsj.com/article/SB 121538754733231043. html?mod= hps_us_pageone .

Daniels, Tom and Deborah Bowers (1997), *Holding Our Ground: Protecting America's Farms and Farmland*, Washington, D.C.: Island Press.

Daniels, Tom and Mark Lapping (2005), "Land Preservation: An Essential Ingredient in Smart Growth," *Journal of Planning Literature* 19, 316-329.

Downs, Anthony (1998), "How America's Cities are Growing: The Big Picture," *The Brookings Review*.

Dresch, Marla and Steven Sheffrin (1997). *Who Pays for Development Fees and Exactions?* San Francisco, CA: Public Policy Institute of California, available at http://www.ppic.org/main/publication.asp?i=106 .

Economic and Technology Advancement Advisory Committee (2008), *Technologies and Policies to Consider for Reducing Greenhouse Gas Emissions in California,* Sacramento, CA: California Air Resources Board, available at: http://www.arb.ca.gov/cc/etaac/ETAACFinalReport2-11-08.pdf .

Ewing, Reid (1997), "Is Los Angeles-Style Sprawl Desirable?" *American Planning\Association Journal. 63,* 107-126.

Ewing, Reid (1994), "Characteristics, Causes, and Effects of Sprawl: A Literature Review," Environmental and Urban Issues, 1-15.

Ewing, Reid and Robert Cervero (2001), "Travel and the Built Environment: A Synthesis," *Transportation Research Record.* 87-114.

Ewing, Reid, Rolf Pendall, and Don Chen (2003), "Measuring Sprawl and its Impact," Washington, D.C.: Smart Growth America.

Ewing, Reid, Keith Bartholmew, Steve Winkleman, Jerry Walters, and Don Chen (2008), *Growing Cooler: The Evidence on Urban Development and Climate Change*, Washington, D.C.: Urban Land Institute.

Friends of the Earth (2001), "Estate Tax = Conservation of Real Estate," Washington, D.C.: Author, available at http://www.foe.org/policy/51e4e.pdf .

Frumkin, Howard (2002), "Urban Sprawl and Public Health," *Public Health Reports.* 117, 201-217.

Frumkin, Howard, Lawrence Frank, and Richard Jackson (2004), *Urban Sprawl and Public Health: Designing, Planning, and Building for Healthy Communities*, Washington, D.C.: Island Press.

Governor's Office of Planning and Research (2003), California *Land Conservation (Williamson) Act Technical Advisory Document*, Sacramento, CA: Author, available at http://www.assembly.ca.gov/ruralcaucus/documents/Williamson_Act_Fact_Sheet-FINAL_10-30-03%20.doc .

Innes, Judith E. and David E. Booher (1999), "Metropolitan Development as a Complex System: A New Approach to Sustainability," *Economic Development Quarterly,* 13(2), 141-56.

Institute for Local Self Government (2002), *Farmland Protection Action Guide: 24 Strategies for California*, Sacramento, CA: Author, available at http://water.lgc.org/resource-tools/Farmland%20Protection%20Action%20Guide.pdf .

Johnston, David (2000), "Despite Benefits, Democrats' Estate Tax Plan Gets Little Notice," *New York Times*, July 13, available at http://www.agecon.ucdavis.edu/extension/update/articles/v11n5_2.pdfhttp://query.nytimes.com/gst/fullpage.html?res=9C06E4DF1F38F930A25754C0A9669C8B63&sec=&spon=&pagewanted=all .

Keating, Raymond J. (2008), Business Tax Index 2008:Best to Worst State Tax Systems for *Entrepreneurship and Small Business*, Oakton, VA: Small Business and Entrepreneurship Council, available at http://www.sbecouncil.org/uploads/BusinessTaxIndex2008.pdf .

Kovacs, Kent (2008), *Farmland Conversion in California: Evidence from the Williamson Act Program*, University of California: Giannini Foundation of Agricultural Economics, available at http://www.agecon.ucdavis.edu/extension/update/articles/v11n5_2.pdf .

Latham and Watkins (2008), *CEQA and Climate Change: One Year after AB 32*, Client Alert, available at http://www.lw.com/Resources.aspx?page=ClientAlert Detail&publication=2051 .

Legislative Analyst's Office (2008), Analysis of the 2008-09 Budget Bill: General Government Tax Relief (9100), Sacramento, CA: Author, available at http://www.lao.ca.gov/analysis_2008/general_govt/gen_anl08020.aspx .

Levine, Ned (1997), [Letter], *American Planning Association Journal. 63*, 279-282.

Lewis, Paul (2001), "Retail Politics: Local Sales Taxes and the Fiscalization of Land Use," *Economic Development Quarterly* 15, 21–35.

Lewis, Paul and Elisa Barbour (1999). *California Cities and the Local Sales Tax,* San Francisco, CA: Public Policy Institute of California, available at: http://www.ppic.org/publications/PPIC121/PPIC121.pdf/index.html .

Mills, Edwin S. (1999), "The Brawl over So-Called Sprawl," *Illinois Real Estate Letter*, summer, 1-7.

Misczynski, Dean J. (1986), "The Fiscalization of Land Use," in *California Policy Choices,* edited by John J. Kirlin and Donald R. Winkler, Sacramento, CA: School of Public Administration, University of Southern California.

Pauli, Bill (2005), "Repeal the Estate Tax," *Hollister Free Lance Newspaper,* September 6, available at http://www.hollisterfreelance.com/opinion/167642-repeal-the-estate-tax .

Planning Report (2007), *SB 375 Connects Land Use and AB 32 Implementation*, July, Sacramento, CA: author, available at http://www.planningreport.com/tpr/?module=displaystory&story_id=1257&format=html.

PolicyLink (2002), *Building A Healthier Sacramento Region: An Analysis of Assembly Bill 680*, Oakland, CA: Author, available at http://www.policylink.org/pdfs/AB%20680.pdf.

Planning Commissioners Journal (2002), *Sprawl Guide*, available at www.plannersweb.com/sprawl/define.html .

Sierra Club (1998), *The Dark Side of Sprawl*, Washington, D.C.: Author.

Song, Yan and Yves Zenou (2006), "Property Tax and Urban Sprawl: Theory and Implications for US Cities," *Journal of Urban Economics.* 3, 519-534.

Steinbach, Tom (2007), "Technology Alone Won't Tame Climate-Change Juggernaut," *San Francisco Chronicle*, October 21, p. F1.

Wassmer, Robert W. (2008), "Causes of Urban Sprawl in the United States: Auto Reliance as Compared to Natural Evolution, Flight from Blight, and Local Revenue Reliance," *Journal of Policy Analysis and Management.* 27, 536-555.

Wassmer, Robert W. (2002), "Fiscalization of Land Use, Urban Growth Boundaries, and Non-Central Retail Sprawl in the Western U.S.," *Urban Studies.* 39, 1307–1327.

In: Land Use Policy
Editors: A. C. Denman and O. M. Penrod
ISBN: 978-1-60741-435-3

Chapter 2

EFFICIENT LAND USE PLANNING AND POLICIES USING GEOSPATIAL INPUTS: AN INDIAN EXPERIENCE

P.S. Roy and M.S.R. Murthy
Remote Sensing and GIS Application Area
National Remote Sensing Centre
Hyderabad, India

ABSTRACT

The population growth, rapid industrialization and changing life styles in India have made the development of land use policies very critical. The social, economic and ecological imperatives have become the interwoven driving forces of land use planning to meet resources requirements, developmental activities and global change .The challenges of land use policy in India today is to meet the food security for 46 M people living below poverty line through integrated land use management practices, development of scientific planning and mechanisms to resolve conflicting land use systems and conservation of natural habitats, biodiversity and carbon sequestration to sustain ecosystem services and goods.

The paper presents how scientific databases developed using remote sensing and geospatial analysis of retrospective and prospective scenarios using prognostic and diagnostic methods have facilitated the development of land use planning and policies towards sustainable development. These efforts include development of geospatial databases and integrated analysis of natural resources, socioeconomics, infrastructure and environmental data to facilitate natural resources planning, suitability assessment, visualization for alternatives; smart growth planning, impact analysis and land use decision support systems.

Integrated Mission for Sustainable development, watershed development, comparative evaluation and prioritization of tribal areas, urban growth planning studies under taken in India using multi thematic remote sensing based information in conjunction with ancillary information provides how land use planning efforts are facilitated at local and regional level to meet food and water security. Coastal zone regulation, protected area development and monitoring, development of Special Economic Zones and delineation of eco-sensitive areas are a few other examples where land use planning has been effectively facilitated to address environmental security. Studies on river basin ecology, carbon sequestration and biodiversity being conducted at decadal scales for the entire nation using satellite remote sensing and agent based change models are aimed to provide various scenarios of impact of land use planning and policies.

1.0. INTRODUCTION

India has 17% population and 11% livestock of the world on only 2.3% land of the world and pressure on land is 4-6 times more as compared to world average. In the last forty years net sown area is constant around 140 ± 2.0 m ha [1]. In addition, agriculture currently consumes 70 percent of total freshwater used, much of which is accounted due to the rapid expansion of irrigation, which annually withdraws around 2,000-2,500 km^3 of water. India`s urban population has grown phenomenally over the past five decades with about 7-8 million people being added to the urban population each year. Considering the rate of urbanization as a parameter to consider the growth of a city, it is found that eleven cities in India are amongst the 100 fastest growing cities of the world as per the "The Transition to a Predominantly Urban World and its Underpinnings" of the International Institute for Environment and Development.

Rural India constituting 67% of total population of the country needs scientific and technical inputs for over all socioeconomic development. Nearly three fourths of households live in rural areas, accounting for one- third of total national primary energy consumption. The projected water demand of over 980 billion cubic meters in 2050 will require intensive development of ground water resources, exploiting both dynamic and in-storage potential especially in rural areas. [2]. On the other hand, twelve major rivers spread over catchment area of 252.8 million hectares (Mha) cover more than 75% of the total area of the country. Effective utilization of surface water is also a primary concern. **Two hundred thousand villages exist within forests, depending for fuel, fodder, and food.**

India has also reasons to be concerned about the impacts of climate change. Its large population depends on climate sensitive sectors like agriculture and forestry for livelihoods. The total area occupied by coastal districts is around 379,610 km^2, with an average population density of 455 persons per km^2, which is about **1.5 times** the national average of 324 persons per km^2. Under the present climate, it has been observed that the sea- level rise (0.4 – 2.0 mm/year) along the Gulf of Kutch and the coast of West Bengal is the highest. Along the Karnataka coast, however, there is a relative decrease in the sea level. Any adverse impact on water availability due to recession of glaciers, decrease in rainfall and increased flooding in certain pockets would threaten food security, cause die back of natural ecosystems including species that sustain the food production [3].

For inclusive growth and development in various spheres and sectors mentioned above to meet the food and water security for the growing population and to address the issues emerging from the climate change, land need to be optimally used for multitude of purposes. Recognizing these multifunctional requirements of land, various dimensions and relationships of different sectors of the society, land use planning and management is considered as interwoven complex web system (figure 1).

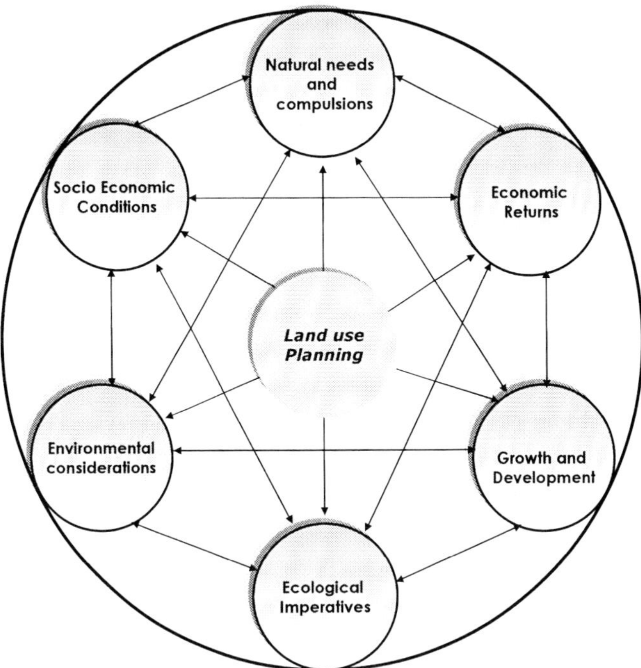

Figure 1. Land Use Planning – An Interwoven Web

In view of this, due attention has been given in India in developing national policies of various sectors of land management [4,5,6,7,8,9].These have been based on the following five principles while keeping sustainability concerns at the core.

- Natural needs / compulsions
- Socio-economic conditions
- Economic returns
- Environmental considerations
- Ecological imperatives

Therefore, for a sustainable land use, agro-ecological, economic, social and energy considerations have been given due priority. The large tract of rain fed and dry land areas, ecological sensitive areas, industrial areas and areas which are vulnerable to climatic change, are specially addressed in the policies. Additionally the policies also addressed the macro level requirements viz., land suitability, land (soil) quality, population supporting capacity (man, animal etc), soils, climatic conditions, trade needs and compulsions and global needs etc. At the micro level domestic needs and demands for different areas (regions) and their populations are taken care of and have enough elasticity and dynamism so that it is (i) buffered against risks (ii) synchronized with climate, (iii) harmonized with environment, (iv) resource consuming and (v) responsive to changes [7,8,9].

While land use policy is governed by socio-politico-economic considerations, land use planning is dictated mainly by scientific and technical considerations based on actual data on land evaluation through surveys and socio-economic parameters within the broad framework of the land use policy. It sets in motion the social processes of decision making and consensus building concerning the use and protection of private community or public areas. Land use planning may be at national, regional, state, district, watershed or village and also at farm level. The techniques and even the strategy of land use planning can be very different at national level, at village level and at any level in between. The process involves the participation of the land users and several other stakeholders.

Thus land use plan can be targeted for increasing the agriculture production, for conservation of soils for improving the productivity in a command area/watershed, or for ensuring livelihood, generating employment and last but not the least for ensuring food security. The methodology and drivers for each of these are different but the ultimate aim is to evaluate the land and present land use and select those combinations that best achieve the desired goals. In its broadest sense, Land Use Planning (LUP) is a tool to support orderly occupation and use of land and to avoid adverse developments. Apart from designating or zoning different land areas, it should specify different interventions necessary for the success of suggested land uses.

Land use planning also need to address problems at multiple spatial and temporal scales or extents, such as land use and land cover change at regional to local settings, and the introduction of new land use policies that have implications across socio-economic, biophysical, and geographical domains and global climate change,. The interchanges between humans and the environment are manifested through land development scenarios and land transformation activities that often create feedbacks and thresholds among people, place, and policy [10].

Lack of application of adequate tools and theoretical understanding across the social, natural, and spatial sciences, has traditionally led to focus on relatively coarse grains of analysis where aggregate data are available. But it is at the finer social, biophysical, or spatial scales where spatially explicit information need to be appropriately collected, derived, and applied because decision-making about the use of the land is often local. Further to adequate data collection at an appropriate spatial scale and in a spatially explicit manner, data analyses need to focus on people and environment, with suitable integration [11]. Considering the extent and heterogeneity of the country, the data collection, analysis and integration in spatial and temporal explicit manner is realized as difficult task .In this context remote sensing and GIS technologies have been adopted as effective tools in complementing the land use planning process in the country. The concept, application and future trends in adopting the geospatial tools towards realizing the efficient land use planning is presented.

2.0. Geospatial Techniques and Land Use Planning

India has 328.73 M ha as total geographical area consisting of twenty-eight states and seven Union territories (figure 2) with 1141 million population. It harbors 5161 towns and 638,588 villages with diverse socio-economic characteristics, indigenous cultures and developmental needs which have greater influence on the life styles and associated impacts on land use. In addition, due to diverse climatic, topographic, hydrologic variabilities, land use planning activities take into cognizance of different agro climatic zones, biogeographical zones, meteorological sub division, bioclimatic zones, watersheds etc as units for assessment and planning. Hence, land use planning is done based on hierarchical administrative and functional thematic units. On the other hand, the planning and management at National, State, District and Village level requires different levels of data at an appropriate scale (Table 1)

Figure 2. India map with administrative state boundraies

Keeping in view of this complexity, Indian Space Programme has coevolved with requirements and demands from user community in developing suitable missions for satellite sensor systems and operational remote sensing applications for sustainable land management [12]. The global coarse resolution satellite data based land use and land cover products, their use and limitations are very many and do not provide necessary inputs for effective regional and local land use planning [13,14]. The Indian Remote Sensing Satellite missions have been built thus based on the spatial and temporal data requirements of the land use planning specific to Indian context in particular and global context in general. The different spatial and temporal process and relevant satellite sensors are given in the figure 3 .Keeping in view of this potential need, an hierarchical land use and land cover classification system is developed which can serve different levels of planning and management (figure 4).

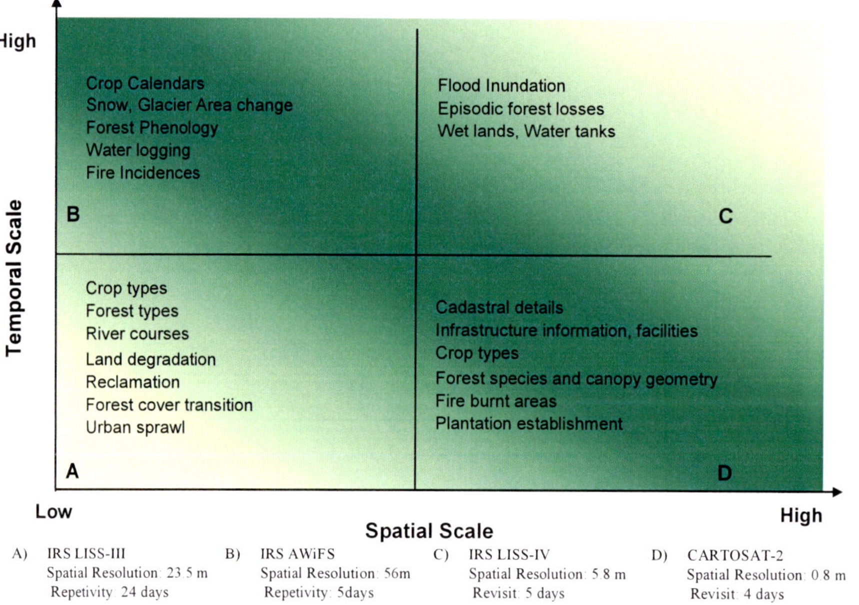

Figure 3. Land Use and Land Cover Information Requirements – Potential of Current IRS Series of Satellites.

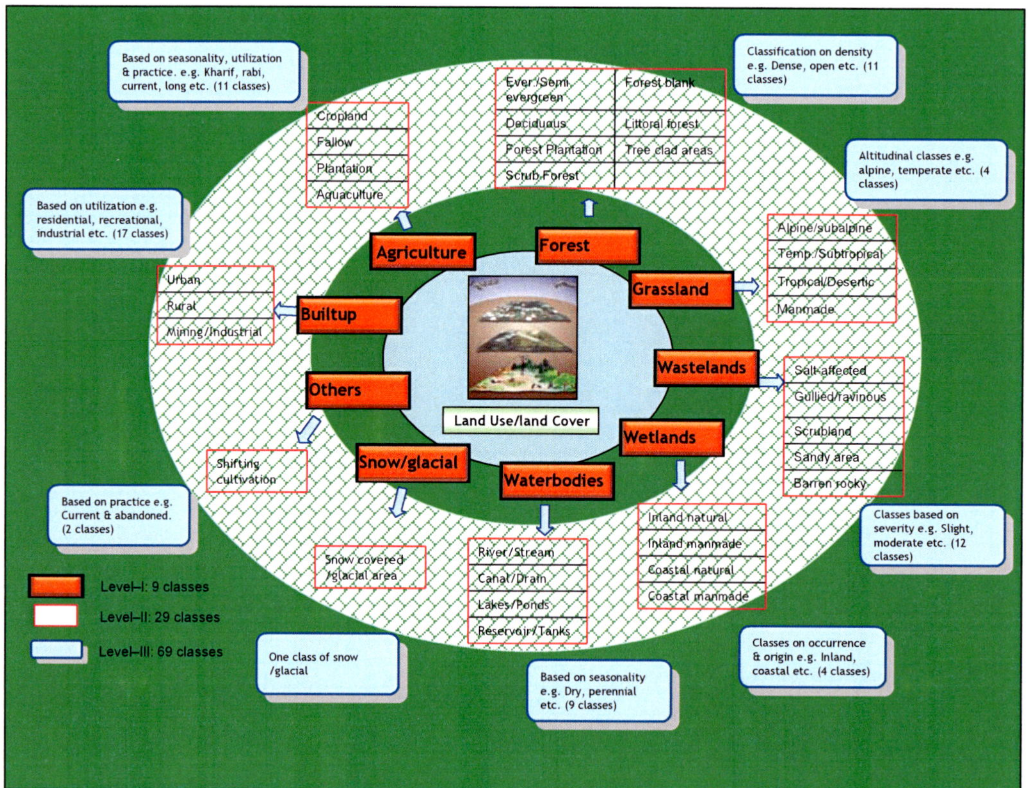

Figure 4. Land Use/Land Cover Classification.

Table 1. Information requirements for land use planning at different scales of operation

S.No	Planning level & Scale	Planning Unit	Information Requirements
1	National		
	1:1 M - 1: 250 M	States Agroclimatic zones Biogeographic zones Bioclimatic zones Industrial zone River basins Soil zonation Meterological sub-divisions	Net sown area Crop Acreages type-wise Forest cover , type areas River discharges Wasteland areas Industrial development Land degradation Rain fed agriculture, Irrigation planning and prioritization
2	States		
	1:250M - 1: 50K	Districts Forest divisions Catchments Watersheds	Crop types, diversity, areas Forest extractions, conservation Rainfed, Irrigation management and monitoring Transportation Urban Planning Land Reclamation and evaluation
3	District		
	1: 50K - 1: 10K	Taluk/Block/Cities/Towns Forest blocks Sub watersheds Micro watersheds Soil/Topography sub-units	Crop rotation, Insurance damage assessment, Productivity, Protection, NTFP Water & Soil conservation Urban Planning Transport Planning
4	Cities/Towns		
	> 1: 10K	Villages Forest Compartments Micro/Mini watersheds	Cadastral level assessment Crop protection, Insurance Rural forest management, Plantation development Water budgeting Field level activities Urban flooding Energy conservation

The sustainable land use planning depends on how the resources are optimally used, while conserving the ecologically unique areas and maintaining the developmental activities. Therefore, rational sect oral planning of resources, conservation and developmental activities is conceived as the primary requirement for land use planning (figure 5).The Indian Remote Sensing application programme during the last three decades has undertaken several national missions and case specific local area studies to strengthen land use planning and management under these sectors (table 2). In addition significant efforts were also made to develop value added services through integration with ground databases for multi criteria based decision making and process understanding in geospatial domain. The different issues, experiences and future challenges in each sector based on the studies conducted are explained:

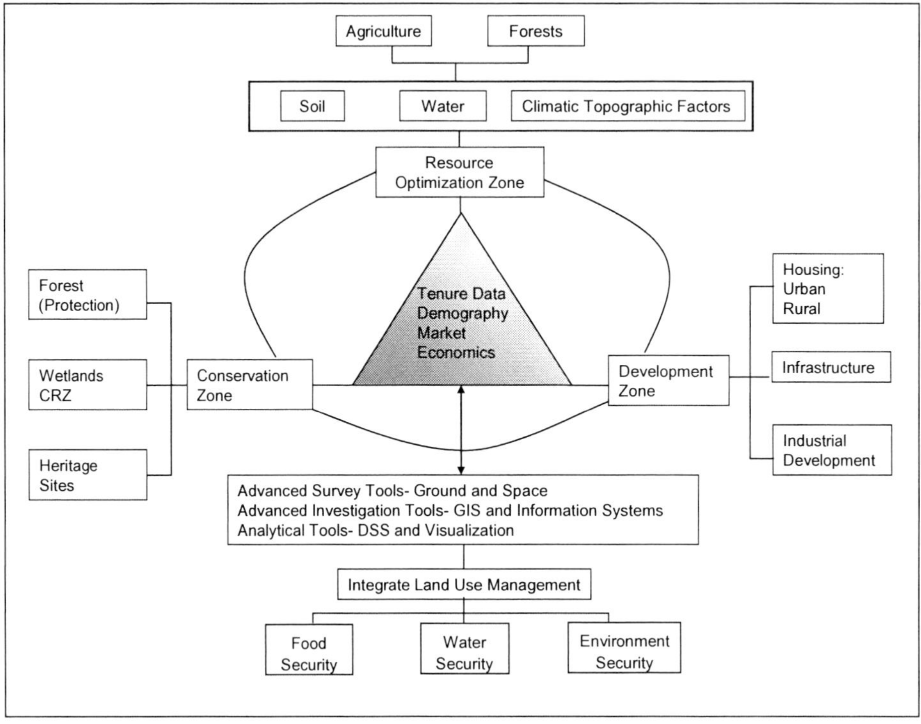

Figure 5. Land use planning and Optimal zonation.

Table 2. National level studies conducted using RS & GIS application in different areas of Land use Planning

S.No	Area	Mission/Study	Scale	Use
I	Resource Optimization zones			
1	Agriculture			
a	Area characterisation, optimisation, trend analysis	Nation level annual LULC assessment	1:250000	Net Sown Area distribution & trends
		Nation crop area acreage assessment		State level estimates for major crop wise areas
		National LULC and Wasteland mapping	1:50000	Culturable wastelands for enhanced cropping areas
b	Production Enhancement			
	Rainfed Agriculture	Integrated Mission for sustainable development	1:50000	
		National Agriculture Technology Programme	1:50000	Action plans for improved land use/soil & water conservation
		Integrated Resource Information System for Desertic Areas	1:50000	

	Irrigation Management	Command area monitoring Augmented Irrigation plan Precision Farming: Pilot studies	1:250000 1:10000 1:10000	Water conservation & crop growth Water conservation & crop growth Improved production
c	Vulnerability Adaptation	National Agriculture Drought assessment Flood damage assessment Climate change (Pilot studies)	1:1 M 1:250000	Fort night drought alerts Crop inundated areas Vulnerability Studies
2	Forests			
a	Area characterisation and trend analysis	Biennial forest cover Vegetation type mapping	1:50000 1:50000	Monitoring hot spots of change Economic and Ecologic perspective
b	Production	Growing stock assessment inputs NTFP assessment	1:25000 1:25000	Forest working plan preparations Rural livelihood
c	Participatory Management	Grassland biomass and productivity Joint Forest Management studies	1:50000 1:25000	Fodder assessment Monitoring and micro plans
II	Conservation Zoning			
1	Protected area and and Biodiversity conservation			
		Landscape level biodiversity characterization National Protected area management and plan	1:50000 1:25000	Disturbance and Biologically richness zones for conservation Management Plans for conservation
2	Coastal zone Regulation			
		Coastal Regulation zone maps Coastal geomorphology, vegetation, hydrology maps (case specific) National Wetland mapping	1:50000 & 1:25000 1:50000	Protection and Development plans Coastal zone management Critical wetlands conservation
III	Development Zones			
1	Cities & Villages			
		Regional city planning Cadstral level mapping	1:50000 >1:10000	Growth and development Village & cadsatral level planning
2	Infrastructure			
		Oil & Gas pipeline routing Power transmission line routing	1:50000 1:50000	Optimal route planning & EIAS Optimal route planning & EIAS
3	Industrial development			
		Mining, Power, Irrigation, Oil and Gas based Industries	1:50000	Rapid & comprehenisve EIA inputs,EMP preparation and monitoring

3.0. Resources Optimization Zones

The agriculture, forests and grassland stand as main stay for food security of India. Constituting 178 M ha (50% of TGA of the country), contributing 21% to the country's GDP, accounting for 11% of total exports, employing 56.45% of the total works and supporting 600 million people directly or indirectly, agriculture is vital to Indian economy and the livelihood of its people. On the other hand, forests covering 67.5 M ha supports directly lively hood of 20 million population in terms of food, fuel and fodder. Apart from this, timber and non timber forests products from forests stand as important market economy and contribute indirectly to livelihood.In view of this forests are treated as productive systems apart from protection perspective through participatory management approaches. The sustainability of these systems also primarily depend on water and soil conservation as 85 million ha falls under the rain fed agriculture and 14 river basins in Himalayas supporting 1.5 billion people for agriculture. The agriculture lands suffer from land degradation and need of fertilization. The sustenance of catchments and command areas at various hydrological levels is very necessary to maintain currently available land under agriculture and forests be productive, develop measures to enhance production and draw additional land for production. In view of this sustainable use of land for agriculture and forests to meet the food security is need to be achieved through scientific and technical inputs and interventions.

3.1. Agriculture

The system of fragmented land holdings, diverse cultural practices, coexistence of multiple crops, and intricate control of rainfall and irrigation regimes make the management of Indian agro ecosystem more complex. 85 M ha area under rain fed agriculture and 58 M ha area under irrigated agriculture faces different challenges in sustaining the efficient use of agriculture land and enhanced production. Decrease in per capita water availability, unassured production, productivity, and market support extension systems, low productivity, impact of global climatic change, scope of investments and crop diversification are a few challenges of rain fed crops. On the other hand set cropping patterns, input intensiveness, increased salinity/alkalinity, unabated chemical degradation, and fall in ground water tables and decline of glaciers are different kind of challenges of irrigated agriculture.

Sustainable agriculture involves improving agricultural productivity of the existing cultivated lands, rehabilitation / restoration of fertility of degraded lands, and adoption of eco-friendly alternate / optimal land use plans. Information on various aspects related to the cropping systems analyses, crop intensification, crop diversification, crop suitability and conformity analyses, etc. could be derived from the space borne spectral measurements. Monitoring of natural resources that are of significance to agriculture, such as soil, surface and sub-surface waters, weather, land use / land cover and land degradation and agricultural drought conditions, aid substantially towards evolving as well as evaluating agricultural systems for sustainability (table 3).

Table 3. Inputs For Resource Optimization Zoning – Agriculture and Forests

Parameters	Processes	Utility
Area Seasonality Crop Type Rotation Yield Acerage Water Requirements Water Utilisation Degraded Lands Soil Relations Soil Degradation Damage Assessment	Monitoring Production Irrigation management Growth Models Crop, Insurance Damage Assessment Crop Diverssification Multifunction Analysis	Trend Monitoring Area Optimization Production Efficiency Area Enhancement Production Models Disasters Preparedness
Climate		
Forests Crown Cover Greeness Vegetation Type Species Assessment Fire Spread Degraded Landscape NTFP, Timber	Cover Monitoring Stock Assessment Carson Biodiversity Habitat Assessment Resources	Afforestation Reforestation and Sheltering Ecosystem Goods and Livelihood Protected Area Planning
Water and Soil		
Surface Water (Area & Distance) Tanks/Catchment River Sn % Morphology Type Terrain Climate	Catchment Treatment Command Area Monitoring Irrigation Scheduling	Watershed Improvement Soil and Water Conservation Catchment Command Area Protection

3.1.1. Area Characterization, Optimization and trend analysis

The area utilization for cropping extensively varies in India both intra and inter annually in rain fed and irrigated agriculture systems due to climatic and soil conditions, irrigation scheduling, local agriculture practices and socio economic conditions. The spatial and temporal explicit database on the inter and intra annual variations in terms of single and double crop areas, current fallows and crop types helps in identification of critical areas of change and undertake appropriate management interventions in sustaining the agriculture land use. Considering the diverse crop types and small land holdings, generating national databases on variation in extent and type of crops grown annually is found to be a cost and time intensive process. The conventional field based databases lacks spatial explicitness, geospatial characteristics and limits to undertake integrated analysis. In this context satellite remote sensing based characterization of cropping patterns in terms of area characterization, optimization and trend analysis carried out on national basis has provided scientific inputs for planning and management. The crop area assessment in terms of net sown area and crop acreage estimation for major crops are the major two initiatives taken up at national level.

(A). Net Sown Area (NSA) Assessment and patterns

The present net sown area reporting system based on sample surveys and up scaled information from ground level in the country has limitation of near real time reporting and lack of spatial explicitness. In order to bring down the turn around time and reliability in net sown area reporting over the entire country, as part of the mission on Natural Resources Census of Dept.of Space the net sown area at the end of each cropping season is being generated for the entire country since 2004 using multitemporal IRS AWiFS data. The project objective is to provide on annual basis interim *kharif* crop area statistics at the end of season and integrated LULC map at the end of each year starting from 2004-05. The project so far completed four cycles of assessment (2004-05, 05-06, 06-07,07-08) and 5th assessment 2008-09 is in progress. In order to precisely capture intra annual changes and prepare spatially and temporally explicit LULC map, multi-temporal data acquired during August- May of each crop calendar year (*kharif*, *rabi*, and *zaid* seasons) was used. Hierarchical decision tree (See 5), maximum likelihood and interactive classification techniques were adopted for classification of the data. Total Net Sown Area (NSA) estimated in first, second and third and fourth cycles is 140.17, 141.87, 141.06 and 139.72 M ha respectively and all India LULC image is shown in figure 6

Response of NSA to rainfall changes found significantly varying in command and irrigation intensive regions, hilly/high rainfall regions, arid and semi arid regions. Out of 33 meteorological subdivisions, 14 have shown an increase in NSA with increasing rainfall from cycle-1 to cycle 2. Moderate drought conditions and seasonal rainfall deficiency of 26 per cent to 50 per cent were reported in 2006 (cycle-3) in North Eastern states, Western UP. The NSA during the period 2006-07 (cycle-3) also has shown reduction in relation to 2005 in these states (figure 7 and figure 8). Consistent double crop and fallow areas were delineated based on 3 cycle's data and consistent fallow areas are present especially in areas having less than 750 mm rainfall. Significant reduction of forests due to shifting cultivation was also observed in NE states.

(B). Crop Acreage Assessment – Major Food and Cash crops

The remote sensing based national and regional level crop inventories have been one of the significant achievements in the management of agro ecosystems of our country. With the cognizance of growing operational and management requirements of crop inventories, the satellite sensor programme has been evolved. The first two satellite missions viz., IRS 1A and IRS 1B owing to the absence of middle infrared channels and low temporal coverage potential were found to have limitations in delineation of multiple crops and assessment of cropping patterns. Accordingly the subsequent satellite missions IRS IC, IRS ID, and RESOURCESAT have been designed to provide better spatial, temporal and spectral resolutions. This has facilitated in progression of crop inventory program to address spatial and temporal (intra annual) variations of cropping systems. In addition conjunctive use of agro meteorological and ground based crop information along with satellite data has been also done to improve the precision of forecasting of crop production. The details of crop inventory and associated satellite data application and methodologies have been standardized with respect to district, state and regional levels.

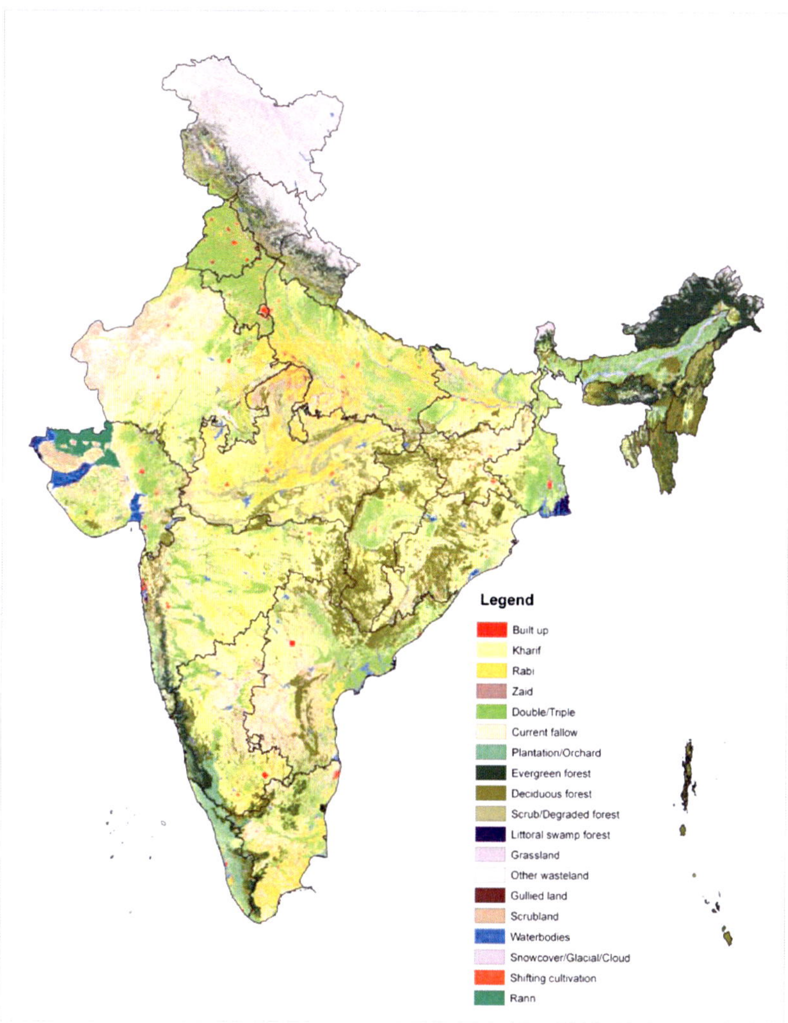

Figure 6. All India LULC Classified map (2006-2007).

Accordingly under the Crop Acreage and Production Estimation (CAPE) project, using **single date cloud free IRS LISS III satellite data** the pre harvest acreage estimates at district level for major crops viz, paddy, wheat, sorghum, ground nut, rapeseed, mustard, cotton and mesta / jute occupying about 80% of the cropped area, are annually carried out. Further multiseason satellite data, agro meteorological information and land based observations were used for the state and national level forecasting of rice and wheat crops at three intervals over an year as part of FASAL (Forecasting of Agriculture outputs using Satellite, Agriculture meteorology and Land based observations) programme. These projects are taken up in collaboration with Dept. of Agriculture, Govt. of India and the outputs are regularly used by the concerned state and central government departments. Methodology has been developed for regional level cotton production estimation using geo-informatics techniques in association with crop modeling and implemented in four districts namely Sirsa, Bharuch, Nagpur and Dharwad district in association with CICR, NBSS and state Agricultural Universities.

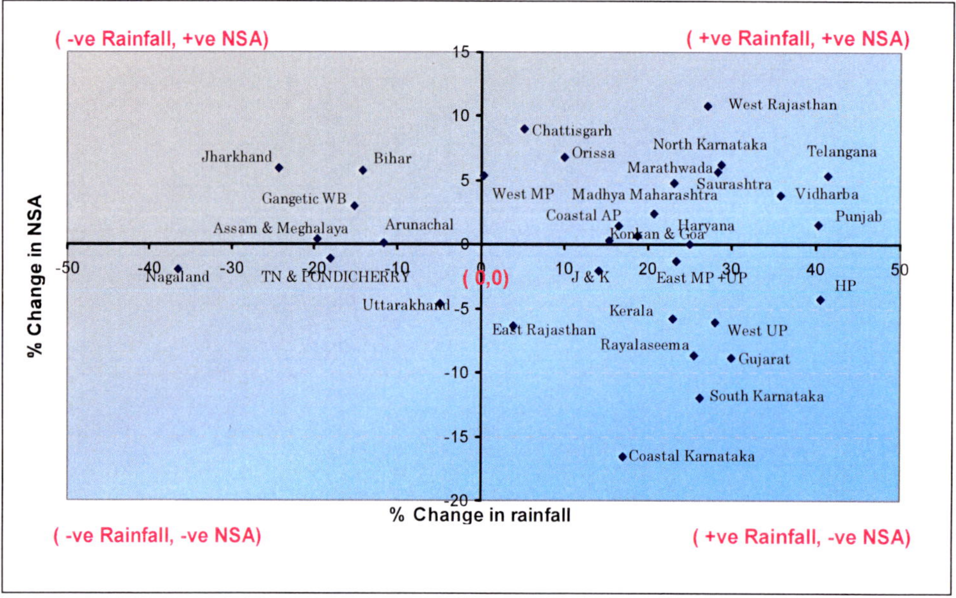

Figure 7. Changes in NSA with Rainfall patterns in 2004-05 and 2005-06.

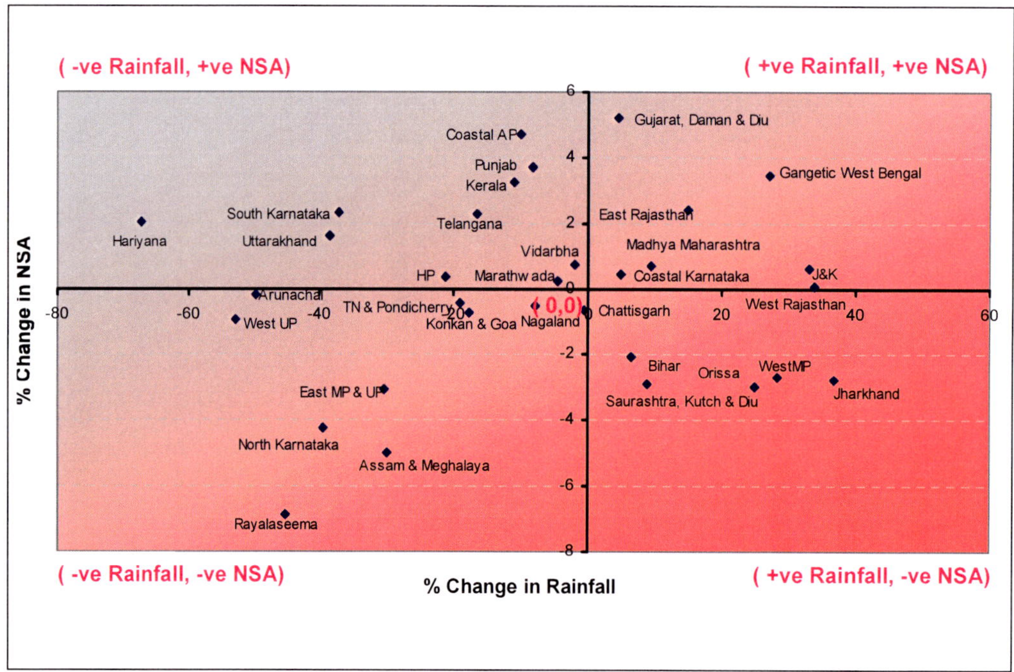

Figure 8. Changes in NSA with Rainfall patterns in 2005-06 and 2006-07

3.1.2. Production Enhancement

Soil and water conservation measures are one of the essential inputs for increasing agricultural output in the country. The arid and semi-arid regions are particularly sensitive to processes of climatic and environmental change and land degradation. Mechanisms that initiate land degradation include physical, chemical, and biological processes. Important among physical processes are decline in soil structure leading to crusting, compaction, erosion, desertification, anaerobism, environmental pollution, and unsustainable use of natural resources. Significant chemical processes include acidification leaching, salinization, decrease in cation retention capacity, and fertility depletion Biological processes include reduction in total and biomass carbon, and decline in land biodiversity.,. A comprehensive assessment of the factors responsible for degradation and their inter-actions, in terms of their impacts, enables realization of the sustainable production. Spatial variability and temporal responses as discerned from geospatial data play a pivotal role in this regard due to the geographical context of the ecosystems.

(A.) Rainfed Agriculture

Rain fed farming is complex, diverse and risk prone and is characterised by low levels of productivity and low input uses. The Government of India has accorded high priority to the holistic and sustainable development of rain fed areas through integrated watershed development approach. The key attributes of the watershed approach are conservation of rain water and optimisation of soil and water resources in a sustainable and cost-effective mode. Improved moisture management increases the productivity of improved seeds and fertilizer.

Realizing the vast potential of remote sensing in achieving the development objectives of the watersheds on a sustainable basis, a large programme called Integrated Mission for Sustainable Development (IMSD) for 174 districts covering 84 M ha was carried out in India. As a part of this, various thematic maps viz., soils, geology, geomorphology, ground water, land use/ land cover, generated from satellite data were generated on 1:50,000 scale. Specific action plans were drawn up indicating alternate land use systems, soil conservation, surface water harvesting and ground water exploitation/ recharge for sustainable development of land and water resources (figure 9). Similar study focusing the desertic areas was also carried out in another project called Integrated Resource Information System for Desertic Areas (IRIS-DA).An integrated model evolved under a project called, SUJALA, has enabled better policy formulation, implementation of suitable action plans and assessment of short term and long term impacts etc. As part of National Agriculture Technology Project (NATP), identification of critical areas for land treatment was done in the watersheds of rain fed rice, cotton, oilseeds, and pulses over 7 states of India (figure 10). The prioritization of micro watersheds over Maharastra, Orissa, and Chattisgarh states is taken up to support rural poverty alleviation programme of Govt.of India.

Landsat MSS / TM, IRS-LISS data have enabled generation of soil resource maps ranging from 1:250000 to 1:50000 with the abstraction level of subgroups/ association thereof and association of families, respectively. High-resolution stereo data were found to be useful for generating information on soil resources at 1:12500 scale, necessary for micro-level optional land use planning. Derivative information such as land capability, irrigability, erodability / retentivity and suitability for different crops to generate optional land use planning could also be generated.

(B). Irrigation Management

Under the programme for the Catchment Management of River Valley Projects and Flood Prone Rivers, 53 Catchments are covered, spread over in 27 States. The total catchment area is 141 million ha. with Priority Area needing urgent treatment in 28 million ha.. National Mission on Reclamation of Alkali Soil aims at improving physical conditions and productivity status of alkali soils for restoring optimum crop production. The major components of the scheme include, assured irrigation water, farm development works like land leveling, bunding and ploughing, agriculture, community drainage system, application of soil amendment, organic manures, etc.

In India, while enormous irrigation potential has been created at huge cost, the gap between created potential and utilization is significantly large (around 9 M. ha). Thus, along with the thrust towards creation of higher irrigation potential, efforts are also need to be directed to optimal utilization of created potential. The anticipated increase in irrigated area, equitable distribution and crop productivity under programmes such as the centrally sponsored Command Area Development (CAD) scheme and National Water Management Project, have been studied using satellite data in some of the major irrigation command projects in India.

Nearly 3.3 M ha of irrigated cropland is annually monitored with moderate resolution multispectral data for irrigation performance evaluation across 14 river commands on an operational basis (figure 11). Apart from performance evaluation of irrigation systems, multi-temporal satellite data have also been used to map current status and to monitor the spatial extent of water logging and soil salinity and/ or alkalinity through the years in most of the irrigation projects. Very High-resolution satellite data from Cartosat-1, Cartosat-2, has been used for identifying and mapping irrigation infrastructure for assessing irrigation potential in new irrigation projects under Accelerated Irrigation Benefit Program (AIBP).

(C). Precision Farming

Development of Geomatics is facilitating integration of Remote sensing,GIS and GPS spatially, temporally and economically to assist farm producers in effectively managing their valuable resources. Precision agriculture with the main objective of economic optimization of crop production maintaining eco balance is an ideal option to meet the objectives of the sustainable agricultural development. Towards this objective, specific studies to explore the role of remote sensing technology in different agro ecological situations of India are taken up on pilot basis. Information on soil spectral variability and yield maps, correlated with ground observations enable generation of crop management options. In places like Punjab and Haryana states, where intense farm management practices are followed, information generated from the remotely sensed satellite data on the spatial and temporal variability of the soil and crop growth patterns can be used for efficient input application. This reduces the excessive use of agrochemicals, which would otherwise cause soil-chemical pollution. Diversified cropping using rotations involve several potential advantages compared to monocultures. These include synergestic yield interactions, reduced operating inputs, and reduced machinery ownership and labor costs.

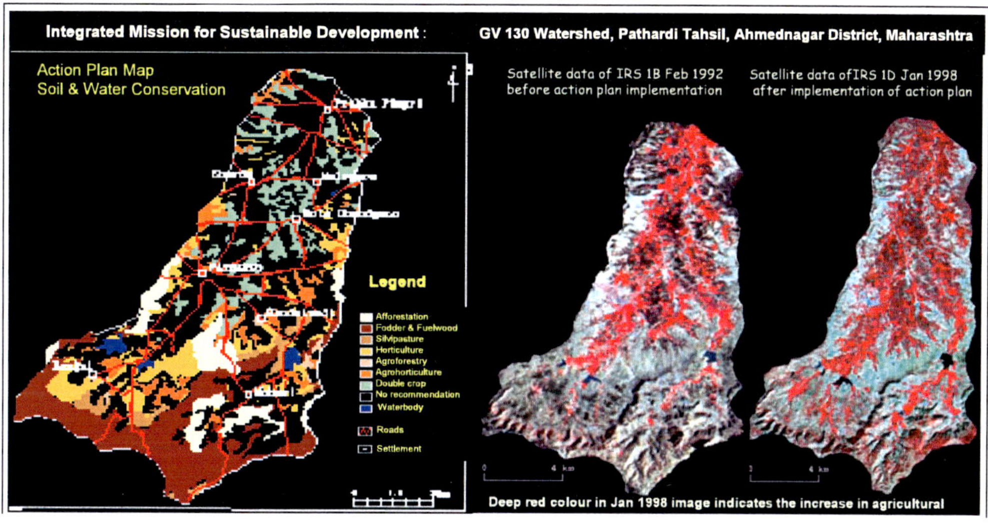

Figure 9. Integrated Mission for Sustainable Development.

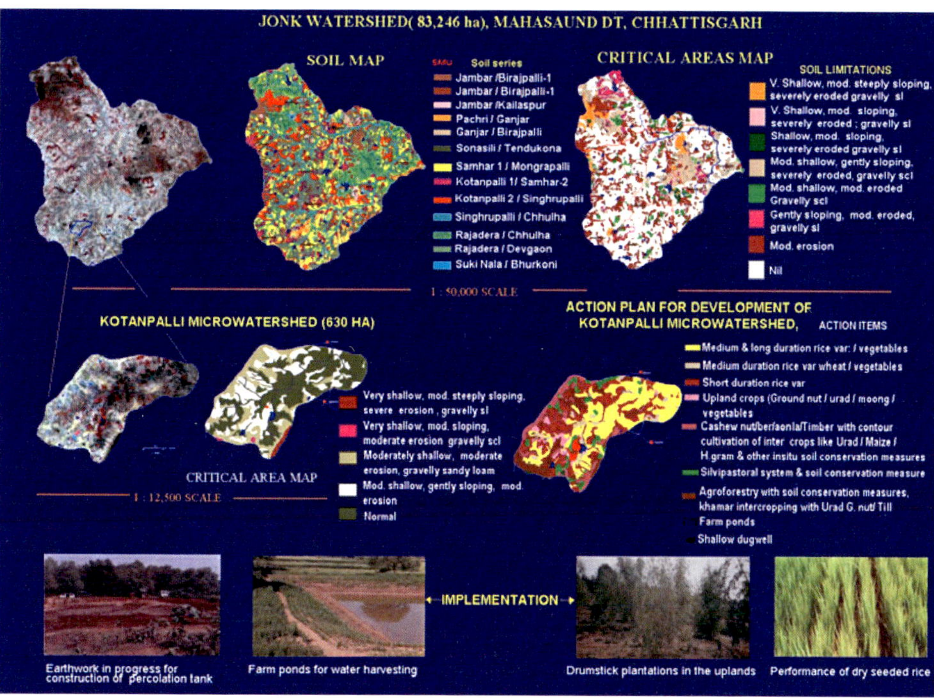

Figure 10. Identification of critical areas for dvelopment of watersheds.

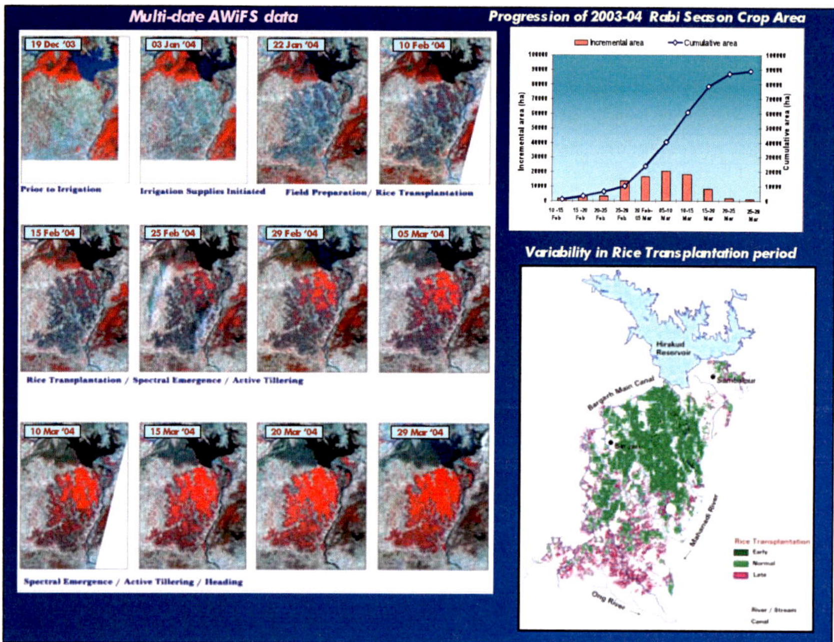

Figure 11. Monitoring of irrigated cropland near Hirakud project site.

(D). Growth Models

Multi temporal earth observation satellite data provides information on cropping patterns in spatial and temporal domains at both micro and macro levels. Interface with the crop growth models would provide information on the utilization patterns of the resources in achieving the sustainable agricultural production from a cropping system perspective. Using multi-temporal remote sensing data, along with soil, physiographic rainfall and temperature information, through modeling provides a framework for cropping systems analysis. These studies indicate the suitability of different crops and cropping systems for different agro-climatic situations under different levels of management practices. The following items could be studied, duly incorporating the weather variability and management interventions:

- Characterization of crop growing environment
- Characterization of *in situ* field and crop canopy parameters' variability to optimize crop management practices
- Crop productivity response across different agro-climatic situations through cropping systems modeling
- In season monitoring of crops for abiotic stress

3.1.3. Vulnerability and Adaptation

The studies related to vulnerability to factors such as drought, floods, land degradation and changes in climatic regimes is very important as the incidence and impact of these factors is going to increase in the context of climate change. In view of this several initiatives to study the vulnerability and adaptation strategies for agriculture ecosystems are taken up.

(A). Agriculture Drought

Being a semi-arid tropical country, India faces severe agricultural drought periodically due to infrequent rainfall. Realizing the potential of satellite-derived vegetation index (VI) which is sensitive to vegetation stress and serves as surrogate measure to assess agricultural drought, a nation-wide project titled "National Agricultural Drought Assessment and Monitoring System (NADAMS)' was launched in 1987 to monitor the drought during Kharif (South-West monsoon) season which is agriculturally more important and is also rain dependent, by generating Normalized Difference Vegetation Index (NDVI) from temporal NOAA-AVHRR data. Bulletins on fortnightly & seasonal crop conditions – depicting agricultural drought status - are issued at State/District levels, based on vegetation indices and ground-based information for 14 States, and at sub-district level for 2 States during the kharif season. Further improvements are being made with the expanded database, vegetation condition indices, mid infrared information and temperature etc. in agricultural drought assessment and monitoring.IRS-P6 AWiFS data with 56m resolution is being used for drought assessment in two states of A.P. and Karnataka. From 2006 onwards, it is planned to include Maharashtra as the third state for sub-district level agricultural drought assessment using AWiFS data. As a demonstrative study, rabi agricultural drought situation was assessed using AWiFS data over 4 selected districts of North Interior Karnataka at Tehsil level.

(B). Land Degradation and Water Logging

The information on the extent, spatial distribution and magnitude of eroded lands, salt-affected soils, waterlogged areas, shifting cultivation, to name a few, at 1:250,000 scale has been generated. This information has been used for planning land reclamation and soil conservation programmes. Soil resources maps are generated using Landsat-MSS/TM, IRS-1A/1B LISS-I and II data at scales ranging from 1:250,000 with the abstraction level of sub-groups/association thereof and association of families, respectively. Land use / Land cover information generated using satellite data in association with the land degradation information and soil maps with the relevant field data enables us to identify the areas that are vulnerable for further degradation. The multi-temporal datasets, in a modeling framework also enable the total diagnostics of the situation, in terms of the nature and severity of the problems and support generation of appropriate management strategies.

(C). Climate Change

Climate change impacts must be studied holistically, requiring integration of climate, plant, ecosystem and soil sciences. Knowledge of spatial soil diversity and landscape dynamics is fundamental to understanding of global biogeochemical cycles. Soil Organic Carbon (SOC) represents a significant pool of carbon within the biosphere. Climatic shifts in temperature and precipitation have a major influence on the decomposition and amount of SOC stored within an ecosystem and that released into the atmosphere. It is possible to link net primary production (NPP) and impact of enhanced atmospheric CO_2 on plant growth to estimate changes in SOC for different scenarios of climate change. These changes are more prone to happen in arid and semi arid areas and hence vulnerability and adaptation of cropping systems need to be understood.

The traditional agriculture land use system in Indian Himalayan region is an integral part of the society and local environment as the crop husbandry, animal husbandry and forests constitute interlinked systems. But due to variety of factors the land use under traditional crops is changing very fast in parts of Indian Himalayan region. This kind of land intensification is a severe threat to the environment of the region. Agriculture is highly dependent on weather and changes in global climate have a major effect on crop yield and food supply. Weather also impacts soil and plant growth; and animal growth and development. Horticulture is an important source of income of the Himalayan people. Irregular rainfall and snowfall; change in climatic condition; and rising temperatures affect fruit production. The quality and quantity of tea production is also affected by irregular rainfall. Hence concerted efforts need to be made in understanding the cropping distribution and adaptation to climate change conditions.

3.2. Forests and Bioresource Potential

The natural terrestrial ecosystems like forests, grasslands and scrub lands, provide immense potential in terms of bioresources. India has forest cover of 67.8 million ha (covering 20.64% of total geographic area).Much of the demand for timber, fuel wood and fodder are met through these forests as bioresources. Wood products removed from forests and other wooded land constitutes an important component of the productive function. The standing stock (timber volume) and the volume of wood removed indicate the condition of the forests and economic and social utility of forest resources to national economies and local communities. This information contributes to monitoring the use of forest resources by comparing actual removal with the sustainable potential.

Besides there has been growing recognition of the role of Non Wood Forest Products (NWFP) as an integral part of sustainable forest management in developed and developing countries. A wide variety of products are collected from forests, woodlands and trees outside forests – a major portion of which are consumed by households or sold locally, while some find export markets. Understanding the potential contribution of NWFPs to sustainable rural development, especially in poverty alleviation and food security, requires good statistical data, which in most cases are gathered sporadically and are often unreliable. In India the knowledge about medicinal value of plants has evolved in the form of traditional systems of medicinal sciences like, Unani, Ayurveda and Siddha. More than 8,000 species are used in some 10,000 drug formulations. It is estimated that about 0.5 million ton (dry weight) of plant material is collected each year from the forests.

Managing this important spatially as well as temporally dynamic resource base due to numerous factors affecting its spread and quality can be a daunting task without the utilization of proper spatial tool. Space technology has immense influence in the decision-making processes especially in areas like forest resource management. Remote sensing as a tool has facilitated systematic and hierarchical approach of forest resources assessment and its monitoring using sensors of different spatial and spectral capabilities, the characterization, quantification and monitoring including specific efforts towards understanding the structure, composition and function of different natural habitats/ecosystems. These studies have provided key inputs for the regulation of the impact of developmental activities and to maintain forest cover areas and sustain the delivery of natural ecosystem goods and services (table 4).

Table 4. Inputs For Resource Optimization Zoning – Forests

Parameters	Processes	Utility
Protected Areas		
Area Type Connectivity Resources Biotic Pressures Habitat Maping	Monitoring Habitat Suitability Remoteness Fringe Effects	Sustainability Ecodevelopment Plans - Fringe management (PWC)
Reserved Forests		
Area Type Resources Degradation Biotic Pressures	Supply-Demand Scenario Productive Potential	Area Conservation Development Plans (RWC) Area Optimization
Coastal Zones		
Area Characterization Habitat Characterization Development Potential	Habitat Monitoring Growth & Development Trends Feasibility Analysis	Developmantal Plans
Heritage Sites		
Geospatial Database Corridor Characterization		Corridor Preservation and Protection

3.2.1. Areas Characterization and Monitoring

At the backdrop of increased developmental activities and demand for land and forest as bioresource, the reliable and repeat assessment of forest cover has become important as bench mark survey for policy planning and scientific management. India has diverse climatic, geological, topographical and anthropogenic disturbance gradients. This has resulted in the formation of diverse vegetation communities. Major eco-regions like Eastern and Western Himalayas, Shivaliks, Vindhyans, Eastern and Western Ghats and Coast constitute region specific vegetation types Champion & Seth (1968) based on extensive ground surveys brought out forest type classification based on forest structure, composition and environment (climate, topography).Grasslands and savannas cover nearly one third of the earth surface, providing livelihoods for nearly 800 million people, along with forage for livestock, wildlife habitat, carbon and water storage. As the milk production increased rapidly over the years (from 21MT in 1968 to 78MT in 2001), the pastures on the other hand, has not increased, instead they were getting reduced or degraded. In this context development of spatially explicit information on extent and distribution and subsequent monitoring of forest cover and its cover types has been achieved through application of satellite remote sensing

(A). Forest Cover Assessment as Baseline on Forest Area

Forest cover mapping provides total forest area information in terms of crown density classes, an index of condition of forests. Forest crown density refers to the % area covered by tree crown per unit ground area. National forest cover mapping initiated by NRSA for the periods 1972-75 & 1981-83 using Land Sat MSS data at 1:1 million scale. In addition, the study has also established the operational methodology for national cover mapping and technology was transferred to FSI. Since then Forest Survey of India (FSI) has made ten biennial assessments. Forest cover was interpreted visually for two crown density classes 10-40% and >40%. for first seven cycles at 1:250,000 scale, and then digital approaches are followed for the subsequent cycles (1:50,000) As spatial resolution of satellite data improved, classes > 70 %, 40 – 70%, 10-40 % and scrub have been delineated in addition to the tree cover outside the Reserve forest areas (figure 3). The present assessment [15] represents >70 %, 40-70%, 10-40 % crown density classes,scrub and tree cover with total forest area reported as 67.7 Mha of the country. Govt. of India envisaged for 33% of total geographical area of the country need to be brought under forest cover. A comparative analysis of % area to be brought under forests for meeting 33% criteria and available culturable wasteland which can reclaimed for development of vegetation is shown in figure 12. The analysis show significant scope of area availability for potential increase in forest cover.

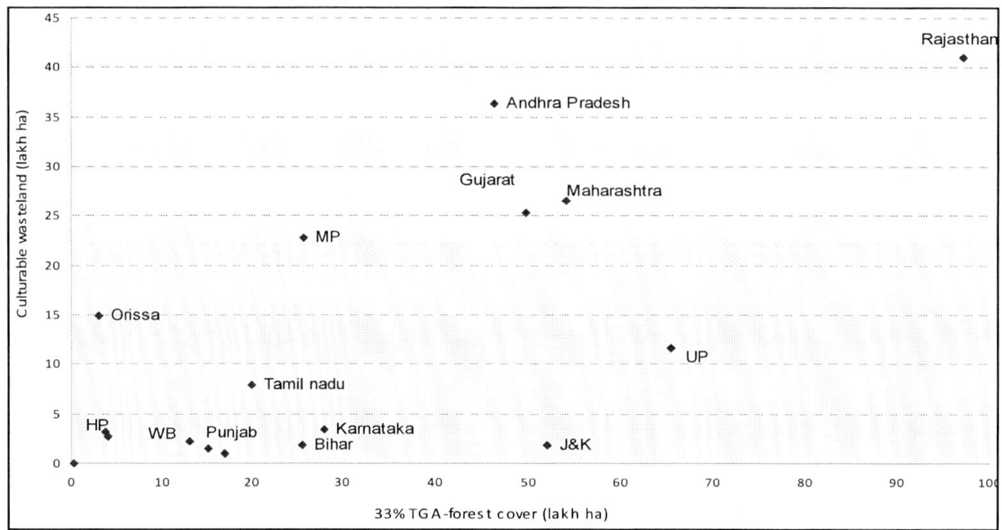

Figure 12. Deficit in forest cover with reference to maximum envisaged area (33% of total geographical area of a state) and available cultivable wasteland in different states of India

(B). Forest Type Mapping as Potential Base of Bioresource

Champion & Seth classification scheme (1968) which is in vogue in the country for characterizing forest type does not have spatial explicitness and with the increasing pressure on forests during the last three decades, enormous changes were noticed in forest composition. In view of this satellite remote sensing is used as one of the effective tools to delineate forest types for better management. Forest types based on unique structure (canopy, height, branching, and tree density), composition (species mixture) and phenology (leaf onset/offset – leaf fall) provides unique spectral signatures. Based on the phenological/structural properties, 16 major type groups of the country were mapped using multi temporal SPOT and IRS AWiFS data [17,18].Using IRS LISS-III data, in addition to type groups, locale specific formations (Red Sanders), gregarious formations (single species formations occurring over larger areas – Sal) were mapped for entire country [19]. Currently FSI is preparing detailed forest type map for the entire country on 1:50,000 scale. These forest types have unique species composition having different economic and ecological value which can be effectively quantified using optimal ground surveys.

(C). Grassland Resources Assessment

Conservation of grasslands/savannas has become major concern due to their rapid degradation, in terms of reduction in productivity, invasion of weeds an d land cover changes. In case of India, it is very critical that 80% of Indian grasslands/pasture is considered as very poor in their productive potential. This has created a wide gap between the availability of fodder and demand for it, which in turn will have wide ranging consequences on the balance of the ecosystem. In this regard, Satellite Remote Sensing offers an effective tool to monitor and assess them periodically in time and cost effective manner. In view of this, a study had been undertaken for mapping (1:50,000 scale) of grasslands/grazing resources using IRS LISS-III data for which 3 different bio-climatic regions namely, Western Himalayas (humid tropics), Gujarat (semi-arid) (figure 10) and Tamil nadu (tropical) were chosen.

3.2.2. Production Systems

(A). Bioresources Assessment as Fodder, Fuel and Commercial Timber

India has enormous biomass potential trapped in different ecosystems. 65.7 M ha of forests has 2400 M T biomass. 12 M ha of grassland / scrub has 30 M T biomass. 224 M ha of cultivable non forest area has ~11 trees/ha. 170 M ha of cultivated land contributes large biomass of crop residue. In addition satellite remote sensing technique is used to estimate the fodder biomass, fuel wood availability enabling to understand the supply demand gaps and identify appropriate measures for regulation of extracts, pressure on forest lands, minimize forest degradation [20].

(B). Commercial Timber Resource Assessment

In India management plans of 750 forest divisions need updation every 10 years. The management plan preparation requires detailed stock maps which show the type of standing forest crop and its timber volume. Ground based conventional methods take 4-5 years with ~5% ground sampling intensity. High resolution satellite data used for forest canopy and type stratification optimizes ground sampling intensity and proper distribution of sample points. Hence using RS and GIS inputs work is accomplished in 2 years with 0.01-0.2% sampling. Several state forest departments are adopting these approaches. National Forest Working Plan code committee envisaged the use of RS & GIS in Forest Working Plan. Outputs provided include stands tables (number of trees distributed across different species and diameter classes), stock tables (total timber volume across species and diameter classes) and stock map. These inputs are used by forest departments to make operational plans for suitable harvest and conservation scenarios. The preparation of working circles like Selection Working Circle using geoinformatics tools helped in sustainable extraction of wood (figure 13).

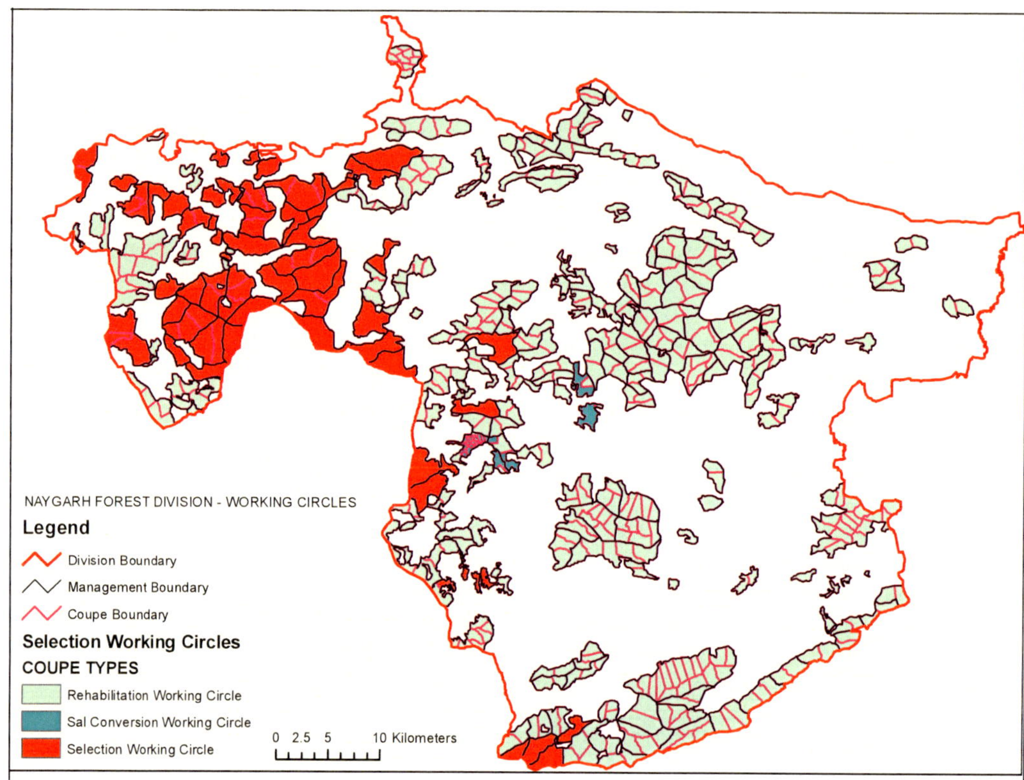

Figure 13. Working plan input preparation using Remote Sensing and GIS.

(C). Species Level Mapping as Potential Information as Bioresource

The economically and medicinally important species like Teak, Sal, Dipterocarpus (Plywood) and medicinally important species like Hippophae, which grows in large extents as single species dominated formations can be identified and mapped using remote sensing sensors like IRS LISS-III [21,22]. Sal forests cover 9 Mha of Indian forests and serve as bioresource in terms of wood, fodder, NTFPs etc. and are almost mapped for the entire part of the country. The spatial information on the distribution of these species could be used as source to prepare scientific assessments on quantification, extraction and conservation systems. In addition using high resolution satellite data like IRS-LISS-IV and Cartosat could be used to map assemblage of species which can give the relative abundance of a species.

3.2.3 Community Forest Management – Sustainable Use of Bioresources

In India, 226 million population depend on forest energy resources. 26 M ha open forest areas are linked with 1,70,000 villages. 96% of rural households use biofuel. Still a gap of 184 M T/annum of firewood and 125 M T/annum of green fodder exists. In view of this, reliable accounting of forest resources and sustainable resources extraction has become critical and a new paradigm of "Forest Management" with rural participation has evolved. Several joint forest management and community forest management programmes are launched in different states over 25 M ha forest area and Joint Forest Management activities are monitored and evaluated using remote sensing data.. RS & GIS based approaches provide means to assess potential biomass, NTFP resources, perspective planning and monitoring. In this scenario the sustainable resources extraction has become critical.

JFM activities involve active participation and involvement of the rural people in developing plantation on marginal and degraded lands, building water and soil conservation structures as bunds on barren lands, fire control, weed removal regulation of forest production and overall forest protection. Rural communities in turn share the benefits accrued from these activities. Satellite remote sensing helps in site identification, resources assessment, monitoring and evaluation. Site identification includes delineation of degraded forests over suitable slopes/terrains and accessibility. Satellite remote sensing data also helps in monitoring and evaluation in terms of changes in greenness, crown closure improvements, new species formations (Weeds/Bamboo/plantation).

4.0. Conservation Zoning

National Environmental Policy, 2006 [5] envisages protecting and conserving critical ecological systems and resources, and invaluable natural and man-made heritage, which are essential for life support, livelihoods, economic growth, and a broad conception of human well-being. It also addresses to ensure equitable access to environmental resources and quality for all sections of society, and in particular, to ensure that poor communities, which are most dependent on environmental resources for their livelihoods, are assured secure access to these resources.

It also defines Environmentally Sensitive Zones as areas with identified environmental resources having "Incomparable Values" which require special attention for their conservation. Significant risks to human health, life, and environmental life-support systems, besides certain other unique natural and man-made entities, which may impact the well-being, broadly conceived, of large numbers of persons, are considered as "Incomparable" in that individuals or societies would not accept these risks for compensation in money or conventional goods and services. A conventional economic cost-benefit calculus would not, accordingly, apply in their case, and such entities would have priority in allocation of societal resources for their conservation without consideration of direct or immediate economic benefit.

With the help of multi resolution satellite remote sensing data and customized data collection and integration systems, concerted efforts were made to facilitate implementation of environmental and socially sustainable conservation planning in the areas of protected area management, coastal zone management and heritage site preservation.

4.1. Biodiversity Characterization and Protected Areas

The status of biodiversity and wildlife in a region is an accurate index of the state of ecological resources, and thus of the natural resource base of human well-being. This is because of the interdependent nature of ecological entities, in which wildlife is a vital link. Moreover, several charismatic species of wildlife embody "Incomparable Values", and at the same time, comprise a major resource base for sustainable eco-tourism. Conservation of wildlife and biodiversity, accordingly, involves the protection of entire ecosystems. However, in several cases, delineation of and restricting access to such Protected Areas (PAs), as well as disturbance by humans on these areas has led to man-animal conflicts.

While physical barriers and better policing may temporarily reduce such conflict, it is also necessary to address their underlying causes. These may largely arise from the non-involvement of relevant stakeholders in identification and delineation of PAs, as well as the loss of traditional entitlements of local people, especially tribals, over the PAs. There is also a strong need for creation of corridors to ensure proper genetic flows across habitats. Since wildlife does not remain confined to particular areas, there is also need to ensure greater protection, and habitat enhancement outside the PAs. A comparative analysis of % area under forests and % area under protected areas is shown in figure 14. The analysis show significant scope of for potential increase in protected areas.

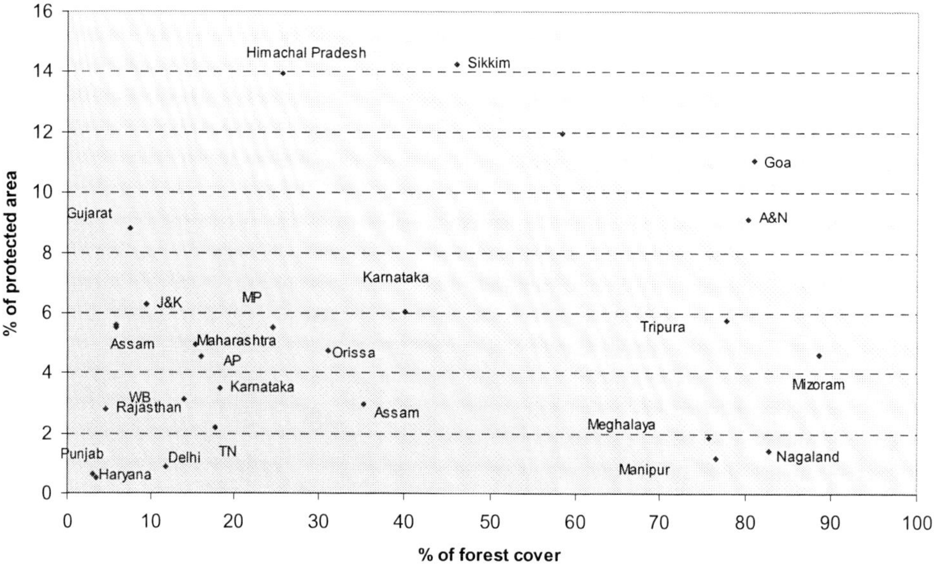

Figure 14. Percent forest cover area and percent forest cover under protected area net work in different states of India

In a major initiative, 50 Mha (80%) forests were characterized for intact and critical habitats of biodiversity under the project 'Biodiversity Characterization at Landscape Level'. The project was carried out in two phases and in the first phase Western Himalayas, North East, the Andaman and Nicobar Islands and the Western Himalayas were covered. In the second phase central India, West Bengal and Eastern Ghats and East coast was covered. The study was an outcome of the efforts of 27 Universities and 11 National institutions involving 63 scientists and 56 research scholars.10 spatial layers comprising Vegetation types derived from remote sensing data, forest fragmentation, settlement and road buffers, ecosystem uniqueness, species diversity and economic value derived from 12,000 sample plots among others were integrated in geospatial domain to derive index of Biological Richness (figure 15). The data is organized in web based 'Biodiversity Information System' facilitating query and analysis. The data provides spatial extent and relative abundance of vegetation patches of medicinal and economic value for prioritizing the areas for conservation and plan for sustainable bioprospecting [19].

With increasing pressure on the pristine forest ecosystems the concept of "Protected Areas" is introduced in the country under the Wildlife Protection Act (1972). Around 500 wildlife sanctuaries, 90 National Parks constituting 15.6 Mha of the forests exist as per date. National Mission to generate spatial databases on vegetation type (1:25,000) using IRS LISS IV data and large mammal density distribution was launched for all protected areas under the aegis of Standing Committee on Bioresources, Ministry of Environment & Forests. Satellite Remote sensing provides inputs in terms of vegetation type, habitat maps, water holes, management zonation prepared using rule based criteria.

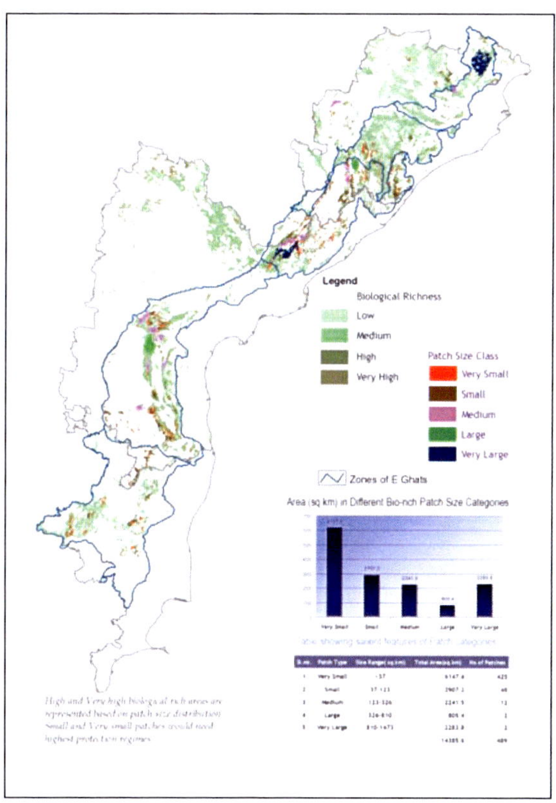

Figure 15. Biologically Rich areas for Conservation Priortisation and Bioprospecting in Eastern Ghats and East Coast.

4.2. Coastal Zones

Coastal environmental resources comprise a diverse set of natural and manmade assets, including mangroves, coral reefs, estuaries, coastal forests, genetic diversity, sand dunes, geomorphologies, sand beaches, land for agriculture and human settlements, coastal infrastructure, and heritage sites. These provide habitats for marine species, which, in turn comprise the resource base for large numbers of fisher folk, protection from extreme weather events, a resource base for sustainable tourism, and agricultural and urban livelihoods. In recent years there has been significant degradation of coastal resources, for which the proximate causes include poorly planned human settlements, improper location of industries and infrastructure, pollution from industries and settlements, and overexploitation of living natural resources. In the future, sea level rise due to climate change may have major adverse impacts on the coastal environment. The deeper causes of these proximate factors lie in inadequate institutional capacities for, and participation of local communities in formulation and implementation of coastal management plans, the open access nature of many coastal resources, and lack of consensus on means of provision of sanitation and waste treatment.

In view of the degradation of coastal environment and uncontrolled construction activities along the Coastal areas, MOEF issued the Coastal Regulation Zone (CRZ) notification, 1991declaring coastal stretches as Coastal regulation Zones and regulating activities in the CRZ [8]. As per this 500 M on the landward side from the High Tide Line and the land area between the Low Tide Line and High Tide Line including 500 M along the tidal influenced water bodies subject to minimum of 100M on the width of the water body whichever is less is declared as CRZ areas. Based on several ecological parameters, the CRZ areas are classified into four categories namely CRZ I (Sensitive and intertidal) CRZ II (urban or developed), CRZ III (Rural or Undeveloped) and CRZ IV (Andaman, Nicobar and Lakshadweep islands). This notification has clearly regulated activities in the CRZ area prohibiting unwarranted activities and permitting essential activities.

In order to facilitate these activities in coastal areas, information on present land use conditions and precise delineation of HTL and LTL was generated using Indian Remote Sensing (IRS) data,having moderate (23-36 m) and high (6 m) spatial resolutions, Database on wetland conditions (mangroves, coral reef,mudflats, beach) between HTL and LTL, land use (agriculture, forest, barren land, built up land) up to 500 m from HTL as well as delineation of HTL and LTL on 1:25,000-scale for the entire country was done [23]. A Classification system has been evolved such that these maps can be used to define coastal regulation zones highlighting ecologically sensitive zones (CRZ I), developed areas (CRZ II), undeveloped areas (CRZ III) and Islands (CRZ IV). These maps provided baseline information for planners and decision-makers and have been used for management plans. Separate maps for identifying areas under erosion and deposition, coral reefs and mangroves were also prepared. The classification accuracy have been achieved is 85 per cent or better at 90 per cent confidence level. The important achievement has been the acceptability of satellite-based information on CRZ by both the executive and judicial authorities. It is now almost mandatory for all industries, governmental as well as non-governmental agencies to use satellite-derived information for the coastal regulation zone activities.

5.0. Development Zones

5.1. Urban Expansion

India's urban population in 2001 was 286.1 million, which was 27.8% of the total population. Over the previous five decades, annual rates of growth of urban population ranged between 2.7 to 3.8%. One-forth of the country's total urban population (80.7 M) belongs to category of poor population and 99% of the housing shortage of 24.7 million at the end of the 10th Plan pertains to the Economically Weaker Sections (EWS) and Low Income Groups (LIG) sectors. 79% of the new jobs totaling 19.3 million between 1991-2001 were generated in urban areas and only 5 million jobs were generated in rural areas It is, therefore, of vital importance that a new National Urban Housing and Habitat Policy [9] carefully analyses ways and means of providing the 'Affordable Housing to All' with special emphasis on the EWS and LIG sectors. In this context availability of non culturable land which can be potential used for developmental activities like housing, infrastructure and industrial activities is one of the prerequisite.

5.1.1. Regional Planning

As India's labour force witnesses a rural to urban shift; it is of critical importance that the rural and urban areas develop in a symbiotic manner. The way to bring about such a symbiotic development between rural and urban areas is by adopting a "Regional Planning approach." The objective of such an approach is to develop a symbiotic rural-urban continuum, which is ecologically sustainable. As part of national wasteland mapping project of India, spatial databases on culturable and nonculturable wastelands have been developed. Using these maps and statistics therein, in conjunction with relevant socioeconomic parameters, the dynamics of relationship between the incidence of poverty and natural resources degradation in the different States of India, representing the diverse ecosystems as well as different economic and social policy regimes and institutional mechanisms has been studied [24]. The study examined how macro-economic variables could determine the dynamics of poverty and natural resources degradation relationship in rural India. The study identified the various states and the potential for utilizing wasteland for different developmental processes.

In view of the fact that 50% of India's population is forecasted to be living in urban areas by 2041, it is necessary to develop new integrated townships. These townships should generally be located on comparatively degraded land excluding prime agricultural areas growing more than one crop with the help of assured irrigation. These townships should be located at a reasonable distance from medium or large existing towns. Further, it is also important to develop mass rapid transport corridors between existing medium and large towns and new green-field towns so that the relationship between industry and commerce is developed to an optimum level. A comparative analysis of socioeconomic index, % industrial growth and availability of non culturable in different states is shown in figures 16 and 17 revealing the scope for further development in different states.

Development of sustainable habitat is closely related to the adoption of 'the Regional Planning approach' while preparing Master Plans of towns/ cities, District Plans and Regional/Sub-Regional Plans. It involves maintenance of the ecological balance in terms of a symbiotic perspective on rural and urban development while developing urban extensions of existing towns as well as new integrated townships. Promotion of sustainable habitat is closely linked with reserving a significant proportion of the total Master Plan area as 'green lungs of the city' (e.g. Master Plan for Delhi 2021 provides 20% of green areas), protecting water bodies with special emphasis on the flood plains of our rivers and developing green belts around our cities. It will be desirable to pursue a goal of 20-25% recreational land use area (excluding water bodies) which has been prescribed for Metro-cities by the Urban Development Plan Formulation and Implementation Guidelines (UDPFI) in order to enhance the sustainability of human settlements. [9]

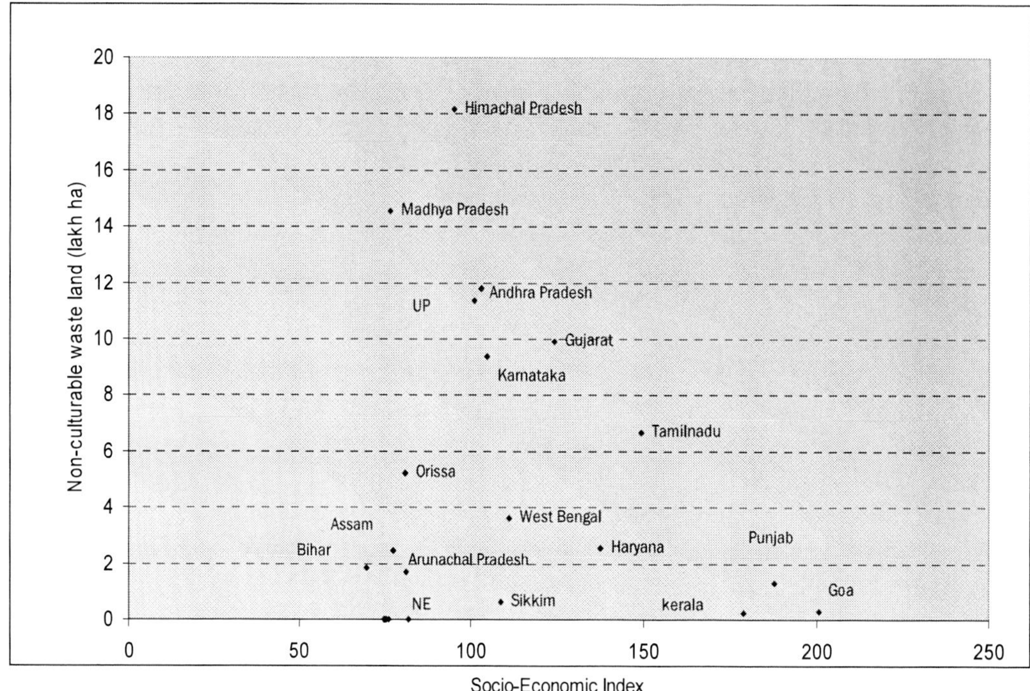

Figure 16. Socioeconomic Index and Non cultivable wasteland available (Potential land for developmental activities) in different states of India

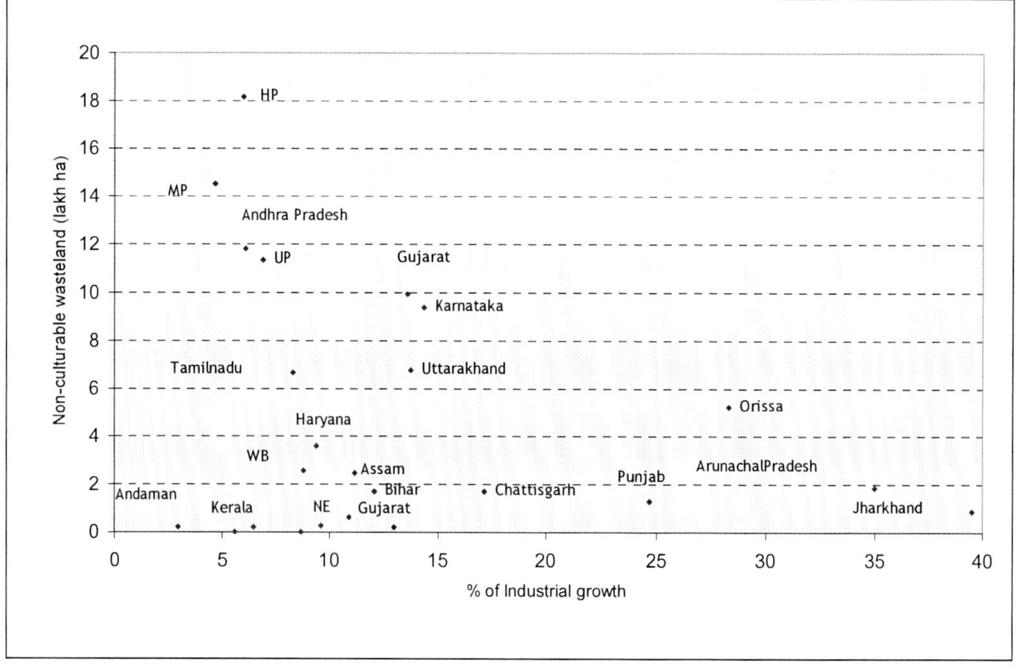

Figure 17. Industrial growth status and Non cultivable wasteland available (Potential land for industrial growth) in different states of India

LULC mapping and creation of GIS database and master plan inputs for major cities are provided in terms of spatial maps including land use/land cover, transport network, administrative boundaries using high resolution IRS satellite data. The remote sensing and GIS inputs provided for the development of plan for National Capital Region (NCR) covering an area of 30,242 sq km is worth mentioning. The inputs provided helped to develop proposed Land use of 2021, Policy zones for development, Settlement Plan of 2001 and 2021, Transport Plan (Road and Rail) of 2001 and 2021, Ground water rechargeable area, Environmental sensitive and Ground water rechargeable areas.

Airborne data is also used for large scale mapping at scales ranging from 1:500 to 1:10000 or higher for applications such as urban planning, rural infrastructure development, base map preparation, cadastral mapping, infrastructure developments, and Utility GIS projects. The expertise also has been put in preparing large scale base maps using High resolution satellite images from sub-meter imagery and presently migrating to exploit the potential of Cartosat-1 and Cartosat-2 data. Realising the need for reliable information, Min. of Urban Development has been funding in phased manner to cover nearly 5600 cities and towns for generating National Urban Information System (NUIS). Under NUIS scheme multi-scale urban Geospatial database for 158 towns of India covering 55, 755 sq. km for urban planning, management, infrastructure development and e-governance. For these cities, four thematic layers viz., LULC, Soil, Geomorphology, and Ground water are addressed. It also generates base details of urban fringe areas generated at 1:10000 scale with Cartosat-1, and urban core area base line information using Aerial data at 1:2000 scale and utility information at 1:1,000 using ground observations (with GPR for sewerage and drainage lines etc.).

A study being conducted on Cadastral level mapping in Nizamabad district in Andhra Pradesh is going to demonstrate development of total Land Information System (LIS) thereby replacing the existing obsolete system with an effective land management system. The LIS coupled with a Village Resource Information System (VRIS) will be immensely useful in managing and developing rural India.The main themes are Urban land use, geomorphology, geology and soils along with spatially integrated socio-economic database. The scientific urban GIS database would help us to establish the ecological footprint of resource, energy and infrastructure for sustainable development of urban environment.

5.2. Infrastructure Development

With the rapid growth of the economy in recent years the importance and the urgency of removing infrastructure constraints have increased. Infrastructure also has backward and forward linkages with the rest of the economy. The transport sector presents India as one of the largest road networks in the world, aggregating to about 3.34 million kilometers at present. The alignment of power transmission lines and oil pipelines, development of new road net works has challenges in developing optimal routes with minimal development and environmental costs. Several studies were conducted to identify optimal routes and its associated impacts on land use. The high resolution satellite data based land use and land cover maps in association with ecological, environmental and socio economic information were geospatially modeled to provide such inputs for optimal path selection .

5.3. Industrial Development

The industrial development sectors like power, mining, paper and pulp (natural resource based industries) and developmental activities like irrigation and river valley projects have a significant influence on land use and land cover. The development of these industries not only has impacts due to land acquisition but also due to associated impacts of development on land use and land cover. In view of this rapid and comprehensive environmental impact assessment of the proposed activities to assess the feasibility of development, preparation of environment management plans and regular auditing has become mandatory. Accordingly natural life sustaining systems and specific land uses which are sensitive to industrial impact because of the nature and extent of fragility are identified (table 5) to regulate the development and are as follows:

a Ecologically and/or otherwise sensitive areas: At least 25 Km depending on the geo-climatic conditions the requisite distance shall have to be increased by the appropriate agency.
b Coastal areas: At least ½ km from high tide line.
c Flood plain of the riverine systems: At least ½ km from flood plain or modified flood plain affected by dam in the upstream or by flood control system.
d Major settlements (3,00,000 population) : Distance from settlements is difficult to maintain because of urban sprawl and ;
e Comprehensive list of land use areas /zones which need to be avoided are given in table 5

Table 5. Ecological Sensitive Areas

1	Religious/Archaelogical/Tourist Importance	
		Religious and Historic places Archaelogical Monuments (e.g.) Identified zone around Taj Mahal Scenic Areas Hill Resorts Beach Resorts Health Resorts
2	Natural - Fragile Systems	
		Coastal Areas rich in Coral, Mangroves, Breeding Grounds of Specific Species Estuaries rich in Mangroves, Breeding Ground of specific Species Gulf Areas Biosphere Reserves National Parks and Sanctuaries Natural Lakes, Swamps Seismic Zones Tribal Settlements
3	Sensitive Establishments	
		Areas of Scientific and Geological interest Defence Installations, specially those of security importance and sensitive to pollution Border Areas (International) and Airports

These eco sensitive zones along with resources information, air and water quality, socio economic factors were used to develop industrial zoning atlases providing shelf of sites which meet minimum ecological criteria. The thematic maps developed on agriculture, forests, biodiversity, geomorphology and soils using remote sensing data were analyzed in conjunction with other relevant non spatial information in geospatial domain to develop atlases on industrial zoning. Subsequently remote sensing based information has been used to assess the feasibility against specific site requirements viz., open cast mines, reservoir submergence area analysis, hydro power and coastal thermal power plant site selection, assessment of potential wood availability for paper and pulp industries, pipe line alignment studies for oil and gas based industries and power line transmission studies. Extensive studies are conducted on ecological monitoring of coal based thermal power plants in terms of mining and ash pond impacts and assess the efficacy of environmental management plans.

5.4. Natural Resources Census – An Integrated Database

In order to make the spatial information on natural resources available to user community and facilitate integrated analysis, the Department of Space, Govt. of India has launched a programme titled "National Natural Resources Repository (NRR)". The NRR consists of data generation, database organization and spatial data services. The natural Resources Census (NRC) project addresses the database generation element of NRR. The NRC envisages generating spatial information on (i) Land use / land cover (ii)Land degradation (iii) Soils (iv) Geomorphology (v) snow cover or glaciers (vi) wetland and (vii) vegetation cover at 1:50000 scale using high resolution satellite data.

6.0. LULC Change - Land Development Scenario

Landdevelopment scenarios as a means of representing the future have been in the planner's toolkit for several decades. . This is evidenced by the inclusion of land-development scenarios in many high-profile planning documents published since the 1960s. At root, landdevelopment scenarios are composed images of an area's landuse patterns that would result from particular landuse plans, policies, and regulations if they were actually adopted and implemented at a certain point of time. Common to landdevelopment scenarios are five components: (1) alternatives, the range of potential choices of landuse plans, policies, and regulations; (2) consequences, the immediate and cumulative effects (physical, ecological, economical, and social) that each alternative would have on an area's land-development futures; (3) causations, the causal bonds between alternatives and consequences; (4) time frames of the periods of time between implementation of the alternatives and the unfolding, either full or partial, of their consequences; and (5) geographical footprints, the place-oriented blueprints of alternatives, and the anticipated marks of their ramifications on the geography of an area [25,26].

In order to understand and quantify these complex relationships, the recent gains in computing resources and techniques need to be adopted. These could be (a) extend dynamic spatial simulation techniques to model the distinct temporal and spatial patterns of land-use and land-cover change; (b) connect these models pending theoretical frameworks that accommodate to the complexity of, and relationships among, socioeconomic and environmental factors (c) establish common validation and replication protocols necessary for determining the robustness of model outcomes under different assessment scenarios; (d) consider the value of information and the role of uncertainty in determining model outputs; and (e)examine the utility of dynamic spatial simulation models for land managers and government decision makers [27].

A number of theoretical approaches are considered as the principles and basis to integrate population-environment interactions as drivers of land use and land cover dynamics. For instance, Complexity theory examines systems that contain more possibilities than can be actualized, where descriptions are not constrained by an a priori definition. The goal of application of this theory is to understand how simple, fundamental processes can be combined to produce complex holistic systems. Non equilibrium systems with feedbacks can lead to non-linearity and may evolve into systems that exhibit criticality. Complex systems generally embody hierarchical linkages that operate at different spatial and temporal scales. Hierarchy theory developed in general systems theory and now incorporated into ecology is used to describe the structure of ecological systems through their spatial and temporal organizations. Spatial and temporal grains and extents frame the studies, and scale, pattern, process interrelationships are fundamental. Hierarchies can change with time thereby making issues of resilience and adaptability of critical importance.

Political ecology theory involves the nesting of local decision-making at finer scales framed within a broader set of issues operating at coarser scales. Interactions between local endogenous factors and regional, national, global exogenous factors are considered, often within a land science context where time-lags are examined and directional flows between direct and indirect consumers and producers are considered. Human ecology theory sees people as active agents on the landscape that shape and are shaped by the environment. Feedback mechanisms with possible thresholds or triggers may be observed where human behavior shifts in relation to real or perceived environmental and/or land use/land cover patterns and dynamics.

Analyzing changes and its causes are the most challenging areas of landscape ecology especially due to the absence of temporal ground data and comparable space platform based data for the historical tome frames. Considering the complexity of heterogeneous landscapes and lack of reliable historical data in India, the predictive modeling of land use scenarios has to go a long way in providing an operational system of predictive modeling and scenario development. A very few important studies were conducted recently on predictive modeling for forest protection and carrying capacity of fuel and fodder supplies.

6.1. Case Studies – LULC Changes

North Eastern (NE) region of India harbours 83.5% forest cover and dominated by varied forest types and associated land use. Indigenous shifting cultivation has long been practiced in all parts of NE region over the past several decades and has impacted land use patterns and compositional and structural changes in forests. In view of this, predictive anlysis of forest cover changes in Meghalaya state of NE region was conducted .The trends in LULC changes were analyzed using remote sensing based LULC maps generated for 1980, 1989, 1995 and were used to develop predictive forest cover for the years [28,29] (figure 18).

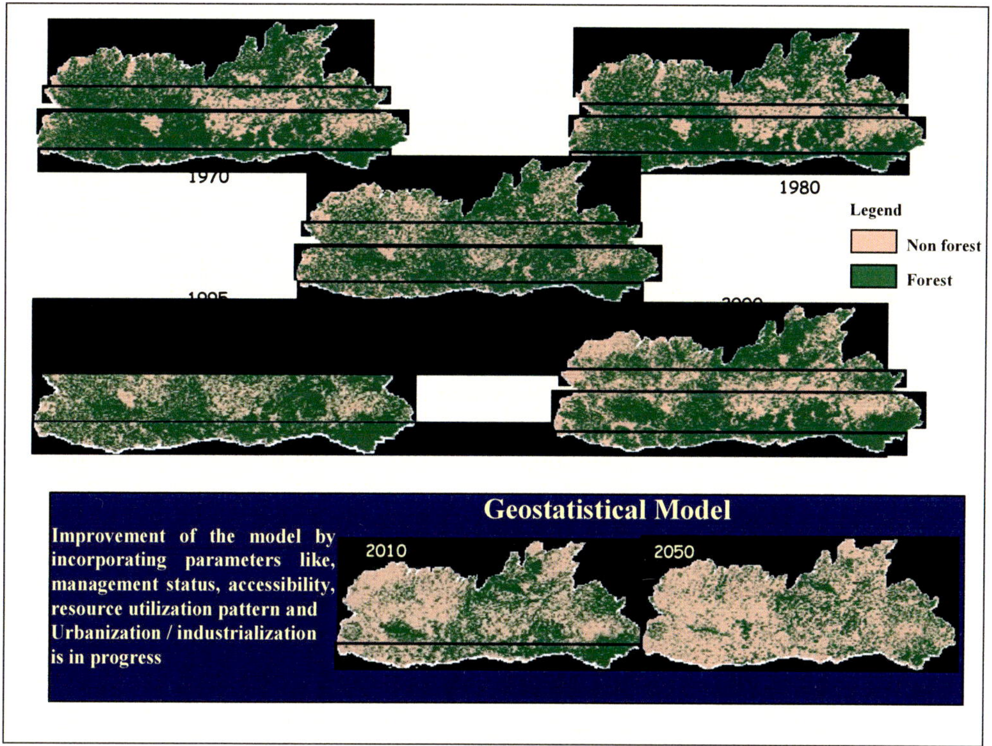

Figure 18. Forest dynamics and predictions.

A time series of remote sensing data from 1973, 1990 and 2004 were used to assess spatial patterns of forest cover change in Kalakad-Mundanthurai Tiger Reserve (KMTR), Southern Western Ghats (India) [30]. Time-series maps were combined with biotic and abiotic factors in GIS for modelling its future change. The landcover change has been modelled using GEOMOD for the study region and predicted for year 2020 using the current disturbance scenario. GEOMOD is a simple unidirectional linear change modelling tool that uses suitability image/s, produced by combining a variety of driver images to predict locations of change for given quantity of change between two time periods. After comparing its performance between the past and the present, using satisfactory suitability image/s, one can actually simulate future change for varying scenarios of change between two categories. The most interesting part of this type of change modelling is in its ability to model location specific change for different quantities of change.

Comparison of the forest change maps over the 31-year period shows that evergreen forest loss (16%) being degraded primarily in the form of selective logging and clear felling to raise plantations of coffee, tea and cardamom. The natural disturbances such as forest fire, wildlife grazing, invasions after clearance and soil erosion induced by anthropogenic pressure over the decades are the reasons of forest cover change in KMTR. The study demonstrates the role of remote sensing and GIS in monitoring of large coverage of forest area continuously for a given region over time more precisely and costeffective manner which will be ideal for conservation planning and prioritization.

6.2. Scenario Prediction for Sustainable Production

With the enormous demand on forests for fuel, fodder and food, the development of future scenario for perspective planning has become very much necessary. The various ongoing programmes on people participatory management on forest based products and Clean Development Mechanism (Forestry) requires inputs for evaluation of sustenance of such activities. Spatial Resources Growth Model (SPRGDM) was used to predict the sustainability of fuel and fodder for the coming 25 years in one of the Joint Forest Management (JFM) programme areas in Karnataka, India [31], which are taken as locking periods of JFM programmes. The study used the databases on forest cover, type prepared using remote sensing data and field based data on biomass, mean annual increment of forest resources as well as the rate of growth of population. The model predicted the degeneration of supply potential of fodder as a consequence to the increased livestock signaling the unsustainable fodder potential in the region. In order to cope with the deficiency of fodder supply the model identified the minor forest areas which can be used on priority for fodder bank programmes.

7.0. Geospatial Information Systems and Models

Decision-making for sustainable development is a complex process and often involves studying trade-offs that need to be made for conflicting goals of different sectors. GIS provides a convenient platform to integrate multi-sector data in different formats for analyzing `what-if' scenarios of alternative developments. Spatial decision support systems (SDSS) integrating process-based models with scenario analysis greatly aid the process of decision-making. There are possibilities of developing SDSS by tight coupling of GIS tools with those for modeling, simulation, optimization, statistical analysis, image processing and expert reasoning (Densham 1991). Besides allowing spatial analysis, GIS is a powerful tool for empowering communities by enabling people's participation in decision-making. Geographic Information System (GIS) is a powerful tool in which spatial information can be stored, organized, and retrieved in a user-friendly environment. Conjunction of satellite remote sensing data, ancillary data in GIS environment and Global positioning system (GPS) data has a huge potential for environment management.

Geoinformatics, a new word coined combining the GIS and Information technology (IT) has been a path-breaking concept with immense possibility and potential. Three major objectives of Geoinformatics includes: Organization/development and management of geospatial data; spatial modeling and data analysis; development and integration of computer tools for visualization and analysis of real time geospatial problems in decision making process. Internet has facilitated three major changes in GIS: (i) Access to data; (ii) Transmission of data; and (iii) GIS Data analysis. The Internet GIS can also link with real time information, such as satellite images, traffic movements and accident information by real time connection with the relevant information sources. The applications developed are cross-platform and accessible through any web browser.

Visualization is one of the most attractive tools for participants to be effectively involved in planning processes. The development trends in Urban Planning and Management to more strategic planning lays emphasis on a more collaborative planning process. Particularly the integration of Remote Sensing and GIS for use in spatial data management, and specifically in Urban Planning, lead to the development of several visualization tools which can be useful for participants in the planning process. These new visualization tools have the advantage, as these can be easily understood by the participants from varying levels of education and at same time can be easy integrated planning process.

Currently the environmental and natural resource database is in a distributed environment and also in a form which are non-compatible among themselves. In such form the database is of no use for efficient retrieval, sharing, updation and analysis for appropriate environmental management and disaster mitigation. Most of the earlier models developed in the last decade are point based models which are today linked to spatial information to bring it to a common GIS platform so that accurate spatial statistics and spatial process models are generated for decision making. So it was envisaged that all the database available in the country should be brought together will all the ancillary databases in a geospatially linked platform where it can be queried and appropriate information can be extracted for the available database.

In this regard Department of Space has compiled an immense amount of data generated as a part of the numerous user based projects over the last 20 years. The biodiversity based data products are available through the web portal BIS and IBIN [32]. The wasteland database has been arranged in the WALIS where the wasteland information can be queried according to administrative boundaries as well as watershed boundaries. The database generated as a part of LULC project is available in BHOOSAMPADA where different queries based on the ancillary database like census data are possible. INFFRAS, a near real time fires detection and response information system has been developed for dissemination of the forest fire information to the respective forest departments. In addition GEOLAWNS, GEOSMART, FORIS and wetland Information systems have been develop to meet the different resource management activities.

The development of on-line integrated multimedia-GIS tools to assist in bottom up decision-making have become important in the context of scenario planning to enable the community to actively explore different land use options and the implication of government structure and strategic plans. National Natural Resources Repository (NRR) is being developed to position consistent means to share spatial data among all users to produce significant savings for data collection, utilization and enhance decision making. The goal of this repository is to enable a consistent repository of spatial information, reduce duplication of effort among agencies, improve quality and reduce costs related to spatial information, to make spatial data more accessible to the users, to increase the benefits of using available data, and to establish key partnerships amongst agencies from the central government, state government, academia and the private sector to increase data usability through National Resources Data Base Management (NRDBM) system.

Rural land use planning in India mainly employs prescriptive planning on a watershed basis. An executive-level PC-based spatial decision support system for rural land use planning (SDSS/LUP) has been developed under a joint program between the Indian Government's Department of Science and Technology and the UN Development Program to assist rural development decision-makers at a district/sub-district level to identify priority watershed sites for different mandated schemes, site selection for infrastructure; and land evaluation for changes in land use [33]. SDSS/LUP addresses a single district only and is not sufficiently robust for the entire agricultural extension community to use for decision-making.

As a sequel to the PC-based Spatial Decision Support System for rural Land Use Planning (SDSS/LUP), a mock-up 'Web-based Decision Support System on rural Land Use Planning 'Web LUP' has been developed, using HTML image maps [33]. The proposed system assists district-level agricultural extension community in their decisions on selection of watersheds for various mandated schemes by displaying maps and making useful queries to aid decisions. Web LUP is also intended to provide suggestions and hazard warnings for land use sustainability by combining data from the existing sources. The proposed system will be developed after involving and obtaining the informed-opinion from the users. This will be valuable to extension agents in disseminating information and will allow them to make effective decisions in solving soil and water conservation problems. However, the socio-economic and marketing components of watershed conservation and management also need to be considered in order to provide more comprehensive, productive and profitable alternatives to the users.

8.0. Areas of Concern

For the last three decades, significant development has been made in the context of preparation of spatial databases at various scales which have been quite useful for planning and prioritization of natural resources management activities. However, all the decision supports in these areas of working have to be data-driven and dependent on various resolutions and scales of spatial and temporal data, multi-thematic information, and locale specific characteristics. This would enable to provide a spatial decision support system as a solution provider enabling to monitor, characterize, and manage a given system. In this regard significant progress need to be made to provide near real time satellite databases, data processing and value addition. This necessitates involvement of multi mission satellite data acquisition, advanced data processing and dissemination, spatial explicit data analysis and modeling, process models, capacity building and user assimilation.

The development of constellation of geo and polar satellite systems facilitating to respond to highly episodic disaster events, alert mechanisms, cropping pattern analysis and ecological hotspot detections is one of the major concerns of the day. In this regard, apart from multi mission satellite data acquisition systems, reliable atmospheric data and development of suitable algorithms for deriving aerosol properties for a wide variety of situations for more accurate atmospheric correction are required to bring out radio metrically consistent databases in temporal sequences. Such kind of databases is crucial for temporal change assessment and simulation, retrieval of bio and geophysical parameters.

Scientific understanding of various land surface processes requires locale and region specific ecosystem process models in order to analyze and predict various ecological processes like crop growth and yield , terrestrial productivity, evapo-transpiration, and regional climate models. Very limited ground based database in the Indian context is available to understand the various processes and upscale to ecosystem models. In this context, spatially explicit well organized field observatories are required to provide geo and biophysical coefficients regulating the various processes to develop region specific process models. The databases development using hyper spectral, airborne lidar and high resolution satellite data is to be standardized and validated to enable to link various locale specific information to upscale through coarse resolution satellite data.

In the coming decade, assessment of ecosystem vulnerability and adaptability in relation to natural disasters, anthropogenic disturbances and climates change is one of the critical areas of research and application to facilitate integrated land use management. The explicit organization of locale specific characteristics both in terms of growth and biophysical parameters would drive the models for deriving meaningful outputs to understand and predict the ecosystem responses. In this context the question that always remains unanswered in the context of the burgeoning role of geoinformatics is the precision of information gathering and efficiency of information sharing. It is in this direction that future perspectives of geoinformatics are going to be a tightly integrated information system of remote sensing, GIS and GPS. In this regard, the synergy of satellite data from high spatial resolution, hyper spectral, and high temporal satellite sensors along with advanced differential GPS systems, and object-oriented GIS, plays a vital role. However, with regard to information dissemination, the strength of communications, especially the internet GIS (Web GIS) and the possible pervasive role of wireless GIS implemented through Internet and geo-stationary satellite communications through VSAT's (e.g. INSAT systems, etc.) may find a long way into the sustainable ecosystem management. Simultaneous targeted efforts for capacity building and outreach should be organized to educate various segments of users and as a service to users necessary free ware tools of data access and processing should be made available.

8.1. Future Directions

"Integrating EO products and services with multi-institutional framework and people's participation in decision-making processes relevant to society" stands as the principle for future direction of EO program. This would turn the direction of working from being a Data Provider to Service Provider by giving end-to-end solutions. As part of this, food security, water security, environmental monitoring and infrastructure development are going to be the main stay of applications with focus on rural development. On the other hand, the ecosystem responses and management to disaster and climate change would also stands as important activities as it would ultimately impact the overall development. In view of these, following programs would take more relevance in the context of optimizing natural resources supply and demand, vulnerability and adaptability of ecosystems to change.

- Natural Resources database development & monitoring
- Food security (Cropping System and patterns, Non timber forest products, fodder, fish stock etc)
- Water security (Surface water management, snow and glaciers, ground water budgeting and , water quality)
- Natural and human-induced disasters (early warning, pre-cursors, hazard zonation)
- Infrastructure Development, Urban & rural planning,
- Protection of ecosystem & biodiversity (coastal, marine, terrestrial)
- Climate Variability and Change (biogeochemical cycles , aerosol transport, energy and water balance)

- Popularize and disseminate remote sensing based products
- Develop innovative applications of dynamic spatial simulation techniques.
- Developing and customizing applications/information for grass root-level users on issues related to the last mile problem

The priority of these programs would involve the need for continuing of existing operational missions and initiate new operational missions in tune with the user requirements. However this would also depend upon the scientific understanding and feasibility in terms of theory methodology and application. The level of application of several areas is given in the figure. Based on this it can be mentioned that several areas need to be strengthened in terms of research and development enabling to provide better operational solutions. The area specific research areas which are mentioned in corresponding sections would be addressed through in-house R&D, technology development programmes, ISRO/DOS Respond and ISRO GBP programmes with the active collaboration from universities and relevant national institutes.

On the other hand with specific reference to satellite missions, the directions are in terms of continuing existing sensor systems and develop new sensor programs to fill the observational gaps and scientific parameter retrieval system. In this context, the earth observation sensors addresses characterization and monitoring land and natural resources, oceans, cartography and large scale mapping, disaster monitoring and mitigation. The new missions would include filling the gaps in terms of spectral, spatial and temporal resolutions in both optical and microwave regions. The constellation of polar and geosynchronous satellite missions is also envisaged to improve detection, monitoring and assessment of various processes with special reference to disasters. The space borne microwave and hyper spectral sensors would form the important basis in ecosystem quantification, retrieval of geophysical and biophysical parameters.

ACKNOWLEDGMENTS

Authors thank Director, NRSC for giving an opportunity and encouragement in preparation of this article. Thanks are also due to different colleagues who have provided inputs, suggestions and preparation of the article.

REFERENCES

[1] Economic Survey of India, Oxford University Press N Delhi, 2007. http://indiabudget.nic.in.

[2] India's Initial National Communication to UNFCC, NATCOM, Ministry of Environment and Forests, Government of India, 2002. http://www.natcomindia.org/book.htm

[3] National Action Plan on Climate Change, Government of India, 2008. http://pmindia.nic.in/Pg01- 52.pdf

[4] National Agriculture Policy, Min. of Agriculture, Government of India, 2000. http://agricoop.nic.in/

[5] National Environment Policy, Min. of Environment and Forests, Government of India, 2006. http://envfor.nic.in/

[6] National Forest Policy, Min. of Environment and Forests, Government of India, 1988. http://envfor.nic.in/

[7] National Conservation Strategy and Policy Statement on Environment and Development, Min. of Environment and Forests, Government of India, 1992. http://envfor.nic.in/

[8] Costal Regulation Zone Notification, Min. of Environment and Forests, Government of India, 1991. http://envfor.nic.in/

[9] National Urban Housing and Habitat Policy, Ministry of Housing & Urban Poverty Alleviation, Government of India, 2007. http://urbanindia.nic.in/

[10] Veldkamp, T. and Lambin, E.F., 2001. Predicting land-use change, Special issue on Agriculture, Ecosystems & Environment, Grand Challenges in Environmental Sciences, http://www.nap.edu/catalog/9975.html

[11] Navalgund, R, R., Jayaraman, V., and Roy, P.S., 2007, Remote Sensing Applications: An Overview, Current Science, Vol.93 (12).

[12] Ian, M., Obersteiner, M., Nilsson, S., Shvidenko, A., 2006, A spatial comparison of four satellite derived 1 km global land cover datasets. *International Journal of Applied Earth Observation and Geoinformation,* Vol 8, 246–255.

[13] Philippe, M., Eva, H., Gallego, J., Strahler, A, H., Herold, M., Agarwal, S., Naumov, S., De Miranda,E,E., Di Bella, C. M., Ordoyne, C., Kopin, Y and Roy, P.S., (2006) Validation of Global Land Cover 2000 Map, *IEEE Transactions on Geosciences and Remote Sensing,* Vol. 44 No. 7. July 2006.

[14] State of Forest Report, Min. of Environment and Forests, Government of India. 2005. http://envfor.nic.in/

[15] Stibig, H.J., Belward, A.S., Roy, P.S., Rosalina, U., W., Agrawal, S., Joshi, P.K., Beuchle, R, S., Mubareka, S, F., and Giri, C., (2006), A land cover map for South and Southeast Asia derived from SPOT-4 VEGETATION data, *Journal of Biogeography,* Volume 34 (4), Pages 625 – 637.

[16] Roy, P.S., Joshi, P.K., Singh, S. , Agrawal,S., Deepshikha Yadav and Jeganathan, C., 2006. Biome mapping in India using vegetation type map derived using temporal satellite data and environmental parameters. *Ecological Modeling,* Vol. 197, Issues 1-2, August 2006, pp- 148-158

[17] Joshi, P.K., Roy, P.S., Singh, S., Agrawal, S. and Deepshikha Yadav 2006. Characterization of vegetation covers in India, using multi-temporal IRS Wide Field Sensor (WiFS) data. *Remote Sensing of Environment,* Vol. 103, Issue 2, July 2006, pp-190-202.

[18] .Biodiversity characterization at Landscape level in Eastern Ghats and East Coast using remote sensing and GIS, National Remote Sensing Agency, 2007. ISBN-978-81-7525-877-8.

[19] Kale, M.P., Sarnam Singh and Roy, P.S., 2002. Biomass and productivity estimation using aerospace data and Geographic Information System. *Tropical Ecology.* Vol. 43 No. 1, pp 123-136.

[20] Roy, P.S., Porwal M.C., and Lalit Sharma, 2000. Mapping of *Hyppophae rhamnoides* Linn. In the adjoining areas of Kaza in Lahul and Spiti using Remote Sensing and GIS. *Current Science,* Vol. 80 No. 9.

[21] Behera, M.D., Srivastava, S.,. Kushwaha S.P.S., and Roy, P.S., 2000. Stratification and Mapping of *Taxus baccata L.* bearing forests in Talle Valley using remote sensing and GIS. *Current Science,* Vol 78, No. 8, pp 1008-1013.

[22] Shailesh Nayak, 2004. Application of remote sensing for implementation of coastal zone regulations: a case study of India, 7th Conference on Global Data Infrastructure, Feb2004, India.

[23] Srivastava, S. K., Dutt, C. B. S., Nagaraja, R., Bandyopadhayay, S., Meena Rani, H. C., Hegde V. S., and Jayaraman, V., 2004. Strategies for rural poverty alleviation in India: A perspective based on remote sensing and GIS-based nationwide wasteland mapping. *Current Science,* VOL. 87, NO. 7, 10 OCTOBER 2004.

[24] Kennedy, R, E., Cohen, W.B., Schroeder, A.T., 2007. Trajectory-based change detection for automated characterization of forest disturbance dynamics. *Remote Sensing of Environment,* Vol 110, 370–386, 2007.

[25] Verburg, P, H., and VELDKAM, A. Introduction to the Special Issue on Spatial modeling to explore land use dynamics. *International Journal of Geographical Information Science,*Vol. 19, No. 2, 99–102, February 2005.

[26] Xiango, W., and Clarke, K., C., 2003. The use of scenarios in land-use planning. *Environment and Planning B: Planning and Design* .Volume 30, pages 885- 909.

[27] Roy, P.S., and Sanjay Tomar, 2001. Landscape cover dynamics pattern in Meghalaya. *International Journal of Remote of Remote Sensing*, Vol. 22 No. 18, pp 3813-3825.

[28] Sarnam Singh, Porwal, M.C., Jeganathan, C., Gautam Talukdar and Roy, P.S., 2001. Vegetation Cover Mapping using Hybrid Approach in Digital Classification. *Asian Journal of Geoinformatics*. Vol. 2 No. 2, pp 37-45.

[29] Giriraj, A, Irfan-Ullah, M., Murthy M.S.R., and Beierkuhnlein, C.,. 2008. Modelling spatial and temporal patterns of forest cover change (1973 – 2020): *A case study from Southern Western Ghats* (India).Sensors 8(1).

[30] Udaya Lakshmi.V. ,and Dutt.C.B.S.,1998. Micro level planning and sustainable forestry through GIS. *Current Science,* Vol.75, No.3, Page No. 245-251.

[31] Indian Bioresources Information Network, 2007, www.ibin.co.in

[32] Adinarayana, J., Maitra, S., and David, D., (2000). A spatial decision support system for land use planning at district level in India, The Land*: Journal of the International Society of Land Use,* FAO/NRI-UK, 4.2, 111-130.

In: Land Use Policy
Editors: A.C. Denman and O.M. Penrod
ISBN: 978-1-60741-435-3

Chapter 3

URBAN SPRAWL AND LAND USE POLICIES

Marialuce Stanganelli
University of Naples–Federico II, Naples, Italy

ABSTRACT

During the last century, a deep discontinuity occurred in urban growth patterns: a break between the pre-existent urban development model, where building growth was led by the planning rules typical of compact cities, and the following model characterizing the contemporary town where growth has exponential speed, and incoherent and chaotic forms. This phenomenon, commonly called urban sprawl, interests almost all the main urbanized areas of the world, even if its evolution has had different origins and paths in the diverse geographic areas. Studies that until now have examined the history of contemporary urbanization appear varied and composite in relation to the different cultural and social settlement situations in which urbanization took hold. Each context seems to be the result of a different creative process, of several heterogeneous stories describing diverse events, knowledge and habits. It is important to highlight, as this chapter observes, how territories of deeply different cultural, economic, and social points of view, through different evolutionary trajectories, have produced spaces with similar characteristics. The homologation of the results seems to be in contrast with the multiplicity of trajectories that produced them, but different stories could have common threads that can be tied again to build one single story. This chapter rewrites the fragmentary history of urban sprawl in the light shed by those who can be considered the homogenizing factors helping to define the domain of any trajectory of urban evolution. To reconstruct a single story from all different urban histories is needed to define action systems and strategies aiming at imposing an organizing structure on the spaces of the urban sprawl. Current strategies are discussed and some new ones are proposed for the existing suburbs. The thesis intervention in diffused urbanization can't be reduced to the identification of spaces to be transformed and activities to be introduced. It is a more complex work requesting active involvement of the community to define spaces able to give rise to new identities.

The main results include a new approach to urban sprawl study, the identifying and the role of the forces underlying urban sprawl, and the identifying of a system of actions on different levels to intervene in urban sprawl.

1. Introduction

The studies carried out on urban sprawl in different geographic areas of the world show that the phenomenon has different origins and developments linked to the conditions of the context in which they occur.

Indeed, the variety of the names through which the several forms of urban sprawl are often referred gives evidence of the perception of these new forms of contemporary cities. The description of the new morphologies of the contemporary urbanization produced, in Italy, several toponyms, such as *diffused city*, *urban diffusion*, and *urbanized country*. The same trend toward a variety of names can be found also in the most consolidated American literature, where the classic term *sprawl* is declined in several subtypes.

That multiplicity, on one hand, represents the plurality of forms and articulations with which the new settlement phenomena take place in the territory; on the other hand, it stresses the different paths of urban growth followed by each community. Each word refers, in fact, to a different settlement story connected to the social expectations, cultural habits, law bounds and economic capacity of the territory. "As we make our history or history tout-court, Marx pointed out, we do not choose the circumstances in which we do so, since the past always conditions our present as it determines the pattern of our thinking and feeling" [1, pag.9]. The history of a territory defines different origins and paths of urban growth. The production of spaces destined to dwelling brings several factors into play, linked to the single context, which start from the economic conditions to the individual aspirations.

1.1. The Origins: Urban Culture and Rural Life

In the United States, where the phenomenon of urban sprawl first occurred on a broad scale, the sprawl was influenced by the desire for living in strict contact with uncontaminated nature, a strong desire in the US culture as well as in the Anglo-Saxon one:

> "Unlike every other affluent civilization, Americans have idealized the house and the yard rather than the model neighborhood or the ideal town" [2, p.5].

That desire is deeply rooted in US history, as shown by noting that, even at the height of his career, George Washington defined himself mainly as a farmer and as such he managed a model estate where he tested new techniques of cultivation. The US culture is connected with the English one, where there is a strong interest too in rural life. Unlike the other European monarchies, until the 18th century the English Crown did not succeed in creating a centralized court capable of attracting nobles to the capital city and involving them in urban life. Between the 17th and the 18th centuries, many English nobles became brilliant farmers able to improve production processes and the breeding techniques [1]. In England, the centralizing trend to urbanization occurred only with the industrial revolution, but, even in this case, despite the creation of an urban society produced by the strong growth of the cities, English culture still remained linked to rural life. During all of the 19th century and the beginning of the 20th century, the English upper class spent part of their time in country houses and part in their city homes, where they spent only the period between February and the beginning of summer, corresponding to the work of Parliament.

The industrial revolution did not produce the same effect on American society, which remained linked to rural life. In *Notes on the State of Virginia* [3], another president of the United States, Thomas Jefferson, exalted life in nature, stressing the damage that industrialization and urban life could cause to the American people by way of corruption, venality and unhappiness:

> "Those who labour in the earth are the chosen people of God, if ever he had a chosen people, whose breasts he has made his peculiar deposit for substantial and genuine virtue" [3, p.291].

On the contrary, continental European society has always been linked to urban life. The European culture is a culture made of cities moreso than States or Regions. The rebirth of Western civilization, after the collapse of the Roman Empire, occured during the low Middle Ages, starting from urban rebirth. It took place through the establishment of new merchant and craft classes which set up a new form of autonomous power in the city ambit: the municipalities. Starting from the year 1000 in Europe, territory was organized through a wide and articulated urban structure. Most of the cities were small commercial centres having fewer than 2,000 inhabitants. Then medium-sized towns followed, with fewer than 10,000 inhabitants, containing local and regional administrative functions. There were very few towns with more than 10,000 inhabitants, whose big sizes were linked to the presence of complex administrative, religious, cultural and economical functions. Many of those big cities had universities such as Barcelona, Colonia or Prague, but in any case their success was due to the multiplicity and diversification of functions [4].

The phenomenon of urban autonomies has characterized the European territory, making its development different from the eastern one. In China, and under the Islam, urban development took place two centuries before, but there the cities had to compete with a bigger socio-political entity, which in Europe would have arisen later: the Central State [5]. In those differences between the prevalence of hierarchy in the East and the spread of urban autonomy in the West, some historians find the causes of the European greater business and industrial development in the 2nd century [6].

Even when cities loosened their autonomy for the rise of new forms of centralized power, in Europe there would always be the idea of a social structure mirrored in a specific urban order. That idea is at the base of several urban utopias developed from the Renaissance onwards. In actual fact, many utopias aimed at solving social problems and/or suggesting new political models; but it is emblematic of the central role played by the city in the European culture, the fact that the authors of those utopias have always felt the need for contextualizing the proposals regarding a new social order describing ideal cities. The city becomes, in the utopian texts, the conceptual image of a possible state of the society [7].

In the 20th century, the social utopias were substituted by the proposals of new ideal urban layouts, with social issues, conceived by the great masters of modern architecture. While the European proposals by Le Corbusier and Tony Garnier, representing the starting point of the CIAM statements, still belonged to an urban view characterized by compactness and high density, the proposal suggested by Wright started from criticizing urban civilization. In Broadacre City, Frank Lloyd Wright suggested a city based on the frontier myth and the right to land, where environmental urban quality was looked for in the fusion between city and country. Broadacre City represented the American way of life, through a settlement based on single-family houses with gardens distributed in lots of at least four acres of land [8].

The different starting point between Europe and United States led to different evolution trajectories of sub-urbanization in the two areas which, however, coincide in the final outcome.

1.2. The Different Paths: Housing Policies

Sprawl has followed different paths in various geographic areas, due to the divergences existing among cultural, social and political contexts.

In USA, for example, there was first the displacement of housing and then the transfer of work. Until the 1970s in America, the building spread over the territory was almost completely made by houses. Fishman [9] describes the classic American suburb, built between 1920 and 1960, as the representation of the American middle-class utopia. It developed along the main railway lines and was characterized by a commuter population of protestant, upper middle-class, white people.

On the contrary, in Europe, a first push to sub-urbanization issued from moving job out from cities. Starting from the 1960s, around the main urban areas, the bigger industries arranged into poles placed in pre-existing small towns near the main cities. However the urban development resulted was limited to the industrial settlement areas, following a concentric model, according to traditional schemes, around small pre-existing towns. Although it cannot be defined a suburban development yet, since it was more a fast growth of centres adjacent to the principal urban area, this phenomenon laid the foundations of suburbanization of the territory, giving rise to the awareness of life styles different from the urban one.

Therefore the first forms of suburbanization in Europe were based on the suburban workers district in contraposition to the spreading of the US single-family houses with garden. On the other hand, in the two continents the housing policies followed two different paths: in many European Countries with market economy, public intervention in housing has represented a very important sector, while in the United States, both for economical, juridical and ideological reasons, this did not happen [10].

It is well known the role played by the Federal Housing Administration (FHA) in promoting the building of single-family houses and fostering racial segregation. In 1934, the National Housing Act introduced the FHA targeted to allocate funds for subsidized loans to be used for building new houses by private initiative. The FHA guaranteed the banks so that they could pay the 80% money down to the building contractors. These last bought the land, subdivided it and built single-family houses with a minimum investment of their own capital. While plans and projects of the houses had to be submitted to the approval of the FHA. In order to fix the values of the credit, the FHA followed the directions given by another federal agency: the Home Owner Land Corporation, which represented the value of the real estate through maps of different colour. The worst areas of the classification, corresponding to the loan interdiction, concerned the ambits close to the coloured people houses. The best class was given to the areas close to protestant white people's districts. [11].

Policies to promote a different use of federal funds for housing were always strongly thwarted. For a long time the conservatives hindered the 1937 Housing Act, which introduced the first program for financing public housing building. It was approved only after strong economic cuts and under condition of slums clearance before building new houses [11].

The 1949 Housing Act too, which entailed to finance about 800,000 council houses by 1955, was hindered for long time and the following negotiations reduced the number of authorized units year after year. In this case too, the new public housing realization was linked to the slums clearance. Contextually, supported by the FHA, the banks allotted credits for building 10 million new single-family houses from 1946 to 1953. This was possible also thanks to the special fund constituted in 1944 in order to guarantee special loans for buying house to the war veterans, giving rise to a huge private corporation based on house building activity [11].

In the United States, Sica notices [8], public action has always been keeping at safe distance from the market borders within which the private initiative could have still found lucrative profits, the limits for the USA public housing policies can be found in the insufficiency of the supply, and in the calculated attention to damage no interest of the entrepreneurial corporations, financial and insurance companies, and building workers unions.

Instead in Europe, at the beginning of the 20th century, all the cultural debate in architectural and town planning field was based on the urban housing articulated in multi-storey buildings and realized by public intervention. It wasn't a case that England kept its distance from the theoretic and cultural debate, slowly developing the detachment from tradition [12].

As well known, the debate was developed by the Congrès Internationaux d'Architecture Moderne (CIAM), constituted in 1928, with the contribution of architects coming from all over Europe. The crucial subject of the CIAM was the mass housing in the framework of public intervention in order to solve the housing problem. In Europe, the problem of houses for workers revealed itself starting from the industrial revolution and developed during the 19th century without finding adequate solutions, except for some experimentations carried out by philanthropists. The CIAM program went on according to successive aggregations and ranged from the study of the minimum living unit (2nd CIAM Congress, 1929, organized by Ernest May in Frankfurt), to its aggregation into urban districts (3rd CIAM congress, organized by Victor Bourgeois in Bruxelles) until the consideration of urban structure (4th CIAM Congress, organized as a work trip from Marseille to Athens). The interest was focused on subsidized multi-storey building and had as counterpart the clear aversion against the single-family house and private housing estates. The single family housing model of the garden city was considered as an expression of a dissipating individualism which contrasted the urban concentration model representing the social spirit and collective will [13].

The opposition to private housing estates and land system based on private enterprise was one of the basilar concepts of the CIAM: "the messy subdivision of land, produced by housing estates, sales and speculations, has to be substituted by a rational system of land subdivisions. This subdivision into groups, base of any urban planning meeting the present needs, will guarantee, to owners and communities, the impartial division of the plus-values deriving from works of common interest" [14, p.535].

At the second Ciam Congress there was also Richard Neutra from the US, who described the market reasons that transformed the single-family house into the most diffused building type in the United States: building speed; easy possibility of sale through payment by instalments and so low risk for the entrepreneur, larger possibility of meeting the demand.

After the Second World War, increased by war destruction, a housing emergency dramatically appeared again all over Europe, transforming the housing question into the hard core of all the European urban policies. In many cases, Countries tried to solve the problem with policies targeted to fastly increase the house supply through a strong industrialization of building, which produced huge districts of subsidized building: the Grand Ensamble in France, the Groβensiedlungen of the centre-east Europe, the 167 Districts in Italy. Apart from the urgency caused by the house deficit, in almost all policies of great interventions in this field, a basic role was played by the intention of using building industry as a mean for absorbing manpower and pursuing the full employment [15].

In the 1960s and 1970s big suburban districts were built around the most important European cities. In Italy, at first, the construction of suburban districts goes on following the morphologic rules of the traditional city, in terms of road ranging, relations between empty and built spaces as well as between public and private spaces [16]. The legislative measure by which Italy passes the policy for social housing, approved in 1949 and being effective until 1963, was called "Measures for increasing workers employment by facilitating building of workers' houses", this title points out that the law main target consisted in facing the unemployment problem, by developing the building sector, recognized as tool for promoting the renaissance of the post war Italian economy [17]. Accordingly, in Italy, at least in the popular district plans until 1962, considerations about the unemployment levels, the education levels of the workers to be emploied, the limitation of import activity determined the use of traditional techniques and material instead of those coming from the building industry [18, p.100]. Only later, with the increase of the house need, linked to an exponential increase of urban population, in the new suburban districts began appearing several morphological characteristics which radically distinguished the new ambits from the traditional city: the predominance of open space on the built space; the free arrangement of buildings; the significant lack of structured public spaces notwithstanding the great size of "public voids". In the suburbs of the 1960s and 1970s big cities, buildings were freely placed in big sized public spaces lacking in any formal quality and so not perceived as spaces but just as emptinesses. The interest was completely focused on the inside space, on the private dwelling, while the outside space, being often shapeless and derelict, was the evidence of the incapability of the present society to express new forms of collective life through a new urban shape.

The big suburban districts of subsidized building, built in the thirty-year period after the war, changed the morphology of the European cities. Those districts, placed in areas far from the built-up centres, in order to take advantage of the land low cost, stimulated property speculation which relied on infrastructures created for public districts. In this way, cities spread beyond the traditional boundaries. Even if it was still an high-density sub-urbanization there still were some of the main characteristics of urban diffusion: more voids than builds, no public spaces, weak relationships among spaces.

2. Transformation Dynamics of the Contemporary City in Italy

As Secchi pointed out [18], transformations of city and territory are super-determined, they are namely the result of a great number of concurrent causes, among which it is difficult to establish orders of importance and priority. Also the push to suburbanization issues from the joined action of more solicitations, some on national level, others on international one which have been absorbed and elaborated in a different way in each territorial context. There, these solicitations have been mixed with other determinant factors due to specifically local phenomena.

Even in the same national context, where there would be probable conditions of greater social and cultural homogeneity, several paths of urban evolution can be found, as in the Italian case.

2.1. Specific Trajectories: Second-Home Suburbs

In Italy, a first very huge incentive to suburbanization took place with the beginning of the second-home tourism, led by economic prosperity and growing motorization. Between the 1950s and the 1960s, Italian economy grew in a fast and intense way producing structural changes in the social composition and life styles. From 1954 to 1964 the per capita income increased by 63% producing a dizzy increase in consumptions. From 1959 to 1963 the diffusion of refrigerators in the houses passed form 370,000 to 1,500,000 units, televisions from 88,000 to 634,000, car output from 148,000 yearly units to 760,000. The circulating cars, in a ten-year period (1954–1964), passed from 700,000 to 5 million units. In 1962 there was one car every 11 Italian people, in 1972 the ratio was 1 to 4 [19]. An ever-increasing income rate could be invested in consumptions apart from the subsistence goods, privileging the new consumptions: electric household appliances, travels, holidays. These were the years in which the external forms of needs satisfaction became more explicit, identifying the belonging to a social status through the possession of determined consumption goods [19]. Objects become status symbols, car and holidays-house became the sign of a new social condition to be shown.

The "Giardinetta", one of the best sold cars of that period, was launched in 1960 through advertising posters showing a family loading luggage in the car ready to leave for holidays.

The demand for vacation houses produced the first wave of low-density suburban buildings near existing urban centres, along coastlines, on the hills, near the lakes, everywhere there were environmental value to exploit. The huge edification gave rise to new ways of using territory, a territory to consume during spare time, whose use is linked to the first forms of extra-urban commuting (tourism commuting).

This process of building linked to tourism reached its peak in the 1960s–1970s, but it went on with no interruption even in the following decades. The estimate is that, in 1997, 32% of the Italian real estate was assembled in the coast municipalities: "they were 7,765,172 houses corresponding to 3 billion and 150 million of cement cubic metres" [20].

That buildings, when placed near big urban areas, has represented the first step to residential colonization of natural and rural areas. The phenomenon was stronger in the South than in the North. Where the building has developed near the big cities there was, in the following decades, the transformation of vacation houses into suburban homes for commuters.

Starting from the 1960s, near Naples, along the Phlegrean coast, an intense tourist colonization of the coastline has been developed, carried out through creating several private real estates developments with single-family houses. "Second home suburbs" reached their peak during the 1960s and the 1970s, but development went on also in the following years, through forms of individual unauthorized building, when the tourist thrust had changed into a settlement thrust due to the closeness and the relative accessibility to the regional capital. The process of tourist exploitation of the coast area from being exogenous has never become endogenous; the coast area has been exploited until saturation, destroying that same natural heritage (sea–dunes–pinewood) which was targeted to become possession. When the tourist demand was exhausted—both because of the strong environmental decay produced, and because the intense building of second houses was not met by a contextual and endogenous rearrangement of local economy targeted to offer an adequate supply of tourist services and differentiated attractors—a part of the existing real estate was used for stable residences although with no services at all.

2.2. Specific Trajectories: Small Enterprise Suburbs

In other cases, it is still clearer the way by which uniform solicitations can determine specific trajectories according to the context and its peculiarities. An example is given by the way in which the crisis of the traditional industry of the 1970s affected the different areas of our country.

In Italy, the effects of the crisis were damped by the presence of a thick and articulated tissue of medium and small industries that gradually has been developing in several north and central areas. The reduced industry size (from 20 to 500 workers) and the innovative use of new technologies made those firms flexible enough to face the market becoming more and more fragmentary and changeable. New technologies played a crucial role in producing the success of those firms, which used them both in the production process and in the distribution one. In the 1960s and 1970s, the local districts of medium and small industries were about 250, half of which in the North [21]. Among the Italian small and medium industries, from 1985 to 1988 [21]:

- 51% worked on new products;
- 70.6% improved the installations;
- 34% introduced computer science in the output processes;
- 65% started export activities.

The numbers shown give evidence of an entrepreneurial model that invested both in product innovation as well as in process one, its success was evidenced also by increasing exporting. Indeed, it was just in these local production districts that the new multinational corporations grew (the most famous case is the Benetton one).

In the widespread industrialization flexible systems dominated by the small and medium industries, houses developments soon grew also. In the North-East and in the centre of Italy, one of the main interpretation of urban sprawl is indeed linked to the economic development of small and medium industries that would have then driven closer the residence of entrepreneurs and workers [22]. Among the causes of the success of local districts of small and medium industries, some "local conditions" are very important: a close local society with no big conflicts; the presence of entrepreneurial attitudes and skills; a familiar networks capable of supporting the market processes; an ideal of realization through work; a territory densely populated [16]. Then, the territorial conditions corresponding to this development model are original and specific and they themselves become economic development factors [16].

In the South, on the contrary, the small and medium industries have never affirmed in such a way that a settlement spread would be justified.

At the beginning of the 1980s, in Campania almost the 70% of production units of the region were placed in 38 municipalities out of 544; the municipalities lacking in any industrial initiative were almost one half of the administered areas [23]. In municipalities characterized by industrial presences, the factories were often no more than three, and never exceeded 19 workers.

The southern industrialization in the 1970s was mainly made by big state-controlled factories and by production plants of northern corporations whose local settlement was motivated by the state incentives for South of Italy development. This kind of industrial structure was fully affected by the economic crisis of the 1970s producing large brownfields and increasing the already high level of unemployment.

2.3. Specific Trajectories: "Post-Emergency" Development

In this context, it is emblematic the Neapolitan case of 1980 linked to the damages caused by the Irpinian earthquake. The earthquake and the following reconstruction struck together with the crisis of traditional industry making it worse. According to the first post-seism appraisal, in Campania about one half of the manufacturing plants were damaged (1,369 out of 2,606), they employed a total of 97,651 workers. The main economic damages took place in the Naples province, with 611 damaged factories, where there was the greater industrial concentration of the Region [24]. The Naples province, in particular, was hit by a so-called "cold earthquake": without many deaths or collapses, but with many damages caused by the scarce maintenance of the building heritage and by its old age. In the city 6810 residential buildings were declared unfit for use, this caused 174,050 people to be evacuated: 138,700 of them, i.e., the 70%, came from historical downtown. To face that situation an "Extraordinary housing program for building in the metropolitan area of Naples" bill was passed (Law n.219/81). It entailed the realization of 20,000 houses and relative urbanization infrastructures placed in the following way: 653 dwellings in the urban tissue; 12,295 in the suburban areas; 6,422 in the areas outside the municipality, later raised to 7,056. The accomplishment of the extraordinary program intended to mitigate the house situation in Naples, which in the seism found its collapse. According to the Prime Minister, it was a work that for its dimensions, for its targets, for the reality it affects, for the powers granted, never occurred in the past (Letter of directions given by the Presidency of the Council of Ministers, 22nd May 1981).

The first effect of this extraordinary plan of residential building was the birth of huge urban suburbs and the move of the needy segment of population from historical downtown to these new suburbs. Contextually the building of over 30,000 dwellings in the municipalities neighbouring Naples gave rise to a violent and uncontrolled growth of urbanization in that area.

In very short time (10 days starting from the approval of the Law n.219/81), the areas to be built were determined. Their individuation entailed the declaration of undelayable situation and urgency of the works, and could then be done also departing from the rules established by master plans in force, even as regard the destination of use and the index of suitability for building (art.81, L.219/81). The percentage of houses produced by urban recovery was irrelevant in comparison to the percentage of new urbanizations realized outside the built-up centre (see table 1). Only in five municipalities, out of 17, were some recovery operations provided.

Outside the built-up centre, the new residential settlements represented isolated areas aimed only at residential use, lacking in the necessary functional mix, but supplied with primary urbanization works. The new residential districts soon attracted other buildings provided by private real estates enterprises. The whole process took place without any territorial planning both on regional and provincial level. The attention was mostly focused to the residence only, i.e. the plan provided only for dwellings. For dwellings built in the city, it was tried to alleviate the lack of other functions by destining the ground floors to commercial use; in the neighbouring municipalities only residential buildings were provided for.

It was, the document of Directions by the Premier that stated as follows: " As regards the characteristics of the to-be-realized buildings, there must be a clear difference between those built inside the Municipality of Naples and those placed outside it; the first ones, with a purely urban characteristic, have to be not only simple residences but, with the destination of the ground level to handicraft, trade, services, will have to meet the needs for autonomy of the residential blocks and, at the same time, the working needs of residents. The residence settlements placed outside the city of Naples will have to be different from the inside ones for the lower house density, for the high percentage of co-ownership green areas and sport equipment".

The works were carried out by giving a "concession" to private building companies and enterprises. The institute of the concession to privates, by Italian law, delegates competences and power of Public Administration to private entrepreneurs: they would have to care not only for the realization of buildings but also will have to manage: land expropriation procedures, allowances payment, executive projects, allotment of houses to the assignees (art. 81, L.219/81).

In the letter of directions by the Presidency of the Council of Ministers, dated 22nd May 1981, it was pointed out that the choice of concession met, on the one hand, the need for promptness in building, on the other hand, it allowed to realize wide economies of scale. Through the intense post seism building activity it was tried to encourage the Campania economy by promoting the allied activities related to building. It should be mentioned that the big residential-only suburbs produced by the earthquake recovery plan, where the needy classes were placed, have become areas characterized by strong social decay, pockets of organized crime and territories of urban guerrilla warfare.

The history of contemporary urbanization appears, therefore, varied and composite in relation to the different cultural and social, settlement situations where it happened. Each context seems to be the result of a different creating process, of several heterogeneous stories telling diverse events, knowledge and habits.

Table 1. Dwellings and rooms realized after the earthquake

Municipality	Resident population				New buildings		Area of urban recovery		Total	
	1911	1971	1980	1991	n. dwellings	n. rooms	n. dwellings	n. rooms	n. dwellings	n. rooms
Pozzuoli	27,576	59,813	71,165	75,706	300	1,200	-	-	300	1,200
Quarto	-	8,295	15,286	30,436	250	1,000	50	200	300	1,200
Melito	4,407	10,090	13,291	19,410	600	2,400	250	1,000	850	3,400
S. Antimo	10,370	21,447	25,747	34,690	356	1,457	-	-	356	1,457
Casoria	14,220	54,785	68,023	79,315	452	1,810	-	-	452	1,810
Casalnuovo	6,031	17,721	20,526	31,974	315	1,260	-	-	315	1,260
Afragola	23,156	50,769	59,354	59,940	937	3,750	2475	990	1,185	4,740
Caivano	12,986	27,457	31,469	35,752	750	3,000	-	-	750	3,000
Cercola	4,547	14,475	17,617	16,262	483	1,930	-	-	482	1,930
Volla	-	6,868	10,140	19,044	202	810	52	210	255	1,020
Pomigliano d'Arco	11,079	30,057	37,961	42,685	462	1,850	-	-	462	1,850
Brusciano	4,176	8,612	9,571	13,778	265	1,060	-	-	265	1,060
Castello di Cisterna	1,728	2,928	3,545	6,420	265	1,060	-	-	265	1,060
Marigliano	12,464	21,138	25,050	27,477	402	1,610	-	-	402	1,610
S. Vitaliano	2,349	2,863	3,272	5,016	261	1,045	50	200	211	1,245
Boscoreale	10,282	18,741	23,292	27,319	653	2,615	-	-	653	2,615
Striano	2,072	4,974	5,956	6,979	100	434	-	-	100	434
TOTAL	147,445	361,053	441,265	532,203	7,055	28,291	650	2,600	7,705	30,891

Anyway, it is interesting to observe that territories being deeply different from cultural, economic, social point of view, through different evolution trajectories, have produced spaces with similar characteristics.

3. Convergence of Different Evolution Trajectories

If from the level of historical reconstruction we pass to the analysis of spatial production, a general homogeneity of forms and structuring characteristics of the contemporary urbanization spaces clearly appears.

> "Sprawl is hard to define, but most definitions involve low density, single–purpose residential or commercial constructions in locations distant from existing public services and infrastructure, as well as ugly, over-scale, automobile-oriented development" [2].

Whatever the evolution trajectories guiding the sub-urbanization would have been, everywhere it is possible to recognize the same common characteristics:

- low density;
- single-functionality and segregation of spaces strictly separated by barriers, fences and enclosures;
- lack of a formal structure supporting the production of spaces;
- absence of public services supporting both residences and transport; absence of public spaces and their substitution with private spaces with public use such as shopping mall or thematic parks;
- a road network destined only to cars circulation without any pedestrian structure;
- car-oriented lifestyle of citizens;
- lack of spaces and places giving rise to forms of identity.

The homologation of the results seems to be in contrast with the multiplicity of trajectories which produced them. Indeed the different trajectories could actually be less heterogeneous than they could appear at a first analysis, or at least their different stories could have common threads that can be tied again to build one single story.

While doing so, it is necessary to consider the epistemological difficulties of the present culture that induce the expert to move on an extremely uneven ground. In the last decades, society has lost the collective dimension giving rise to a society of individuals, who in recognizing all the specificities and differences points out the single elements instead of the connecting ones. Also in the way of reading the reality, there is the tendency to stress the particular instead of the general, to favour the reading of the differentiation elements instead of the homologation ones, the reading of the minimum local swings instead of the big driving forces of change operating on global and international level.

Getting rid of the modern scientific thought that divides, distinguishes and hierarchizes, according to a privileged point of view and perspective, there is a recovery of pre-modern forms of knowledge based on individual experience, on the absence of separation between subject and object, on the impossibility of comparing and summing the experiences. The only form of analysis is then the description, inventory, cataloguing, archives; techniques in which each single element preserves all its peculiarities and the richness issuing from these differences. It maintains uniqueness and irreproducibility, but at the expense of the possibility of reading its connection with the rest, of comparing it with the other elements through a selection of the main characteristics. So doing, many forms of truth, issued from different forms of knowledge, are legitimated.

The absence of hierarchy and privileged points of view determines the difficulty of distinguishing a leading structure in the evolution of the different phenomena.

How are the urban transformations interpreted in this context? How does the city evolve? And through which mechanisms does it change?

From the historical point of view, town planners can be divided into those who think that the great historical movements drive urban change, and those who give more importance to the market forces. More recent positions regards the way in which the decisions about the city are taken and how they affect its change.

Secchi [7] states that territories and cities we observe are the result of a long process of cumulative selection where the huge archives of tangible signs left in the territory by us or by our ancient is the outcome of the accumulated decisions. Those decisions, according to Secchi, can be the result, not always desired, of the intentions and decisions, not always coordinated among each other, of a whole society, taken according to rules prescribed by beliefs and imagery incorporated into tradition. Or else, other signs result from decisions and intentions of one single person, of a caste or a group, eventually of experts, who produced images and arguments aspiring to be shared and incontestable. In this view the evolution of city and territory is linked to the decision-making process and to the balance of forces characterizing a community. According to this hypothesis, Secchi read urban history as characterized by an alternation of moments in which choral decisions prevail and others in which the decisions made by single persons dominate.

Also Rykwert [1] places the problem of urban evolution on the decision-making level, but giving more evidence to individual decisions. He argue "that these vast and seemingly impersonal historical and/or economic 'forces' have always been aggregate products of the choices that were made by individuals. If you think of any historical process in the graphic terms as the vector resulting from any number of forcesacting in different directions, you will see that any alteration in their alignement will deflect the angle of the vector". Each of us take decisions that affect urban morphology, even if they are little decisions: "What sometimes looks like an impersonal force is often a vector such as I have described, resulting from all our decisions whose exact angle or direction as well as impact we inevitably modify by our everyday activities, however subtly" [1, pag.6]

The way by which decisions are taken is, therefore, crucial in building urban space. Another fundamental question regards who are the decision-maker and how the decisions take by single persons interact with the institutional decisions, namely how much freedom each society gives to individual decisions and initiatives. Anyway, it is useful to observe how each decision ranges within a field of action circumscribed by habits, beliefs, prevailing culture, rules, contingences and structural factors. If the great forces of history and economy as well as the several local solicitations contribute to define the impact point of a trajectory, we could suppose that while the first ones define an impact area, the second ones determine the impact points within this area. It comes, than, that the metaphoric vector described by Rykwert moves within an impact area strictly defined by the great international forces of history. Inside this domain the paths can be different and the impact points can diverge each other but they range always within this circumscribed area. This fact would explain the converging results of differentiated paths and how it is possible to read history both as one or as composed by many tellings. It depends on having chosen to follow the whole concatenation of single solicitations or having preferred the study of the driving forces which delimit the domain.

According to this second view, the history of the Campania Region hit by the seism, is interwoven with the general history of Italy under economic crisis and still under the pressure of housing emergency, while the political climate and prevailing culture were based on neo-liberalism of Reagan and Tatcher's imprint.

In this context, all over Italy, the private real estate developers was mostly fostered even by passing over urban and territorial planning. Actually the so much declared insufficiency of housing was then confuted by the census data of 1981, notified only in the second half of the decade. In the 1970s a very big number of flats (about 4,500.000) had been built, but the existing heritage was used in irrational and unbalanced way: many vacant flats on the one hand, and over one million families forced to co-habitation on the other hand. The supported policy, almost based on quantity, showed its limits.

In the following part of this chapter, the fragmentary history of urban sprawl is rewritten in the light shed by those that can be considered as the homogenizing factors helping to define the domain of any trajectory of urban evolution that occurs in a determined historical period in a specific cultural area.

3.1. Political Convergences: The Decision-Making Context

Although with different causes, in Italy, the thrust to sub-urbanization took place in a homogeneous political decision-making context, partly shared by the rest of Europe. In the policy developed by the Italian State during the last two decades of the previous century, the trends and problems that affected the whole Western area are present: the passage from welfare-state to a neoliberalist policy and the following evolution toward a pluralist decision-making process, which introduces forms of negotiated planning where the financial intervention of privates becomes more and more important. These changes coincide with the twenty-year period characterized by the wider increase of urban sprawl in Europe. In Italy, the spread of the 1960s and 1970s was still mostly an high-density increase spreading in all directions around the most important urban areas. It is from the 1980s that the settlement development becomes more and more a low-density spread.

During the 1980s, in West Europe and USA the rediscovery of the classic liberal ideas caught on. "Liberal theorists attributed the economic malaise of social democracy to excessive state of intervention which led to inefficient 'bureaucratic' decision-making and stifled private enterprise, competitiveness and efficiency." [25] According to that theory, urban development too should be considered as part of the economic context where it occurs; therefore it should have been governed by the market forces rather than be planned by the State [26].

The Reagan and Thatcher governments were the first to carry the neoliberalist view out.

In his speech at the Royal Town Planning Institute in 1979, Heltsine, the Secretary of State for Environment in the Thatcher government, outlined the program of English neoliberism planning:

> He "held that planning authorities should take a much more favourable view of applications for planning permission; in other words, that planners should take a 'positive' view of market-led-development. He was keen to see a planning system which did "not act as a drag on the necessary processes of development", and he famously added that "thousands of jobs every night are locked away in the filing trays of planning departments" because of delays in issuing approvals for development" [25, pag.137].

During the Thatcher government in England, several new changes were introduced, which were targeted to liberalize the real estate developer by releasing it from the "excessive" town planning controls: the categories of urbanizations allowed with no building licence was enlarged; the "enterprise zones", were introduced, where the normal town planning regulations were suspended; the Urban Development Corporations were established, targeted to the requalification of some urban areas inside the main English cities, these Corporation were allowed to operate outside the town planning logic.

The most evident act of the English deregulation was the abolition, in 1985, of the Greater London Council, the historical body in charge of planning London metropolis. The main section of County Hall was, symbolically, sold off to an hotel operator, while the other parts were rented or sold to different trade enterprises [1].

An example of town planning development left to market is the one of Houston, city taken by the neoliberism supporters [27] as positive example of urban area without a town planning system. It is not a chance that Houston is one of the city with the lowest density of population all over the world, lacking in pedestrian structures and urban centre. It is therefore characterized by those feature that can be defined as the peculiarities of urban sprawl. Until 1999, the guiding regulations of building activity in Houston concerned the minimum lot and car parks. Houston exacted 5,000-square-foot minimum lots. Apartment buildings must have 1.25 parking spaces for an efficiency and 1.33 spaces for each bedroom, with similar mega-parking requirements for offices, supermarkets and other business, all of which not only discourages walking but also depletes land for homes and other uses.

Also in the Italian town planning system, in the 80's, elements such as "market" and "spontaneity" were introduced. The "expediting of procedures" became one of the main ruling strategies, it was considered as necessary to relaunch private enterprise, releasing it from the "normative cage" formed by the laws in force [20, pag.71]. In the undertaken policies, the building exploitation of territory played a crucial role in reconstructing the economy in crisis. In line with that philosophy, in 1982 the law n. 94/82 ("Regulations for residential building and measures on eviction") passed, which showed many similarities with the strategies implemented in Great Britain: simplification of procedures in municipalities under 10,000 inhabitants and expansion of those interventions not requiring explicit concession. But the most evident law intervention of this period was the first amnesty for infringement of building regulations, in 1985, unfortunately destined to be just the first one of three. By the above-said amnesty, the State intended to exploit unauthorized building in order to face public deficit. The already lively unauthorized building activity found an incentive for relaunching in those measures. The events of those years demonstrate how the Italian State considered building activity: a drive of economic development, an employment source, a taxes source.

In the following decade things seemed to go better with a wider opening to participation in planning processes; actually the models followed gave more and more space to private enterprise, by completely involving it in the decision-making process.

In the 1990s, local authorities were required a greater entrepreneurial skill. The cut of public resources was a circumstance that joined all Europe in this period. With scarce resources, the effectiveness of the actions carried out by local administrations mainly depended on the capability of cooperating with non-institutional actors and joining private capitals and public resources. Public (State or European Union) funds can be obtained through competition procedures, announced on specific topics or determined areas. Those funds, however, cover only part of the necessary resources, asking the local authorities for funding the remaining part with its own resources or private ones. The need for using partnerships has widened the sphere of the actors taking part in the decision-making process, involving also private subjects and producing a pluralistic decision-making model.

This fact has often produced a consequent behaviour of the local authorities, who conceived projects and programs following each time purposes and contents defined by the announcements of the public financing of the moment (in this sense the State has gained again the role of decision-maker it had partly delegated to local governments). In other cases, mainly in the needy territories, local authorities tended to consider as economic development possibility whichever private enterprise would be started over their territory: from the shopping mall, to real esate development, to thematic park, without critically assessing the results on a wider scale.

The new pluralist decision-making model starts from the assumption that the public government is not more the only interpreter and custodian of the common good.

The common good is not considered as an heritage belonging to a single actor of the decision-making process, i.e. each actor is allowed to follow his own interpretation of "common good" which can correspond to an economic advantage, a social progress, an environmental need [28]. Social interaction among the different actors is seen as a moment of knowledge production which integrates the analysis based on technical knowledge, giving rise to shared reference frameworks which records the terms of the agreement reached each time.

In Italy, the process has developed according to the introduction of several planning and programming tools (Complex programs, tools for negotiated programming), in which the qualities (flexibility, operativeness, multisectoriality) clash with limits such as fragmentariness and inconsistency with the structural nature of the problems. Those limits issue from their nature of detailed tools (as in Complex Programs) or sectorial ones (as in Territorial Pacts and Area Contracts). As regards the (spatial or thematic) partiality of the considered problems, these tools, when introduced as support or complementary element to a general plan, do not require the setting up of a global strategic view which should be defined by the planning tool. In many cases they have been used in conflict with the plan foresights or even without any plan in place.

A greater important role to local governments was given by the globalization process: the "global networks (entrepreneurial, trade, financial, cultural, etc.) in looking for their most opportune territorial "anchorages" deal directly with local systems (cities, small municipalities, tourist districts, industrial districts, etc.) which are induced to develop strategic actions where the higher territorial authorities (regions, state) are seen as possible allies or as obstacles to bypass" [29].

The contents of the action carried out by local government on urban and territorial system have been increased: the traditional task of planning the territorial physical layout has been joined by initiatives of social and economic development. Therefore, the spatial transformation does not represent the main core of decisions, but indeed, often represent one of the means to reach different goals, always according to the assumption that economic development is capable of orienting an adequate territorial development. Urban projects are promoted as catalysts for economic development as means to improve the financial and functional efficiency of the city. It seems meaningful that "sprawl is particular evident where Countries or regions have benefited from EU regional policies" [30]. Economic development and sprawl advance together in these years.

The phenomenon is internationally widespread:

> "Competition among municipalities for new income generating jobs and services is great and many municipalities can be tempted to relax controls on development of agricultural land and even offer tax benefits to commercial and industrial enterprises to invest in the municipalities. Competition of this nature between municipalities fuels urban sprawl" [30].

While in west nations there is a strong public opinion reacting against excessive private proposals, in the developing Countries the results of that kind of policy have had a stronger impact. It is in those areas that the phenomenon of megacities have mostly occurred, these are cities with more than ten millions inhabitants that have been fast developing at the beginning of the new millennium.

The fin de siècle megacity represents the society of flexibility, of competitiveness, of a market ideology based on competition, of disparity as stimulus to emulation among individuals, social groups, cities and territories, of who runs risks and is rewarded in case of success [1].

In all asian cities, governments that are already heavily in debt are seeking loans and funds from international profit-seeking enterprises.

> "Urban development in Asia is largely driven by the concentration of local, national and increasingly, international enterprises" [31].

An example is the new Master Plan of Karachi in Pakistan. Karachi, with a population of about thirteen million, aims to develop an "investment-friendly infrastructure" and, in its Master Plan, projects have replaced planning. Among the projects funded by foreign holding there are housing developments along the coasts, carried out by investments from companies from Dubai, Malaysia and USA. The projects includes elite townships, exclusive clubs, theme parks and expo centres.

> "Experience in Karachi shows that such parks are too expensive for the poor and expo centres are not used by them", these kind of projects "is further dividing the city into rich and poor areas both physically and socially" [31].

Also in Latin America, local governments have looked for strategies that could attract investment, new employment and tourism in association with the private sector. "The result of such projects is a widened gap between privileged and less-privileged areas" [32].

3.2. Cultural Convergences: The Absence of a Territorial Project

The previously said events outlines the spreading absence of a general reflection on the territorial layout in all the geographic areas.

In all the European legislations, the town planning tools had remained linked to the single dimension of Master Plan until the 1960s, when the clear need for giving space to a super-municipal dimension came out. The town planning laws in some of the most important European countries were modified in order to work out a territorial planning tool: Structure Plan in Great Britain and Holland, the Scheme Directeur d'Amenagement Urbaine (SDAU) in France. Only in the UK there was the consequent reorganization of the power system, in order to match the levels of government and the levels of planning. Where that did not occur, the concept of territorial planning was disregarded [33]. In Italy the Planning Law of 1942 already entailed the drawing up of a super-municipal Territorial Plan of Coordination, but for long time there was no territorial reference authorities for this type of planning. Until the 1970s, in fact, the town planning competences were subdivided between State and Municipalities. At the beginning of the 1970s the process of regional self-government started. In 1972 there was the first decree about powers transferring to Regions in planning issues. The transferred powers included lawmaking and the administrative functions entailed by the national town planning law. The first passage of authorizations was fragmentary and, besides, in the town planning field the competences were more of administrative type (regarding the plans approval) than of planning type. Moreover, the passage of functions had not occurred by organic and comprehensive matters. This fact produced a new redefinition of competences in 1977. The Regions were able to implement their powers in the field of land use government only between the end of the 1970s and the beginning of the 80's. In the first period of activities, the Regions applied themselves to reorganize their territorial competences specifying the contents. They issued planning laws that reproduced the national law in the general structure, by pointing out and defining the relations of Regions with the other territorial bodies. Besides, until the end of the 1980s, the Regions were to face a new centralizing thrust by the State which issued several special laws overcoming the sphere of regional competence, like the case of areas hit by earthquake, by ecological disasters, of special events (Italia 90, soccer world championship). It is only starting from the 1990s that a territorial planning period started, even thanks to the introduction of new tools (Provincial plans introduced in 1991, Plan of Basin in 1989, Plan of Natural Parks in 1991) as well as to a more proposing and driving role played by the Regions in governing their territory, as shown by new urban and regional planning laws enacted.

In the 1960–70 ten-year period of maximum building development in Italy, the super-municipal planning was carried out by central government bodies: the State or its peripheral bodies. The State intervened on the territory mainly through plans of big infrastructural works (motorways, railways, industrial areas), without any territorial study.

The absence of a wide overall strategic view, inside a territory having infrastructures, caused a growth of urbanization lacking any form or pre-arranged directions. The settlement developed according to logics imposed by local contingencies, transitory opportunities and limited interventions, because completely contained in the municipal framework. Besides, there was an excessive territorial fragmentation: just in some areas of greater conurbation, Italy has many Municipalities with very small dimensions. Without any rule and strategy, the new urbanization relied on the existing territorial supply: to the existing urban centres and their services; to road infrastructures; to railway lines. These pre-existent territorial supply more then determining suburbanization make it easier.

The absence or the scarce efficiency of regional planning as well as administrative fragmentation in land use decion-making, are some of the factors that join the town planning experience both of the European countries and the US ones [30, 2].

3.3. Economic Convergences: The Urban Real Estate Market

The lack of attention to territorial themes, to all that occurred outside the traditional city has fostered forms of chaotic and messy growth. Contextually, the policies implemented in the traditional city have encouraged the sub-urbanization, making the urban real estate market more and more inaccessible for wide segments of population.

In the ten-year period 1980–1990, the financial and project attention was mainly based on the traditional city or on its opposite: the natural areas. State and community funds were available, project experimentations were carried out mainly on the recovery of historical centres, urban re-qualification and re-use of urban brownfields. In the re-qualified and equipped historical centres the cost of dwellings has grown at dizzy speed, making it difficult to buy a house not only for the needy people but increasingly also for the middle class. The recovery took place with lack of interest in the problem of original inhabitants safeguard, even when the interventions were carried out partially funded by Municipalities. In Milan, the 73% of the agreements stipulated between private and municipality to promote urban requalification during the 1980s did not contain neither regulations for the safeguard of the existing tenants, not the control on the tenancy or sale prices after intervention [20].

Moreover, in Italy, to worsen the situation provoked by the rise in the real estate market there was a policy on tenancy which produced the lock of the urban rents, followed by a subsequent excessive increase of rents. This produced the lack of an effective alternative to the house ownership.

In 1978, while trying to provide for lack of public houses through rented houses at low cost, the law on controlled rent passed (L.392/78). The controlled rent was to be used as rent price in at least four-year contracts. The rise of the controlled rent did not corresponded to the market rules but was fixed according to indices that made it inferior to the real rental value. The owners, considering the rent as inadequate, chose to keep the houses vacant, readily available for sale. Otherwise, the houses were rented not for residential uses, because other uses were not subjected to controlled rent. Besides, a "black market" of rentals aroused with costs being higher than those fixed by law, using ways of payment that left no trace. The law produced the end of the rental market. At the beginning of the 90's, almost the 75% of Italian people lived in their own houses [34]. In 1992 the financial law broke the deadlock, by introducing the possibility of freely fixing location rental and the duration of contract. The end of controlled rent caused the sudden increase of rent coasts making the urban rent market prohibitive for many families. Contextually, the urban real estate market has become of crucial importance in the financial operations made either by single privates, who invest by buying and selling houses; or by real estate operators through re-qualification operations; or by financial holdings through the management of the house loans. The financial transformation of urban market has made the purchase of a house difficult also for the middle class.

A house market characterized by an increasing rise in prices, together with a static and little generous rents market, sees more and more frequent phenomena of speculation that made the city available either to those who have great financial availability, or, on the contrary, to those who want to remain in the city paying high costs (house sharing, low levels of services endowment, overcrowding, high buildings decay, unofficial contract conditions) and scarce living qualities, conditions that often characterize the immigrant segment of population [35].

Urban re-qualification and rental policy made the real estate market inaccessible for wide segments of population which are almost "expelled" from the city and look for new locations in the suburbs where the real estate operators suggest charming formulas: residences "plunged into green", in blocks of flats "rich of sport equipment", in a "peaceful and protected" environment, " ten minutes far from downtown".

For wide segments of population, the transfer to suburban areas was not caused by a desire for rural life, by the intention of going away from congestion and city problems, by considerations on the advantage of the supposed closeness to the city due to the development of infrastructural networks. All those factors have only played the role of sirens to attract the population expelled from the traditional city to an amorphous and scattered territory, where the real estate operators promised new houses at good prices.

All the above-said assumptions point out the strict interdependence between city and its surrounding territory: the city re-qualification fosters urban sprawl; the commercial mall placed in the sprawling city produces difficulties in small trade and craft activities of the traditional city; the lack of services of the sprawling city increases the congestion of the compact city. The policies concerning the traditional city affect the sprawling city and the absence of rules of the sprawling city affect traditional city. By this the reason why the policies of the two contexts are to be coordinated and integrated in order to obtain better results: the actions on the sprawling city regeneration should be linked to the urban policies related to the compact city.

4. To Build Future-Shared Trajectories

Starting from the 1970s in the Unites States, there have been opinion movements against the sprawling diffusion which have produced different contrast strategies. The first implemented strategy was the Urban Growth Boundary (UGB), introduced for the first time in 1973 in the Land use Act of the State of Oregon: 236 municipalities were required to define an impassable limits for urban growth under the State supervision. This strategy, useful only as preventive strategy, was proposed even by other Countries such as Canada and Australia, while in Europe has become part of the compact city policies during the 90's. Compact city policies were promoted by the "Green Paper on the Urban Environment" (Commission of the European Community, 1990). The Paper, analyzed the environmental problems of contemporary cities and underlined that it was necessary "to avoid escaping the problems of the city by extending its periphery: it was necessary to solve urban problems within existing boundaries". Compact city policies are based on three main strategies: strict urban growth boundary, mixed land use and denser development. The critics of urban densification strategies argued that the inevitable result of restricting the supply of land, while doing nothing about the demand for new houses, is a rise in prices [36, 37].

Other strategies have been proposed within the American movement of New Urbanism based on new neighborhoods provided of a town centre with market, shops and post office; dedicated open spaces and a walkable distance dimension. Therefore, each neighbourhood has tight building codes to reconnect designer of houses to vernacular building traditions. A pattern proposed, conceived and developed by Peter Calthorpe and Douglas Kelbaugh, concerns the construction of nodes around light rail stations (TOD, Transit Oriented Development or Pedestrian Pockets). These nodes are mixed used areas limited in extent by walking distance to the transit stop and are surrounded by a residential hinterland [38]. In both cases the logic seems to be yet oriented to new real estate expansions, the concern is on *new* residential neighbourhood, *new* mixed use areas, *new* light rail transit stations, the attention seems focused on the attempt to avoid that new suburbs had the same negative limits of the existing ones. But what kind of strategies can be worked out for the existing suburbs?

Usually for the existing urban sprawl, infilling development is proposed, a strategy of densification through which new buildings are put into the already existing fabric of diffused city. Infilling can't be efficacious without a general framework strategy to define which spaces with which functions and criteria should be used to make the infilling. Without this general framework infill become a sum of limited actions which are not able to face the structural nature of the urban diffusion, it ends to add "things over things" in an already chaotic context.

Recently, in order to create this general framework to support densification action of urban diffusion, planning proposes the creation of polycentric systems trough the realization of new centralities within diffuse city [39]. It could be useful a reasoning on what kind of centralities could be of interest in the urban diffusion.

> "They should be meant as magnets logically spread over the territory in order either to attract non residential functions of urban level (having a strategic and general function for the whole city) or to constitute new points of urban clot, of "urban hearts in the outskirts" (having also a local function targeted to rebuild local identities)....The new urban poles represent city injections into the non-city, a distribution of values of the city downtown inside the outskirts carrying those functions being absent by tradition: public and private directionality, cultural equipment, shopping centres, accommodation capacity, universities" [40].

About that point it should be pointed out that they are not the big facilities which lack in the sprawling city, but the small utilities necessary for the everyday life. The suburban inhabitant does not feel the need for university, but for the primary school. Generally speaking , the seating of a big urban activity ends up by becoming the umpteenth attractor of people flows who pass on the territory without living it and so without producing the expected effect of revitalization.

As Rykwert states [1], in the last decades all over the world, public buildings are more and more isolated from their context, separated by it by means of wide parking, green and protection barriers. The present public building is often completely targeted to interiorize the space excluding connections or even references to the surrounding context. Public buildings are more and more often places for "only authorized persons" : students, sportsmen, employee or buyers. Neither the shopping centres, nor the university campus, nor the stadium are capable of producing a "community effect" as well as of transmitting processes of identification.

4.1. Spaces and Identity

The described strategies have as reference the traditional city and aim at producing again the same conditions inside the new urban suburbs. Some authors criticize the fact to have as only future perspective the one of coming back to the past, proposing the model of traditional city again. In order to give again a sense to this shapeless magma in which we are put, wrote Decandia [41], we should start from new concepts, it is not enough to repeat lost orders or superimposing an "external mechanical order" separated from the present and then put into the territory [41].

In my view, the problem is misleading: it is not a question of choosing which formal or managerial model is to be followed in order to intervene in urban spread, but of defining what the people living in the sprawling city care for.

Suburbia inhabitants are forced everyday to increasingly long transfers, they are devoted to a completely car-oriented life in order to go to work, to school, to shop, to meet friends.

"On fringe both adults and teenagers needed cars to drive in different directions to work and school" [2, pag.190]. Women are the category more disadvantaged from this lifestyle:

> "to deal with fringe locations, American women doubled their miles driven between 1984 and 2000, making many more trips to serve other family members than men did. Marketer coined a new term 'taxi parent', to sell goods to the family trapped in the car. [...] Taxi parents bought containers for storing and serving hot or cold foods and beverages in their cars. They added televisions and CD players, plus minilockers for sports gear, back seat organizers, and trash containers" [2].

In suburban contexts, the need for moving greatly affects the daily cost of life, causing problems for the needy segments of population. In Lyon the demographic development of the inter-municipal suburban areas is characterized by the arrival of people who are to make long daily transfers within a range of 40–50 Km. [42]. In this area the incidence of travel cost on inner city inhabitants budget is around the 6–7%; this rate increases until 20-30% of suburbs inhabitants budget.

In the Asiatic South-East to Thai commuters who pass most of their time into cars, they are suggested to transform their car into a "small house on wheels" [1].

Suburbs inhabitants need for services adequately localized in order to reduce the number and the length of daily necessary travels. They need for usable and enjoyable spaces even outside their home gate. They need for dailiness and usages that go beyond the everyday queue in the traffic. They need for a social life developed in the territory where they live, made of habits and events able to create the sense of community. They need for shared spaces and a community to share these space.

This strong relationship between space and community has always marked urban spaces. At the begin of the VII century, Isidoro da Siviglia, in the text founder of the medieval Encyclopedism, outlined the importance of the human component within the city: "*Civitas*", the latin word from which the Italian *città* derives, "is a multitude of men gathered together by a social tie, it is so called for the *cives*, its inhabitants; in fact, with the word *urbs* we intend the walls, with the word civitas instead we intend not the stones but the men who live there" (Etimologiae, XV, II, 1). Therefore, an urban space is made of stones and community. An urban space is a public, open, accessible to everyone, relational space. An urban space is a polyfunctional and polysemic space, it has many functions and many meaning for people who live there. An urban space has different roles at the same time: it is possible to pass through it to go working, it could be a meeting point with friends, a place for shopping, for a walk or even all these activities at the same time. An urban space or better an urban place, as Augè [43] remarked, keeps memory of the events and the facts that along the time have happened within it, therefore it assumes more meanings and generates more kind of identities: individual or collective identities.

On the relationship among urban spaces and memory is focused one of the invisible cities of Italo Calvino [44]: the city of Zaira. The city is made of "relationship between the measurement of its space and the events of its past (...). A description of Zaira as it is today should contain all the past of Zaira", but a city don't tell its past just contain it "like the lines of a hand, written in the corners of the streets (...) every segment marked in turn with scratches, indentations, scrolls"

The memory of big and little daily events creates the tie between a community and the space. Memory gives identity to places.

> "Identities are built up trough the stratification of usages and meanings sedimented in places in agreement with the evolution of communities lifestyles. Territories with diffused urbanization, which are the clear expression of the speed alternating of land use destination and lifestyle changes, are increasingly spaces without identities" [45].

Is it possible to carry out actions and strategies oriented to generate a collective identity?

Collective identity refers to shared usages and shared meanings. Shared meaning could be due to a common cultural heritage which identify in some places symbolic elements where community recognize itself. Shared usages could be referred to ritual activities but also more simply to collective daily usages such as elderly meeting place to chat and play bowls or the place where to have a walk on Sunday morning. These kind of places do not exist in suburban city.

Even if the absence of an historical sedimentation process in these areas make it impossible to define identities strongly rooted in culture and tradition, it should be possible to start processes of spaces possession, meanings attribution, small daily memories accumulation in order to give rise to new identities for these territories. To reach this target two things must be considered. The first one is that identity is strongly rooted in the relationship between community and space, then it request an active behaviour of the social component; without the active involvement of inhabitants every initiative is destined to failure. In fact, it is possible to contribute to the emerging of new form of identities just promoting the built up of a collective "project of meanings" [46]. The second one is that spaces possession request flexible and polyfunctional spaces which could gave rise to different recurrent occupations. Contemporary cities is full of monumental spaces which are impressive, huge and public but also deserted and empty since they didn't succeed in stimulating any form of possession in population.

> Often, "urban landscape is constructed as a collection of oversized and competing design objects, proposing itself as the realm of the diffuse and competitive aesthetic: landmarks instead of monuments, the private versus the collective" [39, pag.7].

Space possession is generated by distinct characteristics which are obsolete in contemporary architecture:

> "Shade, shelter, amenity and convenience are the usual causes of possession. The emphasizing of such places by some permanent indication serves to create an image of the various kinds of occupation in the town, so that instead of a completely streamlined and fluid out-of-doors a more static and occupied environment is created, ... where a periodic occupation (chatting after church?) is woven permanently into the town patterns" [47, pag.23].

Moreover, "efficient services and environmental quality, togheter with ordered and calm spaces that are environmentally accommodating and located in physical proximity to interacting components. This can be achieved through the use of simple, organic architecture that establishes clear relationships with the processes of urban planning. This is the only way of guaranteeing the openness of the social imagination, without making aesthetic imitations of strange hybrid structures and constructing spaces that are able to house new functions as well as ancient feelings, memories and passions." [39].

Intervention in diffused urbanization can't be reduced to the identify of spaces to be transformed and activities to be introduced. It is a more complex work requesting an active involvement of collectivity to define spaces able to give rise to new identities.

5. Conclusion

Urban sprawl impacts in increasing ways all geographical regions. Origins and paths followed by this phenomenon may vary in each context; this notwithstanding, common threads exist through which the different stories can be linked again to become a single one: the globalization process, the urban neo-liberism, the lack of territorial project, the administrative fragmentation, the transformation of urban real estate in a financial market, and the policies built around the traditional city, considering this one as a separate entity from the new diffused urbanization. These common threads have generated settlement spaces without shape and identity, characterized by low density, single-purpose residential constructions in locations distant from existing public services and infrastructure, and automobile-oriented development. Reconstruction of a single story from all different urban histories is needed to define action systems and strategies aiming at imposing a structure on the spaces of urban sprawl.

From the proposed unified view it is possible to extract some factors that have contributed to define the phenomenon (table 2). They can be classified as:

- *Determinants:* These are the factors that gave birth to the settlement creation pressure during the last century.
- *Facilitating factors:* These are the factors that, under settlement creation pressure, made suburban areas the selected target for new settlements.

- *Shape factors:* These are the factors that determined the morphology of the diffused city.

Table 2. Factors underlying sprawl

DETERMINANTS	FACILITATING FACTORS	SHAPE FACTORS
- urban population growth - economic expansion - transformation of urban real estate market into a financial market - competition between municipalities - increasing weigth of private sector on land use policies	- inner city problems - housing preferences - increased car ownership - new technologies development and diffusion	- lack of large scale planning of land use - fragmentation of territorial control - development of transportation facilities and infrastructures

The arguments presented here show that policies to be implemented have to be taken at different levels and have to include not only a general change of paradigm, putting settlement problems as the centre of the land management actions, but also specific policies both for the traditional city and the diffused one. It has been highlighted here that the traditional city and the diffused city are strictly interlinked, so that one's evolution has spawned the other, and now a strict relationship still exists between them; problems arising in one are having effects on the other, in both directions.

As general policies it is important to promote:

- *Coming back to focus on regional planning:* land use changes have to be again the main focus of territorial policies; they are not to be intended as a mean or way to achieve other goals.
- *Financing actions for qualifying diffuse urban growth.* During the last years, a large amount of money has been spent in financing improvements in the compact city, while urban sprawl has been only marginally considered in public appropriations. This trend has to be switched in the opposite direction, giving money to the operations aimed at structuring the diffuse settlements.

Policies for traditional city should be oriented to:

- *Avoiding evinction,* through contributions, incentives, public owned homes, there is a need to contrast gentrification processes that are acting in the inner cities; these processes boost the chaotic sprawl of settlements on territory.
- *Rationally managing existing real estate heritage*; in the globalization era, intensely-built areas are opposed to extinguishing historical urban areas. In Italy, there are a lot of municipalities risking extinction; through policies aimed to make these areas more accessible and centers of development, a better use of the existing built spaces could be achieved.

Policies for the diffused city should deal with promoting projects oriented to:

- *Creating "spaces for people":* It is necessary to promote projects whose aim is not to sum "things over things", activities on spaces, or builds on voids, but to realize spaces for people. It is necessary to create places that can give rise to forms of possession, meanings attribution, and small daily memories accumulation in order to favour the emerging of new identities for these territories. It is necessary to involve the local community in order to give a structure to anonymity working on image and identity.
- *Extracting a morphological structure from existing spaces:* Starting from what is already on the territory, a project must fit it into a structure adequate to population needs, through actions as the realization of a system of open spaces with small services.
- *Extracting variables and walkable spaces:* Through small links and connections in existing spaces, it is possible to create variable and path-oriented spaces, removing anywhere it is feasible the fences and barriers separating single-function areas, in order to allow passage by foot or by cycle from house to shopping centre to fruit-growing woods; and creating transit paths alternative to car use, breaking the sequences with public spaces that could attract social uses.

Strategies have acted until now, when involving existing diffused urbanization, to privilege the insertion of large urban functions, trying to generate new centralities. But large attraction poles are not what is missing in the sparse city; what is really missing are the small poles for everyday life, which may become attraction centers for self identification processes. This brings again the discussion, on one side, to small-scale things, to small but everyday needs, more than to large emergencies by lacking functions; on the other side it advocates strongly for going back, in urban planning, to using urban design going over the sole definition of land uses and quantification of use.

It is necessary to go back to the design of urban space, moving from public spaces to private ones, in which, then, built spaces (buildings with their dimensions and shapes) result from the design of open spaces (roads, squares, public gardens), contrary to what happens now in the diffused city in which external space is only a leftover among buildings.

Throughout this process, residents have to be strongly involved, for the design of open spaces has to be derived by the needs and wants of people living in the diffused city, not by an a priori ideological choice.

REFERENCES

[1] Rykwert, J. (2003). *La seduzione del luogo. Storia e futuro della città.* Torino, Italy: Einaudi.

[2] Hayden, D. (2004). *Building suburbia.* New York, USA: Pantheon Books.

[3] Jefferson, T. (1781-82), *Notes on the State of Virginia,* http://etext.virginia.edu/toc/modeng/public/JefVirg.html

[4] Petralia, G. (1998). Crescita ed espansione. In: Artifoni, *E. Storia Medioevale*. Roma, Italy: Donzelli editore,

[5] De Landa, M. (2003). *Mille anni di storia non lineare*. Torino, Italy: Instar libri.

[6] Mc Neill, W. H. (1982). The Pursuit of Power. Technology, Armed Force, and society since A.D. 1000. Chicago, USA: University of Chicago Press.

[7] Secchi, B. (2000). *Prima lezione di urbanistica*. Bari, Italy: Laterza.

[8] Sica, P. (1978). *Storia dell'urbanistica*. Il Novecento. Bari, Italy: Laterza.

[9] Fishman, R. (1987). Bourgeois Utopias: the Rise and Fall of Suburbi New York, USA: Basic Books.

[10] Tosoni, P. (2002). Introduzione: leggere la città diffusa. In Dal Pozzolo L., *Fuori città, senza campagna*. Milano, Italy: Franco Angeli.

[11] Hayden, D. (2002). *Redisigning American Dream: The Future of Housing, Work and Family Life*. New York, USA: W. W. Norton.

[12] De Fusco, R. (1974). *Storia dell'architettura contemporanea*. Bari, Italy: Laterza editore.

[13] Le Corbusier (1930). La parcellizzazione del suolo urbano. In: Aymonino, C. (Ed.), *L'abitazione razionale. Atti dei Congressi CIAM 1929-30*. Padova, Italy: CLEAN

[14] Benevolo, L. (1993). *Storia dell'architettura moderna*. Bari, Italy: Laterza.

[15] Calabi, D. (2005). *Storia della città. L'età contemporanea*. Venezia, Italy: Marsilio.

[16] Lanzani, A. (2003). *I paesaggi italiani*. Roma, Italy: Meltemi.

[17] Di Biagi, P. (2001). La grande ricostruzione. Il piano Ina-Casa e l'Italia degli anni '50. Roma, Italy: Donzelli.

[18] Secchi, B. (2005). *La città del ventesimo secolo*. Bari, Italy: Laterza.

[19] Gorgolini, L. (2004). Un mondo di giovani. Culture e consumi dopo il 1950. In: Sorcinelli P., *Identikit del Novecento*. Roma, Italy: Donzelli editore.

[20] Canevari, A. (2001). Il territorio "trasparente": tra regola e indifferenza. In: Canevari, A. & Palazzo, D., *Paesaggio e territorio*. Milano, Italy: Franco Angeli.

[21] Colicelli, C. (2004). *Le transizioni sommerse degli anni 90*. Soveria Mannelli CZ, Italy: Rubettino editore.

[22] Indovina F., Matassoni F., Savino M., Sernini M., Torres M. & Vettoretto L. (1990). *La città diffusa*. Venezia, Italy: Iuav-Daest.

[23] Maggioni, V. (1982). L'assetto territoriale dell'industria. In: Sciarelli, S., Maggioni, V., Stampacchia, P., *L'industria in Campania all'inizio degli anni ottanta*. Napoli, Italy: CCIAA Napoli, ISVEIMER.

[24] Mangoni, F. & Pacelli, M. (1981). *Dopo il terremoto la ricostruzione*. Roma, Italy: Edizioni delle autonomie.

[25] Taylor, N. (1997). *Urban Planning Theories since 1945*. London, UK. SAGE

[26] Hayek, F.A. (1960). *The Constitution of liberty*. London, UK: Routledge& Kegan Paul.

[27] Jones, R. (1982). *Town and Country Chaos: A Critical Analysis of Britain's Planning System*. London, UK: The Adam Smith Institute.

[28] Crosta, P. (1998). *Politiche. Quale conoscenza per l'azione territoriale*. Milano, Italy: Franco Angeli.

[29] Dematteis, G. (1999). Presentazione. In: Salone C., *Il territorio negoziato*. Firenze, Italy: Alinea Editrice.

[30] EEA, European Environment Agency (2006). *Urban Sprawl in Europe*. EEA Report No10/2006. www.eea.europa.eu

[31] Hasan, A. (2007). The New Urban Development Paradigm and the Changing Landscape of Asian Cities In *Urban Trialogues: Co-productive ways to relate visioning and strategic urban projects*. Isocarp review 03.
[32] Vescina, L. (2007). Experiences from Periphery. In Urban Trialogues: Co-productive ways to relate visioning and strategic urban projects. Isocarp
[33] Marcelloni, M. (1993). Il regime dei suoli in Europa. In Campos Venuti, G.,& Oliva, F., *Cinquant'anni di urbanistica in Italia*. Bari, Italy: Laterza.
[34] ISTAT, Istituto Nazionale di Statistica (1991). 13° Censimento della popolazione e delle abitazioni. www.istat.it
[35] Granata, E. & Lanzani, A. (2008). La fabbrica delle periferie. Produzione collettiva della scarsità, disagio e conflitti latenti a Milano. In: Fregolent L. (Ed.), *Periferia e Periferie*. Roma, Italy: Aracne.
[36] Cooper, I., Jason, P. (1999). Il programma di ricerca sulle città sostenibili nel Regno Unito. *Urbanistica*, 112
[37] Bruegmann, R. (2005), *Sprawl: A Compact History*. Chicago, USA: University of Chicago Press
[38] Duany, A. & Plater-Zyberk, E. (1996). The lexicon of New Urbanism. *Urbanistica,* 108.
[39] Gregotti, V. (2005). Urban Futures: continuities and discontinuities. In: 49° IFHP World Congress, *Urban Futures: continuities and discontinuities*, Summary Report. Rome, Italy.
[40] Marcelloni, M. (2003). *Pensare la città contemporanea. Il nuovo piano regolatore di Roma*. Bari-Roma, Italy: Laterza.
[41] Decandia, L. (2008). *Polifonie Urbane*. Roma, Italy: Meltemi.
[42] Rosales-Montano, S. (2006). Territoires à l'épreuve, table ronde. In: *Revue Urbaniste*, n.347. review 03.
[43] Augé, M. (2005). Nonluoghi. Introduzione ad un'antropologia della surmodernità. Milano, Italy: Eleuthera.
[44] Calvino, I. (1972). *Le città invisibili*. Milano, Italy: Einaudi.
[45] Petroncelli, E. (2008). Transformation Processes and Spirit of the Place: historic hambits. In *Proceeding of the Scientific Symposium of the 16th General Assembly ICOMOS*, Quebec, Canada.
[46] Decandia, L. (2000). Dell'identità. Saggio sui luoghi per una critica della razionalità urbanistica. Soveria Mannelli CZ, Italy: Rubbettino
[47] Cullen, G. (1961), *Townscape*. London, UK: The Architectural Press.

In: Land Use Policy
Editors: A. C. Denman and O. M. Penrod

ISBN: 978-1-60741-435-3

Chapter 4

DYNAMICS OF LAND USE CHANGE IN THE MEDITERRANEAN: IMPLICATIONS FOR SUSTAINABILITY, LAND USE PLANNING AND NATURE CONSERVATION

Julia Martínez-Fernández, Miguel Angel Esteve, M. Francisca Carreño and Jose Antonio Palazón
Departamento de Ecología e Hidrología. Universidad de Murcia.
Campus de Espinardo, 30100-Murcia, Spain.

ABSTRACT

During the last decades Mediterranean systems are being affected by important land use changes which are transforming the entire landscape. Traditional irrigated lands have constituted one of the most characteristic agro-landscapes in the Mediterranean and have played a relevant socio-economic, ecological and environmental role. However, these valuable agro-landscapes are progressively decaying due to recent socio-economic changes which, at the same time, are promoting new irrigated lands outside the river valleys. These new irrigated lands have a major effect on land, water resources, landscape and the biodiversity value of extensive tracts of the Mediterranean area. At the same time, Mediterranean drylands are quickly disappearing due to land abandonment. In addition, Mediterranean areas are suffering a quick urbanisation process affecting both natural and agricultural areas. These trends may be considered as a reduction of the most characteristically rural Mediterranean landscape to favour ecologically extreme landscapes: on one side the natural areas and on the other side the new irrigated lands and urban areas. It is necessary, therefore, to understand the factors driving the land use changes in the Mediterranean, to analyse their ecological effects and to explore the potential implications of several policies regarding land use and natural resources.

To this aim, we have analysed the land use changes and their socio-economic and environmental context in three study cases in Southeastern Spain, an arid Mediterranean area where the four above-mentioned land use changes are taking place. These study cases are the traditional irrigated land of Murcia, the agricultural system of Mazarron-Aguilas and the land use changes in the Mar Menor watershed. The ancient Murcia irrigated lands constitutes a paradigmatic example of the loss of this valuable agro-landscape and its highly fertile soils due to the urbanisation process and spread of infrastructures. The Mazarron-Aguilas new irrigated lands may be considered as representative of the most intensive agricultural systems in the Mediterranean area, which are quickly spreading at the expense of drylands and natural areas. The Mar Menor watershed have suffered important agricultural and urban-tourist land use changes affecting the hydrological and nutrient dynamics and the biological communities of the coastal lagoon and associated wetlands. An integrated approach has been applied combining GIS, Remote Sensing, spatial and environmental modelling and dynamic system models to analyse the sustainability of these three case studies, the spatial and temporal patterns of land use, the main socio-economic and environmental driving factors and their ecological implications.

1. INTRODUCTION

The spatial dimension of sustainability is an essential issue which is generating an increasing interest both in the scientific and social sides. Land use changes constitute one of the dimensions of global change linking the local, regional and global levels. The importance of land as resource and the analysis of the spatial dimension of change emerge as a key point in many places, especially in insular systems and where there is an strong dynamics of land use change, as occurs in the Mediterranean coastal areas, where the Murcia region is located.

Mediterranean landscapes have evolved under traditional models of use of resources and territory in which environmental conditions and productive systems have been closely connected. However, during the last decades strong socio-economic changes have affected these traditional systems and, therefore, the associated landscapes. The new socio-economic context is decoupling the Mediterranean production systems from the environmental conditions, resources and limits of local ecosystems. As a result, traditional Mediterranean landscapes are suffering intensive and generalised transformations, especially in coastal areas. These changes affect to the conservation of biodiversity and cultural values, to the allocation of resources and to the general sustainability of the territory.

It has been pointed out (Burel and Baudry, 2002) that past trends cannot merely be extrapolated into the future, except for short periods. It is necessary a deep understanding of the causes explaining the land use changes and the use of models capable of taking into account the interactions of the environmental and socio-economic subsystems, in order to simulate the expected behaviour of the system and the state of the territory in the long run. An important effort is being devoted to the construction of models for understanding landscape and land use changes (Fresco et al., 1994; Ramírez et al., 1999; Martínez Fernández and Esteve Selma, 2002; ESPON, 2007). These models allow an integrated approach to consider the effects of land use changes in a given territory in terms of resource requirements, nature conservation and social needs. In this sense, the study of Murcia Region is of high interest due to its location in a coastal area in which the most important processes of land use change in the Mediterranean are taking place. In this chapter we analyse such land use changes at two spatial scales: the regional level (the entire Murcia Region) and the local level, in three case studies: the traditional irrigated land of *Huerta de Murcia*, the agricultural system of Mazarron-Aguilas and the land use policies in the Mar Menor watershed (figure 1).

Figure 1. Location of Murcia Region and the selected study cases.

The *Huerta de Murcia* is a traditional irrigated land located in the middle lowland area of the Segura river around the city of Murcia (Spain). The Huerta is a traditional irrigated land considered by Meeus et al. (1990) as open agricultural landscapes in the river valleys along the Mediterranean coast and characterised by irrigation, intensive use and high crop diversity. Along century XX several factors such as the creation of new irrigated lands and the urbanisation of traditional irrigated lands have given rise to a growing imbalance between water resources and irrigation demands and to a loss of fertile soil and other environmental and cultural values of this traditionally agricultural area.

The irrigated land of Aguilas and Mazarron, in Southeastern Spain, constitutes a good example of the new intensive Mediterranean agriculture. They are located close to the coast and have arid (260 mm mean annual rainfall) and warm (17 ^{0}C mean annual temperature) conditions. This agriculture is based on groundwater exploitation and makes full use of technological advances. The intensive use of groundwater resources has led to the over-exploitation of local aquifers and to seawater intrusion, water salinisation and the falling off water tables. Moreover, the continued expansion of irrigated lands has meant the transformation of areas with high ecological value, threatening the habitat of endangered protected species. Some of these effects constitute full environmental externalities whereas others also negatively influence the profitability of irrigated lands. All these factors establish complex relationships which condition the general behaviour of the system.

The Mar Menor, with an area of 135 km^2, is the largest coastal lagoon in the Western Mediterranean. During recent decades several land use changes in the Mar Menor watershed are threatening its conservation. Important agricultural and urban-tourist changes have taken place in the watershed, affecting the lagoon and its coastal wetlands. Changes in land use are one of the main factors driving the hydrological dynamics and the quality of waters (Mander et al., 1998, Tong and Chen, 2002). This is also the case in the Mar Menor site, where the expansion of irrigated lands in the watershed and the urban and tourist development have led to significant hydrological changes and to the increase in the nutrient inputs reaching the lagoon and associated wetlands from diffuse (agricultural drainage) and point sources (wastewater).

These cases illustrate the main trends of land use change in the Mediterranean: the abandonment of traditional agro-landscapes, in particular drylands and traditional irrigated lands along the river valleys; the increase in the area occupied by intensive irrigated lands and the transformation of extensive tracts of the territory into urban uses and infrastructures. These three processes characterise the basic land use changes in many other Mediterranean areas, especially along the coast, as in Marina Baja in Eastern Spain (Peña et al., 2008). The entire Murcia Region and these three cases have been studied using an integrated approach to understand the dynamics and driving factors of land use changes, the environmental effects and the expected implications in terms of sustainability of several scenarios and policy options. Such integrated approach combines spatial analysis, environmental modelling and dynamic simulation, making use of data provided by a variety of sources: field surveys, Remote Sensing and statistical databases. In the following sections we present the main results and insights obtained at the Murcia Region level and at the selected study cases.

2. General Methodological Approach

At the Murcia Region level, it has been studied the spatial dimension of sustainability through the analysis of land use, the recent trends of change and their environmental implications, by means of a set of sustainability indicators. Results also allowed a first conceptual model of sustainability in the use of land and water resources in Murcia Region. In the three study cases, quantitative dynamic system models were developed to understand the specific trends of change.

There is a growing interest to include the temporal dimension in the analysis and modelling of landscape and land use. The consideration of both, time and space constitutes a challenge but also an increasing need to adequately understand the underlining dynamics of change and its implications for sustainable land use policies. Several methodologies have been applied, including transition matrices of landscape change (Mouillot et al., 2005), the spatially explicit landscape simulation (Constanza and Voinov, 2004; Aurambout et al., 2005) and the use of integrated approaches which combine several methodological tools, in particular GIS, Remote Sensing, environmental response models and dynamic simulation models. Such approach, applied in this work, has revealed useful in several studies, as the combined use of environmental modelling and socio-economic scenarios to study the biodiversity at landscape level (Gottschalk et al., 2007); the environmental modelling of land use changes detected by Remote Sensing (Geoghegan et al., 2004); the use of decision models, GIS-based agricultural models and simulation models to analyse the environmental and socio-economic interactions involved in the long run changes of agricultural areas (Wu et al., 2007) and the integration of GIS, environmental modelling and dynamic simulation in the study of land use changes under different scenarios (Larson et al., 2004; Martínez Fernández and Esteve Selma, 2002).

A dynamic system model was developed in each case study: the traditional irrigated land, the agricultural system of Mazarron-Aguilas and the land use changes in the Mar Menor watershed. Dynamic system models (Roberts et al. 1983, Vennix 1996; Jorgensen & Bendoricchio, 2001) are of special interest for the study of problems related to sustainability and the integration of social, economic and environmental factors. The dynamic system model describes the structure of the system by reference to the main factors, interactions and feedback processes which simulate its dynamic behaviour. The structure is defined by a set of variables, basically levels and rates, and the relationships and feedback loops they establish. Feedback loops, a central concept in the structure of dynamic system models, constitute closed cause-effect relationships inducing exponential processes (positive loops) or tendencies to some type of equilibrium (negative loops). Non-linear relationships and delays are other elements which add complexity to the system.

The dynamic models were developed making use of the software VENSIM (Ventana Systems, 2007). The modelling process involved several stages (figure 2): conceptualisation, data acquisition, formulation of model equations and calibration. In the final stage the models were iteratively improved through calibration against the historical data of main variables. Finally, the models were validated using different structural tests (Barlas 1996), including dimensional consistence tests, sensitive analysis and extreme condition tests. The models were used to define and explore the expected effects of several policy scenarios.

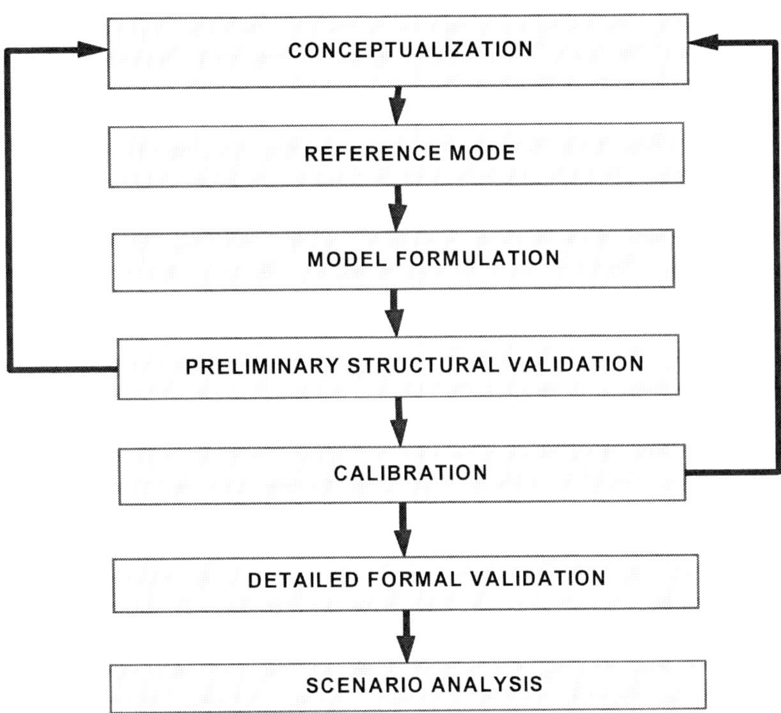

Figure 2. Methodological steps in the construction of dynamic system models.

3. Sustainability of Land Use in Region De Murcia

3.1. Land Use and Sustainability. Methodological Approach

The development of indicators on the spatial dimension of sustainability is not free of difficulties, taking into account the multiple questions to consider regarding the spatial patterns and the directions of change. In relation to landscape complexity, indicators dealing with diversity and functionality of land cover have been proposed (Papadimitriou, 2002). Venturelli and Galli (2006) emphasises the need of indicators based in multidisciplinar approaches integrating the ecological, socio-economic and agronomic dimensions. Such indicators may help in a better description of the relationships among the techno-systems, the agro-systems and the natural and semi-natural systems, along with their trends of change.

One important line of research refers to the formulation of indicators based on information provided by remote sensing and image classification at different scales. The application of indicators based on remotely-sensed information is receiving an increasing attention due to the widespread use of remote sensing and GIS techniques, which facilitate the monitoring of spatial and temporal patterns. Remotely-sensed land use indicators at watershed scale have been proposed (Tiner, 2004) regarding the extension, perturbation and integrity of habitats. Other works have applied land use indicators based on remote sensing at the European and regional scale (Bock et al., 2005). This has also been applied to assess the land use patterns in Murcia Region and the recent trends of change. The European project CORINE Land Cover provided land use maps based on remote sensing and image classification, covering Europe in years 1987 and 2000 with 100 m spatial resolution.

A number of land use indicators have been proposed to assess the spatial dimension of sustainability. However, prior to the selection of the appropriate indicators it is necessary to identify the strategic questions which should be addressed regarding the sustainability in a given territory . In Murcia Region these strategic questions are the following:

- Does the territory keep an adequate proportion of natural and semi-natural systems?.; Are rural systems with active environmental functionality maintained?
- Is maintained as non-fragmented an adequate proportion of natural and semi-natural systems?
- Is there an efficient use of land allocation for artificial uses?
- Is there a sustainable management of the coastal areas?
- Is designated and protected as natural site an adequate proportion of the territory?

The above questions have been addressed by means of the application of the appropriate indicators. The results obtained provided a deeper understanding of the dynamics of land use change in Murcia Region, the relationship between land and other critical resources such as water and the implications for overall sustainability. This has allowed a first conceptual model on sustainability of land and water in Murcia Region. In the following sections the main results are shown.

3.2. Main Results

3.2.1. Area Occupied by Natural and Rural Systems

Figure 3 shows an overview of the land use pattern in Murcia Region in year 2000, according to data provided by the Corine Land Cover project. Natural and semi-natural systems occupy around 40% of territory, agricultural uses 56%, artificial uses around 3% and water bodies (reservoirs and the Mar Menor coastal lagoon) around 1%. Table 1 presents the area occupied by the basic land uses and their increase respect to 1987.

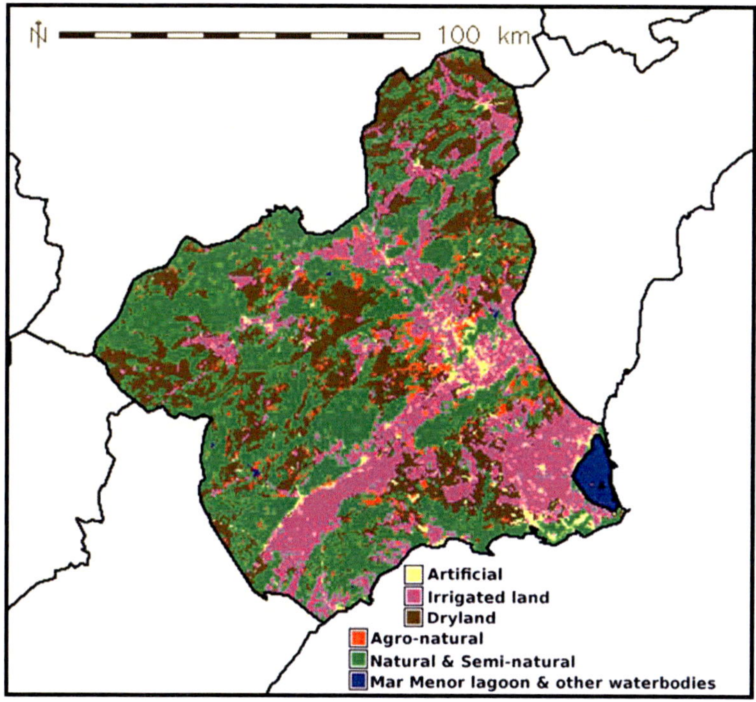

Figure 3. General pattern of land use in Murcia Region in Year 2000. Source: Corine Land Cover and own elaboration.

Table 1. Basic land use in Murcia Region in year 2000 and increase respect to 1987. Source: Corine Land Cover and own elaboration

Land use	2000 (ha)	Increase respect to 1987 (%)
Natural and semi-natural	450,230	- 1.46
Agro-natural	55,041	- 15.52
Dryland	322,649	- 10.09
Irrigated land	265,271	+ 17.14
Artificial areas	36,634	+ 62.16
Mar Menor lagoon and other waterbodies	14,873	+ 1.06

The comparison between 1987 and 2000 reveals a significant increase in artificial areas and in irrigated lands, an important loss of drylands and agro-natural systems and also reductions in natural and semi-natural areas. In 13 years the environmentally active landscape, constituted by drylands and agro-natural systems, has lost around 46,000 ha, a 11% of its area in 1987. Mediterranean drylands play important ecological functions, which include their trophic role for many species, even those typically associated to forest areas as forest prey birds. In addition, drylands constitute the optimum habitat for species linked to traditional Mediterranean agrolandscapes, such as steppe birds and for species typical alternating patches of natural vegetation and crops, which is the case for the terrestrial tortoise *Testudo graeca*.

The loss of agricultural and natural areas is partially explained by the increase in artificial areas. In addition, there are important internal changes among the agricultural uses according a gradient of increasing intensification from drylands and agro-natural systems to irrigated lands. This double process of intensification and abandonment (Antrop, 1993; Vos, 1993; García Novo, 1999; de Aranzábal *et al.*, 2008) means the loss of extensive drylands and agro-natural systems, the environmentally active rural areas, to favour to extreme landscapes: the natural one and the areas with a very intensive use of land and natural resources, represented by the artificial areas and the new irrigated lands

The decrease in drylands due to the loss of their socio-economic functionality and the associated polarization of landscape is a general trend in many European areas (Meeus et al. 1990, Fjellstad and Dramstad, 1999). This process is generating several environmental effects, such as the degradation of natural landscapes, fragmentation and loss of natural habitats and loss of biodiversity (White et al. 1997; Poudevigne et al., 1997; Burel and Baudry, 2002). The fragmentation and loss of habitats are two of the main threats for the conservation of endangered species and constitute key processes in conservation biology (Groom et al. 2006).

The reversibility of agricultural uses to other type of land use is also linked to the degree of intensification. Dryland is the agricultural use with a highest proportion of change into other uses and, in fact, it changes in opposite directions, into semi-natural areas due to abandonment and into irrigated lands. On the contrary, the reversibility of irrigated lands to less intensive uses as dryland or semi-natural is very low. This should be taken into account in the assessment of irrigated lands, whose area increases by around 17% in Murcia Region between 1987 and 2000. Moreover, this increase occurs far from the river valleys and areas naturally adapted to irrigation, what generates several environmental effects which will be discussed in more detailed in the study cases.

3.2.2. Fragmentation of Natural and Semi-Natural Systems

The maintenance of the environmental functionality of natural and agro-natural systems requires not only a certain proportion of land but also a high degree of connectivity by means of large patches and elements acting as ecological corridors. Infrastructures, in particular roads, one of the main causes of land fragmentation, are quickly spreading in Murcia Region, especially in the case of motorways. It has been carried out an analysis of the regional road system and its effects on land fragmentation taking into account roads equal to or higher than 10 m width. In 2003 motorways and high capacity roads (50 m width) represented a 9.25% of total road length but were responsible for the 41,6% of total land uptake by roads. Figure 4 presents the effect of roads on fragmentation of natural and agro-natural systems.

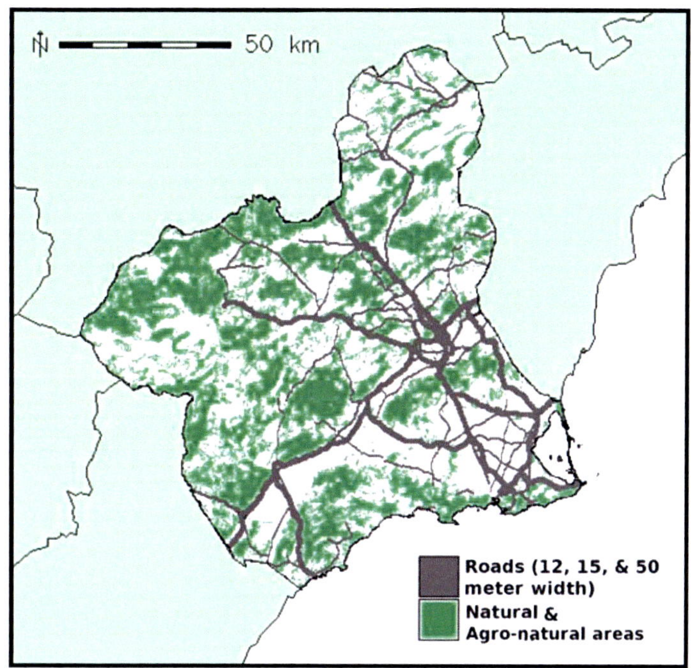

Source: Corine Land Cover 2000 and own elaboration.

Figure 4. Roads network and patches of natural and agro-natural areas in Murcia Región.

Available studies on the relationship between species richness and size of natural patches in Murcia Region as salt marshes (Pardo *et al.*, 2003), allow to estimate the minimum patch size of natural vegetation with an interest for conservation. It has been considered all patches with an area equal to or greater than 10 ha, since under such threshold the species richness quickly decreases. Using the map of natural and agro-natural systems elaborated from the Corine Land Cover 2000, the roads network and the GIS, it has been calculated the number and size of patches with natural and agro-natural use before and after taking into account the effect of roads. Roads generate (table 2) an increase in the number of patches, a decrease in the average size and above all, a significant (55%) reduction of the maximum size of patches. As expected, the main effect of roads is linked to the fragmentation of the large units of natural and agro-natural systems, those which present a highest interest for the ecological processes, the conservation of biodiversity and the environmental functionality of territory. This constitutes a very relevant issue since land fragmentation is extremely difficult to reverse.

Table 2. Number, average size, maximum size and standard deviation of patches of natural and agro-natural systems with and without taking into account the effect of the roads network. Source: Own elaboration

	Without roads effect	With roads effect
Number of poligons	604	652
Average size per poligon (ha)	824.00	763.31
Maximum poligon size (ha)	195,562	88,244
Standard deviation	8,475	5,284

3.2.3. Efficiency of Land Uptake by Artificial Uses

Land uptake by artificial uses, especially for urban settlements and transport infrastructures, is quickly increasing at all scales: global, national and regional. The Mediterranean countries presented, in general, a moderate to low proportion of land uptake due to a traditional urban design based on compact cities (the Mediterranean city model) and a relatively low degree of development of transport infrastructures, especially high capacity roads. However, this is quickly changing in the last decades. To analyse such changes in Murcia Region, it has been calculated several indicators regarding artificial uses in 1987 and 2000 (table 3). Total area of artificial uses increased by 62%, the highest rate in Spain, which is also the country with a highest rate in Europe (Fernández Durán, 2006). The increase in total area of artificial uses and total urban area doubles the respective average values in Spain. This is especially the case of scattered urban settlements, which increases a 83%, almost three times the average value in Spain.

Table 3. Indicators of land uptake by artificial uses in Murcia Region in 1987 and 2000

Artificial uses	1987 (ha)	2000 (ha)	Net change (ha)	% Change respect 1987
Total area of artificial uses	22,592	36,634	14,042	62
Compact urban area	10,460	11,246	785	8
Scattered urban settlements	1,902	3,480	1,578	83
Total urban area	12,362	14,725	2,364	19
Ratio Scattered/Total urban area (SS/TU)	0	0	0	54

Source: Corine Land Cover.

The ratio SS/TU, this is, the proportion between scattered settlements to total urban area constitutes a good indicator of the efficiency with which the needs for residential purposes are satisfied: low values indicate that urban needs are mainly satisfied using the Mediterranean compact city model, which requires a low land consumption and therefore represents a more sustainable land management policy. The ratio SS/TU was 15,38% in 1987, whereas it reached 23,63% in 2000, what represents a significant reduction in the efficiency of land uptake for urban development. The increase in this indicator by 53% points out to a more unsustainable land management.

Figure 5 presents other indicators of efficiency of land uptake. A sustainable land management should decrease the per capita land consumption for artificial uses by means of more efficient models of land allocation to fit the social and economic needs. In Murcia Region the per capita area of artificial uses increased by 47% between 1987 (0.02 ha per person) and 2000 (0.03 ha per person). However, the per capita land uptake for total urban uses increased only by 8% despite the strong increase in scattered urban settlements, since most of urban areas still belong to the Mediterranean compact model. However, between year 2000 and 2008 the scattered settlements have experienced an unprecedented rate of growth due to the generalised sprawl of the "Californian model", characterised by scattered residential areas disconnected from the existing cities and traditional towns and characterised by low density uni-familiar housings with large areas for gardens and golf courses. This process affects the SS/TU ratio and the per capita land uptake for urban uses. These trends of land uptake are general in Spain, although the per capita rates in Murcia double the respective average values in Spain (figure 5).

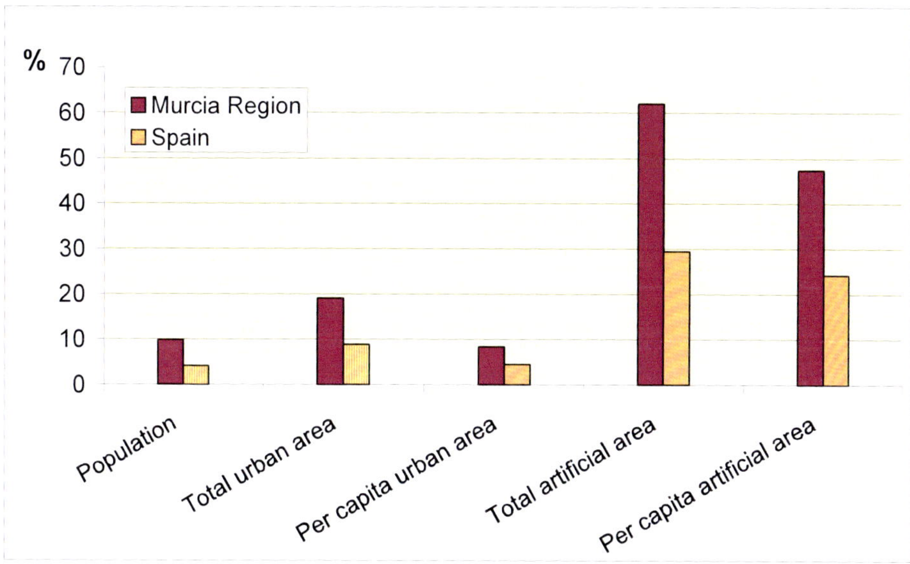

Figure 5. Percentage of change between 1987 and 2000 in population and in the total and per capita area of artificial uses and urban area in Murcia Region and in Spain. Data sources: Corine Land Cover, and population census of INE (National Institute of Statistics).

The current process of urban sprawl is affecting the entire Murcia Region and is generating a series of direct and indirect effects on land, natural resources and other environmental issues (figure 6), which are briefly described.

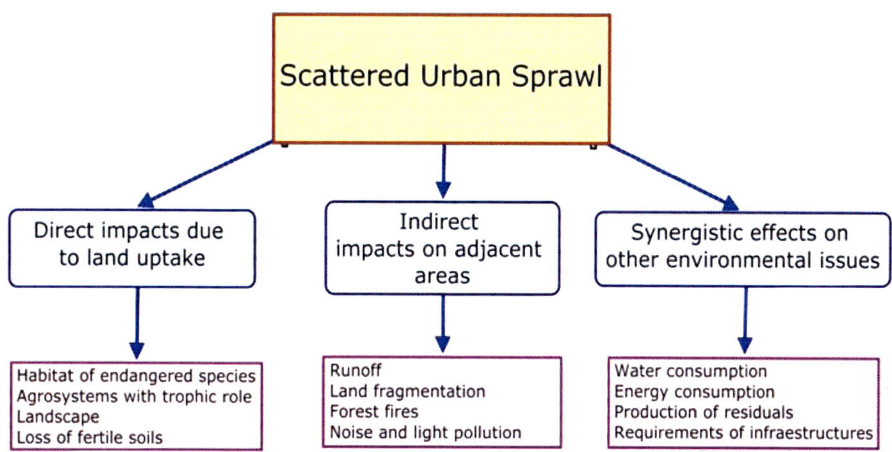

Figure 6. Direct and indirect effects of the scattered urban sprawl in Murcia Region.

Regarding direct impacts due to land uptake, the spread of residential settlements, infrastructures and golf courses generate loss of biodiversity, landscape degradation and sealing of fertile soils. Biodiversity is affected by direct transformation of habitats of relevant species and by the loss of extensive drylands close to natural sites. These agrolandscapes present a key trophic role as breeding areas for prey-birds and other protected species. The quality of landscape is also degraded by the spread of new urban settlements and associated infrastructures and golf courses. Finally the traditional irrigated lands along the river valleys, which present soils with high natural fertility, a scarce non-renewable resource in Murcia Region, are being affected by soil sealing due to the spread of residential areas and infrastructures.

There also indirect environmental effects on adjacent areas regarding land fragmentation and the creation of barriers affecting the population of some species. Other indirect effects refer to the alteration of runoff and the drainage network. Increased runoff coefficients due to soil sealing and changes in the drainage networks due to infrastructures increase the problems associated to big rainfall events and overland flow, whose frequency will increase, according to the expectations of available scenarios of climate change for this Mediterranean area (Eisenreich, 2005). Water consumption also significantly increases since the low-density unifamiliar residential model presents a per capita water consumption around 400 litres person day, three times higher than in the case of the Mediterranean compact city, around 110-140 litres person day (Capellades et al., 2002). The per capita water consumption substantially increases in low density residential settlements due to a different pattern of water consumption and the spread of private gardens and swimming pools. One emerging indirect effect on adjacent areas refers to the increase in the frequency of forest fires and in the seriousness of their consequences, due to the increased direct contact between natural areas and urban settlements generated by the low-density residential model, in contrast with the Mediterranean city model in which such direct contact is kept to a minimum. This has already occurred in other Spanish Mediterranean areas where the spread of this low-density residential model is well developed, as Catalonia and Valencia.

3.2.4. Sustainable Management of Coastal Areas

Figure 7 and table 4 present the area occupied by artificial uses in 1987 and 2000 in a series of strips parallel to the coast. The proportion of land uptake by artificial uses is higher in the strips very close to the coastal line (over 30% of land in the 100 m and 200 m strip width). From 200 m width onward the proportion of land uptake decreases until the strip located between 2 and 5 km distance from the coastal line, which in year 2000 presented around 10% of land uptake by artificial uses (figure 7).

However, when the relative increase is considered, the trend is the opposite: the ratio at which land uptake is taking place is highest in the coastal strips located at a certain distance from the coastal line (table 4), whereas the 0-100 m and 0-200 m strips present a low proportion of land uptake between 1987 and 2000. This is explained by new acts and rules widening the public coastal domain to cover the entire 0-100 m strip and by the existence of broad tracts of non-urban land located in the 0-2 and 2-5 km strips available for low-density residential settlements and associated golf courses.

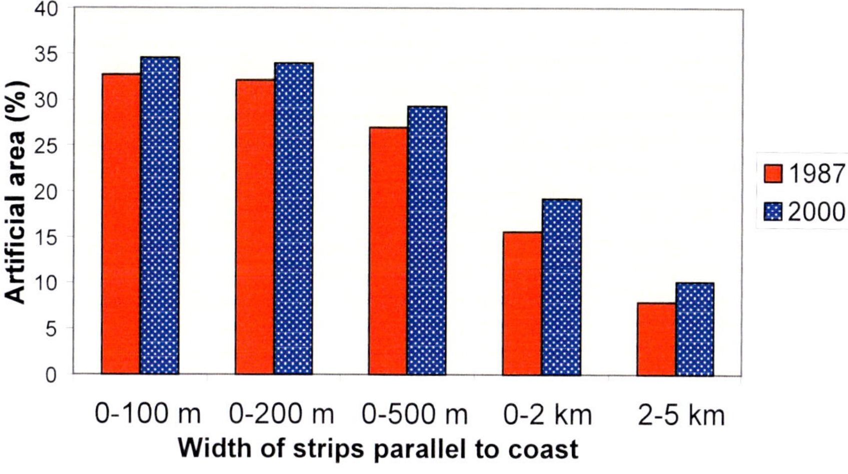

Figure 7. Proportion of land uptake by artificial uses in a series of strips parallel to the coast with varying width. Source: Corine Land Cover.

Table 4. Area occupied by artificial uses in a series of strips parallel to the coast in Murcia Region

Strip width	1987 (ha)	2000 (ha)	Increase 1987-2000 (%)
0-100 m	863.45	911.99	5.62
0-200 m	1,489.45	1,575.03	5.75
0-500 m	2,596.78	2,820.80	8.63
0-2 km	4,703.97	5,800	23.3
2-5 km	2,932.86	3,757	28.1

Source: Corine Land Cover.

3.2.5. Designation and Management of Protected Sites

Murcia Region presents high values of species richness and ecological diversity, explained by its location in the only arid Mediterranean area existing in Europe and as a transition zone between the Mediterranean forests and the arid sub-tropical systems (Esteve and Calvo, 2000). The degree of conservation in the habitats with European interest, according to the Habitats Directive, is optimum in 56% of such habitats and 68% of total habitats present a degree of conservation over the corresponding average values in Spain (Esteve Selma et al, 2003). Biodiversity includes rare species as the terrestrial tortoise *Testudo graeca* and prey birds whose populations present one of the highest densities in Europe. In 1992 a regional network of protected sites was established and in 1999 it was designated a set of Sites of Community Importance (SCI). Moreover, Special Protection Areas for Birds (SPAB) were designated to contribute to the European network Natura-2000.

Table 5. presents the protected area, number and average size of protected sites in Murcia and Spain.

Table 5. Total protected area, number and average size of protected sites in Murcia and Spain.

		Protected area (ha)	Number protected sites	Average size (ha)
Murcia	2001	80,238	19	4,223
	2006	68,736	19	3,617
	Change 2001-2006	-11,502	0	-605
Spain	2001	3,957,973	620	6,384
	2006	5,952,226	1,186	5,023
	Change 2001-2006	+1,994,253	+565	-1,361

Source: Fundación Europarc-España.

In 2001 the protected area in Murcia was around 7%, close to the average in Spain. However, five years later both values substantially differ due to an almost 50% increase in Spain and a 14% reduction in the protected area in Murcia. As a consequence, in 2006 the proportion of protected area in Murcia is only 6% whereas it reaches 11,79% as average in Spain. This atypical process by which part of the protected area became unprotected, has affected agrolandscapes and habitats of European interest and is favouring the urbanisation processes.

In synthesis, Murcia region lacks an adequate land use policy to maintain the natural systems and main agrolandscapes, to minimise land fragmentation and land uptake by artificial uses, to apply a sustainable management of coastal areas and to adequately protect the natural sites. These processes and trends of land use change interact with other important environmental and socio-economic factors such as the dynamics of population and the management of water resources, interactions which should be taken into account for a comprehensive understanding of the whole system. This integrated approach has been applied to the detailed analysis of the three study cases presented in the following sections, focusing on the traditional and modern agricultural systems, their recent trends of changes and their environmental effects.

4. The Traditional Irrigated Land of *Huerta De Murcia*

4.1. Introduction

Irrigated lands constitute a characteristic Mediterranean agrolandscape. Historically irrigated lands developed in areas with available water, especially in lowlands along the main river valleys. These areas are well adapted to this productive function due to several factors: availability of renewable water resources and soils with a natural high fertility, adequate topographic conditions and the existence of close spatial and functional connections with the hydrological dynamics of the river regarding water flows between the irrigated land, the river and the alluvial aquifer. These agro-landscapes are, therefore, located in areas naturally pre-adapted to this productive function. The spatial and functional proximity of traditional irrigated lands respect to natural riparian ecosystems determines a close integration between irrigated lands and the adjacent ecosystems regarding landscape, basic ecological processes and environmental functions.

In relation to landscape, the traditional irrigated land, called "huerta", resembles the role of riparian natural systems that they substitute, showing a similar scenic contrast with the surrounding arid ecosystems. Regarding basic ecological processes, water flows in the system river-lowland-alluvial aquifer are not severely modified. Finally, the huerta agrosystem presents valuable environmental functions as the conservation and sustainable use of soils with a high natural fertility, the maintenance of a high biological diversity of species linked to riparian systems and wetlands and the conservation of a high agro-diversity with hundreds of traditional varieties.

The Huerta de Murcia (figure 8) is located on the middle lowland area of the Segura river around the city of Murcia. The high crop diversity of this agro-system includes citrus groves and many other fruit trees combined with potatoes, peppers and a great variety of other vegetables. There are also occasional mulberry trees, pomegranate trees and date-palms and relict elements of the original riparian vegetation along the traditional irrigation channels like elms (*Ulmus minor*) and poplars (*Populus alba*). The traditional irrigation channels present other helophytes, like *Imperata cilindrica* and *Arundo donax*, aquatic species like *Potamogeton pectinatus* and some interesting botanical rarities in the context of the Murcia region like *Ceratophyllum submersum*. In addition, the agro-landscape constitutes the habitat of more than a hundred different bird species.

The sustainability of the Huerta de Murcia and the rest of the traditional irrigated land of the Segura basin along its lengthy history has been based on adaptive strategies of irrigation and crop management. Traditional elements like the irrigation channels (dating from before 1000 AD) exist alongside modern elements associated with urban development.

Figure 8. General view of the Huerta de Murcia traditional irrigated land.

However, the preservation of this agrosystem is seriously threatened in the short and long term by different social, economic and environmental factors, all of which present complex interactions and relationships, leading to the decreasing viability and finally to the degradation and progressive disappearance of these valuable agro-landscapes. Such factors include the creation and growth of new irrigated lands which have increased total water demand and generated an increasing water scarcity, the competition between agricultural and urban land uses, the increasing pollution of irrigation water and the progressive reduction of the average size per farm, all affecting the profitability of traditional irrigated lands in several ways.

The loss of fertile soils due to land uptake by artificial uses is a worrying issue and subject of special consideration by the European Commission, which pointed out that the areas more seriously affected by this problem are the river lowlands of Southern Europe. The most seriously threatened country is Spain, which is both the country where soils of high agricultural quality are most scarce (only 7 % of total soils) and where the proportion of high quality soils lost due to urbanisation is highest (7.1 % of total high quality soils) (Comisión de las Comunidades Europeas 1992). This loss is three times higher than that occurring in medium quality soils and fourteen times greater than in low quality soils.

It has been developed a dynamic model to understand the driving factors involved in the decaying viability of these traditional irrigated lands and to evaluate the effects of some policy scenarios regarding land use and other management options.

4.2. Model Description

Figure 9 presents a simplified diagram of the dynamic model of Huerta de Murcia. The model simulates the system starting in 1932 with a monthly time resolution. The main variables are grouped into four sectors: water resources, irrigated area, population and farmers, although there are links between the whole set of model variables.

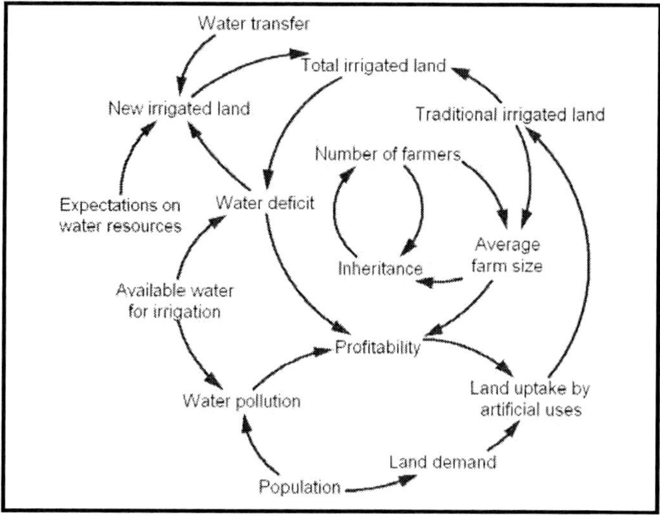

Figure 9. Simplified diagram of the dynamic model of Huerta de Murcia.

In 1932 the Huerta de Murcia had 13,500 ha, area which progressively decreases as a consequence of the increase in population, which demands land uptake for artificial uses, and due to a reduction of profitability of traditional irrigated lands. In 1995 14% of the initial area of traditional irrigated lands had been lost, value which doubles the proportion of high quality soils lost in Spain. The key factor in the reduction of profitability is the increase in the number of farms and, consequently, the decrease in the average size per farm. Figures 10, 11 and 12 present the observed and simulated values of the area of traditional irrigated lands, number of farmers and average size per farm between 1932 and 1995. Water deficit and water pollution constitute other factors which also affect negatively, although to a lesser degree, the profitability of traditional irrigated lands.

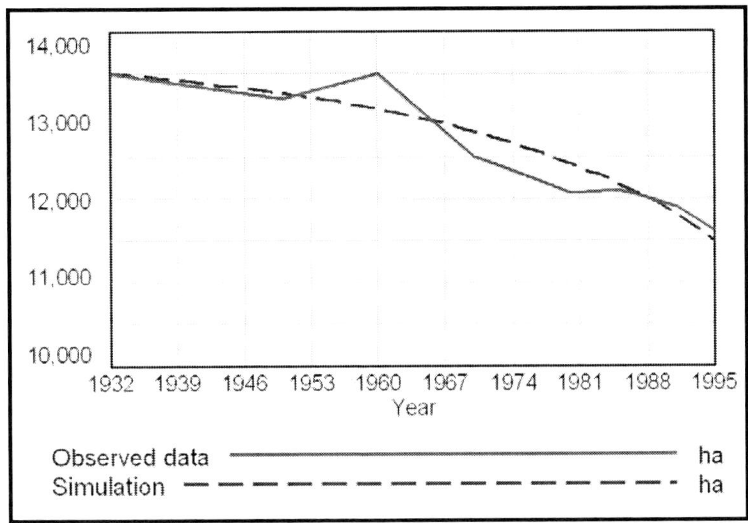

Figure 10. Area of traditional irrigated land in Huerta de Murcia between 1932 and 1995. Observed data and results of the simulation model.

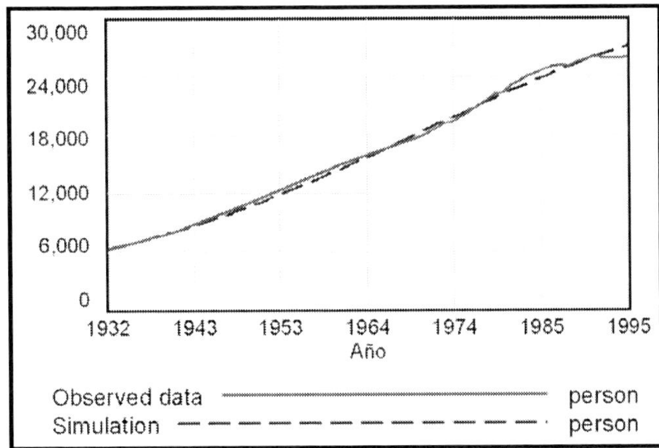

Figure 11. Number of farmers in Huerta de Murcia between 1932 and 1995. Observed data and results of the simulation model.

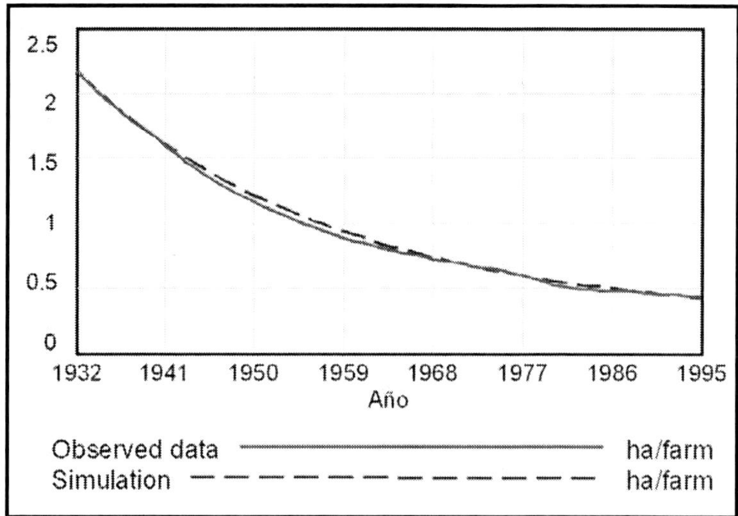

Figure 12. Average size per farmer in Huerta de Murcia between 1932 and 1995. Observed data and results of the simulation model.

4.3. Scenario Analysis

It has been used the dynamic model to analyse the potential effects of several policy scenarios during the period 1995-2025. Figure 13 presents the expected results under two scenarios: Base trend, under which model parameters are not changed, representing the maintenance of the observed trends regarding population and profitability, and the Conservation policy scenario, under which several management measures are implemented to conserve the Huerta de Murcia.

Under the Base trend scenario the traditional irrigated land decreases to around 8,500 ha by the end of the simulation period due to the reduction of profitability generated by a combined effect of a small average size per farm, water deficit and water pollution and due to the population increase.

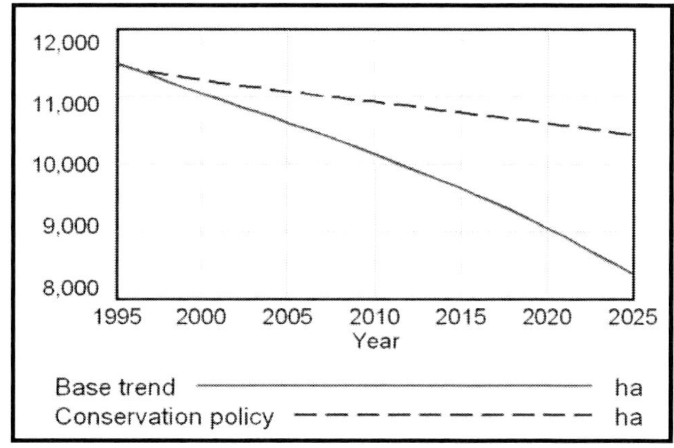

Figure 13. Expected values of traditional irrigated land in Huerta de Murcia between 1995 and 2025 under the Base trend and the Conservation policy scenarios.

Under the Base trend scenario 3,100 ha of traditional irrigated land would be lost between 1995 and 2025, equivalent to 100 ha annual loss in average, a rate which doubles the land uptake between 1965 and 1995. By 2025 around 38% of Huerta de Murcia would be transformed into artificial uses. This Base trend scenario corresponds to the maintenance of current situation, characterised by no measures to promote profitability of traditional irrigated lands and no control regarding land uptake. Land use policy at municipal level has maintained this weak control on land use change. In 1995 the updated municipal land planning recognised the traditional irrigated land in Huerta de Murcia as an important agrolandscape which should be conserved, but at the same time allowed the potential transformation into urban areas of around 1,500 ha of huerta.

The Conservation policy scenario (figure 13) considers several measures to slow down the land uptake by urban uses and infrastructures and to increase the average size per farm, joined to an improvement of the amount and quality of available water for irrigation. Under this scenario the traditional irrigated land in 2025 would have around 10,500 ha. Although there is still some land transformation, the rate of loss is a third respect to the Base trend scenario.

Which has been the observed trend since 1995?. It has been estimated the area of traditional irrigated land in Huerta de Murcia between 1995 and 2007 by land use sampling using aerial photographs and remote sensing images. Results obtained show that actual values have been well below the expected values under the Base trend scenario (figure 14), which means that the actual trend has accelerated his rate of land use change.

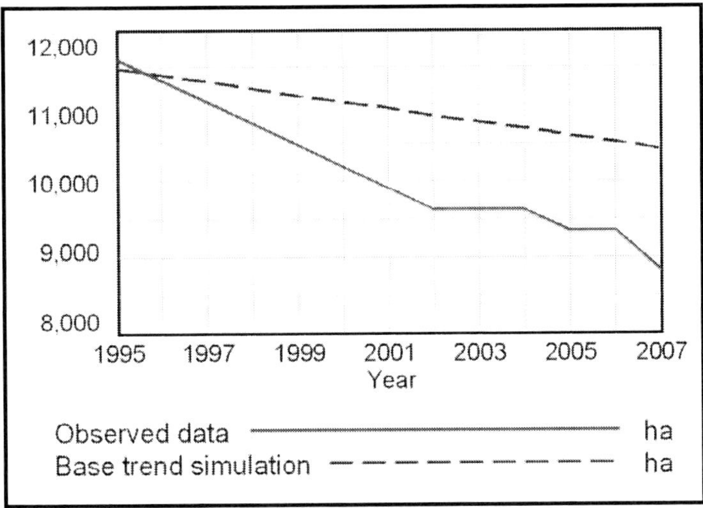

Figure 14. Actual values of traditional irrigated land in Huerta de Murcia between 1995 and 2007 and expected values under the Base trend scenario.

In 2007 the actual area of traditional irrigated land in Huerta de Murcia was around 8.800 ha (figure 14), very close to the expected value under the Base trend scenario by 2025, 18 years later (figure 13). The municipal land use planning has proved useless to conserve the Huerta de Murcia and, in fact, the rate of loss has substantially increased as a response to the current high land demand for urban uses and infrastructures affecting the whole Murcia Region, as described in earlier sections. Existing land use policies at the regional and municipal levels have shifted from weak controls on land uptake to actively promote the transformation of traditional irrigated lands into urban areas and infrastructures.

Despite this, traditional irrigated lands have multiple and important functions. In addition to their productive role, these agrosystems allow the maintenance of high quality landscapes, the preservation of cultural and environmental heritage and the conservation of the soils with a highest fertility, a non-renewable and scarce resource in Murcia Region. It is necessary to reverse current land use policy and implement new land planning instruments with effective measures to conserve the Huerta de Murcia and other traditional agrolandscapes with outstanding environmental, cultural, historical and landscape values.

One of the processes affecting the decreasing viability of traditional irrigated lands is the creation of new, modern and highly profitable irrigated lands outside the river valleys. This is the case of the Mazarron-Aguilas agricultural system, described in the next section.

5. The Agricultural System of Mazarron-Aguilas

5.1. Introduction

The area of Mazarron and Aguilas, in the southern coast of Murcia, constitutes a good example of the new and highly intensive Mediterranean irrigated lands. They apply all kind of technological advances regarding varieties, automatic fertilisation and irrigation and use of greenhouses and present a profitability between ten and twenty times higher than that of drylands. These irrigated lands began to be opened up in the 1960s due to a growing fresh vegetable market in Europe. The irrigated lands of Mazarron-Aguilas have been studied in an integrated framework by means of dynamic system models, environmental modelling and GIS, in order to analyse the spatial model of this system, the land use changes during the last decades, the main environmental effects and the key socio-economic and environmental factors driving the whole system.

In order to understand the Mazarron-Aguilas irrigated land system, the following methodological steps were followed:

- Analysis of land use in 1981 and 1999 and main land use changes on a geo-referenced basis.
- Environmental modelling of each type of irrigated system and its response to the climatic, topographic and lithological conditions.
- Spatial modelling of irrigated lands by means of a GIS.
- Elaboration of a dynamic model describing the key environmental and socio-economic factors driving the system and the main land use changes.
- Use of the dynamic model to evaluate the potential effects of several policy scenarios
- Combined use of the simulation results, the environmental model and the GIS to analyse the expected spatial distribution of irrigated lands under the considered scenarios and their environmental effects.

5.2. Spatial Modelling of Mazarron-Aguilas Irrigated Lands

5.2.1. Specific Methodology

An extensive and detailed systematic sampling of land use was carried out in the Mazarron-Aguilas area. The sample includes 1,211 units covering the whole study area with a total extension of 72,500 ha at two different times: 1981, through aerial photographs, and 1999, through direct fieldwork. The land uses considered include, among others, forests, natural shrubland, horticultural and tree crop drylands, open-air horticultural irrigated crops, irrigated tree crops and greenhouses. Data acquired were combined with a geo-referenced environmental database with forty ecological, topographic and lithological variables. This allowed the environmental characterisation of each type of irrigated land in 1981 and 1999, the construction of a land use transition matrix and the elaboration of environmental response models for the different types of irrigated land using GLM (Generalised Linear Models). Finally the environmental models and the geo-referenced database were combined with a GIS to build up the potential distribution map of irrigated lands in both studied years.

5.2.2. Results

During the last two decades the area of irrigated lands in the study area has increased from 10,000 ha in 1981 to 17,000 ha in 1999. This 70% increase in irrigated land has occurred at the expense of areas previously occupied by dryland and shrubland. Of particular relevance is the growth in the area covered by greenhouses, which in less than twenty years has increased to 6,000 ha, an area eight times greater than its initial extension. The analysis of the land use transition matrix shows the intense dynamics of change affecting dryland, 43 per cent of which has become shrubland (due to land abandonment and natural succession) or has changed into new irrigated lands. This trend may be interpreted as a reduction of the most characteristically rural area, associated with a loss of functionality, to favour two ecologically extreme landscapes: the natural one and that characterised by the agriculturally intensive use of land and natural resources.

Irrigated lands also exhibit an important internal dynamics of land use change. The main changes are the transformation of tree crops into open air horticultural crops and the transformation of open air horticultural crops into greenhouses. Figure 15 shows the main land use transitions during the study period.

The general pattern in all these land use transitions represents a clear trend to the most intensive uses following the gradient: natural vegetation-dryland-irrigated land-urban use. Within the irrigated areas there is another gradient of intensification: tree crops-open air horticultural crops-greenhouses. The degree of reversibility of agricultural uses is related to the intensity of such use: drylands show a high rate of change in the two opposite directions (natural vegetation and irrigated land), whereas irrigated tree crops and open-air horticultural crops usually shift to greenhouses. Finally greenhouses show a degree of irreversibility similar to that of urban use, at least in the time span considered in this study. This is a distinctive characteristic, which in conjunction with other factors makes greenhouse-based agriculture more similar to some industrial activities. This has deep implications in relation to agricultural and land use policies, since the spread of greenhouses implies a more intense and qualitatively different transformation of land.

The environmental response models of irrigated lands in 1981 and 1999 include topographical (slope), climatic (winter rainfall) and lithological (presence of siliceous materials) variables. Figure 16 shows the increased trend of irrigated lands to occupy steep slopes. In these areas the new irrigated lands give rise to a risk of erosion processes and to the occupation of areas with high ecological value.

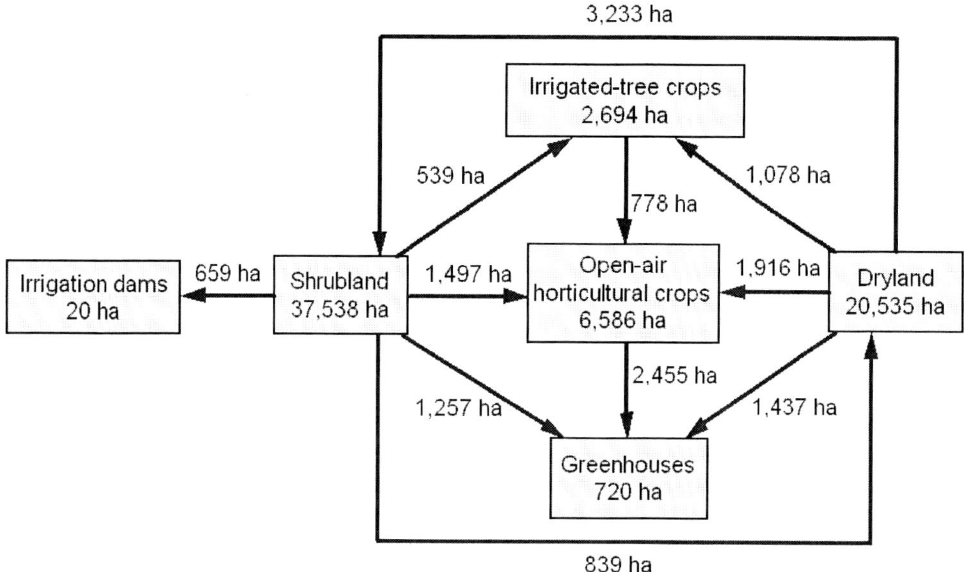

Figure 15. Main land use transitions between 1981 and 1999 in Mazarron-Aguilas, indicating the area covered by each land use in 1981 (boxes) and the area involved in each land use change (arrows).

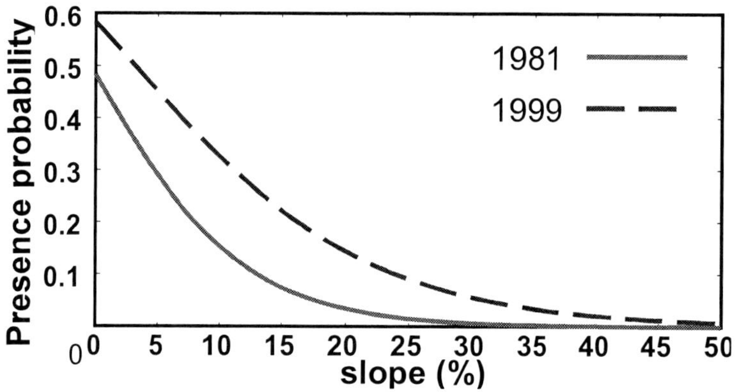

Figure 16. Presence probability of irrigated lands in 1981 and 1999 in Mazarron-Aguilas as a function of slope.

Figure 17 shows the model as a function of slope and winter rainfall whereas figure 18 presents the potential distribution map of irrigated lands by means of the environmental response model and the GIS.

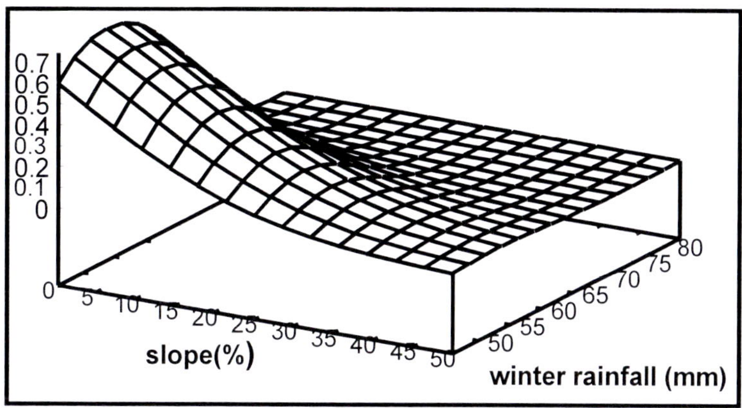

Figure 17. Probability of presence of irrigated lands as a function of slope and winter rainfall.

The land use transition matrix and other results obtained with the spatial analysis were used to develop the dynamic model, in particular to define the structure and parameters of the land use sector.

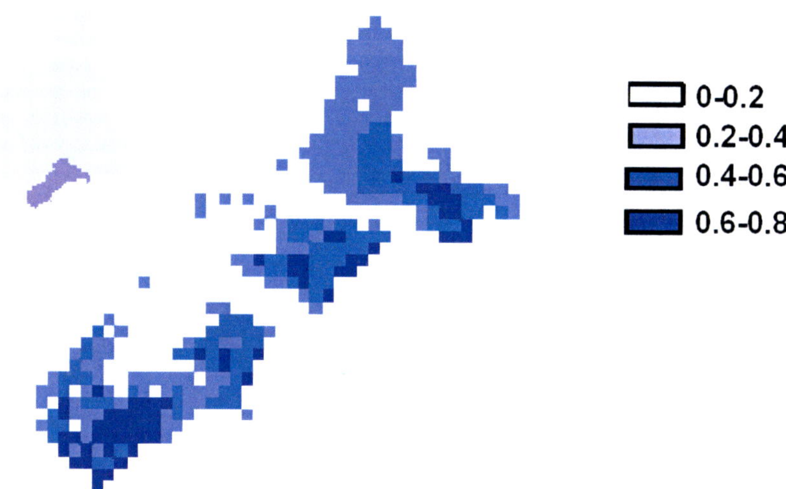

Figure 18. Potential distribution of irrigated land in Mazarron-Aguilas indicating the presence probability in each cell unit.

5.3. The Dynamic Model of Mazarron-Aguilas

5.3.1. Model Description

The dynamic model considers five sectors: Land Use, Profitability, Available Area, Water Resources and Pollution. The model starts in 1960 and has a monthly time resolution. Figure 19 presents a simplified diagram showing the main factors and relationships.

Figure 20 shows a simplified diagram of the land use sector with the area of irrigated tree crops, open air horticultural crops, greenhouses, dryland, natural vegetation (shrubland) and dams for irrigation. The whole set of variables and parameters was determined using data obtained from the fieldwork and the environmental and spatial modelling. The area occupied by each one of the three types of irrigated land varies with time through 12 land use changes. The rate of change of each land use depends on several variables, especially the difference of profitability between each land use and the aggregated costs index (which depends on other model variables such as the cost and quality of water for irrigation and the available area for new irrigated lands).

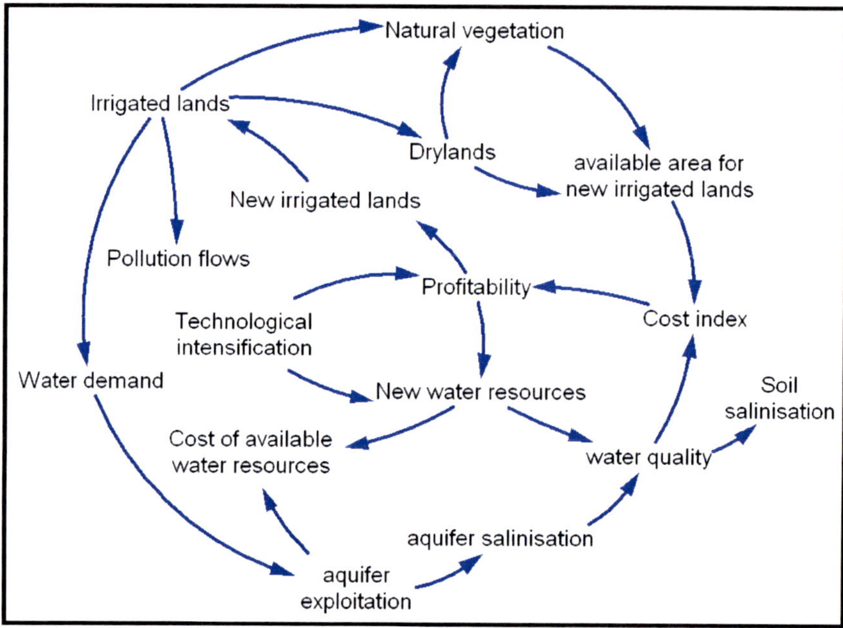

Figure 19. Simplified diagram of the Irrigated Lands dynamic model.

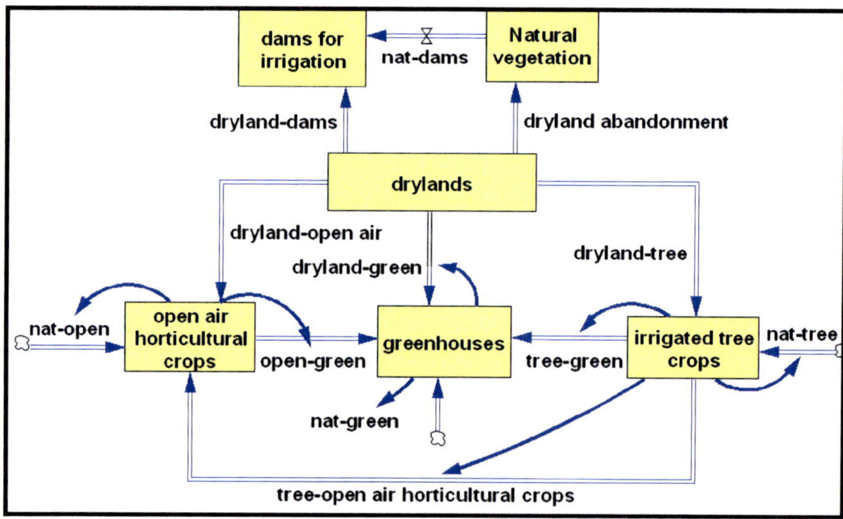

Figure 20. Simplified diagram of the land use sector representing the main uses and land use changes. nat-dams: natural vegetation to dams for irrigation; nat-open: natural vegetation to open air horticultural crops; open-green: open air horticultural crops to greenhouses; tree-green: irrigated tree crops to greenhouses; nat-tree; natural vegetation to irrigated tree crops.

The simulation gives results similar to the observed data series, showing an increase in irrigated lands from 1,200 ha in 1960 to 17,000 ha in 1999 (figure 21) and the exponential growth of greenhouses. The model shows a shift from the initial prevalence of positive feedback loops promoting exponential growth to the dominance of negative feedback loops, when the system begins to perceive the local restrictions in key factors like the quantity and quality of water resources.

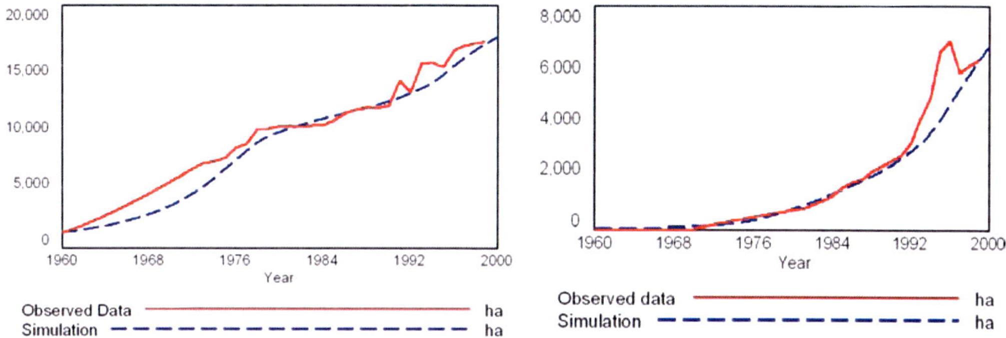

Figure 21. Area of total irrigated lands (left) and greenhouses (right) in Mazarron-Aguilas between 1960 and 2000. Observed data and simulation results.

Structural validation tests, the basic approach in the validation of dynamic system models (Barlas, 1996) were applied to validate the *New Irrigated Lands* model, including statistical tests and comparison with observed data series, analysis of dimensional consistency, extreme condition tests and sensitivity analysis. The sensitivity analysis assess the model robustness to parameter changes. Robust models should present smooth, generally quantitative but not qualitative changes in their general patterns of behaviour. Figure 22 presents a Montecarlo simulation with the response of total irrigated lands to a simultaneous variation in all tested model parameters, showing a smooth change and the maintenance of the basic pattern.

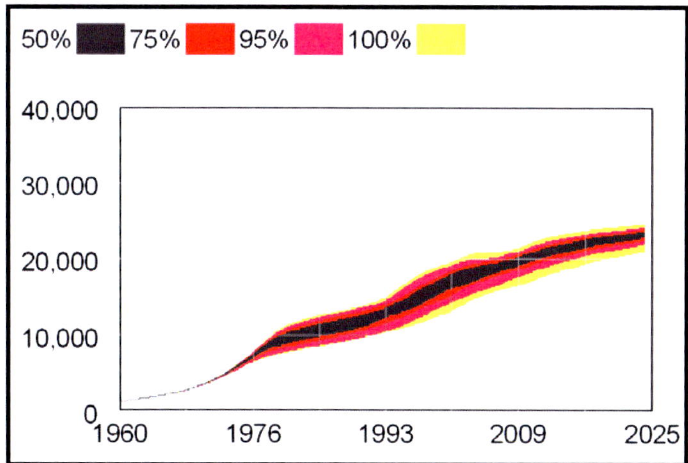

Figure 22. Montecarlo simulation. Response of total irrigated lands to a simultaneous variation in all tested parameters. Tones indicate the confidence intervals including 50, 75, and 100 per cent of simulation runs.

The environmental effects of land occupation were analysed by reference to four indicators: area of irrigated lands inside a protected natural site, the area inside a Natura 2000 site, the habitat of terrestrial tortoise (*Testudo graeca*) lost due to its transformation into irrigated land and the habitat of *Periploca angustifolia* (an ibero-african endemism) lost due to irrigated lands.

Around 14% of the area of Mazarron-Aguilas has been designated as protected natural site, a value over the average in Murcia Region and which reflects the ecological relevance of the arid coastal Mediterranean ecosystems, as those existing in Mazarron-Aguilas. In 1999 irrigated lands occupy 17 % of such natural sites, whereas a 22 % of the area susceptible to further land transformation into irrigated land (areas of dryland or shrubland with a presence probability of irrigated land higher than 50%) is also located inside a protected natural site. This susceptibility to land use change constitutes a potential threat to such sites and their ecological value.

Mazarron-Aguilas falls within the distribution area of *Testudo graeca*, a singular terrestrial tortoise with a very restricted European distribution. About 57 % of Mazarron-Aguilas corresponds to the optimum habitat of this endangered species (Giménez et al., 2001; Anadón et al., 2005, 2006). Irrigated lands occupied around 3,900 ha of this optimum habitat in 1981, which means a loss of 9.4% of the original total in the study area. In 1999 the optimum habitat lost due to irrigated lands had reached 22%. This loss is caused not only because of the increase in area of irrigated lands but also because of the higher habitat quality of the areas being transformed (Martinez et al., 2002). Greenhouses have contributed most to this loss of optimum habitat. In total, 1,137 ha, 43 per cent of the areas highly susceptible to transformation into irrigated lands, constitutes optimum habitat of *Testudo graeca*. This means that any scenario of increase in irrigated lands will negatively affect the conservation of this threatened species.

Mazarron-Aguilas also presents habitat of *Periploca laevigata*, one of the most singular and scarce European Mediterranean shrubs. It is a Priority Habitat according to the 92/43 Habitats Directive. Murcia Region contains more than half of the total habitat in the Iberian Peninsula. Around 64% of habitat in Murcia Region is located in Mazarron-Aguilas (figure 23), area which emerges as a key factor for the conservation of this species.

In 1999 irrigated land had consumed 3,250 ha, around 29%, of the habitat of *Periploca angustifolia*, a high value taking into account its restricted distribution. The areas with a high probability of transformation represent another 600 ha of this optimum habitat.

5.3.2. Scenario Analysis

Several scenarios concerning the available area and water resources for new irrigated lands have been defined and explored. All scenarios were projected over the time horizon for which the model was validated, covering the period 1999-2024. Three of such scenarios are here presented:

1. *Base Trend.* All model parameters remain unchanged, assuming the continuation of trends over the next 25 years. This scenario attempts to overcome water scarcity, the main limiting factor to the increase in irrigated lands. No special environmental policies are adopted.
2. *Technological Intensification and Partial Increase in Water Resources*. It is assumed a reduced rate of increase in the external water supply. It is also considered an

increase in the technological innovation in irrigated lands, which partially counterbalances the increased costs due to scarce water resources.

3. *Strong Nature Conservation Policy*. In addition to the hypothesis of the previous scenario, a strong policy on nature conservation is adopted, which excludes new irrigated lands in the protected natural sites and in the high quality habitat of *Testudo graeca* (areas with a presence probability higher than 70%) and *Periploca angustifolia* (areas with a presence probability higher than 25%).

Under the base scenario the increase in the area of irrigated land would continue to reach 23,500 ha by the end of the simulation period, around 80% of total available area for such use in Mazarron-Aguilas, at the expense of dryland and shrubland. This growth is caused by the spread of greenhouses, whereas tree-crops and open air horticultural crops suffer a slight reduction (Figure 24).

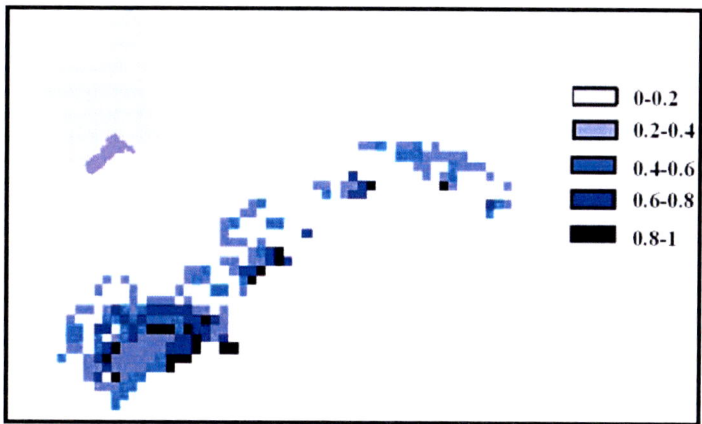

Figure 23. Potential distribution of *Periploca angustifolia* in Mazarron-Aguilas. The presence probability in each cell unit is indicated.

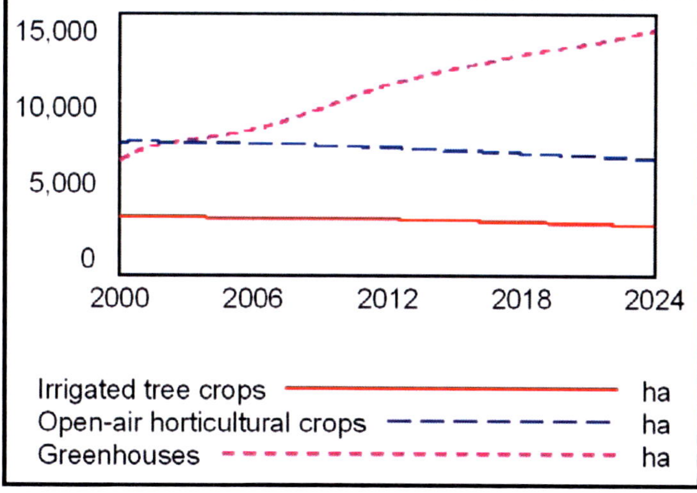

Figure 24. Base Trend scenario. Expected area occupied by each type of irrigated land.

The effects of the Base Trend scenario on the occupation of areas with a high ecological value were explored by the combined use of the dynamic model, the environmental model and a GIS. Figure 25 shows the potential distribution of irrigated lands by year 2024 under the Base Trend scenario.

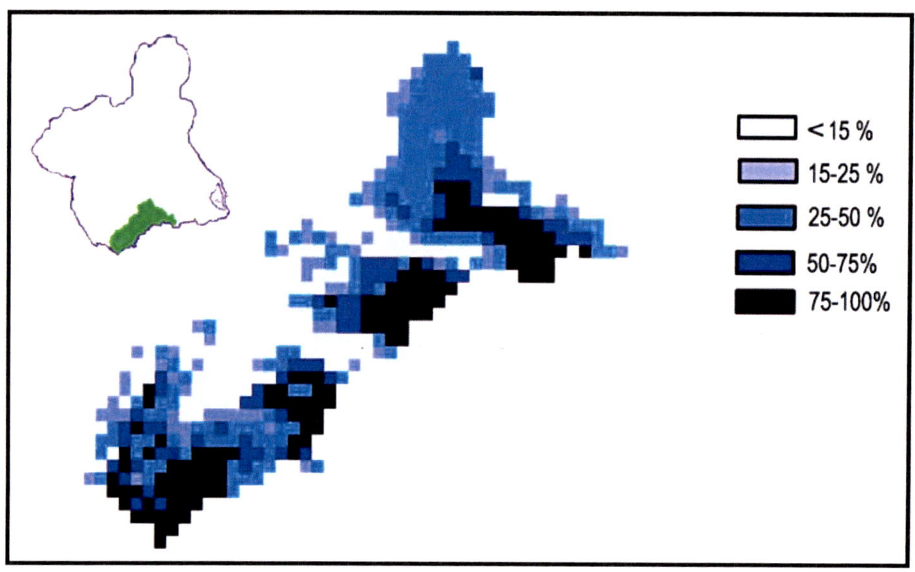

Figure 25. Potential distribution of irrigated lands by year 2024 under the Base Trend scenario. The presence probability in each cell unit is indicated.

The habitat loss of each species was obtained as the product of the presence probability of irrigated lands by the presence probability of the habitat in each cell unit. This can be interpreted as a risk analysis of habitat loss. By the end of the simulation period the loss of optimum habitat of *Testudo graeca* would increase by another 2,400 ha to reach 26% of total optimum habitat in Mazarron-Aguilas (table 6).

Table 6. Actual and expected loss of optimum habitat of *Testudo graeca* due to the increase in irrigated lands under the Base Trend scenario

Year	Irrigated lands (ha)	Affected optimum habitat (ha)	% Total optimum habitat
1981	10,000	3,890	9.4
1999	17,000	8,440	20.3
2024	23,500	10,835	26.1

Figure 26 presents the spatial distribution of risk of habitat loss, which would reach values higher than 75 per cent in a considerable number of cell units, especially along the coastal hillsides.

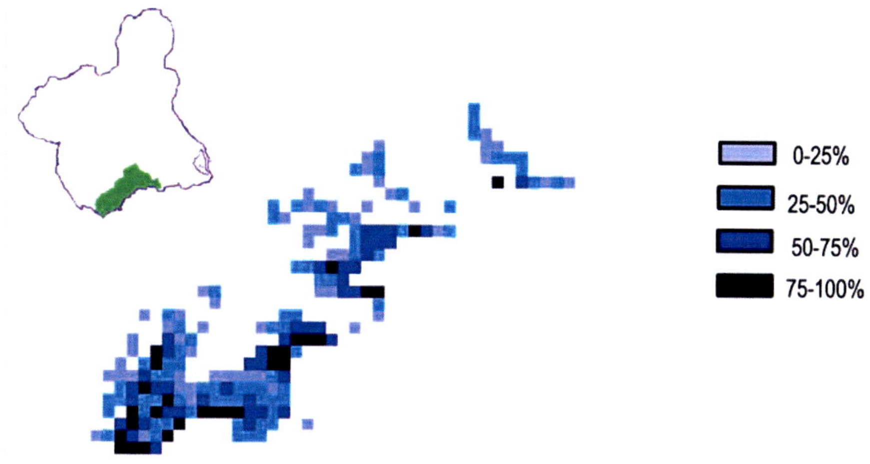

Figure 26. Base Trend Scenario. Spatial distribution of risk of habitat loss of *Testudo graeca*.

Moreover, there would be an important additional habitat loss of *Periploca angustifolia*, which would increase from 3,250 to 4,800 ha (figure 27).

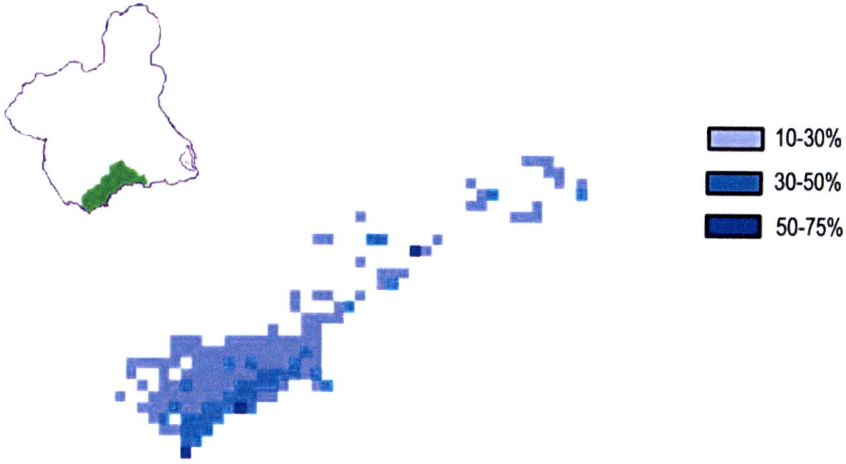

Figure 27. Base Trend Scenario. Spatial distribution of risk of habitat loss of *Periploca angustifolia*.

Results expected under the Base Trend scenario would break the Habitats Directive, which establishes quantitative criteria for some rare habitats and in particular it requires the conservation of 100% of the habitat of *Periploca angustifolia* (Esteve and Calvo 2000) and 75 per cent of the habitat of *Testudo graeca* (Giménez et al., 2001).

In relation to non-trend scenarios, the Strong Nature Conservation scenario leads to significantly different results: total irrigated land at the end of the simulation period reaches 18,300 ha, an increase of only 1,400 ha in 25 years. Under the scenario Technological Intensification and Partial Increase in Water Resources the irrigated land reaches intermediate values (figure 28).

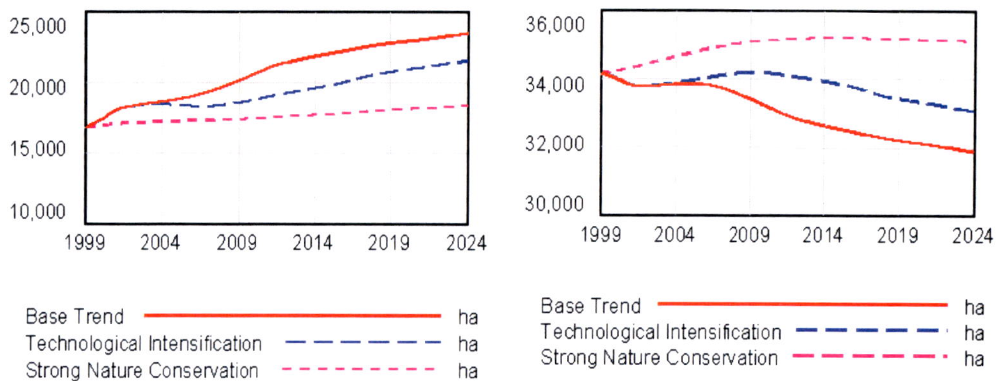

Figure 28. Irrigated lands (left) and area with high quality natural vegetation (right) under several scenarios.

The Strong Nature Conservation Policy requires the effective fulfilment of actual legislation which, starting in 1988, prevents, with few exceptions, the increase in irrigated lands. It is also necessary a further development on the control measures of land use change, such as the environmental impact assessment, in which the irreversibility of the process should be incorporated as part of the criteria. In this sense, the environmental caution in the case of land transformation into greenhouses should be stricter than in the case of drylands or even other irrigated lands, since greenhouses present a degree of irreversibility closer to the urban and industrial uses than to more traditional agricultural uses.

The Mazarron-Aguilas area needs a socio-economic development model based on a sustainable use of water and land. It cannot be based on an continued increase in irrigated lands at the expense of drylands or natural area nor in a generalised spread of urban-tourist uses under the actual expansion of low-density residential settlements. This last option is actively promoted in the area with big projects such as the Marina de Cope urban-tourist project, which would include, in a coastal area protected as nature reserve until 2001, five golf courses, 10,000 housing units and 22,000 hotel beds, among other commercial and tourist infrastructures. Besides the environmental effects caused by the actual spread of artificial uses in Murcia Region, discussed in previous sections, in the case of Mazarron-Aguilas this would affect the landscape and biodiversity values of one of the scarce natural, non-urbanised Spanish Mediterranean coastal areas which presents habitats of European Interest, endangered species as the terrestrial tortoise *Testudo graeca* and ibero-african endemisms with restricted distribution as *Periploca angustifolia*.

6. Land Use Policies in Mar Menor Watershed

6.1. Introduction

The Mar Menor lagoon and associated wetlands are an important site for wintering and breeding waterfowl, with the presence of flamingos, herons, waders, gulls, terns, grebes and seaducks (Martínez Fernandez et al., 2005). The lagoon and wetlands maintain 18 habitat of European interest, according to the Habitat Directive. The ecological value of the Mar Menor lagoon and wetlands have been recognised in a series of rules and resolutions, at regional, national and international level (Ramsar site, Special Protection Area for Birds, Site of Community Importance and Special Protection Area for the Mediterranean).

The Mar Menor watershed (figure 29), constitutes a wide sedimentary plain slightly inclined to the Mar Menor lagoon. It has approximately an area of 1,200 km^2 and it is drained by several riverbeds running into the Mar Menor lagoon. More than 80 % of total area is used for agriculture, especially for open-air horticultural crops, citrus fruits and greenhouses.

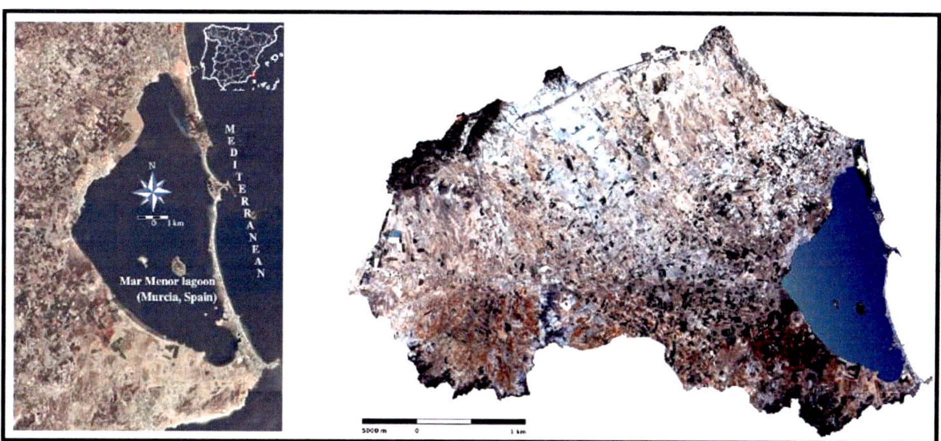

Figure 29. The Mar Menor coastal lagoon and its watershed.

The Tagus-Segura water transfer system, which opened in 1979, has given rise to a significant increase in the total area of irrigated lands at the expense of drylands. These irrigated lands are characterised by a very intensive use of fertilisers. As a result, there has been a significant increase in the nitrogen and phosphorus load reaching the Mar Menor lagoon-associated wetlands complex.

Urban settlements and population in the area of influence of Mar Menor have shown a very high increase during the last decades. There is also a strong seasonal dynamics, leading to very high increases of total population during summer, which generates problems to manage wastewater and leads to direct spillage into the lagoon.

The increase in irrigated lands and the urban-tourist development are changing the trophic state of the lagoon, favouring eutrophication processes and the jellyfish blooms, which have not only environmental but also socio-economic effects due to their impact on the quality of bathing water and, therefore, on the tourist activities in the Mar Menor. Therefore, land use in the watershed is a key factor driving the dynamics of nutrients and the hydrological and ecological changes affecting the Mar Menor lagoon and wetlands (Martínez Fernández et al., 2005; Martínez Fernández and Esteve Selma, 2007; Carreño et al., 2008; Pardo et al., 2008). Remote Sensing and dynamic modelling were applied to understand current and future trends in land use and their environmental effects. The next sections present the main results and findings.

6.2. Analysis of Land Use Changes through Remote Sensing

It has been carried out a supervised classification of Landsat images of summer 1996, winter 1997 and summer and winter 2000 using the Maximum Probability Algorithm (Michelson et al, 2000). All bands except thermal infrared were used. The NDVI index was computed and also used in the classification. Twelve land cover types were considered: dense forest, open forest, dense shrubland, open schrubland, tree-dryland; herbaceous-dryland, open-air horticultural crops; irrigated-tree crops, greenhouses, urban uses and infrastructures, water bodies and salt ponds. Resulting land cover maps in 1996/1997 and 2000 were validated using training areas by means of cross-validation in 626 stratified random points. The confusion matrix was used to compute overall confidence and the Kappa statistics, which measures the adjustment explained by the accuracy of the classification. Both overall confidence (higher than 70%) and Kappa statistics (0.9) pointed to the accuracy of the classification.

Results show important land use changes. Dryland losses 14,600 ha (26% of area in 1996/1997) whereas irrigated lands increases around 11,000 ha (30% respect to the 1996 values), especially due to the spread of open-air horticultural crops (figure 30). Data on land cover and main land use changes were used to develop the land use sector of the dynamic system models, described in the next section.

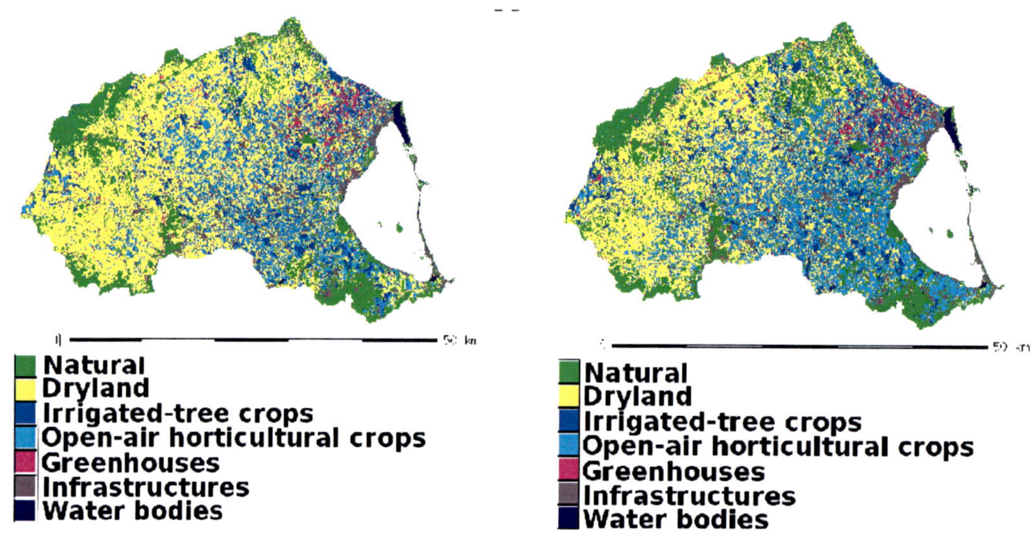

Figure 30. Land cover maps in 1996/1997 (left) and 2000 in Mar Menor watershed obtained by supervised classification of Landsat images.

6.2. Model Description

A dynamic model was developed to understand the linkages between land uses at watershed scale and their effects regarding the inflow of nutrients into the Mar Menor lagoon and coastal wetlands. Several sectors have been considered: i) land-use changes between main uses; ii) nitrogen flows and compartments; iii) phosphorus flows and com-partments; iv) role of wetlands on nutrient removal; v) nutrient inputs from urban sources and vi) economic costs of management measures. All model sectors are interconnected through several variables and linkages. Figure 31 presents a simplified diagram of the main model sectors.

The land use sector (figure 32) considers the area and main land use changes between natural vegetation, drylands, urban areas and each type of irrigated land (irrigated-tree crops, open-air horticultural crops and greenhouses). Each land use presents specific characteristics regarding the amount and dynamics of nitrogen and phosphorus and therefore land use changes strongly affect the nutrient sector. Land use changes basically depend on two socio-economic factors: the water availability, which substantially increased after the opening of the Tagus-Segura water transfer, and the difference in average profitability between land uses, with drylands and greenhouses exhibiting the minimum and maximum profitability respectively.

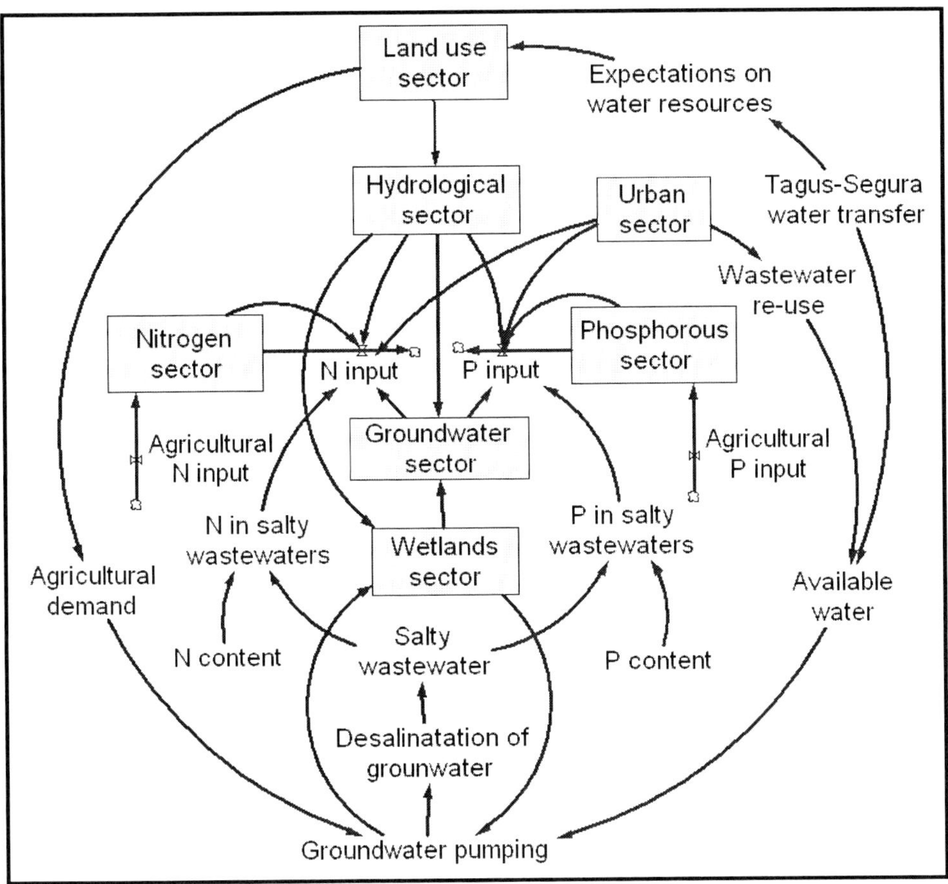

Figure 31. Simplified diagram of the Mar Menor watershed model.

The urban sector takes into account the resident population, the seasonal dynamics of tourist population, the wastewater production, the efficiency of wastewater treatment plants, the amount of wastewater reused for agriculture and the load of nutrients in the spilled wastewater. Finally the Costs sector determines the costs associated to the considered management options and computes several indicators of interest for the socio-economic analysis.

The model simulation for the period 1970-2003 shows a good adjustment with the actual values of available data series. The model shows the pronounced increase in irrigated lands favoured by the water transfer system which opened up in 1979 and the higher profitability of such agriculture, especially in the case of greenhouses (figure 33). This has generated an increased input of nutrients from diffuse sources into the Mar Menor (figure 34). The estimated load of nutrients shows strong fluctuations due to the high variability in rainfall and the occurrence of flood events, when large amounts of nutrients and materials from the watershed are flushed out and enter into the lagoon and wetlands.

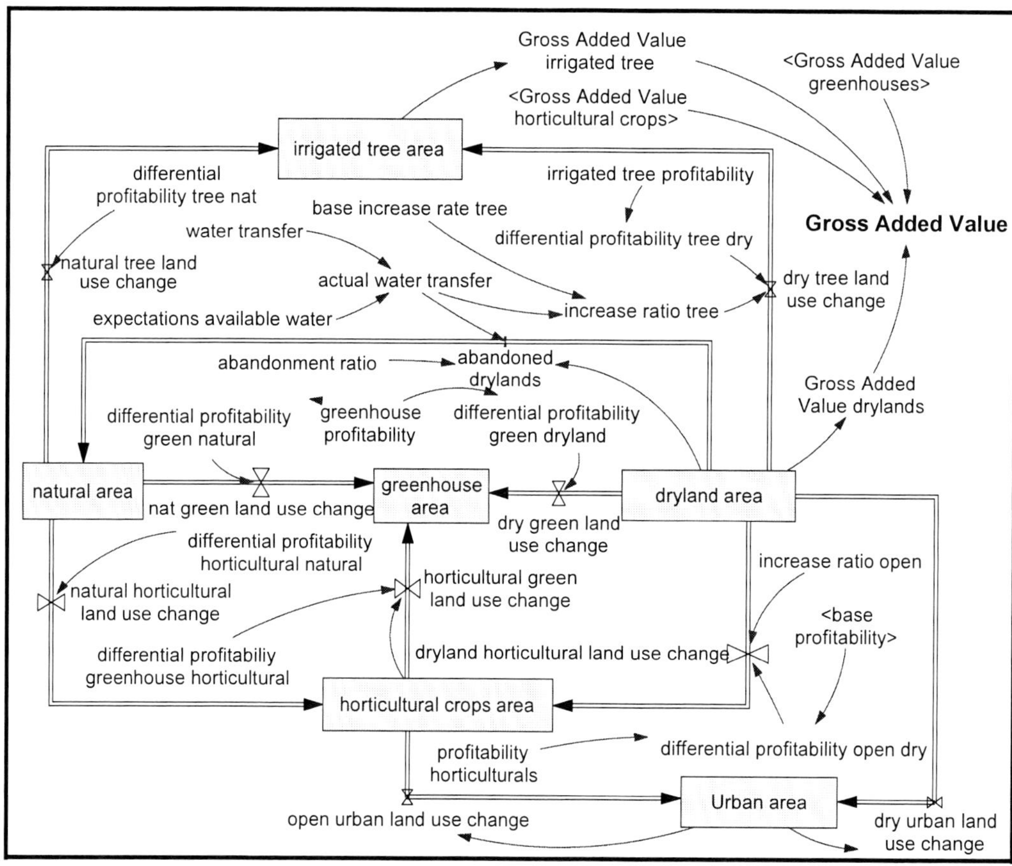

Figure 32. Land use sector of the Mar Menor watershed model.

According to the simulation results for the period 2000-2004, an average annual load of 900 ton year-1 of DIN (dissolved inorganic nitrogen) and around 200 ton year-1 of DIP (dissolved in-organic phosphorus) from diffuse sources can be estimated. These values fall within the ranges obtained in other agricultural watersheds (Mattikalli and Richards, 1996; David et al., 1997; Jordan et al., 1997).

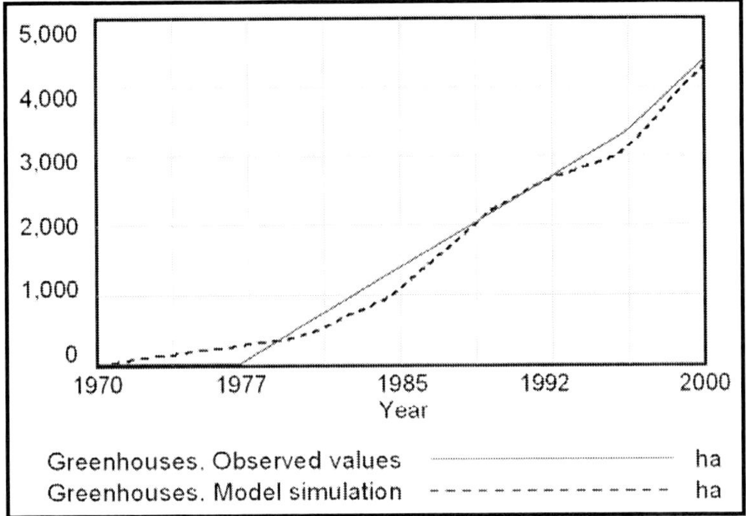

Figure 33. Area occupied by greenhouses in the Mar Menor watershed model between 1979 and 2000. Observed and simulated values.

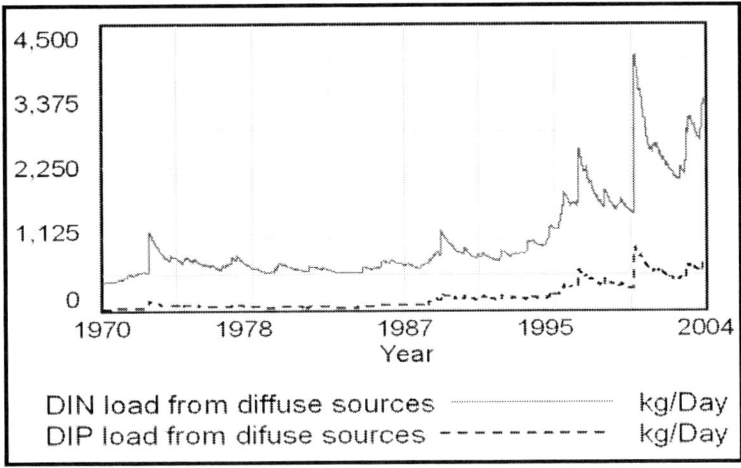

Figure 34. Simulated pattern of daily DIN (Dissolved Inorganic Nitrogen) and DIP (Dissolved Inorganic Phosphorous) input (kg day^{-1}) from diffuse sources using a 365 days moving average period.

The population of the Mar Menor area has also shown a rapid growth in recent decades due to tourism. Despite the existence of treatment plants, this has led to a high increase in wastewater and the input of nutrients from urban sources, especially during summer. The estimated average urban input is around 130 ton year-1 of DIN and 17 ton year-1 of DIP, which represents a 12% and 8% taking into account all sources (point and diffuse).

This high nutrients inflow may aggravate the initial eutrophication process in the Mar Menor lagoon and might lead to dramatic changes in its ecological state if water transparency diminishes to such an extent that it causes a massive collapse *of Caulerpa prolifera* beds and subsequent oxygen depletion phenomena (Lloret et al., 2005). In addition, a clear relationship has been established between the long-term trend of nutrient inputs into the Mar Menor lagoon and the response of aquatic birds assemblages. Opportunistic species such as grebes are being favoured whereas other species such as *Mergus serrator*, a typical piscivorous bird, shows some decline (Martínez Fernandez et al., 2005). Therefore, conservation of the ecological and natural values of the Mar Menor will require the control of the nutrient inputs into the lagoon.

6.3. Scenario Analysis

The model has been used to explore a set of scenarios and management options aiming at reducing the input of nutrients into the lagoon from both point and diffuse sources. The base trend is assumed by the *Urban and Tourist Development* scenario, which implies a shift from the increase in irrigated lands to rapid and intense urban and tourist development. Indeed, this is already occurring and new urban settlements and tourist facilities, especially in the form of golf-resorts, are being built-up. This scenario points to a high increase in the permanent and seasonal population which, by 2015, would double present day values. Because of the lack of coordination between policies, all these new urban-tourist developments will increase the urban pollution reaching the lagoon. Assuming that the overall performance of current and future wastewater treatment plants will be similar to present, and according to the simulation results, this would mean a significant increase in the input of nutrients from urban sources, especially during summer (figure 35). The estimated load from urban sources by 2015 would double actual values.

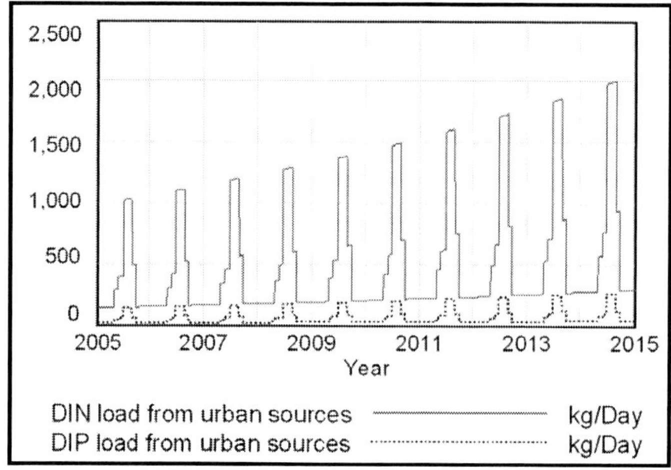

Figure 35. Simulated DIN (Dissolved Inorganic Nitrogen) and DIP (Dissolved Inorganic Phosphorous) inouts from urban sources under the scenario Urban and Tourist Development.

Several management options, dealing with the reduction of nutrient inputs from point and diffuse sources, have been considered and analysed: the improvement of wastewater management, the reuse of agricultural drainage, rich in nutrients, coming from the intensive irrigated lands of the watershed, and the recovery of wetlands to enhance its functionality to remove part of the nutrient inputs contained in the water flows reaching the lagoon.

The scenario *Improved Wastewater Management* assumes a significant increase in the proportion of wastewater reused for irrigation (from 65 to 85%) and in the overall efficiency of the treatment plants (from 68 to 88%). Under this scenario a significant reduction (about 60%) in the nutrient input from urban sources would be achieved. However, when all sources, point and diffuse, are considered, the estimated overall reduction is lower than 10%, since most of the nutrients come from diffuse sources.

The scenario *Reuse of Agricultural Drainage* simulates the expected effects of several hydraulic facilities to collect part of the agricultural drainage coming from the irrigated lands. The drainage water would be collected through a system of drainage channels and then pumped to a desalination plant, after which it would be reused for irrigation. Under this management option, total nutrient input into the Mar Menor might be reduced by around 10%, slightly higher than in the case of the Improved Wastewater Management scenario.

The *Recovery of Wetlands* scenario is based on the recovery of part of the wetland area lost due to land use changes and its reconnection with the Albujon ephemeral channel, the main watercourse draining the Mar Menor watershed, in order to remove part of the nutrients load of such watercourse. This measure would achieve a significant reduction in total nutrients input which doubles that achieved by the management option of Reuse of Agricultural Drainage (Figure 36). This reduction of the nutrient inputs from the Albujon watercourse might lead to a substantial improvement in the ecological state of the Mar Menor lagoon.

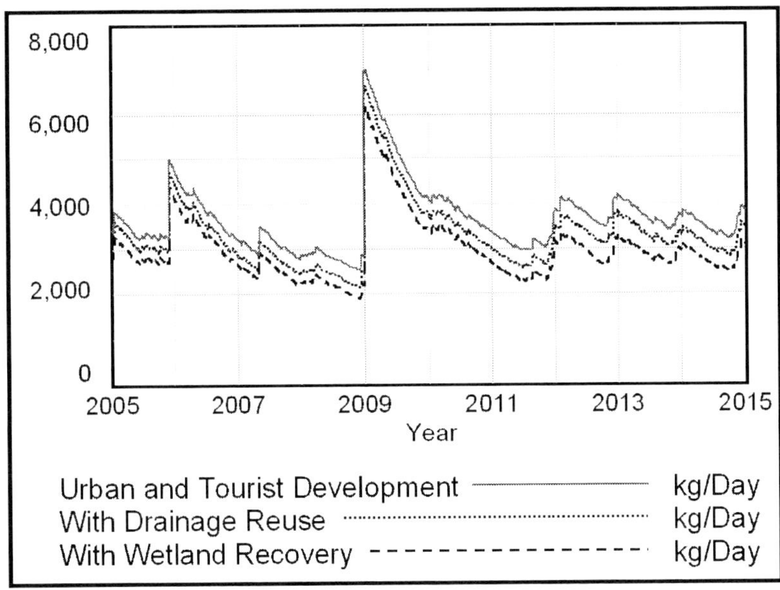

Figure 36. Pattern of daily load of DIN (Dissolved Inorganic Nitrogen) from surface water using a 365 days moving average period under the scenarios Urban and Tourist Development, Drainage Reuse and Wetlands Recovery.

As shown, land use in the watershed is a key factor for the actual and future state of the Mar Menor lagoon. The lack of coordination between land use and other policies regarding agricultural measures and the conservation of environment leads to an ineffective management and to the degradation of the lagoon and their coastal wetlands. This lack of coordination is also counterbalancing some management measures aiming at reducing the input of nutrient into the lagoon. In this sense, the important increase in irrigated lands has counterbalanced any effort to control the input of nutrients from agricultural sources, as voluntary agreements according to the designation of the Mar Menor as Vulnerable Zone, under the European Directive 91/676/EEC, concerning the protection of waters against pollution caused by nitrates from agricultural sources. Similarly, urban pollution reaching the lagoon and coastal wetlands fails to comply with the designation in 2001 of Mar Menor as Sensible Zone under the European Directive 91/271/EEC, on treatment of urban wastewater, by which the load of nutrients must fit specific standards. One of the key factors is again the absence of controls on the land use dynamics, since the effectiveness of the program to improve the wastewater treatment plants in the Mar Menor keeps low due to the continued spread of urban-tourist settlements around the lagoon.

In synthesis, the absence of a sustainable land use policy and the sprawl of residential settlements around the Mar Menor lagoon are affecting not only the landscape, natural areas and the conservation state of the coast, as described in earlier sections, but also the quality of water, the ecological state of the lagoon and associated coastal wetlands and the fulfilment of European Directives regarding the control of water pollution. It is therefore necessary to implement an integrated management of this coastal area and its watershed to achieve a more sustainable use of land and the effective conservation of the Mar Menor lagoon and its coastal wetlands.

7. Conclusion

Land use changes constitute one of the dimensions of global change linking the local, regional and global levels. The importance of land as resource and the analysis of spatial dimension of changes emerge as a key point in many places, as occurs in the Mediterranean coastal areas, where the Murcia region is located. A set of indicators on the spatial dimension of sustainability has been applied in Murcia Region. These indicators reveal a trend to the reduction of the environmentally active rural areas, represented by dryland and agro-natural systems, to favour to extreme landscapes: the natural one and the areas with a very intensive use of land and natural resources, represented by the artificial areas and the new irrigated lands. The proportion between scattered settlements to total urban area show a decreasing efficiency of land uptake to satisfy the urban needs, due to the sprawl of low-density residential areas disconnected from the existing cities and towns and with large areas for gardens and golf courses, contrary to the model of the Mediterranean compact city. This process is giving rise to land fragmentation, loss of biodiversity, landscape degradation and sealing of fertile soils.

The traditional irrigated land of Huerta de Murcia is progressively decreasing as a consequence of the population growth, which demands land uptake for artificial uses, and due to a reduction of profitability of traditional irrigated lands. The dynamic model has shown that under the base scenario the loss of huerta is maintained at a high rate, whereas a set of measures to slow down the land uptake by urban uses and infrastructures and to increase the average size per farm would reduce the loss of huerta by a third part. However, actual land uptake by artificial uses between 1995 and 2007 has been well over the expected values under the base scenario, due to existing land use policies at the regional and municipal levels, which have shifted from weak controls on land uptake to an active transformation of traditional irrigated lands into urban areas and infrastructures. It is necessary to apply specific measures to conserve this traditional agrolandscape, whose environmental, socio-economic and landscape values remain unattended.

The spatial analysis and dynamic model of Mazarron-Aguilas showed the environmental effects of land occupation by the new and highly intensive irrigated lands. These effects include the loss of habitat of protected species as the terrestrial tortoise *Testudo graeca* and the ibero-african endemism *Periploca angustifolia*. Results on the risk of habitat loss, obtained with the combination of the dynamic, the habitat and the spatial models, show that the base trend scenario would break the Habitats Directive, which establishes quantitative criteria for these species and habitat. A sustainable use of land and water requires a further development on the control measures of land use change, such as the environmental impact assessment, to incorporate new criteria as the irreversibility of the process. In this sense, the environmental caution in the case of land transformation into greenhouses should be stricter than in the case of drylands or even other irrigated lands, since greenhouses present a degree of irreversibility closer to the urban and industrial uses than to more traditional agricultural uses.

Land use generates also indirect effects and changes at different spatial scales, as revealed in the Mar Menor and its watershed. Remote Sensing showed significant land use changes in the watershed of this valuable coastal lagoon, in particular the increase in open-air horticultural crops. Nutrients reaching this coastal lagoon and associated wetlands have increased due to the spread of irrigated lands in the watershed and the increase in urban-tourist settlements around Mar Menor. According to the dynamic model simulations, under the base scenario, which assumes a shift from the increase in irrigated lands to rapid and intense urban and tourist development, the estimated load from urban sources by 2015 would double actual values. Land use in the watershed is a key factor for the actual and future state of the Mar Menor lagoon, what demands an effective coordination between land use and other policies regarding agricultural measures and the conservation of the environment.

Finally results obtained in this work show the need of integrated analysis to tackle the synergistic effects of land use changes in a given territory and their implications in terms of resource requirements, nature conservation and other environmental effects, in order to assess the sustainability of current and future land use scenarios. To this aim, it is needed to take into account both, time and space, to adequately understand the underlining dynamics of change and its implications for sustainable land use policies. The combined use of different methodological tools such as GIS, Remote Sensing and Dynamic System Models may contribute to apply such integrated approach.

ACKNOWLEDGEMENTS

The research has been partially supported by the European project DITTY: *Development of Information Technology Tools for the Management of European Southern lagoons under the influence of river-basin runoff* (EVK3-CT-2002-00084), support which is acknowledged. The research has also been partially supported by the scientific national project: *Análisis y seguimiento de indicadores en el marco de un observatorio de la sostenibilidad de la Región de Murcia*, Spanish Ministry of Environment, support which is gratefully acknowledged.

REFERENCES

Anadón J.D., Giménez A., Pérez I., Martínez M. & Esteve M.A. (2005). The role of relief in local abundance patterns of spur-thighed tortoise Testudo graeca graeca in southeast Spain. *Herpetological Journal.* 15: 285-290.

Anadón JD, Giménez A, Martínez M, Martínez J, Pérez I & Esteve MA. (2006). Factors determining the distribution of the spur-thighed tortoise Testudo graeca in southeast Spain: a hierarchical approach. *Ecography.* 29: 339-346.

Antrop, M. (1993). The transformation of the Mediterranean landscapes: an experience of 25 years of observations. *Landscape and Urban Planning*, 24: 3-13.

de Aranzábal, I.; Schmitz, M.F.; Aguilera, P.; Díez Pineda, F. (2008). Modelling of landscape changes derived from the dynamics of socio-ecological systems A case of study in a semiarid Mediterranean landscape. *Ecological Indicators*, 8: 672-685.

Aurambout, J.P.; Endress, A.G.; Deal, B.M. (2005). A spatial model to estimate habitat fragmentation and its consequences on long-term persistence of animal populations. *Environmental Monitoring and Assessment.* 109: 199–225.

Barlas, Y. (1996). Formal aspects of model validity and validation in system dynamics. *System Dynamics Review*, 12: 183-210.

Bock, M.; Rossner, G.; Wissen, M.; Remmb, K. (2005). Spatial indicators for nature conservation from European to local scale. *Ecological Indicators*, 5: 322-338.

Burel, F.; Baudry, J. (2002). *Ecología del Paisaje. Conceptos, métodos y aplicaciones.* Ediciones Mundi-Prensa. Madrid.

Capellades, M.; Rivera, M.; Saurí, D. (2002). Luces y sombras en la gestión de la demanda urbana de agua: el caso de la Región Metropolitana de Barcelona. In: *III Congreso Ibérico de Planificación y Gestión de Aguas.* Fundación Nueva Cultura del Agua. Sevilla. 13-17 Noviembre 2002.

Carreño, M.F.; Esteve, M.A.; Martinez, J.; Palazón, J.A.; Pardo, M.T. (†). 2008. Dynamics of coastal wetlands associated to hydrological changes in the watershed. *Estuarine, Coastal and Shelf Science*, 77: 475-483.

Comisión de las Comunidades Europeas. (1992). *Programa Comunitario de Política y Actuación en materia de Medio Ambiente y Desarrollo Sostenible.* Madrid: Instituto de Investigaciones Ecológicas.

Constanza, R.; Voinov, A. (Eds.). (2004). *Landscape simulation modeling. A spatially explicit, dynamic approach.* Springer. New York.

David, M. B.; L.E. Gentry; D.A. Kovacic & K.M. Smith. 1997. Nitrogen balance in and export from an agricultural watershed. *Journal of Environmental Quality* 26: 1038-1048.

Eisenreich, S.J. (Ed.). (2005). *Climatic change and the European Water Dimension.* European Commission-Joint Research Centre. Office for Official Publication of the European Communities. Luxembourg.

ESPON. (2007). *Scenarios on the territorial future of Europe.* European Spatial Planning Observation Network. ESPON Project 3.2. Luxembourg.

Esteve, M.A. and Calvo, J.F. (2000). Conservación de la naturaleza y biodiversidad en la Región de Murcia. In: Calvo, J.F.; Esteve, M.A. y López Bermúdez, F. (Coord.). *Biodiversidad. Contribución a su conocimiento y conservación en la Región de Murcia.* Instituto del Agua y Medio Ambiente. Servicio de Publicaciones Universidad de Murcia.

Esteve Selma, Lloréns Pascual, M.; Martínez Gallur (Eds.). (2003). *Los recursos naturales de la Región de Murcia. Un análisis interdisciplinar.* Servicio de Publicaciones de la Universidad de Murcia. Murcia.

Fernández Durán R. (2006). *El Tsunami urbanizador español y mundial.* Editorial Virus. Madrid.

Fjellstad, W. J.; Dramstad, W. E. (1999). Patterns of change in two contrasting Norwegian agricultural landscapes. *Landscape and Urban Planning,* 45 : 177 – 191.

Fresco, L.O.; Stroosnijder, L.; Bouma, J.; Van Keulen, H. (Eds). (1994). *The future of the land grating agriculture and conservation.* University of Warwick, Coventry.

García Novo, F. (1999): Los paisajes transitorios. El futuro de los paisajes tradicionales en una sociedad urbana. En: Homenaje a D. Angel Ramos Fernández (1926-1998). Madrid. Real Academia de Ciencias Exactas, Físicas y Naturales.

Geoghegan, J.; Schneider, L; Vance, C. (2004). Temporal dynamics and spatial scales: Modeling deforestation in the southern Yucatan peninsular region. *GeoJournal,* 61: 353–363.

Giménez A, Anadon A D, Martínez J, Palao M.M, Pérez I, Esteve M A. (2001), *Estudios básicos para el diseño de una estrategia de conservación de Testudo graeca en la Región de Murcia.* Murcia: Consejeria de Medio Ambiente, Agricultura y Agua

Gottschalk TK, Diekotter T, Ekschmitt K et al . Weinmann, B.; Kuhlmann, F.; Purtauf, T.; Dauber, J.; Wolters, V. (2007). Impact of agricultural subsidies on biodiversity at the landscape level. Landscape Ecology, *Landscape Ecology,* 22 (5): 643-656.

Groom, M.J., Meffe, G.K. & Carrol, C.R. (2006). *Principles of conservation biology* (3ª ed.). Sinauer Associates.

Jordan, E ; Correll, D ; Weller D. 1997. Effects of agriculture on Discharges of Nutrients from Coastal Plain Watersheds of Chesapeake Bay. *Journal of Environmental Quality* 26: 836-848.

Jorgensen, S.E. & Bendoricchio, G. (2001). *Fundamentals of Ecological Modelling.* Elsevier. Amsterdam.

Larson, M.; Thompson, F.; Millspaugh, J.; Dijak, W.; Shifley, S. (2004). Linking population viability, habitat suitability, and landscape simulation models for conservation planning. *Ecological Modelling* 180 (1) : 103-118.

Lloret, J.; Marin, A.; Marin-Guirao, L.; Velasco, J. 2005. Changes in macrophytes distribution in a hypersaline coastal lagoon associated with the development of intensively irrigated ag-riculture. *Ocean & Coastal Management,* 48, 828-842.

Groom, M.J., Meffe, G.K. & Carrol, C.R. (2006). *Principles of conservation biology* (3ª ed.). Sinauer Associates.

Meeus, J. H.; Wijermans, M. P.; Vroom, M. J. (1990). Agricultural landscapes in Europe and their transformation. *Landscape and Urban Planning,* 18 : 289 – 352.

Mander, U., Kull, A., Tamm, V., Kuusemets, V. and Karjus, R. (1998). Impact of climatic fluctuations and land use change on runoff and nutrient losses in rural landscape. *Landscape and Urban Planning,* 41, 229-238.

Martínez Fernández J, Esteve Selma MA. (2002). Un modelo dinámico del regadío de Mazarrón y Aguilas y sus efectos ambientales. In: Martínez Fernández and Esteve Selma (Coord.), *Agua, Regadío y Sostenibilidad en el Sudeste Ibérico.* Bakeaz-Fundación Nueva Cultura del Agua: Bilbao.

Martínez, J.; Esteve, M.A.; Palao, M..; Pérez, I.; Anadón, J.D.; Giménez, A. (2002). Effects of new irrigated lands on habitat conservation of Testudo graeca graeca in the Southeast of the Iberian Peninsula. *Chelonii. International Congress on Testudo Genus*, 3: 349-354.

Martínez-Fernández, J.; Esteve-Selma, M.A.; Robledano-Aymerich, F.; Pardo-Sáez, M.T.; Carreño-Fructuoso, M.F. (2005). Aquatic birds as bioindicators of trophic changes and ecosystem deterioration in the Mar Menor lagoon (SE Spain). *Hydrobiologia*, 550 : 221-235.

Martínez-Fernández, J.; Esteve-Selma, M.A. (2007). Gestión integrada de cuencas costeras: dinámica de los nutrientes en la cuenca del Mar Menor (Sudeste de España). *Revista de Dinámica de Sistemas*, 3: 2-23.

Mattikalli, N; Richards, K. 1996. Estimation of Surface Water Quality Changes in Response to Land Use Change: Application of The Export Coefficient Model Using Remote Sensing and Geographical Information System. *Journal of Environmental Management* 48: 263–282.

Michelson, D. B., Liljeberg, B. M. and Pilesjö, P. (2000): Comparison of Algorithms for Classifying Swedish Landcover Using Landsat TM and ERS-1 SAR Data. *Remote Sensing Environment*. 71: 1-15.

Mouillot, F.; Ratte, J.P.; Joffre, R.; Mouillot, D.; Rambal, S. (2005). Long-term forest dynamic after land abandonment in a fire prone Mediterranean landscape (central Corsica, France). *Landscape Ecology*, 20: 101–112.

Papadimitriou, F. (2002). Modelling indicators and indices of landscape complexity: an approach using G.I.S. *Ecological Indicators*, 2: 17-25.

Pardo, M.T.; Calvo, J.F.; Caballero, J.M.; Esteve, M.A. (2003). Relaciones especies-área en los Saladares del Guadalentín (SE Ibérico, España) e implicaciones para la conservación, restauración y gestión. *Anales de Biología*, 25: 91-102.

Pardo, M.T.(†); Esteve, M.A.; Giménez, A.; Martínez-Fernández, J.; Carreño, M.F.; Serrano, J.; Miñano, J. 2008. Assessment of the hydrological alterations on wandering beetle assemblages (coleoptera: Carabidae and Tenebrionidae) in coastal wetlands of arid mediterranean systems). *Journal of Arid Environments*, 72: 1803-1810.

Peña, J.; Bonet, A.; Pastor, E.; Terrones, B.; Constan-Nava, S. (2008). Los Sistemas de Información Geográfica y la Ecología Espacial. In F.T. Maestre, A. Escudero & A. Bonet (ed): *Introducción al Análisis Espacial de Datos en Ecología y Ciencias Ambientales. Métodos y Aplicaciones*. Universidad Rey Juan Carlos. Servicio de Publicaciones. Editorial Dyckinson. Madrid. pp. 496-540.

Poudevigne, I.; van Rooij, S.; Morin, P. Alard, D. (1997). Dynamics of rural landscapes and their main driving factors: A case study in the Seine Valley, Normandy, France. Landscape and Urban Planning, 38 : 93 – 103.

Ramírez Díaz, L.; Esteve Selma, M. A.; Calvo Sendín, J. F. (1999). Pautas de uso agrícola en la Región de Murcia: implicaciones ambientales, in: *Homenaje a D. Angel Ramos Fernández (1926-1998)*. Madrid. Real Academia de Ciencias Exactas, Físicas y Naturales. 869-885.

Roberts, N.; Andersen, A.; Deal, R.; Garet, M. (1983). *Introduction to computer simulation: the system dynamics approach*. Reading: Addison-Wesley.

Tiner, R. (2004). Remotely-sensed indicators for monitoring the general condition of "natural habitat" in watersheds: an application for Delaware's Nanticoke River watershed. *Ecological Indicators*, 4: 227-243.

Tong, S.T.Y., Chen, W. (2002). Modeling the relationship between land use and surface water quality. *Journal of Environmental Management*, 66, 377-393.

Vennix, J.A. M. (1996). *Group Model Building. Facilitating team learning using system dynamics*. Chichester: Wiley.

Ventana Systems Inc. (2007). VENSIM®. Ventana Simulation Environment. Reference Manual. USA.

Venturelli. R.; Galli, A. (2006). Integrated indicators in environmental planning: Methodological considerations and applications. *Ecological Indicators*, 6: 228-237.

Vos, W. (1993): Recent landscape transformation in the Tuscan Apenines caused by changing land use. Landscape and Urban Planning, 24, p. 63-68.

White, D.; Minotti, G.; Barczak, M.; Sifneos, J.; Freemark, K.; Santelmann, M.; Steinitz, C.; Kiester, A. y Preston, E. (1997). Assessing risks to biodiversity from future landscape change. *Conservation Biology*, 11: 349 - 360

Wu, W.; Shibasaki, R.; Yang, P.; Tan, G.; Kan-ichiro Matsumura, K; Sugimoto, K. (2007). Global-scale modelling of future changes in sown areas of major crops. *Ecological Modelling*, 208 (2-4) : 378-390.

In: Land Use Policy
Editors: A. C. Denman and O. M. Penrod
ISBN: 978-1-60741-435-3

Chapter 5

HOW SPATIALLY-DISAGGREGATED LAND-USE MODELS CAN INFORM LAND-USE POLICY: THEORY AND AN EMPIRICAL APPLICATION FOR INDONESIA

***Miet Maertens**[*1] **and Manfred Zeller**[2]*

[1] Division Agricultural and Food Economics,
Department of Earth and Environmental Sciences,
Katholieke Universiteit Leuven, Belgium.

[2] Institute for Agricultural Economics and Social Sciences
in the Tropics and Subtropics, Universität Hohenheim, Germany

ABSTRACT

In this chapter we develop a spatially explicit economic land-use model that gives insights into the determinants of land-use patterns and how these patterns are affected by policy changes. The model explicitly takes into account the decision-making process as to why and where farmers convert the use of forest land. This is different from previous spatially disaggregated models – such as simulation models – where the underlying decision-making process is imposed. The micro-economic focus in this paper is crucial for understanding the ongoing human-induced land-use change process and is essential in the land-use change literature – that is dominated by natural scientists focusing on geophysical and agro-climatic processes. Our model is extremely valuable to inform land-use policy as it specifies how individual decision makers will react to policy and other exogenous changes in their environment and how this response will alter the landscape.

The model is derived from the von Thunen-Ricardo land rent model that describes land-use patterns as a result of variability in geophysical land attributes and differences in location and transport costs. However, this model is valid only under certain assumptions and is less suited to describe land-use patterns in forest frontier areas characterized by semi-subsistence agriculture and imperfect markets. We refine the model to account for

---

* Corresponding author: Miet.Maertens@ees.kuleuven.be

the fact that agricultural prices and wages might be endogenously determined and households cannot be considered as profit maximizing agents.

We empirically estimate the model for a forest-frontier area in Indonesia using a combination of data from satellite image interpretation, GIS data and a socio-economic survey data. The results demonstrate that differences in Ricardian land rent are important in determining spatial land-use patterns. However, we do not find evidence in support of the von Thunen idea that land-use patterns are determined by differences in transport costs. Rather the labor intensity of land-use systems, population levels, the access to technology and household characteristics matter. This has important implications for forest conservation and land-use policy. In addition, the refinement of the von Thunen-Ricardo land rent model – which incorporates more realistic descriptions of economic behavior – is justified by the empirical results.

1. INTRODUCTION

There are two distinct aspects related to land use: the quantity or the rate of land-use change and the location of these changes. From an environmental viewpoint the location of land-use change is as important as its magnitude (Nelson and Geoghegan, 2002). For example, for biodiversity protection it is not only important to know the physical extent of deforestation but also the degree to which it affects critical habitats in specific locations. Also for policy makers it is important to anticipate where land-use changes are likely to take place. For example, road development might trigger land-use changes and the exact location of new roads might have a large impact on the landscape.

In this chapter we develop a spatially explicit economic land-use model that gives insights into the determinants of land-use patterns and how these patterns are affected by policy changes. The focus is on a forest frontier area where agricultural settlers are the main agents in land use conversion. The model explicitly takes into account the decision-making process as to why and where smallholder farmers convert the use of forest land; which is crucial for understanding the ongoing human-induced land-use change process and is essential in the land-use change literature – that is dominated by natural scientists focusing on geophysical and agro-climatic processes. Our model is extremely valuable to inform land-use policy as it specifies how individual decision makers will react to policy and other exogenous changes in their environment and how this response will alter the landscape. We discuss the theoretically derived implications of the model and empirically estimate the model for a forest-frontier area in Indonesia using a combination of data from satellite image interpretation, GIS data and a socio-economic survey data.

The chapter is structured as follows. In the next section we give a brief overview of spatially explicit land-use models. In section three we develop a land rent model that can explain forest conversion and agricultural land expansion in forest frontier areas. Section four deals with the empirical estimation of the derived model for a forest frontier area in Indonesia. In a final section we draw some conclusions.

2. Spatial Land Use Models

Location matters and questions concerning spatial patterns of land use and the location of land use change have been addressed in spatially disaggregated land use models. For a long time geographers and natural scientists have dominated spatially explicit land-use analysis with statistical and simulation models (Irwin and Geoghegan, 2001). Some of these studies have focused solely on the geographic and biophysical explanation of spatial land-use patterns (e.g. Liu *et al.*, 1993; Gobin and Feyen, 2002). In such models the role of geophysical factors such as soil type, topography, etc. and landscape elements such as distance to roads, patchiness of different land-use types, etc. is emphasized. Other geographic studies did include socioeconomic variables such as population, wealth and technology in their spatial statistical land-use analysis (e.g. Fox *et al.*, 1994; Mertens and Lambin, 1997; Serneels and Lambin, 2001). However, the selection of socioeconomic variables is often *ad hoc* and the results do not give insights into the decision-making process. Also spatial simulation models that consider socioeconomic factors are not able to model economic responses because the underlying decision-making process is imposed (e.g. Verburg *et al.*, 1999; Verburg *et al.*, 2000; Verburg and Veldkamp, 2001). Geographers and natural scientists have modeled land use in a spatially explicit way, however with less emphasis on understanding the underlying economic processes that lead to spatial land-use patterns.

More recently, questions concerning the location of land use, have also attracted the attention of agricultural economists. Chomitz and Gray (1996) took the lead in describing the landscape using an economic model. Spatially explicit economic land-use models initially focused on the role of roads and geophysical land attributes in affecting the landscape through influencing households' economic behavior (Chomitz and Gray, 1996; Nelson and Hellerstein, 1997). Later, also the impact of population growth and the role of protected areas were addressed (Cropper *et al.*, 2001; Deininger and Minten, 2002; Müller and Zeller, 2002). Access to credit, tenure security (Deininger and Minten, 2002) and the level of technology (Müller and Zeller, 2002; Vance and Geoghegan, 2002) were also taken into account. Vance and Geoghegan (2002) also included household demographic composition in a spatial land-use model. The strength of spatial economic land-use models is that they give insights into the decision-making process as to where people convert the use of land. They are very well suited to model how individual decision makers will react to policy and other exogenous changes and how this response will alter the landscape.

3. A Spatial Economic Land Use Model

The von Thunen – Ricardo Land Rent Model

Spatially explicit economic land-use studies are generally based on an analytical model derived from the land rent theory of von Thunen and Ricardo. An analytical approach was elaborated by Chomitz and Gray (1996) and applied by Nelson and Hellerstein (1997); Cropper *et al.* (2001); Deininger and Minten (2002); Munroe *et al.* (2002) and Müller and Zeller (2002).

A plot of land is assumed to be allocated to the use that brings in the highest rent. Following von Thunen, land rent decreases with distance to a central market because of increasing transport costs, which result in lower output prices and higher input prices (von Thunen, 1826). Since transport costs differ between crops, the land-use pattern will exist of concentric rings of different land-use types around a central market (figure 1). High value crops that are more difficult to transport (such as vegetables) will be located closer to urban centers than more bulky crops with a lower value and lower transport costs (such as grains). The original von Thunen model assumes a featureless plain surrounding a central market (von Thunen, 1826). This model was refined by Chomitz and Gray (1996) and Nelson and Hellerstein (1997) to emphasize the importance of roads. Transport costs do not only increase with Euclidian distance to the market but also with the difficulty of accessing the market. In addition to the relative location of markets also the location with respect to roads determines land rent.

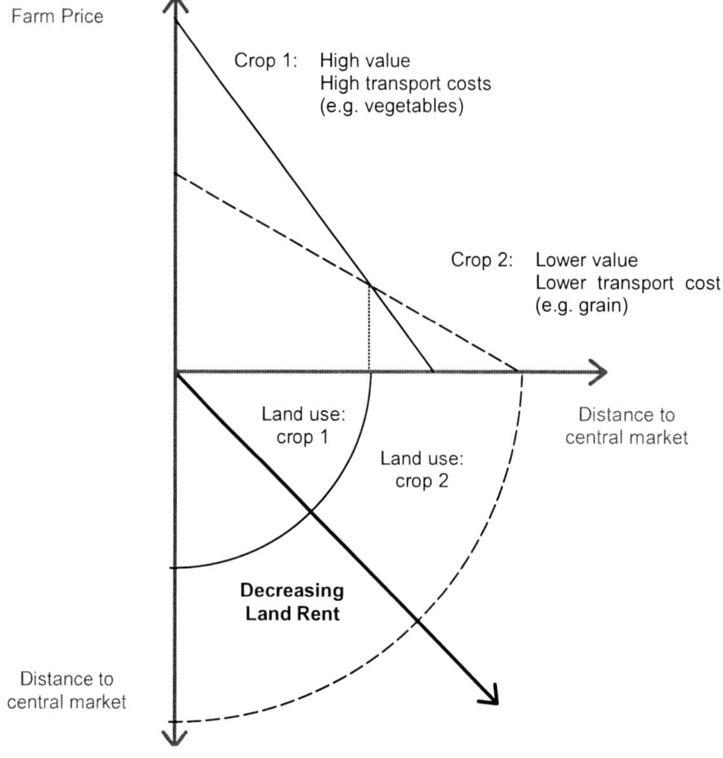

Figure 1. The von Thunen Land Rent – Land Use Model.

The model was further elaborated by adding land-rent features according to the work of Ricardo. Next to access to markets and roads also natural land attributes matter. Differences in geophysical characteristics bring about variability in natural land productivity. This determines (potential) agricultural yields and therefore influences land rent. By adding roads and Ricardian features, the original von Thunen model has become more complex. However, the basic insight of the importance of location and transport costs in determining land rent and land use remains (Nelson, 2002).

Shortcomings of the Von Thunen Ricardo Land Rent Model

The von Thunen - Ricardo land rent model is valid only under certain assumptions (Lambin *et al.*, 2000; Nelson and Geoghegan, 2002). First, it is assumed that a plot of land will be converted if it is profitable to do so. So, perfect markets and profit-maximizing behavior are implicitly assumed (Nelson and Geoghegan, 2002). This assumption is too simplified for the case of rural areas in developing countries. In such areas markets are often highly imperfect or even missing, which makes households' production decisions to be interlinked with consumption decisions? With missing rural labor markets it is more realistic to assume that households trade-off the utility of farm income and consumption with the disutility of labor rather than maximizing farm profits.

Second, the model assumes that there is one central market where all outputs and inputs, including labor are traded. This might resemble peri-urban areas or isolated commercial settlements reasonably well. However, the land-use pattern in forest frontier areas, characterized by smallholder and semi-subsistence agriculture, is likely to be more diffused and not well described by the von Thunen model (Mertens and Lambin, 1997; Lambin *et al.*, 2000).

Third, it is assumed that agricultural prices in the central market are not influenced by changing land use and product supply. One should be aware that this does not at all hold for products with an inelastic demand such as basic food crops. The assumption is more reasonable in the case of export crops with prices determined by world market conditions and not much affected by local supply.

Fourth, spatial differences in prices are solely related to differences in transport costs. The assumption of increasing input costs with distance to markets is very plausible for bulk inputs such as fertilizers but is less clear for labor inputs (Chomitz and Gray, 1996). Wages do not necessarily increase with distance to the market. On the one hand, opportunity costs of labor might be higher closer to markets because of more profitable off-farm employment opportunities. On the other hand, labor might be scarcer and hence more expensive in less densely populated areas further away from urban centers and markets.

In the next section we elaborate on the von Thunen - Ricardo land rent model by adding some new features that allow us to relax some of these assumptions.

A Refinement of the Von Thunen - Ricardo Land Rent Model

As in the spatial land-use model developed by Chomitz and Gray (1996) we assume there is a potential rent attached to each possible land use (k) of each plot of land (i). Each plot will be allocated to the use with the highest rent (R_{ik}). The land rent R_{ik} is the difference between the value of outputs and inputs for land use k at plot i. We assume that the output for each land use k follows a Cobb Douglas production function with capital (k_k), labor (l_k) and land (a_k) inputs, a productivity shifter (S_k) and constant marginal returns to scale.

$$q_k = S_k k_k^{\alpha_k} l_k^{\beta_k} a_k^{\gamma_k} \qquad \text{with} \qquad \alpha_k, \beta_k, \gamma_k > 0 \qquad (1)$$

$$\alpha_k + \beta_k + \gamma_k = 1$$

The output per unit of land (Q_{ik}) for land use k at plot i is then a function of the capital (K_{ik}) and labor (L_{ik}) inputs per unit of land and the plot-specific productivity shifter (S_{ik}).

$$Q_{ik} = S_{ik} K_{ik}^{\alpha_k} L_{ik}^{\beta_k} \qquad \text{with} \qquad \alpha_k, \beta_k > 0 \qquad (2)$$

$$0 < \alpha_k + \beta_k < 1$$

The productivity shifter includes the available technology (S_{1v}) and the natural productivity of the plot (S_{2i}) and can be expressed as the product of these factors:

$$S_{ik} = \lambda_{ok} S_{1v}^{\lambda_{1k}} S_{2i}^{\lambda_{2k}} \qquad (3)$$

The available technology does not vary for single plots but is assumed to be specific to the village (v) in which the plot is located. Natural productivity is plot specific and includes agro-climatic and geophysical aspects that determine the suitability of the plot for cultivation: slope, soil type, climate etc. The way in which the available technology (S_{1v}) and natural suitability (S_{2i}) shift productivity is specific for each land-use type k. Besides the labor inputs on the plot (L_{ik}), we assume there is an additional labor cost related to an increased walking time to distant plots. This costs is plot-specific and increases exponentially with the distance (D_i) to the village. We specify output prices for different crops (P_k), the price of capital inputs (C), wages (W) and express the potential land rent associated with allocating plot i to land use k as follows:

$$R_{ik} = P_k Q_{ik} - CK_{ik} - WL_{ik} \exp(\gamma D_i) \qquad (4)$$

Substituting (2) and (3) in (4) we can derive the optimal amounts of labor and capital inputs for each land use k at each plot i:

$$L_{ik} = \left[\alpha_k^{\alpha_k} \beta_k^{1-\alpha_k} \lambda_{0k} S_{1v}^{\lambda_{1k}} S_{2i}^{\lambda_{2k}} \left(\frac{1}{\exp(\gamma D_i)} \right)^{1-\alpha_k} \left(\frac{P_k}{C} \right)^{\alpha_k} \left(\frac{P_k}{W} \right)^{1-\alpha_k} \right]^{1/1-\alpha_k-\beta_k} \qquad (5)$$

$$K_{ik} = \left[\alpha_k^{1-\beta_k} \beta_k^{\beta_k} \lambda_{0k} S_{1v}^{\lambda_{1k}} S_{2i}^{\lambda_{2k}} \left(\frac{1}{\exp(\gamma D_i)} \right)^{\beta_k} \left(\frac{P_k}{C} \right)^{1-\beta_k} \left(\frac{P_k}{W} \right)^{\beta_k} \right]^{1/1-\alpha_k-\beta_k} \qquad (6)$$

Substituting (2), (3), (5) and (6) in (4) and rearranging, results in expressing the land rent for plot i and land use k as:

$$R_{ik} = P_k \left[\alpha_k^{\alpha_k} \beta_k^{\beta_k} \lambda_{0k} S_{1v}^{\lambda_{1k}} S_{2i}^{\lambda_{2k}} \left(\frac{1}{\exp(\gamma D_i)} \right)^{\beta_k} \left(\frac{P_k}{C} \right)^{\alpha_k} \left(\frac{P_k}{W} \right)^{\beta_k} \right]^{1/1-\alpha_k-\beta_k} \tag{7}$$

Farm-gate output and input prices and local wages are endogenous and unobserved. We assume that households are integrated in agricultural output and input markets, and that differences in local prices are determined by transport costs from the village to the market. In equation (8) we specify that the price of agricultural outputs relative to capital inputs decreases with distance or costs-of-access from the village to the central market (Z_v). The factor δ_{1k} represents transport costs, which are crop specific. The factor is negative indicating that local output prices decrease with distance to the market and input prices increase. The factor δ_{ok} represents the price of agricultural outputs relative to capital inputs in the central market.

$$\frac{P_k}{C} = \exp(\delta_{ok} + \delta_{1k} Z_v) \tag{8}$$

Labor markets might be missing or highly imperfect due to immobility of labor in the short run and lack of off-farm employment opportunities in remote rural areas. We assume that labor is exchanged locally and express village-level relative wages as a function of the village population (equation 8). A higher population (A_v) increases the supply of labor, increases the demand for agricultural products and therefore increases the price of agricultural outputs relative to wages. The specification depends on the type of crop (γ_{3k}). The price of basic food crops is likely to change much more in response to population growth while the price of export crops might be unaffected. The specification additionally depends on village-specific characteristics (γ_{1v}) and characteristics specific to the village population (γ_{2a}). The way population growth affects labor supply and food demand strongly depends on the age composition and the share of workers versus dependents in the population. Also, the functioning of markets matters. If household are integrated in off-farm labor markets, the effect of population growth on relative wages might be weak. In addition, other unobserved village and household characteristics might influence village-level relative prices.

$$\frac{P_k}{W} = \gamma_{1v} \gamma_{2a} A_v^{\gamma_{3k}} \tag{9}$$

Substituting the expressions (8) and (9) for relative prices in (7), taking natural logarithms, combining all constant terms and combining unobserved effects in an error term we obtain:

$$\ln R_{ik} = a_{ok} + a_{1k} \ln S_{1v} + a_{2k} \ln S_{2i} + a_{3k} D_i + a_{4k} Z_v + a_{5k} \ln A_v + \varepsilon_{ik} \quad (10)$$

The model presented here differs in some aspects from the model elaborated by Chomitz and Gray (1996). Instead of considering plot-specific absolute prices for agricultural outputs and inputs, we considered relative prices at the village level. With this specification we are able to not solely attribute differences in local prices to differences in transport costs to a major market. We account for the endogeneity of agricultural prices and wages by assuming local level relative prices to depend on household- and village-specific characteristics. In addition, our model is not necessarily based on the assumption of perfect markets and profit-maximizing behavior. The model can be put in a framework of utility maximization by assuming differences in relative (implicit) wages to be household specific and ascribing them to differences in the marginal rate of substitution of income (or consumption) for leisure.

Implications of the Model

First, equation (10) indicates that the land rent for agricultural land use increases with improved agricultural technologies (S_{1v}). Second, favorable natural characteristics (S_{2i}) leading to a higher natural productivity also increase the land rent for agricultural land use. Third, the coefficients a_{3k} and a_{4k} are negative and the land rent diminishes as the distance from the plot to the village (D_i) and from the village to the market (Z_v) increases. Fourth, a higher population (A_v) increases the land rent. Fifth, since the coefficients a_{3k} and a_{5k} are a function of β_k, population (A_v) and distance to the village (D_i) have a stronger impact on the land rent for crops with a higher labor elasticity. Similarly, the coefficient a_{4k} depends on α_k and δ_{1k} implying that the land rent for capital-intensive land-use systems or for crops with higher transport costs, is much more affected by changes in the accessibility to major markets (Z_v).

4. Empirical Estimation

Research Area

We estimate the above model for an area surrounding the Lore Lindu National Park in Central Sulawesi, Indonesia. The park is located in two districts comprising together five sub-districts and 119 villages. The rural households in these villages depend on agriculture for their livelihoods and cultivate a variety of crops including coffee, cocoa and coconut for the export market and rice for subsistence and for the local market. The national park is increasingly threatened by agricultural encroachment into the park's boundaries and unsustainable agricultural practices in the surrounding areas. This region is our research area and was chosen as a focus site for a collaborative research project.

Understanding the spatial land-use patterns and household behavior that determines these land-use patterns is extremely relevant for this forest-frontier area as the area is recognized as one the most important centers of endemic species in the world and forest protection is extremely important for conservation of the unique biodiversity (Waltert et al., 2003).

The Model

If a plot of land is allocated to the land use with the highest rent as expressed in equation (10), the probability of a plot i to be allocated to land use k can be expressed as:

$$\Pr(ik) = \frac{R_{ik}}{\sum_j R_{ij}} \tag{11}$$

Equation (10) and (11) describe a multinominal logit model that allows us to estimate the coefficients in equation (10) empirically. We estimate this multinominal logit model for the Lore Lindu region using a combination of socio-economic survey data and GIS data.

Data

To estimate the model we use a unique combination of socio-economic and geographic data. We use land-use data derived from satellite image interpretation, other geographic data derived from a variety of maps and socioeconomic data derived from a village-level survey and census data.

First, we use a land-use map derived from the interpretation of a Landsat ETM scene taken on August 24th, 2001 and covering the research area. The interpretation procedure used maximum likelihood classification techniques with ground-truth data, resulting in a land cover map with ten different land-use classes and a resolution of 15 by 15m. The identified land-use classes include open and closed forest, four classes of agricultural land use, grassland, reed, water, settlement areas, clouds and shadow.

Second, along with the land-use map, additional geographic information was compiled in a GID system. This includes a topographic map[3] that was digitized and used to construct a digital elevation model with a resolution of 70 by 70 m and an administrative map with sub-district boundaries, location of populated village centres, and demarcation of the National Park. In addition a detailed road map[4] distinguishing between asphalt roads, gravel or dirt

[3] This is derived from the 1991 edition of the *Peta Rupabumi Indensia* constructed by Bakosurtanal (*Badan Koordinasi Survei dan Pemetaan Nasional* – National Coordinating Agency for Surveys and Mapping). The scale is 1:50,000. The maps are based on aerial photographs of the years 1981,1982 and 1989.

[4] The road map is constructed using information from the topographic map, a recent road map constructed by Bappeda (*Badan Penencanaan Pembangunan Daereh* – Directory of Development Planning Board) and own observations from the field.

roads and walking tracks is included. Also a soil map[5] providing rough information on different soil types was digitized and included in the GIS.

Third, 80 out of the 119 villages in the research area have been selected to be included in a comprehensive village-level survey based on a stratified random sampling method. The villages were classified in ten different strata based on the proximity to the National Park, the population density in the village and the share of migrants among the village population. We selected disproportionately more villages among the villages located close the National Park because the collaborative research project mainly concerns the stability of the rainforest margins. With respect to the other criteria, the selection was proportionate to population size.

The village survey was implemented in the period March-July 2001 using a formal quantitative questionnaire inquiring about the following topics: demographics, land use, agricultural production, agricultural technology, marketing, land and labor institutions, conservation issues, livestock holdings, infrastructure, and household well-being. The interviews were held in group discussions with village representatives and village elders. The village survey data were complemented with socio-economic data from secondary sources, including population and agricultural censuses for several years.

Combining Spatial and Non-Spatial Data

We estimate the model described by equation (10) and (11) using non-spatial socio-economic survey data and spatial geographic data. The way of combining spatial and non-spatial data requires some more explanation.

First, the resolution of our land-use map derived from the satellite image interpretation is 15×15 m^2 while the other grid-based data sources derived from the DEM have a resolution of 70×70 m^2. We take the smallest common multiple of these pixel sizes, 210×210 m^2 as the final resolution of the analysis. This resolution is used to construct new grids from vector data sources and to resample existing raster data. The grids correspond to a plot size of 4.4 hectares.

Second, because of a lack of data on village boundaries (the smallest administrative unit for which reliable maps exist is the sub-district) we need to construct artificial boundaries in order to be able to link village-level socioeconomic data and spaital data. We do so by constructing Thiessen polygons, polygons around each village center such that each location within a polygon is closer to the village center of that polygon than to any other village center. (see e.g. Müller and Zeller, 2002). The boundaries constructed in this way are certainly not to be interpreted as representing real administrative boundaries. Rather they are an artificial spatial unit for linking village-level data to spatial data.

Third, the survey covers only a sample of 80 of the 119 villages in the region. These 80 villages include a total of 104,085 pixels of 210×210 m^2. For the estimation of the model we take a non-random sub-sample of 55,464 observations, which consists of all pixels that are located less than three km from roads, walking tracks and village centers. The sub-sample includes 95 percent of the agricultural area and 47 percent of the forest area of the total

[5] The 1:1,000,000 soil map was constructed by Bakosurtanal (*Badan Koordinasi Survei dan Pemetaan Nasional* – National Coordinating Agency for Surveys and Mapping) in 1995.

sample. This represents agricultural and forest marginal areas where most land-use changes are taking place and which we are most interested in.

Fourth, some of the variables used in the model are spatially explicit and measured at the pixel level while others are measured at the village level. An overview of the variables used in the model is given in table 1. The dependent variable is derived from satellite image interpretation and constitutes a categorical variable with four different land-use types: forest, annual crops, perennial crops and grassland.

Table 1. Overview of the variables used in the multinominal logit model

Dependent Variable	Variable name Categories			Freq.	Perc.	Scale
		Forest		42,717	77.02%	Pixel
		Annual crops		4,165	7.51%	Pixel
		Perennial crops		4,225	7.62%	Pixel
		Grassland		4,357	7.86%	Pixel
Explanatory Variables	Variable name	Mean	Std. Dev.	Minimum	Maximum	Scale
Geophysical variables						
Slope (degrees)	SLOPE	10.79	8.03	0	45	pixel
Elevation (100 m)	ELEV	10.49	3.70	0.25	23.51	pixel
Aspect (degrees)	ASP	187	105	0	360	pixel
Aspect squared (degrees)	ASP^2	45,967	38,822	0	129,598	pixel
Distance to river (100 m)	TORIVER	1.15	1.11	0	9.60	pixel
Location variables						
Distance to road (100 m)	TOROAD	84.29	72.42	0	322.74	pixel
Distance to hamlet (km)	TOVILL	3.47	2.95	0	20.28	pixel
Dummy inside the National Park	PARK	0.33	0.47	0	1	pixel
Distance to city (km)	TOCITY	92	33	9	145	hamlet
Distance to city squared (km)	$TOCITY^2$	9,527	5,937	77	21,091	hamlet
Distance to district capital (km)	TODISTRICT	27	19	0	67	hamlet
Socioeconomic variables						
# years irrigation infrastructure	IRR_YRS	3.80	9.53	0	71	village
ln (population)	lnPOP	6.64	0.67	5.46	8.45	village
% of population in working age	POPWORK	67	8	39	83	village
Spatially lagged variables						
Lagged slope (degrees)	LAG	10.76	6.85	0	35	pixel
Lagged slope * slope	SLOPE_LAG	211.49	222.92	0	1,680	pixel

Source: own calculations.

RESULTS

The results of the estimation of the multinominal logit model are reported in table 2. We estimate the model taking forest as the comparison land-use category and therefore the results should be interpreted as such. We indicate the estimated coefficients as well as the estimated relative risk ratio or odds ratio which are easier to interpret. The majority of the estimated effects is statistically significant and has the expected signs based on the refined von Thunen – Ricardo land rent model.

The probability to find annual crops relative to forest is higher on flatter plots with a higher elevation, on less northward sloping hillsides, on plots closer to rivers and village centers, and outside the National Park. The same is true for perennial crops but the effects of slope and distance to rivers are a lot smaller and not statistically significant. The probability of a plot being allocated to agricultural land use, annual or perennial crops, is higher in villages closer to cities and district capitals and in villages with a larger population and work force. In addition, access to irrigation decreases the likelihood of perennial crops relative to forest cover. The probability to find grassland relative to forest is higher on plots at a lower altitude, further away from roads and in villages closer to cities and district capitals.

Table 2. Results of the multinominal logit model (with forest as comparison)

			Number of observations		55,464
			Wald chi2(42)		12,945
			Prob > chi2		0.000
			Pseudo R^2		0.380
			Log Likelihood		27,211
	Relative Risk Ratio	Coeffcient	Robust Std. Err.	z	P>|z|
Annual Crops					
LAG	0.8788	-0.1292	0.0123	-10.52	0.000
SLOPE	0.9410	-0.0608	0.0244	-2.50	0.013
SLOPE_LAG	1.0023	0.0023	0.0013	1.74	0.082
ELEV	0.8047	-0.2173	0.0357	-6.09	0.000
ASP	0.9939	-0.0061	0.0020	-3.14	0.002
ASP^2	1.0000	0.0000	0.0000	2.11	0.035
TORIVER	0.7828	-0.2449	0.0910	-2.69	0.007
TOROAD	0.9982	-0.0018	0.0018	-1.03	0.304
TOVILL	0.5626	-0.5752	0.1183	-4.86	0.000
TOCITY	0.9351	-0.0671	0.0113	-5.93	0.000
$TOCITY^2$	1.0005	0.0005	0.0001	5.82	0.000
TODISTRICT	0.9862	-0.0139	0.0087	-1.61	0.108
PARK	0.2348	-1.4489	0.2325	-6.23	0.000
lnPOP*	1.2459	0.2199	0.1688	1.30	0.193
POPWORK	1.0206	0.0204	0.0106	1.92	0.054
IRR_YRS	1.0048	0.0047	0.0070	0.68	0.497
Constant		2.9431	1.3890	2.12	0.034
Perennial Crops					
LAG	0.9565	-0.0445	0.0121	-3.68	0.000
SLOPE	0.9760	-0.0243	0.0175	-1.39	0.165

SLOPE_LAG	1.0014	0.0014	0.0007	2.02	0.043
ELEV	0.7016	-0.3544	0.0304	-11.65	0.000
ASP	0.9864	-0.0137	0.0018	-7.44	0.000
ASP^2	1.0000	0.0000	0.0000	4.88	0.000
TORIVER	0.9931	-0.0070	0.0907	-0.08	0.939
TOROAD	1.0008	0.0008	0.0016	0.52	0.606
TOVILL	0.6176	-0.4819	0.0754	-6.39	0.000
TOCITY	0.9383	-0.0637	0.0098	-6.48	0.000
TOCITY^2	1.0004	0.0004	0.0001	5.55	0.000
TODISTRICT	0.9921	-0.0079	0.0080	-0.98	0.325
Perennial Crops					
PARK	0.4452	-0.8093	0.1892	-4.28	0.000
lnPOP*	1.3876	0.3276	0.1835	1.79	0.074
POPWORK	1.0095	0.0095	0.0111	0.85	0.393
IRR_YRS	0.9827	-0.0175	0.0060	-2.93	0.003
Constant		3.7524	1.3486	2.78	0.005
Grassland					
LAG	0.8121	-0.2082	0.0215	-9.67	0.000
SLOPE	0.9841	-0.0160	0.0286	-0.56	0.576
SLOPE_LAG	1.0018	0.0018	0.0016	1.10	0.270
ELEV	0.9086	-0.0958	0.0452	-2.12	0.034
ASP	0.9932	-0.0068	0.0019	-3.59	0.000
ASP^2	1.0000	0.0000	0.0000	3.70	0.000
TORIVER	1.0055	0.0055	0.0692	0.08	0.937
TOROAD	0.9941	-0.0059	0.0025	-2.37	0.018
TOVILL	1.0473	0.0463	0.0497	0.93	0.352
TOCITY	0.9809	-0.0193	0.0218	-0.88	0.377
TOCITY^2	1.0003	0.0003	0.0002	2.02	0.043
TODISTRICT	0.9767	-0.0236	0.0161	-1.47	0.142
PARK	0.1164	-2.1505	0.3463	-6.21	0.000
lnPOP*	0.8251	-0.1923	0.3801	-0.51	0.613
POPWORK	1.0208	0.0206	0.0215	0.96	0.337
IRR_YRS	0.9974	-0.0026	0.0162	-0.16	0.874
Constant		0.6011	3.1487	0.19	0.849

* Instrumented variable.

Source: own estimations.

IMPLICATIONS OF THE EMPIRICAL MODEL

The results of the multinominal logit model indicate that geophysical land characteristics are very important factors in determining the spatial land-use pattern. Other spatially explicit land-use studies also found highly significant effects of topographic features and other geophysical land characteristics on the probability of certain land-use types or land-use changes (e.g. Nelson and Hellerstein, 1997; Cropper *et al.*, 2001; Deininger and Minten, 2002; Müller and Zeller, 2002). The estimated effect of slope and lagged slope on the probability of agricultural land use relative to forest is negative while the interaction term of slope and lagged slope has a positive effect. This means that agriculture is found more often on flatter plots and in less mountainous surroundings. Yet, the probability to find agricultural land on steeper plots is higher in more mountainous surroundings. Further, annual crops are found closer to rivers and on less steep slopes, which indicates that (potential) agricultural yields of annual crops are determined to a large extent by topographic characteristics and access to water. The likelihood of perennial crops relative to forest is less influenced by the slope of the plot. In addition, the estimated effects show that agricultural land use becomes less likely and forest more likely with increasing elevation. The results demonstrate that differences in Ricardian land rent are very important in explaining the present land-use pattern.

The location of a plot in relation to villages and roads is hypothesized to be crucial in determining land use. The results show that the distance to populated centers has a much larger effect on land use than the distance to roads, which is statistically not significant[6]. For each additional five kilometer away from a village center, it is 18 times less likely to find annual crops and 11 times less likely to find perennial crops compared to forest[7]. Further, the accessibility to cities and major towns might matter. We find that with every ten kilometer distance between the village center and the district capital, it becomes 1.15 times less likely to find annual crops and 1.08 times less likely to find perennial crops compared to forest. It is almost two times less likely to find perennial or annual crops on plots in villages located ten kilometer further away from the city. These results indicate that the distance from plots to village centers is much more important in determining land use than the distance from villages to towns and markets.

As in other spatially explicit economic land-use studies, the model for the Lore Lindu region shows that the attributes and the location of plots influence land use. However, most studies find a much larger impact of access to roads (e.g. Deininger and Minten, 2002; Müller and Zeller, 2002). Our results indicate that the location of plots with respect to roads is not important at all in determining the land-use type. Rather, the location of plots in relation to village centers and to a lesser extent the access of villages to markets matters. The land-use pattern in the Lore Lindu region is centered on villages rather than around roads and major markets, which relates to the history of the area. Villages might have a long history of establishment while roads were built more recently to connect villages. The spatial land-use pattern is quite different than for instance in the Amazon regions, which are characterized by road colonization implying clearance and settlement of forested areas after roads have been built.

The land-use pattern is centered on villages with annual crops cultivated closer to the village and perennial crops further away at forest margins. This could be related to the fact that village centers are located in flatter areas, which are more suitable for the cultivation of annual crops. However, differences in topographic features are accounted for in the model. Also in villages without much topographic variation the same land-use pattern emerges. The relation between distance to the village and the likelihood to find annual respectively perennial crops is likely associated with differences in labor intensity. Land-use systems

---

6 To exclude the possibility that the effect of distance to roads is statistically not significant because of multicollinearity problems, we estimated the multinominal regression dropping all other cost-of-access variables that are correlated to some extent with distance to roads. The estimated effects of distance to roads and the level of significance did not change much, which demonstrates that there is no multicollinearity problem for the variable.

7 The variable $TOVILL$ is measured in km and the estimated coefficients for this variable are –0.5752 and –0.4819 for annual crops and perennial crops respectively. So, the odds ratio for a five units (= 5 km) change is

based on the cultivation of annual crops are more labor intensive than systems with perennial crops. More labor-intensive land-use systems are located closer to village centers and less labor-intensive systems further away because this reduces the time spent to reach the fields.

The variable expressing distance to the city and its square have an opposite sign with an inflection point around 70 kilometer. This implies a U-shaped relation between distance to the city and the likelihood of agriculture land use relative to forest. The interpretation of this result is not straightforward and should be done with some caution. On the one hand, in villages closer than 70 kilometer from the city, the probability of agriculture decreases with distance to the city at an increasing rate. Since villages closer to the cities are better connected to the road network this could mean that the cost-of-access rather than the Euclidian distance between villages and cities matters. Better access to markets and lower transport costs increase the profitability of farming and increase the likelihood of agriculture relative to forest. On the other hand, in villages further than 70 kilometer from the city, the probability of agriculture increases with distance to the city. This could imply that in villages further from the market agriculture is more extensive, resulting in a lower probability of forest cover. In addition, remote villages are also more mountainous such that agriculture and forest compete for less suitable land. Further, we find that the probability to find annual crops relative to forest is much more influenced by the distance to district capital towns than is the case for perennial crops. Concerning the accessibility to major cities, similar effects are found for both land-use types. Annual crops constitute food crops such as rice and corn while perennial crops are usually export crops such as coffee and cocoa. Hence, the results suggest that local markets in the district capital towns are more important for trade of food crops while cities are important for the marketing of both food crops and export crops. The original von Thunen model and its application in spatial land-use models emphasize the importance of differences in transport costs for different crops in determining the spatial pattern of land use. Since the effect of distance to the city is not different for annual crops than for perennial crops, we do not find much evidence in support of this idea. The differences in transport costs between rice, the major annual crop, and cocoa beans, the major perennial crop product, might not be that large because these are both bulk products, which are quite easily transported.

Further, the results demonstrate that inside the Lore Lindu National Park it is 4.3 times less likely to find annual crops, 2.2 times less likely to find perennial crops and 8.6 times less likely to find grassland compared to forest. The forest inside the National Park is less likely to be cleared, which suggests that the establishment of a National Park is to some extent effective for forest conservation. Yet, the forest inside the National Park is more likely to be cleared for the cultivation of perennial crops than for the cultivation of annual crops. There are several possible explanations for this observation. First, the borders of the National Park are set along topographic features and the land inside the Park is less suitable for the cultivation of annual crops. Second, the risk of being caught (and fined) is less because plots with perennial crops inside the forest are less conspicuous. Third, the risk of being caught while working on the plot is less because perennial crops are less labor demanding. Fourth, it is easier to avoid fines by claiming to have planted perennial crops already before the demarcation of the National Park.

1/exp (-0.5752*5)=18 for annual crops and 1/exp (-0.4819*5)=11 for perennial crops. Other odds ratios can be calculated in similar way.

Next, we find that access to an improved irrigation system reduces the probability of perennial crops compared to forest. This implies that technical progress for paddy rice cultivation reduces pressure on forests. The results show that the likelihood of agricultural land use compared to forest increases with population and the share of workers in the population. A one percent increase in village population increases the probability of perennial crops and annual crops relative to forest with 33 and 22 percent respectively. With every five percent increase in the share of workers among the village population, it becomes 1.1 times more likely to find annual crops and 1.04 times more likely to find perennial crops relative to forest. Excluding the effects that are statistically not significant, these results point to the importance of population in shaping the spatial land-use pattern. There is not much evidence for a substantial effect of population and other socioeconomic variables in spatial land-use models in the literature. However, the effect might have been obscured due to the difference in aggregation level between land-use data at the pixel level and socioeconomic data at a much more aggregated level. For example, Cropper *et al.* (2001) and Deininger and Minten (2002) included district-level population into a spatial land-use model and find no significant effect. The aggregation bias might have led to an erroneous conclusion about the effect of population and other socioeconomic factors on land-use change and deforestation. Our model using village-level data might be better suited to elucidate the effects of socioeconomic factors on spatial land-use patterns.

5. Conclusion

We can conclude that the refinement of the von Thunen – Ricardo model to let prices (especially relative wages) be determined not solely by transport costs to a major output market, has provided a good basis for a description of the spatial land-use pattern in the Lore Lindu region. Land use is very much determined by differences in geophysical land characteristics and is centered around villages with labor-intensive land-use systems closer to populated centers. Differences in population levels, the available technology and the location of major markets and towns further shape the spatial land-use pattern.

References

Bakosurtanal (Badan Koordinasi Survei dan Pemetaan Nasional). 1991. Peta Rupabumi Indonesia skala 1:50,000. Jakarta, Bakosutanal.

Bakosurtanal (Badan Koordinasi Survei dan Pemetaan Nasional). 1995. Peta Dasar. Digetasi dari Petah Rupabumi. Skala 1:1,000,000. Jakarta, Bakosutanal.

Bappeda (Badan Perencanaan Pembangunan Daerah Kabupaten Donggala dan Kantor Kabupaten Donggala). 2000. Analisa Peta Dasar Neraca Lahan Kabupaten Donggala. Palu.

Chomitz, K.M. and D. Gray. 1996. Roads, Lands Use, and Deforestation: A Spatial Model Applied to Belize. *World Bank Economic Review*. 10: 487-512.

Cropper, M., J. Puri, and C. Griffiths. 2001. Predicting the Location of Deforestation: The Role of Roads and Protected Areas in North Thailand. *Land Economics*. 77: 172-186.

Deininger, K. and B. Minten. 1999. Poverty, Policies, and Deforestation: The Case of Mexico. *Economic Development and Cultural Change*. 47:313-343.

Fox, J., R. Kanter, S. Yarnasarn, M. Ekasingh, and R. Jones. 1994. Farmer Decision Making and Spatial Variables in Northern Thailand. *Environmental Management*. 18: 391-399.

Gobin, A., P. Campling, and J. Feyen. 2002. Logistic Modelling to Derive Agricultural Land Use Determinants: A Case Study from Southeastern Nigeria . *Agriculture, Ecosystems & Environment*. 89: 213-228.

Irwin, E.G. and J. Geoghegan. 2001. Theory, Data, Methods: Developing Spatially Explicit Economic Models of Land Use Change. *Agriculture, Ecosystems & Environment*. 85: 7-23.

Lambin, E.F., M.D.A. Rounsevell, and H.J. Geist. 2000. Are Agricultural Land-Use Models Able to Predict Changes in Land-Use Intensity? *Agriculture, Ecosystems & Environment*. 82:321-331.

Liu, D.S., L.R. Iverson, and S. Brown. 1993. Rates and Patterns of Deforestation in the Philippines: Application of Geographic Information System Analysis. *Forest Ecology and Management*. 57:1-16.

Mertens, B. and E.F. Lambin. 1997. Spatial Modelling of Deforestation in Southern Cameroon - Spatial Desegregation of Diverse Deforestation Processes. *Applied Geography*. 17:143-162.

Mertens, B. and E.F. Lambin. 2000. Land-Cover-Change Trajectories in Southern Cameroon. *Annals of the Association of American Geographers*. 90:467-494.

Munroe, D., J. Southworth, and C.M. Tucker. 2002. The Dynamics of Land-Cover Change in Western Honduras: Exploring Spatial and Temporal Complexity. *Agricultural Economics*. 27:355-369.

Müller, D. and M. Zeller. 2002. Land Use Dynamics in the Central Highlands of Vietnam: A spatial Model Combining Village Survey Data and Satellite Imagery Interpretation. *Agricultural Economics*. 27:333-354.

Nelson, G.C. 2002. Introduction to the Special Issue on Spatial Analysis for Agricultural Economists. *Agricultural Economics*. 27:197-200.

Nelson, G.C. and J. Geoghegan. 2002. Deforestation and Land Use Change: Sparse Data Environments. *Agricultural Economics*. 27:201-216.

Nelson, G.C., V. Harris, and S.W. Stone. 2001. Deforestation, Land Use, and Property Rights: Empirical Evidence from Darien, Panama. *Land Economics*. 77:187-205.

Nelson, G.C. and D. Hellerstein. 1997. Do Roads Cause Deforestation? Using Satellite Images in Econometric Analysis of Land Use. *American Journal of Agricultural Economics*. 79:80-88.

Serneels, S. and E.F. Lambin. 2001. Proximate Causes of Land-Use Change in Narok District, Kenya: A Spatial Statistical Model. *Agriculture, Ecosystems & Environment*. 85:65-81.

Vance, C. and J. Geoghegan. 2002. Temporal and Spatial Modelling of Tropcial Deforestation: a Survival Analysis Linking Satellite and Household Survey Data. *Agricultural Economics*. 27:317-332.

Verburg, P.H., Y. Chen, and T. Veldkamp. 2000. Spatial Explorations of Land Use Change and Grain Production in China. *Agriculture, Ecosystems & Environment*. 82:333-354.

Verburg, P.H., T. Veldkamp, and J. Bouma. 1999. Land Use Change under Conditions of High Population Pressure: The Case of Java. *Global Environmental Change*. 9:303-312.

Verburg, P.H. and A. Veldkamp. 2001. The Role of Spatially Explicit Models in Land-Use Change Research: A Case Study for Cropping Patterns in China." *Agriculture, Ecosystems & Environment.* 85:177-190.

von Thünen, J.H. 1826. *Der Isolierte Staat in Beziehung auf Landwirtschaft und Nationaloekonomie.*

Waltert, M., M. Langkau, M. Maertens, M. Härtel, S. Erasmi, and M. Mühlenberg. 2003. Predicting the Loss of Bird Species from Deforestation in Central Sulawesi. In G. Gerold, M. Fremery, and E. Guhardja, editors, *Land Use, Nature Conservation and the Stability of Rainforest Margins in Southeast Asia.* Springer. Berlin.

In: Land Use Policy
Editors: A. C. Denman and O. M. Penrod

ISBN: 978-1-60741-435-3

Chapter 6

URBAN LAND USE POLICY AND CHILDREN'S DEVELOPMENT – A HONG KONG PERSPECTIVE

Ling Hin Li*

Department of Real Estate and Construction; 5/F Knowles Building
The University of Hong Kong; Pokfulam Road, Hong Kong, China

INTRODUCTION

Studies around the world have shown that there is a significant correlation between children's personal development and the neighbourhood environment in which they are brought up. While the neighbourhood environment is a master set of a vast number of interdependent and intermingled variables, one particular factor, the urban land use environment, sometimes tends to be overlooked. In fact, all other neighbourhood variables work inside the framework of land use settings as all human activities take place on and above land and certainly within some form of physical structure. On the other hand, land use settings are constantly shaped and reformed by the urban land policies devised by the public sector through different channels. This chapter attempts to provide some insights into this particular aspect through a qualitative analysis. A major youth survey is carried out, and the views of young people on two major aspects of land use settings are collated. In the micro-system, the extent to which young people enjoy the urban land use environment is examined through an urban experience analysis. In the macro level, their views on whether and how the physical land use environment affects them are tallied. We find that urban land use environment in the neighbourhood does impose important impacts on young people, and young people do recognise this. However, they seem to be unable to capitalize the benefits of "routine activities" due to various reasons, and the management of public space is a major reason. In general, there is inadequate government effort in trying to stimulate young people's interest in contributing to the debate of urban land use policy, making most young children rather indifferent on a number of socio-economic land use issues.

* Tel: 852-2859-8932; Fax: 852-2559-9457; E-mail: lhli@hkucc.hku.hk

BUILT ENVIRONMENT AND CHILDREN

Studies of children and the built environment can be traced back to the 1960s and 1970s, with the pioneer work made by Jacobs (1964) followed by the influential work of Lynch (1977). Starting from Wilson's *The Truly Disadvantaged* (1987), sociologists have begun to realise that poor environments in inner urban neighbourhoods contribute a lot to the "natural disadvantages" faced by the poor families living in these neighbourhoods. Hence, "*ecological context mattered in very fundamental ways that went beyond individual characteristics or family circumstances*" (Massey, 2001, p.42). The tenet that the environment is an important factor in an individual's personal development is firmly established. In recent decades, research interests in the aspect of the correlation between neighbourhood environment and young people's development have spun off into a variety of foci on the physical environment of urban space for children (Torrell, 1990), on the social (Hart, 1997) and legal view (Eekelaar, 1986) of the youth's participation in urban planning, as well as on the urban safety for young people (Blakeley, 1994). Yet all these imply an apparent inadequacy in the understanding of the needs of our young children who, by no means, should be regarded as second-class citizens as far as decisions on and management of urban space are concerned.

Cairney (2005) justifies that as children grow, their dependence on the built environment and on their parents begins to shift. In the early stages of childhood (ages 12 to 14 years old), children are still fairly dependent on their family and the built environment. However, as children progress through childhood into the middle and late teen years, they are increasingly less dependent on the primary caregiver. Moreover, older children are also apt to spend more time outside the home with peers, both at school and in recreational activities. Thus, the influence of the built environment and the social environment becomes significant for older children. According to Michelson and Levine (1979), the characteristics of the built environment become more important as children grow. During earlier years, they are more dependent upon adults and are more tied to the neighbourhood, since they only go to other parts of the city accompanied by adults. At a later stage when they can be relatively independent, they should be able to expand their use of the environment beyond the neighbourhood alone, and thus reap more benefits from the city and the social environment.

Piaget (1956) views human cognitive development as a specific form of biological adaptation of a complex organism to a complex environment. In Piaget's theory of cognitive development (Piaget, 1952), four major stages of cognitive development are identified:

Stage 1: Sensorimotor period – birth to age 2
Stage 2: Preoperational period – ages 2 to 7
Stage 3: Concrete operational period – ages 7 to 11
Stage 4: Formal operational period – ages 11 onward

Piaget (1956) regards his age norms as approximations and acknowledged that transitional ages may vary. In view of children actively exploring the world around them, the interaction with the environment gradually alters their way of thinking. In the context related to spatial behaviour, the children's world expands to include the neighbuorhood and school in stages two and three. Children in these stages develop abstract notions of social roles and their spatial coordinates as they begin to understand the surroundings and learn to satisfy their needs in a larger environment. In stage four, children are ready to explore and understand the world beyond the neighbourhood and school to the city and world level.

Urban space is essential for young people to experience the path of growing up in the adult's world. Considering that most community activities take place within the settings of urban space and within a physical built environment shaped by urban planning and land use policies, this experience path of young people should be encouraged and be taken more seriously. Simpson (1997) notes some legal and social problems in constraining such experience to be enjoyed by the younger generation. He explained that in most societies, young children are not regarded as legally equal to adults, and children are mostly treated as "future citizens" who should not be given a place in the "current" decision-making process for urban space utilization. As a result, children are often denied access to voice their needs in urban planning and land use policies which affect substantially their childhood development. Simpson remarks this consequence quite concisely when he said that "*empowering 'users' is disconnected from the benefits for children, who apparently are not 'users' in the same sense as other members of the community*" (Simpson 1997, p.918).

In practical terms, such a denial of young people's needs in the production of urban space has excluded young people from the broader category of "public" in the enjoyment of open space for their own activities. Valentine (1996) notes that open space can sometimes be a "closed" space where young people are subject to adults' interpretation of the acceptable mode of behaviour and rules of usage in such areas. This drives young people away from the "adults'" open space, and the results can be more chaotic (Valentine 1996, p. 214). One should come to realize that young people are in fact one of most frequent user groups of open/public space in our society given their less-constrained time management, although it is true that most essential urban economic activities involve adults only, especially in the urban centre, as well as inside the cyberspace.

Even if one may argue that urban space, to a large extent, is more valuable to adults than to young children, one cannot delineate urban open space as an "adult-public" domain only. Lasch (1995) stresses the importance of informal meeting places where children can learn from unrelated adults interacting with each other and can assume responsibilities in the neighbourhood, something which is not taught to young kids in schools.

The measurement of collective neighbourhood effects on children's development has gained tremendous success with the application of econometric and other quantitative methods of analyses (Duncan and Raudenbush, 1999; Sampson, et al., 1997). Brooks-Gunn et al. (1993), for example, applied regression models in their study to explain the correlations between the socio-economic characteristics of neighbourhoods and the developmental outcomes of children with interesting results. While the examination of these socio-economic factors in the neighbourhood is essential and instrumental to understanding neighbourhood effects on children, some researchers on children's development have also agreed that the impact of urban land use patterns/systems on children's well-being has often been overlooked. Sampson (2001) explains very succinctly the potential effect of such "routine activities"[8] perspective when he said that "*… the mix of residential with commercial land use, public transportation nodes… are relevant to organizing how and when children come into contact with other peers, adults, and nonresident activity..*" (p.11).

[8] According to Sampson, the "routine activities" perspective has been well-applied in the field of criminology to study the correlation between the physical environment and motivation of crimes.

Camstra (1997) declares that the urban environment is not the most suitable environment for a child to grow up. As cities are crowded, polluted, and hectic, the urban environment is seen as a less favourable living environment for children as well as grownups.

LAND USE PLANNING AND CHILD DEVELOPMENT

As suggested by Gutenschwager (1995), the crisis-ridden built environment is the setting for child development and growth. The greatest challenge, therefore, is to create a sense of security in such a chaotic environment. Gehl (1996) is concerned that there would be a lack of open spaces and of natural areas in the city. Particularly, the noise level in some parts of the city is likely to be high. Malone (2001) states that ideally, towns and cities should be the place where children can socialize, observe, and learn about how the society functions as well as contribute to the cultural fabric of a community. They should also be sites where they find refuge, discover nature, and find tolerant and caring adults who support them. Unfortunately, it is hard to see how this environment will improve much in the coming century for most of the world's population, given the current rate of urbanization and economic growth, at the expense of good community planning practices. Consequently, there is a tendency to look at the more negative effects built up by our environments on the younger generation.

According to Maxwell (2003), the primary environment is defined as settings where a person spends a great deal of time and establishes important relationships. For children, the home, school, and day-care centres are primary environments which especially have critical effects. When there is a source of stress such as chronic noise or crowding in the primary environment, it is more likely to have negative effects on the individual than if it happens in a transitory or secondary environment such as a bus or stadium.

As supported by Maxwell (2003), it is believed that communities shape children's development. The relationship between the built environment and children's self-identity, self-esteem, and academic performance is identified. If children are given the right start, fewer developmental problems will develop later on.

On the other hand, Berg and Medrich (1980) explain the problems of current land use zoning practices and how they limit the heterogeneity in the environment. For example, the location of the city centre and various resources in the neighbourhoods determine children's ability to make use of these resources. The farther these resources are in one's neighbourhood, the less likely children can have access to them.

Maxwell (2003) warns that the consequences of chronic exposure to a high-density environment for children have generally been documented negatively. These consequences include increased aggression and hostility, poor academic performance, poor family social interaction, and social withdrawal. He examined whether or not home density (the number of people living in the child's home) affects children's classroom behaviour and academic performance. He examined 73 children in the age group of 8 to 10 from two schools in the urban area. The children were asked to describe their living environment and whether or not they feel annoyed and disturbed at home while doing homework and reading. Regression analysis indicated that there was a main effect of household density on the reading measure and word identification such that children from the more crowded homes obtained lower scores on this measure. Furthermore, these children are more likely to feel badly, while children who have their own bedroom are more likely to feel they have a place by themselves. It is concluded that household crowdedness has a negative effect on academic performance.

Evans et al. (2001) confirm this by looking at the psychological health of children. They found that there is a positive relation between household density and psychological symptoms. Children living in more crowded homes are less likely to persist when confronted with a challenging puzzle.

URBAN EXPERIENCE IN HONG KONG

Given the extensive literature in this field, we hope to contribution to the discussion further by looking at the extent to which young people feel about the importance of the built environment and suggest policy implications from the results. In this research, we are going to take a look at how young people in Hong Kong feel about their built environment. Hong Kong is an international city in China with a substantial cultural influence from the West due to the colonial administration for almost one hundred years before 1997. Hence, examination of this city will not only provide an insight into how young people raised in a mixed Western-Asian culture behave, but also lend itself to the analysis of other international cities.

This examination is conducted on two levels. The first level is an examination of "urban experience" of young people in Hong Kong. The second is a more structured analysis, based on a large scale survey, on how young people in this city feel about the physical land use environment.

Urban Experience

For some people, the term "urban experience" may sound intriguingly confusing. When we set out an attempt to "experience" something, we normally try to feel something that does not occur to us daily. We therefore will experience new challenges by trying sky-diving or simply a new hair-style for the graduation party, or experience a new life style when we move to a completely new environment. However, for city dwellers, we do live in an urban environment for most part of our conscious life and we don't regard daily routine matter to be an "experience". Urban space is essential for young people to experience the path of growing up. For example, where would the young people like to have a park, a football stadium and other leisure facilities ? How large and what sort of design would fit their needs ?

The Research

A team of young people from different family background in the age group of 15-18 has been chosen. The were asked to wander around ten different locations in Hong Kong, including their own residential neighbourhood, school area, and other districts such as the CBD, industrial area, run-down residential area, high class housing district and shopping area in Hong Kong. The participants are given a very simple questionnaire to fill in their family background information. In each spot, they are asked to write down their feelings about planning, design, transportation, provision of facilities, and feeling on the local residents/people. The following table shows the background of these participants, which will then be compared with the feeling they recorded after their visit.

	Ching	Mui	Miss C	Miss V	Ray	Ki	Minnie	Me
gender	girl	girl	girl	Girl	boy	girl	girl	girl
Age	15	18	18	16	16	16	16	15
Family size	3	6	3	3	5	5	3	4
2 parents	Y	Y	N	Y	Y	Y	Y	Y
Parent's job	janitor	sales	housewife	technician	---	chef	clerk	Self-employed business
Home	public	private	public	Pubic	Public	private	private	private
Size-house	400	550	300	540	400	800	700	1000

In this paper, we isolate these participants' impression of the CBD in Hong Kong, namely the Central District[9], for examination. Central in Hong Kong (see pictures below) is probably one of the busiest commercial districts in the world.

Mui	Ray	Ki	Me
Central always known as the wealthy district and *only people with good knowledge can work here and they do not wear causal dress.* People over Central walk very fast and they produce a special image to me, people all fighting with time and always in a rush. I seldom visit Central as the things sold in Central are not suitable for me.	I seldom go to Central as the *district gives people a sense of suppression* with all these buildings and the pace of life there. Besides, the goods in these fancy shops in Central are out of our league.	Everybody in Central seems to be carrying the word "busy" on their face and they always move very fast. They cross the road fast and they eat fast. *They feel cold to me though. I guess they cannot afford to notice what is going on around* and even when an old lady trips and falls, they could not care less. The day I visited, there was actually an old lady trying to cross the road without following the light. Nobody seems to feel the need to stop her. *Everybody seems to be talking to themselves and Central is too cold for me*	Ever since I was a little girl, Central gives me a sense of "highness". The buildings are tall, rentals are high and there are a lot of high class shops. *I like Central as it is like a kaleidoscope, it is so colourful and full of different things.* When you walk into Central, you find it fascinating. I feel proud of HK for being a truly international financial hub. *I wish one day I will work here as I think only those who are talented and successful can work here.*

* sentences highlighted by author, not by the participants.

9 For a crash course in Central District, Hong Kong, please read : http://en.wikipedia.org/wiki/Central_and_Western_District

Picture 1. A busy day in Central, Hong Kong.

Picture 2. Central in Hong Kong is one of the important global financial centres.

These four young persons managed to provide elaborate description of their feelings and hence they were selected for the analysis. As we can see from the table, there is a distinct difference between how "Mui", "Ray", "Ki" and "Me" feel about Central. "Me" was the one more positive about the CBD and she apparently aspired to be one of the "Central people". "Mui" and "Ray" felt an inferior complexity in this district with "Mui" tended, relatively, to be more positive than "Ray". "Ki" was the most negative one when it comes to the feeling of CBD in Hong Kong to the extent that it almost repulsed her. She was also a bit sarcastic when it comes to the people in the CBD.

What is more interesting is the distinct difference in the family background between these young persons. The aspired one, "Me" comes from a relatively affluent family with a relative big house (at least by Hong Kong standard). "Mui" and "Ray" live in a relative small flat and "Ray" even refused to disclose his parents' occupation. While "Ki" lives in a comparatively larger flat, her parent is a chef, which by Hong Kong standard is not entirely a socially-aspired occupation. These three kids have at least one common feature in the family that they all have big family and hence per-capita space is relatively small. All of these kids seem to have very minimal personal contact/experience with the CBD in Hong Kong before this exercise. On the other hand, "Me" comes from a middle-class family of four with a per-capita space occupation of 250 square feet per family member, which is the most spacious among all participants. With this glimpse of their urban experience, it is not difficult to see that their personal feeling of a certain urban district is more or less shaped by their family background. The same business and financial district in the city can be either "cold" or "highness", depending on probably how they were brought up and how they value their surroundings. To investigate this issue from a different angle, we analyse their experience in another district in Hong Kong. This is the Shamshuipo district[10] which is a traditionally run-down residential area with retails mainly on second-hand electronic products and low-value garments. The following table is a recollections of "Mui", "Ray" and "Me" on their experience of walking around Shamshuipo (see pictures below).

Mui	1. Shumshuipo, to me is known as a very old district. It has lots of aged buildings there, and their designs are very traditional and simple. Apart from the retail shops, there are lots of many old shops located, you can find some old style food there, like biscuits and electrical shops. Compared to other districts, the goods sell in Shumshuipo always in a lower price, there are lots of street sellers over corners. Another street called "Ap Liu Street" is very famous in Shumshuipo, there are many electrical shops and mobile phone shops here, when people wants to get the electrical utilities, like wires, bulb, torches, they will immediately think of this street and get the thing here, as the price are cheaper than selling outside, but you must be very careful when you buy things in Ap Liu Street, as they famous of cheaper things and also the false or mock. Lots of people also cheated by the tricky shop owners. Apart from few business centres, Shumshuipo has lot of spaces used as residential areas, the buildings are very close and crowded, they all have one characteristic that the stairs are very narrow and dark. *When I was young, I think Shumshuipo is a bad district, as there are lots of triad society members and the hawkers there, and my father told me not to visit there. Now I would only say that Shumshuipo is a funny place, you can get the things which never think of it will have.* 2. Apart from the private car, the vehicles and trucks also land their goods by parking aside the road. Traffic jam isn't common in Shumshuipo. I think the Government should take more control of the parking system in this district, otherwise it will become worse and people cannot use the public facilities as they are all occupied by the vehicles and private cars.

[10] For a glimpse of Shamshuipo, please read : http://en.wikipedia.org/wiki/Sham_Shui_Po

	3. In Shumshuipo, you can easily find the elder people here, the reason is that the buildings over Shumshuipo are very old, and elder people don't want to move from the living district, also there are lots of elder homes (care centres) here, they provide the utilities services and living places for them. They normally chat or wait there for the whole day, I guess the reasons they act like this because they don't have anything to do as their sons and daughters wither go out for work or moved out from this estate, they feel alone and only stay in the park to get a comfortable area for themselves. It is very interesting that you will find more men than women in Shumshuipo, perhaps it is because of the "Men Street – Ap Liu Street", and the men usually shop there alone.
Ray	Shamshuipo is an old area, and long time ago it was an industrial/commercial area before it turned into today's a mainly residential district. It is now a rather large residential district with several large public housing estates. Hence, average income is rather low in Hong Kong standard. *However, with new redevelopment in the neighbourhood, there are several new high class residential projects coming up. I think this is because Shamshuipo has a rather improved public transportation network now that can support a larger population.* Though there are some parks and recreational facilities, because the district was planned long time ago, it is not that well-designed. Most buildings are old, and so are the residents, I think the aging process tops HK average. Though there are some new recreational centres such as the Dragon Centre, it is still limited by land area available. I guess that is why reclamation from sea is essential. There is a street in Shamshuipo where you find many interesting electrical products and parts which attract a lot of male customers. There is also a large second hand market for such products as mobile phones or computers. But recently, underground vice industries are emerging, making local residents rather uncomfortable. Computer centres are landmark in Shamshuipo, where you find a lot of people around, unfortunately, the triad society also use these locations for pirated CDs and CD ROMs retail. I come here very often as I love to shop around for computer and accessories. Though the district feels old, with some redevelopment projects going on in the neighbourhood, I think it will be better planned and things are changing.
Me	I have a feeling that Shamshuipo is a no-go zone. From the news and TV, I learn that there are quite a number of prostitutions working there as well as other underground activities. Hence, I don't come here that often. In fact, I think Shamshuipo is a rather popular district. When you get out of the MTR station, you find a lot of shops selling many different items, such as second hand mobile phones, DVD players, or even high-tech and interesting product such as surveillance devices, and of course there are two large computer centres. Lots of people going there are prices are low with a large variety of choice, though quality is not guaranteed. There are also some "theme" streets that can be found in this district. For example, there are streets with shops selling mainly export fashions, or man-made jewellery, or cloth, or electronic products. As most of these shops sell in wholesale manner, prices are low. That is why you always find buyers from some other countries, especially African countries. My mother used to purchase clothing here, especially red ones. Most of the buildings are old but they are not tall. I guess some of them have been turned into underground activities. I am sure there are problems in fire escapes, among others. My sole purpose of going to this district is to buy electronic products.

* sentences highlighted by author, not by the participants.

Picture 3. Typical dilapidated housing in Shamshuipo, Hong Kong.

Picture 4. Street market is the typical economic activity in Shamshuipo.

Relative to the CBD, all these three young persons recognise that Shamshuipo is a rather unattractive location. "Ray" in this case is more positive about the district, probably because he is a boy and there are more attractions for boys in this district. We notice that both "Ray" and "Mui" paid more attention to the problems in this district and recognised that improvement is undergoing and even suggested actions to be taken by the government. "Me" on the other hand, was rather negative and used the term "No-go zone" to describe it. Apparently, she was very much influenced by TV and media reports about the district until she actually visited the place and found it "popular". Once again, the relatively positive and negative feelings to some extent correlate to their differences in family backgrounds.

Stage Two : Impact of the Built Environment

Urban space is essential for young people to experience the path of growing up in the adult's world. Consider that most of community activities take place within the settings of urban space and within a physically built-environment shaped by urban planning and land use policies, this experience path of young people should be encouraged and taken more seriously. In most societies, young people are not regarded as legally equal to an adult and children are mostly treated as "future citizens" who should not be given a place in the "current" decision making process for urban space utilization. As result, children are often denied access to voice their needs in urban planning and land use policies which affect substantially their childhood development.

We hope to investigate the extent to which young people feel about the importance of the built environment, as shaped by the government urban land use policy. We conducted a series of large scale questionnaire surveys covering six secondary schools in various districts and one private tutoring school. A total of 3128 questionnaires were returned for analysis covering the youngsters in the age group of 13-18. 44% were male students and 56% were female. 82% of the respondents were born in Hong Kong while 15% and 3% were born in mainland China/Macau and other places respectively (see figure 1).

In general, we group the questions into different areas of possible impact imposed by the built environment on young people's development. These areas are the importance of public space in their neighbourhood; management of public space in their neighbourhood; the possible impact the built environment has on their own development ; young people's tendency to get acquainted with their neighbours and young people's interaction with their built environment.

Importance of Public Space

Participants were asked these four questions and the responses from them were collated as follows :

	Public open space is instrumental to fostering interaction among residents	Public open space is instrumental to fostering interaction among family members	Public open space provides a good alternative for families to spend holidays	Public open space induces residents to care about the community more
Strongly Agree/Agree	50%	41%	45%	32%
Neutral/No Opinion	32%	36%	30%	40%
Strongly Disagree/Disagree	18%	23%	25%	28%

Most of the young people who participated in this survey agreed that public space is important to increase interaction among family members and between neighbours in a community. This leads to the second question of how public space should be managed in a neighbourhood in order to serve this role better.

Management of Public Space

	Management should not control such healthy activities as cycling in public areas as this makes the neighbourhood more lively	More activities such as fairs/carnivals should be held in these area for residents' benefits
Strongly Agree/Agree	48%	54%
Neutral/No Opinion	28%	28%
Strongly Disagree/Disagree	24%	18%

From this table, it is also obvious that most young people agree that public space should be more inviting than controlled. Public space should be a forum for interaction, not a territory for the management staff to show off their authority, a path most management staff take especially in public housing estates in Hong Kong.

Impact of the Built Environment on Personal Development

	The design of the built environment in my neighbourhood affects my personal development	The design of the built environment in my neighbourhood always affects my mood	Watching adults interact with each other in my neighbourhood is important for my own personal development
Strongly Agree/Agree	44%	39%	33%
Neutral/No Opinion	36%	38%	46%
Strongly Disagree/Disagree	20%	23%	21%

As built environment as a term is relatively general to young people, we chose to study the impact of the "design" of the built environment. As expected, most young people we surveyed agreed that the design of the built environment in their neighbourhood affected both their personal development as well as their mood (figures 2-3). It is also interesting to note that when it came to the role of adults in their neighbourhood, not that many of them were certain about the effect (figure 4). This maybe due to a lack of use of public space by the adults ourselves (again, a problem of the management of space), or a more serious question that adults cannot exert good influence when we are behaving in public space. This may also explain why not too many of them are willing to stay in their own neighbourhoods during holidays (figure 5).

With this picture in mind, it is now interesting to examine the extent to which these young people make an effort to get acquainted with their neighbours. Figure 6 shows that 19% of the total respondents know most of the neighbourhoods in the community. 15% know about half, 32% know a few and 34% know only the next-door neighbour or nobody at all. If we break down the total number in terms of different types of residential neighbourhoods such as public housing estates, HOS estates and private sector, etc, we have the following :

	I know most neighbours in the estate/community	I know about half of neighbours	I know only a few neighbours	I know only the neighbour next-door/ I know nobody at all
Public Housing	17%	12%	33%	38%
HOS Flats	25%	22%	27%	26%
Private Housing	15%	15%	35%	35%
NDH/Others	25%	15%	26%	34%

Note : NDH means non-domestic housing units.

It is interesting to note that not all the young people living in government-subsidized flats are that aloof. In fact, from the above, HOS kids know more neighbours than their counterpart in the private housing community. This probably contradicts to other studies that usually government-assist housings create a more indifferent environment that young people do not tend to communicate with their neighbours. However, care must be taken here that HOS is a special creature of Hong Kong as this is half-way between welfare housing and the private market. HOS is Home Ownership Scheme that was started in Hong Kong in the 70's when property prices were lifting off and a lot of people who could not be qualified for welfare rental housing could not afford to buy a decent flat. To solve this problem, government grants land to a special organisation to build cheap housing for sale to a certain group of citizens within a fixed salary bracket. Hence, residents in the HOS projects are quite similar in terms of family background as compared to private housing communities. In this way, it may explain why young people find it easier to get acquainted with others in such a neighbourhood where everybody are similar in terms of socio-economic status.

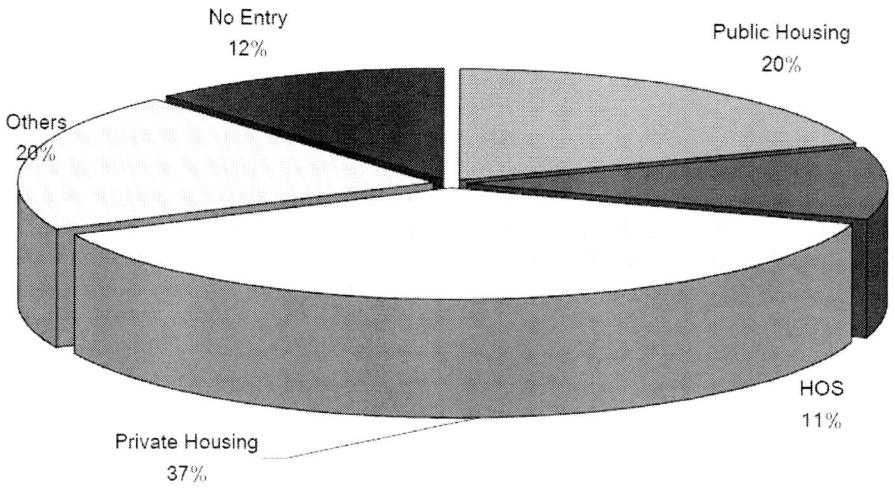

Figure 1. Profile of the respondent by living environment.

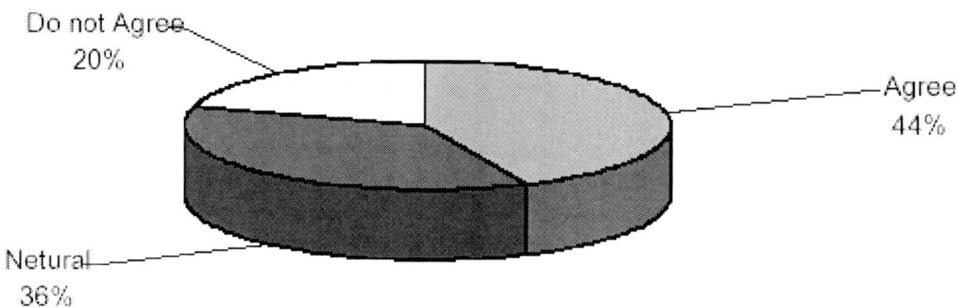

Figure 2. Whether the Built Environment affects personal development.

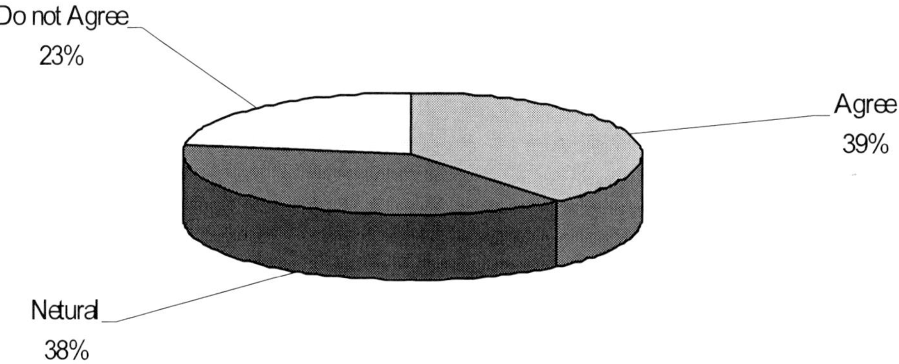

Figure 3. The design of the built environment always affects the mood of the young people.

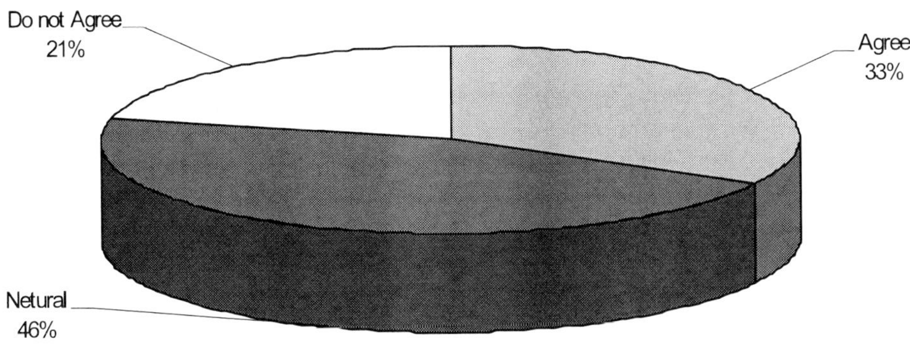

Figure 4. Watching adults interact in the neighbourhood is important.

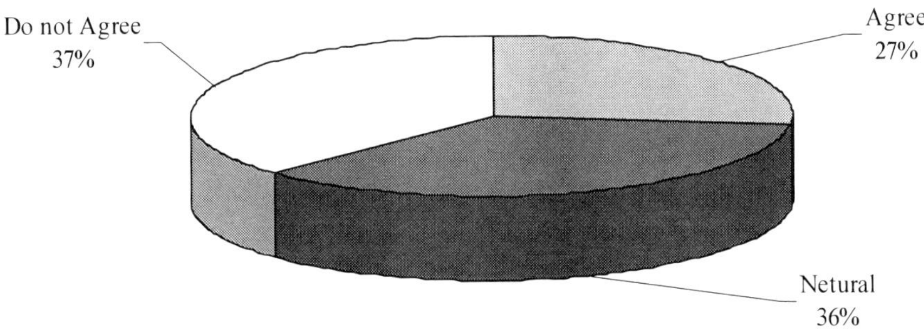

Figure 5. Young People like to stay in their neighbourhood during holidays.

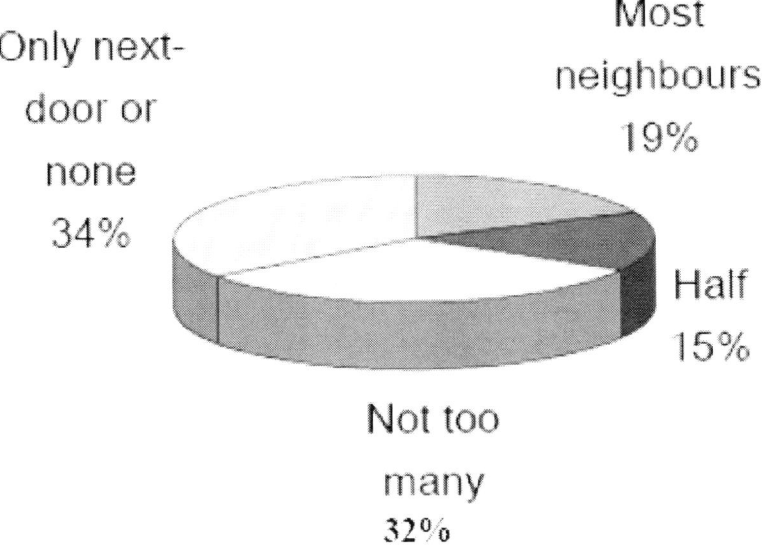

Figure 6. How well do young people get acquanted with their neoghbours ?

CONCLUSION

From above, we find that while young people experience our urban environment based on a set of values passed down by their family and their peer, the physical urban environment also impacts on how our young people behave and perceive their neighbourhood. With the analyses above, we list the following points as crucial areas where our government in Hong Kong can spend more time and effort in raising the awareness of such importance.

Policy Implications

1 From the large scale survey, it seems that a very large number of respondents do not have a strong opinion on the issues that affect them as observed in the relative high proportion of choosing neutral in the survey. These are probably problems in our secondary education training that students are more examination-oriented rather than analysis-oriented.
2 The government should encourage young people to participate more in the formulation of urban land use and planning policies so that it enhances their own sense of belonging. This is because the physical (built) environment is where young people can feel the existence of the society more easily and readily.
3 The artificially-built environment can to a certain extent affect young people's personal development and mood. The government should therefore focus on how we utilize a positive and amiable built environment so that young people can experience more easily the adult's (real) world and, hence a much more healthy way of growing up.
4 The government should not just concentrate on environmental friendly technology and ignore the human side of the environment , ie. how do people, especially young people interact with the environment and how would a much carefully forged urban land policy benefit our next generation.
5 The government should come to realize that good land use and planning policy practice that maximize the benefits of most citizens will achieve not only economic goals, but also some other social objectives. For instance, in the land sale policy, should more larger sites be sold so that communities, instead of just housing, can be built ?
6 The government should open up more channels to receive views from young people on urban land issues

To reiterate our focus here, land use policies help shape our physical environment, which is likely to impact on our future generation as land and infrastructure developments take a long time for completion. There is a need for a more organised effort to bring young people to this awareness so that their needs can be reflected in the formulation of urban land policy, so that a more sustainable environment can be created.

REFERENCES

Berg, M. and Medrich, E. (1980). Children in four neighborhoods. *Environment and Behavior*, 12 (3), 320 – 348.

Blakeley, Kim, (1994), "Parents' Conceptions of Social Dangers to Children in the Urban Environment," *Children's Environments*, Vol.11, 1994, pp.16-25

Camstra, R. (1997). *Growing up in a changing urban landscape.* Assen: Van Gorcum.

Cairney, J. (2005). Housing tenure and psychological well-being during adolescence. *Environment and Behavior*, 37 (4), 552 – 564.

Duncan, G. and Raudenbush, S. (1999), "Assessing the effects of context in studies of child and youth development," *Educational Psychology*, 34 (1), 29-41

Gutenschwager, Gerald (1995), "Ekistic environment and influences on the child," *Ekistics* , Vol. 62, Issue 373-375, pp289-293

Jacobs, Jane (1964), *The Death and Life of Great American Cities*, Harmondsworth : Penguin Books

Eekelaar, J. (1986), "The Emergence of Children's Rights," *Oxford Journal of Legal Studies*, Vol.6, 1986, pp.161-182

Evans, G. W., Saegert, S. and Harris, R. (2001). Residential density and psychological health among children in low-income families. *Environment and Behavior*, 33 (2), 165 – 180.

Gehl, J. (1996). *Life between Buildings.* Copenhagen: Arkitektens Forlag.

Hart, R.A (1997), *Children's Participation: The Theory and Practice of Involving Young Citizens in Community Development and Environmental Care*, London : Earthscan

Lasch, C. (1995), *The Revolt of the Elites and the betrayal of Democracy*, New York : W.W. Norton

Lynch, Kevin (1977), *Growing Up in Cities*, London : MIT Press

Malone, K. (2001), *"Exposing Intolerance and Exclusion and Building Communities of Difference,"*, Keynote Address, Youth Coalition Symposium "Youth and Public Space", Opening of Youth Week, National Museum, Canberra, April 8, 2002

Massey, Douglas (2001), "The Prodigal Paradigm Returns : Ecology Comes Back to Sociology" in Booth, Alan and Crouter, Ann C. (2001) (ed.) *Does It Take a Village ? Community Effects on Children, Adolescents, and Families*, Mahwah, NJ : Lawrence Erlbaum Associates Publishers

Maxwell, L. E. (2003). Home and School Density Effects on Elementary School Children: The Role of Spatial Density. *Environment and Behavior*, 35 (4), 566 – 578.

Michelson, W. and Levine, S. (1979). *Child in the City: Changes and Challenges.* Toronto: University of Toronto Press.

Piaget, Jean (1952), *The Origins of Intelligence in Children*, New York : International Universities Press

Sampson, Robert J.(2001), "How do Communities Undergrid or Undermine Human Development ? Relevant Contexts and Social Mechanisms" in Booth, Alan and Crouter, Ann C. (2001) (ed.) *Does It Take a Village ? Community Effects on Children, Adolescents, and Families*, Mahwah, NJ : Lawrence Erlbaum Associates Publishers

Samson, R. , Raudenbush, S. and Earls, F. (1997), "Neighbourhood and violent crime : A multilevel study of collective efficacy," *Science*, 277, 918-924

Simpson, Brian, (1997), "Towards the Participation of Children and Young People in Urban Planning and Design," *Urban Studies*, Vol.34, Nos. 5-6, 1997, pp.907-925

Torrell, G. (1990), "Children's Conception of Large Scale Environments," *Goteborg Psychological Reports*, 20 (2)

Valentine, Gill, (1996), "Children Should be Seen and Not Heard : The Production and Transgression of Adults' Public Space," *Urban Geography*, Vol.17, No. 3, 1996, pp.205-220

Wilson, W.J. (1987), *The Truly Disadvantaged : The inner city, the underclass, and public policy*, Chicago : University of Chicago Press

In: Land Use Policy
Editors: A. C. Denman and O. M. Penrod

ISBN: 978-1-60741-435-3

Chapter 7

ANALYZING URBANIZATION, SPATIAL AND TEMPORAL LAND USE/LAND COVER CHANGE OF SARIYER DISTRICT, ISTANBUL, TURKEY

Sedat Keleş[1]**, Fatih Sivrikaya***[2]**, Günay Çakır***[3]**,***
Cemil Ün[4]**, Emin Zeki Başkent***[5] **and Selahattin Köse***[6]*

[1] Karadeniz Technical University,
Faculty of Forestry, 61080, Trabzon, Turkey
[2] Karadeniz Technical University, Faculty of Forestry,
61080, Trabzon, Turkey
[3] Düzce University, Faculty of Forestry, Düzce, Turkey
[4] General Directorate of Forestry, Department of Forest
Administration and Planning, Ankara, Turkey
[5] Karadeniz Technical University, Faculty of Forestry,
61080, Trabzon, Turkey
[6] Karadeniz Technical University, Faculty of Forestry,
61080, Trabzon, Turkey

ABSTRACT

Spatiotemporal analysis of land use/land cover is crucial in formulating an appropriate set of actions in landscape management and in developing appropriate land use policies. On the other hand, understanding the interaction between landscape pattern and land use policy is important to reveal the detrimental consequences of land use change on soil and water quality, biodiversity, and climatic systems. This study focuses on the spatial and temporal pattern analysis of land use/land cover change in the Sarıyer

* Email: skeles@ktu.edu.tr, Tel:+90 462 377 28 99, Fax: +90 462 325 7499
* Email: fatihs@ktu.edu.tr, Tel:+90 462 377 37 34, Fax: +90 462 325 7499
* Email: gcakir@ktu.edu.tr, Tel:+90 462 377 37 34, Fax: +90 462 325 7499
* Email: cemilun@ogm.gov.tr, Tel: +90 505 771 10 19
* Email: baskent@ktu.edu.tr, Tel:+90 462 377 28 63, Fax: +90 462 325 7499
* Email: skose@ktu.edu.tr, Tel:+90 462 377 28 63, Fax: +90 462 325 7499

Forest Planning Unit surrounding the district of Sarıyer in a megacity of Istanbul, Turkey. The spatio-temporal pattern of the study area was evaluated with Geographical Information System and FRAGSTATS to assess the change over 31 years. As a result of population increase and urbanization, the Sarıyer district expanded very fast and many changes in land use/land covers between 1971 and 2002 were realized. As an overall change, there was a net decrease of 1243 ha in total forested areas compared to a net increase of 1331 ha in settlement areas. However, both forest areas with full crown closure and regenerated or young forest areas increased due mainly to reforestation of degraded forests and agricultural areas and the conversion of coppice forests to high forests. In terms of spatial configuration, analysis of the metrics revealed that landscape structure in Sarıyer forest planning unit changed substantially over the 31-year study period, resulting in fragmentation of the landscape as indicated by the higher number of large patches and the smaller mean patch sizes. In conclusion, understanding of the factors affecting the land use/land cover is increasingly important for the design and planning of urban areas and the sustainable management of natural resources.

Keywords: Land use/land cover change; Forest dynamics; Urbanization; Geographical Information System.

1. INTRODUCTION

During the last centuries, the forest cover was altered drastically with increasing population pressure, agricultural activities and industrialization. The human impacts on those lands are overwhelming as the growth of the population is directly linked to urbanization, principle cause for depletion of nearby forest ecosystems or agricultural areas. On the other hand, technological, institutional and natural resource policy forces also play an important role in changing land use patterns (Wear *et al.* 1996, Rao and Pant 2001, Alphan 2003). For those reasons, land use/land cover type changes has been a major topic in natural resource management because understanding the historical dynamics, composition, and environmental distribution of land use and forest landscapes provides a context for monitoring changes, describing trends, and establishing reference conditions (Kennedy and Spies 2004).

Over the past few decades, the topic of land use/land cover change has become very important particularly in developing countries. Land-use and land cover change can play an important role in environmental planning and contribute to global change (Chen *et al.* 2001, Kennedy and Spies 2004, Wakeel 2005). Changes in land use/land cover have important effects on biodiversity, soil conservation, water quantity and quality, and world climate (Iida and Nakashizuka 1995, Johnson *et al.* 1997, Chen *et al.* 2001, Dupouey *et al.* 2002, Upadhyay *et al.* 2005, Liu *et al.* 2006). In addition to area coverage, the spatial pattern of land use patches is an important characteristic for evaluating the processes and effects of land use change (Gautam *et al.* 2003, Baskent and Jordan 1995). Spatial structure of forest landscape refers to the size, shape, numbers, and spatial relationship of or configurations of patches as is also critical to ecosystem functioning and habitat quality (Matsushita *et al.* 2006, Baskent and Jordan 1995).

Sustainable management and planning of the natural resources requires spatially accurate and timely information on land use change and their patterns. Determining as well as understanding the problems arising from population growth is very important, especially for crowded areas which have been undergoing rapid changes. Moreover, detection of land use changes provides urban planners and decision makers with essential information about past and current states of development and the nature of changes that have occurred (Musaoglu *et al.* 2005, Musaoglu *et al.* 2006). In this context, timely and reliable data on land use/and cover may facilitate the formation of integrated resource management policies. Good monitoring systems must be introduced to better understand the nature of land use/land cover changes and urbanization (Alphan 2003).

There are various methods that can be used in the collection, analysis and presentation of natural resources data. The use of remote sensing (RS) and geographic information system (GIS) technologies can greatly facilitate the process. Repeated satellite images and aerial photographs are useful for both visual assessments of natural resources dynamics occurring at a particular time and space as well as quantitative evaluation of land use/land cover changes overtime (Gautam *et al.* 2003). Applications of RS and GIS to illustrate spatial and temporal changes in land use/land cover over time have been reported by many investigators (Turner and Ruscher 1988, Iverson *et al.* 1989, Ripple *et al.* 1991, Fioralla and Riple 1993; Spies et al., 1994; Verburg et al., 1999; Kammerbauer and Ardon, 1999; Luque, 2000, Kennedy and Spies 2004, Wakeel *et al.* 2005, Keleş *et al.* 2007, Sivrikaya *et al.* 2007). These studies documented the spatial and temporal land use/land cover changes as well as focusing the factors affecting these processes. On the other hand, complex relationships between environmental, ecological, economic and social factors that induce changes and degradations of land use/land cover should be studied and documented for sustainable development and management of natural resources.

This study analyses the spatial and temporal pattern of land use/land cover change in a forest management area surrounding the strict of Sarıyer in Istanbul during 1971-2002 period based on forest stand map generated with GIS and FRAGSTATS- a spatial statistics program. The region is notable because of its high urbanization and environmental heterogeneity. The study psrticulary focuses on detecting and documenting changes in major land cover from 1971 to 2002. As well, this study analyses patterns of changes in landscape during the period using a few important landscape metrics measuring landscape structure and fragmentation.

2. Methods

2.1. The Study Area

The study area surrounding the Sarıyer district is a typical forest management unit that covers 10,113 ha. It is situated in the Europe side of Istanbul in northwestern part of Turkey (661000-678000 E, 4555000-4570000 N, UTM ED 50 datum Zone 35N) and characterized by a dominantly smooth terrain. The case study area is delimited by the Black Sea in the north, a narrow body of water called Bosphorus or the Istanbul Straits in the west, by the district of Eyüp in the east and by the district of Şişli in the south. Sarıyer has good location for Istanbul's natural life sources such as forests, rivers, green areas, and sand dune in the Kilyos region of the Black Sea coast. The prevalent climate regime is of Black Sea-Mediterranean climate characterized by a mild winter and a cool summer and rainy almost all season. The average annual precipitation is 693.7 mm, the average annual temperature is 14.3

°C and the average relative humidity is 73%. The vegetation type is mainly forest and the dominant tree species of the vegetation are *Quercus sp., Pinus nigra* Arnold., *Castanea sativa* Mill. and, *Pinus pinea* L., *Pinus pinaster* Aiton. in reforestation areas. In the study area, there are one important plant area (IPA) named Kilyos sand dune ecosystem designated by WWF in 2003 (Özhatay *et al.* 2003). The geographic location of the study area is shown in figure 1.

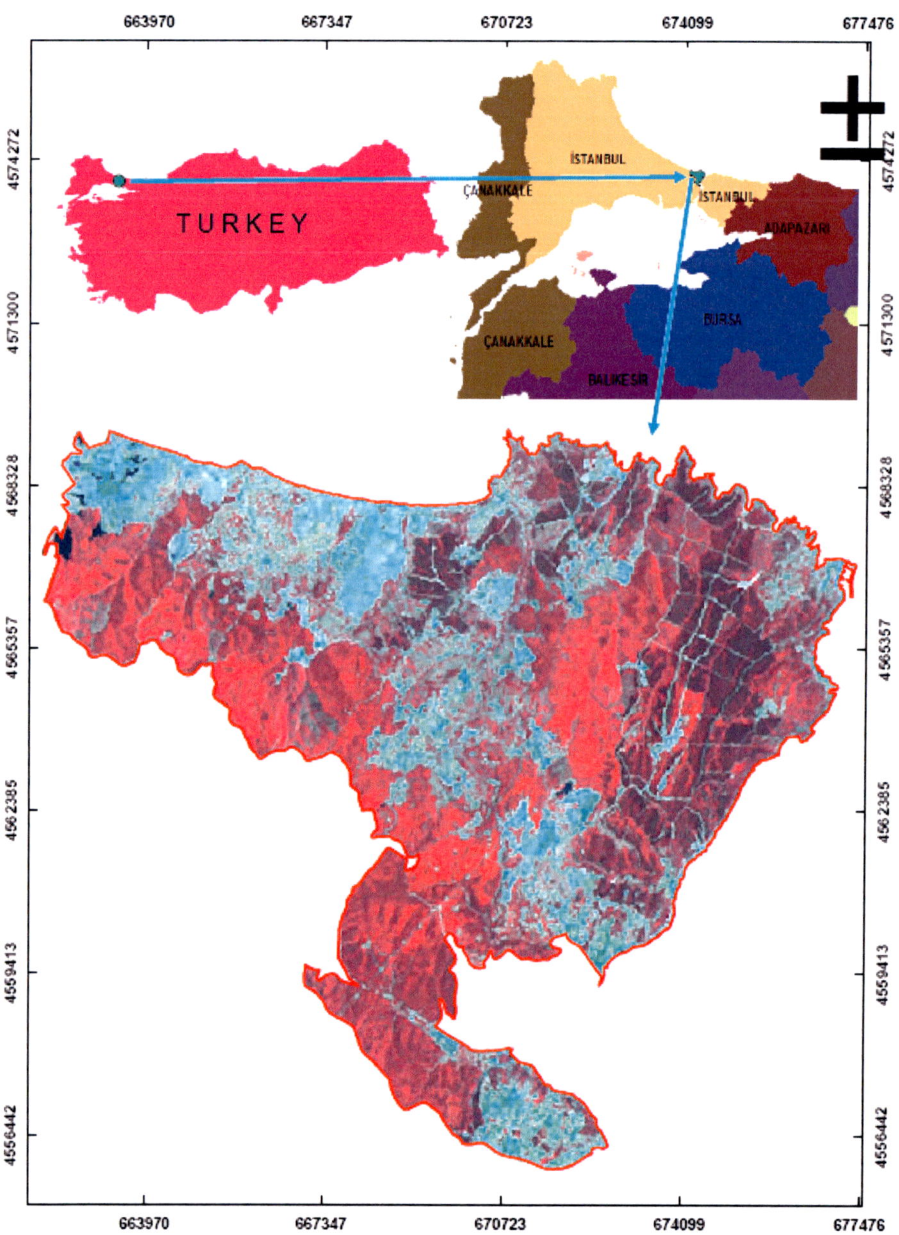

Figure 1. The geographic location of the study area surrounded with solid red lines.

2.2. Database Development

The spatial database, developed as part of this study, consisted of forest cover type map derived from the RS data and field survey in 2001. Remotely sensed data of the study area were obtained from the General Directorate of Forestry (GDF) for the years 1971 (scale 1:22 000 and panchromatic aerial photographs) and 2001 (1:15000 color infrared aerial photographs). Forest stand maps, generated through aerial photographs and field survey, in 1971 and 2002 were qualified with the database of GDF. The paper maps were digitized and processed using GIS (ArcGIS 9.0) with a maximum root mean square (RMS) error under 10 m. and the associated attribute data were punched into the computer to create the spatial database of the area. The following basic categories of land cover were identified from each forest stand map: (1) conifer forest (CF), (2) broadleaf forest (BF), (3) mixed forest (MF), (4) degraded forest (DF), (5) coppice forest (CoF), (6) forest openings (FO), (7) private forest (PF), (8) Settlement (S), (9) agriculture (A), (10) water (W), and (11) other (O, includes sandy and rocky areas).

The transitions were also evaluated using periodic results of forest management plans. The land use polygon themes for 1971 and 2002 were overlaid and the area converted from each of the classes to any of the other classes was computed. The land use, development stage and crown closure polygon themes for 1971 and 2002 were analysed with the same methods. The database consisted of stand types, characterised by species type, crown closure and development stages. Classification of crown closures and development stages in Turkey is given in table 1. However, it is possible to see some mixed development stages in a forest, such as development stage "bc" meaning that the stand has both "b" and "c" development stages dominated by the volume of development stage "b".

Table 1. Classification of crown closures and development stages

Crown Closure Types	Criteria (% cover)	Development Stages	Criteria (average dbh)
0	Regenerated areas	a (regenerated)	< 8 cm
Degraded forest	0-10%	b (young)	8 – 19.9 cm
1 (low coverage)	11%-40%	c (mature)	20 – 35.9 cm
2 (medium coverage)	41%-70%	d (over mature)	>36 cm
3 (full coverage)	>71%		

The spatial dynamics of the forest landscape refers to the temporal change in size, number, shape, adjacency and the proximity of patches in a landscape. We used some metrics or measurements as proxy to quantify and spatially analysis the change in spatial structure as demonstrated by Başkent and Jordan (1995) and McGarigal and Marks (1995); (a) CA; (b) NP; (c) MPS; (d) PERCLAND; (e) LPI; (f) PD; and (g) AWMSI. Specifically, we used FRAGSTATS (McGarigal and Marks 1995) program to quantify landscape structure of Sarıyer forest management unit for each of the land use classes. Brief definitions of the selected metrics are listed in table 2. These landscape pattern metrics involve the qualitative and quantitative measurements that expressed the characteristics of the landscape as a whole (Abdullah and Nakagoshi 2006). In order to study forest fragmentation processes, the land cover maps for 1971 and 2002 were used to calculate the values of spatial landscape metrics with FRAGSTATS (McGarigal *et al.* 2002) for each of the land use class.

Table 2. Landscape metrics used in this study and their brief definitions

Landscape metrics(unit)	Description
CA (ha)	Class area; sum of areas of all patches belonging to a given class, in map units
NP	Number of patches
MPS (ha)	Mean patch size; the average patch size within a particular class
PERCLAND (%)	Percent of landscape
LPI (%)	Largest patch index; percentage of the landscape comprised by the largest patch
PD	Patch density; number of patches per 100 ha
AWMSI	Area-weighted mean shape index, the average perimeter to area ration for a class, weighted by the size of its patches

3. RESULTS

3.1. Changes and Transitions among Land Use/Land Cover Types

Changes in land use/land cover changes were analyzed using the area statistics (table 3) derived from land cover maps of 1971 and 2002 (figure 2). According to the digitized stand type maps from forest management plans between 1971 and 2002, total forested area decreased from 8160 (80.7 % of the study area) ha to 6917 (68.4 % of the study area) ha, with a net loss of 1243 ha. Conifer forest, broadleaf forest and mixed forest increased 1463, 144 and 2536 ha, respectively due mainly to the conversion of coppice forest into high forest.. There was a net decline of 186 ha in agricultural areas as opposed to a net increase of 1331 ha in settlement area. As a good indicator of forest landscape development, degraded forest decreased 2185 ha during the period.

Besides analyzing the changes in the amount of land use/land cover types, the temporal transitions among land use/land cover types were also evaluated to see the inter-temporal dynamics of land use/land cover types. The transitions were evaluated using periodic results of historical forest stand type maps between 1971 and 2002 (table 4).

A broad level analysis showed that about 1347 ha forest areas changed into non-forest areas while 331 ha non-forest areas changed into forest areas. A crucial point here is that 903 ha forest areas converted to settlement area. Other transitions among forest cover types between 1971 and 2002 could be illustrated as; 1254 ha from degraded forest to conifer forest, 2192 ha from coppice forest to mixed forest and 762 ha from private forest and agriculture to settlement. Furthermore, all coppice forests were converted to other forest covers and land cover types due to the recently initiated conversion policy efforts of Turkish Forest Services.

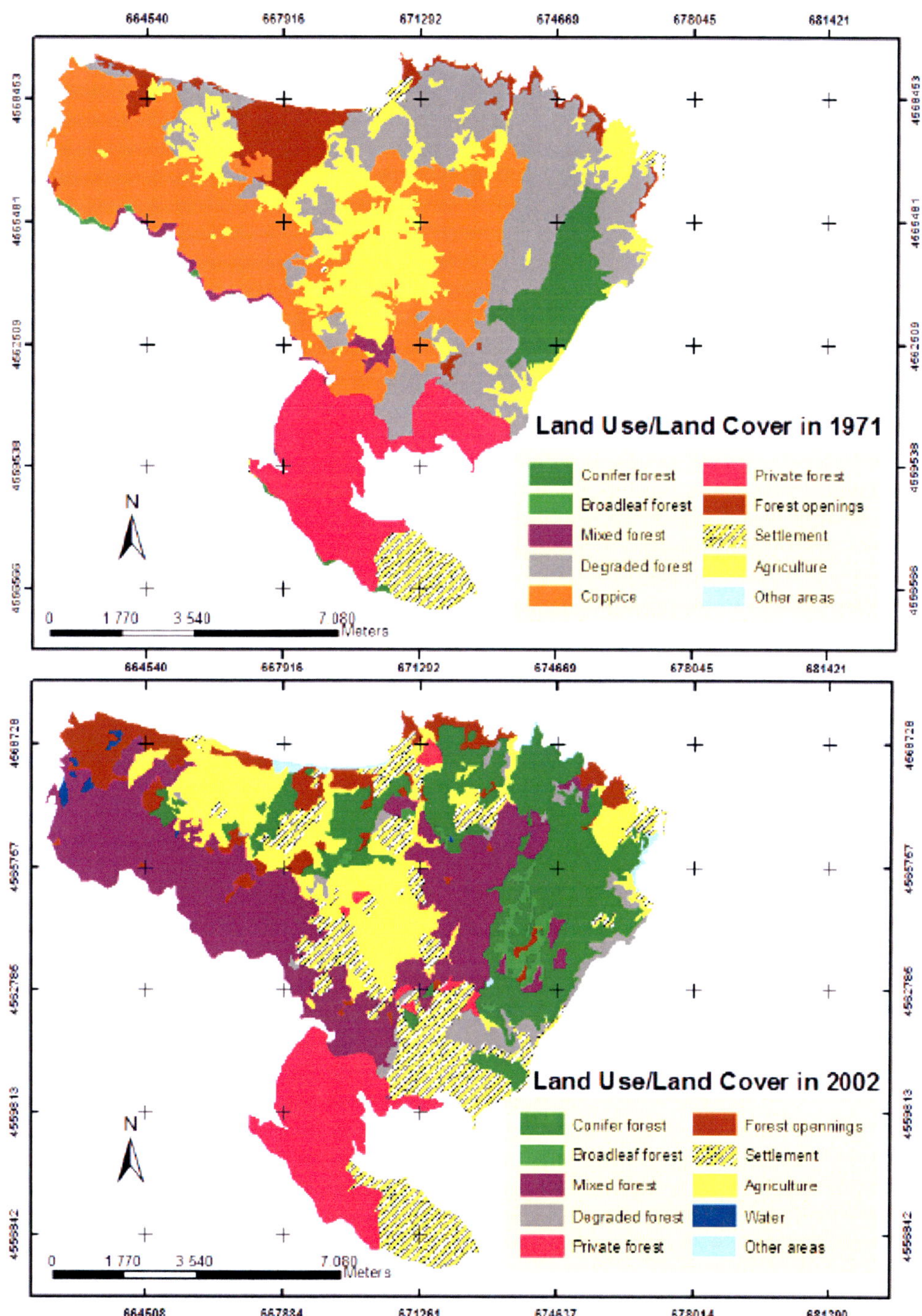

Figure 2. Land use and land cover of the study area over 1971-2002.

Table 3. Evolution of selected landscape variables in the study area from 1971 to 2002

Year	1971		2002	
Total Area	ha	%	ha	%
Conifer forest	561.8	5.6	2024.7	20.0
Broadleaf forest	23.0	0.2	166.9	1.7
Mixed forest	114.1	1.1	2650.1	26.2
Degraded forest	2504.9	24.8	319.9	3.2
Coppice forest	3080.3	30.5	-	-
Forest openings	600.5	5.9	722.2	7.1
Private Forest	1275.7	12.6	1033.7	10.2
Settlement	377.9	3.7	1709.3	16.9
Agriculture	1574.8	15.6	1388.3	13.7
Water	-	-	29.8	0.3
Other	-	-	68.1	0.7
Total	10 113	100	10 113	100

Table 4. Land use and land cover changes during the study period

Changed from	Changed to	Change during
		1971-2002
Conifer forest	Broadleaf forest	45.1
	Mixed forest	47.5
	Degraded forest	32.3
	Forest openings	9.5
	Private forest	7.7
	Settlement	9.5
	Agriculture	0.7
	Other	0.7
Broadleaf forest	Mixed forest	22.8
	Private forest	0.2
Mixed forest	Private forest	2.4
	Forest openings	2.0
	Agriculture	2.2
	Settlement	13.0

Table 4. (Continued).

Changed from	Changed to	Change during
Degraded forest	Conifer forest	1253.9
	Broadleaf forest	102.7
	Mixed forest	212.0
	Forest openings	176.6
	Private forest	43.1
	Settlement	272.7
	Water	1.7
	Other	12.5
Coppice forest	Conifer forest	145.5
	Broadleaf forest	11.0
	Mixed forest	2192.0
	Degraded forest	31.4
	Forest openings	269.2
	Private forest	30.3
	Agriculture	188.8
	Settlement	184.1
	Water	28.1
Forest openings	Conifer forest	83.2
	Broadleaf forest	0.2
	Mixed forest	19.5
	Degraded forest	7.3
	Private forest	0.2
	Agriculture	159.8
	Settlement	100.4
	Other	49.4
Private forest	Conifer forest	2.1
	Mixed forest	7.4
	Degraded forest	1.2
	Settlement	323.4
Settlement	Forest openings	1.1
	Private forest	5.2
	Agriculture	0.2
	Other	4.5
Agriculture	Conifer forest	131.1

Table 4. (Continued).

Changed from	Changed to	Change during
	Broadleaf forest	7.9
	Mixed forest	54.5
	Degraded forest	44.8
	Forest openings	83.2
	Private forest	3.2
	Settlement	439.2
	Other	1.0

Crown closure is also evaluated to see and analyze changes in forest ecosystem structure. Between 1971 and 2002, stands with the crown closure of 3 (71 %-100 %) increased 3348 ha while stands with the crown closure of 0 (0 %-10 %) increased 920 ha. As for the temporal transitions among the crown closures of forest ecosystem over the period, 59 ha changed from low crown closure to full covered stands and 21 ha from medium closure to full covered stands (table 6). The striking point here is that 1440 ha degraded forest and 1648 coppice forest changed to full crown closure forest areas with reforestation of degraded forests and the conversion of coppice forests to high forests.

Development stages of forests were analyzed to see the changes in the quality of forest ecosystem structure (table 7). Between 1971 and 2002, regenerated areas (a) increased 1128 ha, ab increased 1836 ha, b increased 723 ha, bc increased 29 ha, c increased 489 ha. On the other hand, over mature forests were regenerated as they reached to rotation age. As for the transition among development stages between 1971 and 2002, table 8 indicates that 127 ha of stands with development stage a changed to ab, 181 ha from a to b and 57 ha from over mature forest to regenerated forests. As well, 3656 ha degraded and coppice forests changed into young forests because of reforestation and regeneration activities.

Table 5. The change in crown closures of forest between 1971 and 2002

Year	1971		2002		Differences (+/-)	
Crown closure	ha	%	ha	%	(ha)	%
0 (Regenerated areas)			919.7	9.1	-919.7	-9.1
1 (low coverage, 11%-40%)	80.3	0.8			80.3	0.8
2 (medium coverage, 41%-70%)	44.7	0.4			44.7	0.4
3 (full coverage, >71%)	573.9	5.7	3921.9	38.8	-3348	-33.1
Degraded Forest	2504.9	24.8	320.0	3.2	2184.9	21.6
Coppice Forest	3080.3	30.5			3080.3	30.5
Forest Openings	600.5	5.9	722.2	7.1	-121.7	-1.2

Table 5. (Continued)

Year	1971		2002		Differences (+/-)	
Crown closure	ha	%	ha	%	(ha)	%
Private Forest	1275.7	12.6	1033.7	10.2	242	2.4
Agriculture	1574.8	15.6	1388.3	13.7	186.5	1.8
Settlements	377.9	3.7	1709.3	16.9	-1331.4	-13.2
Water			29.8	0.3	-29.8	-0.3
Other			68.1	0.7	-68.1	-0.7
Total	10 113	100	10 113	100	10 113	0.0

Table 6. Transitions among crown closures between 1971 and 2002

CLASS		Crown Closure in 2002										
		0	1	2	3	DF	FO	PF	A	S	W	O
Crown Closure in 1971	0											
	1	4.2			58.7		2.0	0.2	2.2	13.0		
	2	23.9			20.8							
	3	0.7			510.5	32.3	9.5	10.0	0.7	9.5		0.7
	DF	128.3			1440.2	203.0	176.6	43.1	226.7	272.7	1.7	12.5
	CoF	700.0			1648.4	31.4	269.2	30.3	188.8	184.1	28.1	
	FO	41.0			61.9	7.3	180.5	0.2	159.8	100.4		49.4
	PF	0.2			9.3	1.2		941.6		323.4		
	A	21.4			172.1	44.8	83.2	3.2	809.9	439.2		1.0
	S						1.1	5.2	0.2	366.9		4.5

Table 7. The change in development stages of forest between 1971 and 2002

Year	1971		2002		Differences (+/-)	
Development stages	Area (ha)	%	Area (ha)	%	Area (ha)	%
a (regenerated, < 8 cm)	630.1	6.2	1757.6	17.4	1127.5	11.1
ab			1835.6	18.2	1835.6	18.2
b (young, 8 – 19.9 cm)	7.3	0.1	729.8	7.2	722.5	7.1
bc			29.4	0.3	29.4	0.3
bd	0.8	0.0			-0.8	0.0
c (mature, 20 – 35.9 cm)	0.5	0.0	489.2	4.8	488.7	4.8
ca	3.1	0.0			-3.1	0.0

Table 7. (Continued).

Year	1971		2002		Differences (+/-)	
d (overmature, >36 cm)	47.0	0.5			-47	-0.5
da	1.7	0.0			-1.7	0.0
db	8.4	0.1			-8.4	-0.1
Degraded Forest (DF)	2504.9	24.8	320.0	3.2	-2184.9	-21.6
Coppice Forest (CoF)	3080.3	30.5			-3080.3	-30.5
Forest Openings (FO)	600.5	5.9	722.2	7.1	121.7	1.2
Private Forest (PF)	1275.7	12.6	1033.7	10.2	-242	-2.4
Agriculture (A)	1574.8	15.6	1388.3	13.7	-186.5	-1.8
Settlements (S)	377.9	3.7	1709.3	16.9	1331.4	13.2
Water (W)			29.8	0.3	29.8	0.3
Other (O)			68.1	0.7	68.1	0.7
Total	10 113	100	10 113	100	10113	0.0

3.2. Spatial Analysis of the Change in Spatial Forest Structure

In the Sarıyer FPU, the total number of forest fragments increased from 127 to 144 (13%) during the 31-year period as all patch types were taken into account (table 9). Mean forest patch size (MPS) decreased from 79.6 ha in 1971 to 70.2 ha in 2001. This rapid decline in mean patch size was associated with an increase in the patch density (PD) during a 31 year period (from 1.26 to 1.42). The LPI increased from 19.4% to 24.6%. Patch shape changed to more regular one (close to circle with straight lines, no meandering) and variant of patch size and patch density increased. Mixed forest, highly variable patch type, increased from 114 ha in 1971 to 2650 ha in 2002. The LPI in this class increased from 0.5% in 1971 to 24.6% in 2001, reflecting that mixed forest is dominant in the Sarıyer FPU. In the mixed forest class, the increases in the LPI (from 0.5 to 24.6 %) and the MPS (from 6.3 to 265 ha) indicate that this class became more clumped as a consequence of gains from both the coppice forests and degraded classes. By 1971, 11% of the forest area was concentrated in small patches between 0 and 100 ha; the remaining forest area occurred in isolated patches of larger than 100 ha, nine patches were bigger than 100 ha. In 2002, 17% of the forest area occurred in patches of less than 100 ha, eight patches larger than 5000 ha existed.

Table 8. Transitions among development stages between 1971 and 2002

CLASS		Development Stages in 2002											
		a	ab	b	bc	c	DF	FO	PF	A	S	W	O
Developing Stages in 1971	a	21.5	126.9	181.4	21.3	198.8	32.3	11.5	10.2	2.9	22.5		0.7
	b	5.2	2.1										
	bd	0.8											
	c		0.5										
	ca	3.2											
	d	35.9	11.1										
	da	1.7											
	db	5.1	3.3										
	DF	304.7	556.1	458.2	2.3	247.3	203.0	176.6	43.1	226.7	272.7	1.7	12.5
	CoF	1246.9	1063.4	26.9	4.9	6.3	31.4	269.2	30.3	188.8	184.1	28.1	
	FO	92.7	5.5	4.4		0.3	7.3	180.5	0.2	159.8	100.4		49.4
	PF	0.2	9.3				1.2		941.6		323.4		
	A	39.7	57.6	59.0	0.8	36.4	44.8	83.2	3.2	809.9	439.2		1.0
	S							1.1	5.2	0.2	366.9		4.5

Table 9. Change of Landscape Pattern in Sarıyer Forest Planning Unit

Forest Cover Type	CA		NP		MPS		PD		PERCLAND		LPI		AWMSI	
	1971	2002	1971	2002	1971	2002	1971	2002	1971	2002	1971	2002	1971	2002
CF	561.9	2024.7	10	19	56.2	106.6	0.10	0.19	5.6	20.0	5.4	12.4	1.9	4.1
BF	23.0	166.9	7	7	3.3	23.8	0.07	0.07	0.2	1.7	0.2	1.3	2.1	3.8
MF	114.1	2650.1	18	10	6.3	265.0	0.18	0.10	1.1	26.2	0.5	24.6	2.1	4.9
DF	2504.9	319.9	18	17	139.2	18.8	0.18	0.17	24.8	3.2	15.1	1.0	4.0	2.2
CoF	3080.3		16		192.5		0.16		30.5		19.4		3.4	
FO	600.5	722.2	16	31	37.5	23.3	0.16	0.31	5.9	7.1	3.8	2.7	2.3	2.1
PF	1275.7	1033.7	1	8	1275.7	129.2	0.01	0.08	12.6	10.2	12.6	9.5	2.4	2.1
S	377.9	1709.3	6	18	63.0	95.0	0.06	0.18	3.7	16.9	3.2	5.7	1.3	2.4
A	1574.8	1388.3	34	20	46.3	69.4	0.34	0.20	15.6	13.7	9.5	5.4	4.8	3.0
W		29.8		8		3.7		0.08		0.3		0.1		1.4
O	0.0	68.1	1	6	0.0	11.4	0.01	0.06	0.0	0.7	0.0	0.3	1.4	3.0
Total	10 113	10 113	127	144	79.6	70.2	1.26	1.42	100.0	100.0	19.4	24.6	3.4	3.4

3.3. Demographic Development

Demographic and socio-economic conditions play an important role in the land use/land cover changes. Istanbul is one of the oldest and crowded cities in the world, strategically located in a crucial location between two important continents, Asia and Europe. It is ranked as the 22nd mega city among the 100 largest metropolitan areas of the world by population (Musaoglu *et al.* 2005, Musaoglu *et al.* 2006). The study area of Sarıyer is also a big and important district in Istanbul. Demographic dynamics of Sarıyer are mostly related to the immigrant from the poor regions of Turkey, with the increased population between 1971 and 2002 because of attractive characteristics. Table 10 shows that the population of Sarıyer has increased over 30 years. Urban population of Sarıyer increased from 62 957in 1970 to 219 032 in 2000, its rural population also increased from 4 945 in 1970 to 23 511 in 2000.

Table 10. Demographic change in Sarıyer forest planning unit between 1971 and 2002

Years	Urban	Rural	Total	Urban (%)	Rural (%)
1970	62 957	4945	67 902	92.7	7.3
1975	79 329	5933	85 262	93.0	7.0
1980	110 469	7190	117 659	93.9	6.1
1985	138 416	9087	147 503	93.8	6.2
1990	160 075	11 797	171 872	93.1	6.9
2000	219 032	23 511	242 543	90.3	9.7

4. Discussions and Conclusions

This study analyzed the spatial and temporal pattern of land use/land cover change in a forest management area covering the district of Sarıyer in Istanbul over 1971-2002 period based on forest stand map using GIS and FRAGSTATS. Overall analysis showed that in Sarıyer district with a long history of human settlement, human based interventions like urbanization, reforestation and rehabilitation studies has played a vital role in land use and land cover changes. It was observed drastic land use/land cover changes, especially on forest resources in the study area of Sarıyer.

Turkey is one of the most important and the richest countries from natural resources viewpoint, particularly in biodiversity and forest resources in the world. Over the last 50 years, urbanization has increased because of population increase as a result of immigrants from rural areas to urban areas. Increased population and urbanization have caused irregular land use/land cover changes in recent times. Thus, population increase and urbanization have become an important issue of land use/land cover changes in Turkey.

As an overall change, there was a net decrease of 1243 ha in total forested area compared to a net increase of 1331 ha in settlement area because of heavy urbanization in the study area. Even though total forest area decreased between 1971 and 2002, degraded forest area decreased because of reforestation studies in the study area (figure 3). Some degraded forest areas and agricultural areas of 1346 ha in total were reforested with *Pinus pinea* and *Pinus pinaster* species over the period. This is extremely important point showing the improvement of forest resources in Sarıyer forest planning unit.

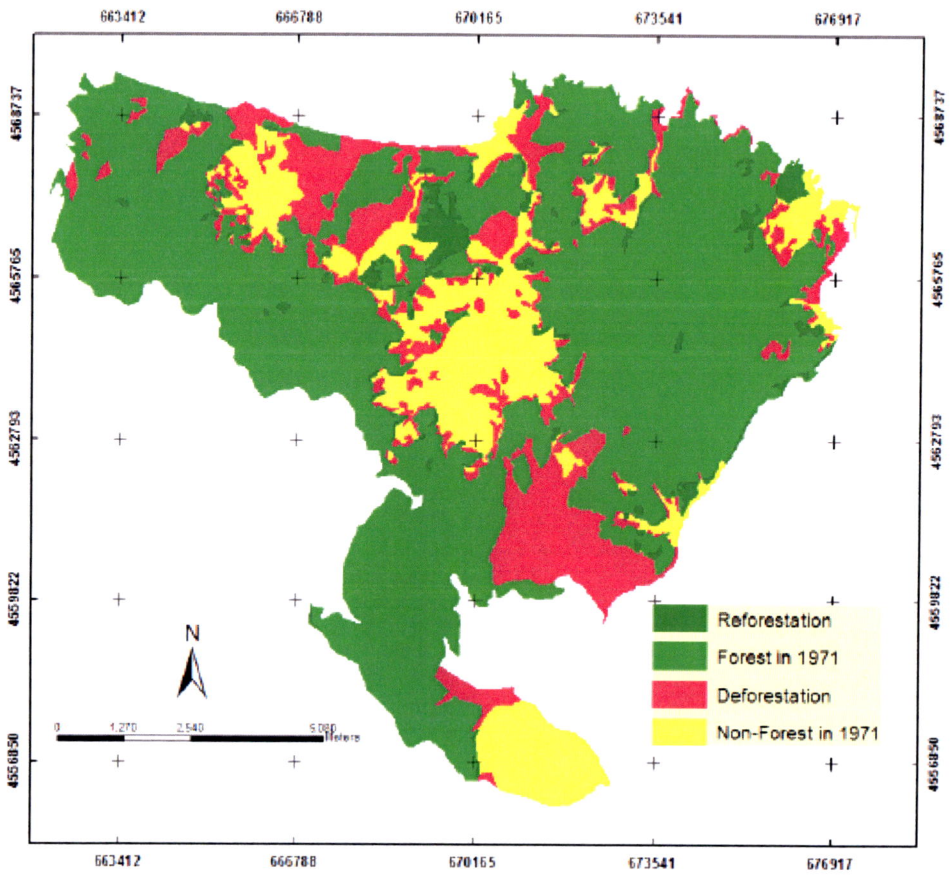

Figure 3. The map of reforestation and deforestation in the study area between 1971 and 2002.

The observed trends could be related to the increase in population and urbanization. Over the last 30 years, total population of the area constantly increased causing the Sarıyer district to expand very fast with many changes in land use/land covers (figure 4). The district was occupied by legal and illegal settlements and industrial developments. Many forest areas including private forests and agricultural areas were converted to settlement areas, specifically luxury apartment blocks demanded by high income groups. Furthermore, some areas of the districts were even occupied by squatters with extremely low income groups (Musaoglu *et al*. 2005, Musaoglu *et al*. 2006). On the other hand, forests near urban areas are very important for welfare of local people as they offer various services to people such as recreation possibilities, clean water, quality air and oxygen production. This point has encouraged Sarıyer forest enterprise to intensify the reforestation and rehabilitation activities in the study area.

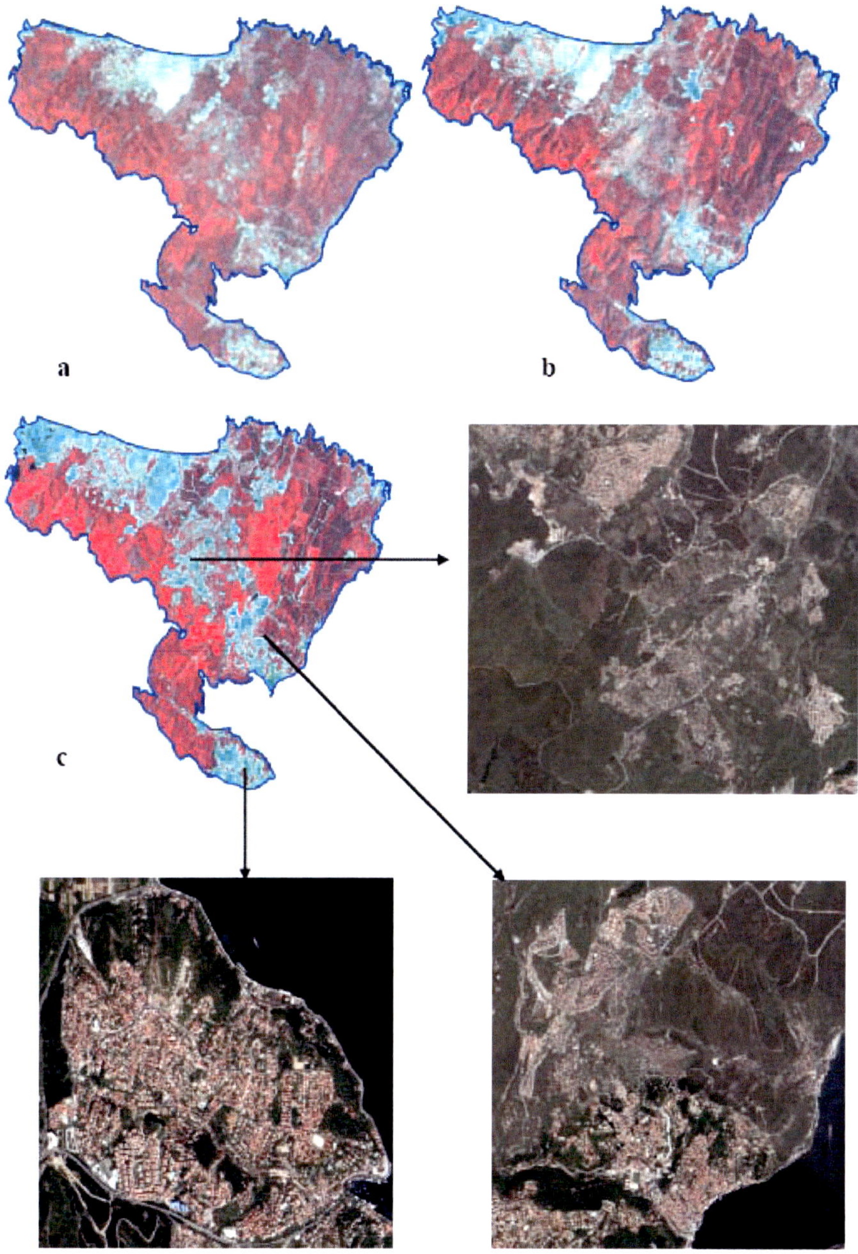

Figure 4. Historical satellite images (a-1975 MSS b-1987 TM c- 2000 ETM+) of the study area and the view of three sections from the study area by 2005 IKONOS.

Forest ecosystems provide many goods and services to public such as water, soil protection, carbon sequestration, recreation, biodiversity other than timber production. However, these values are extremely related to forest ecosystem structure characterized by species mix, crown closure, development stages and the spatial distribution of patches/stands. For example, as stand density increases water production and soil erosion decreases (Keleş *et al.* 2006, Keleş and Başkent 2007). Thus, land-use/land cover changes, especially in forest cover, may have important consequences for all forest values. In the study area, forest areas with full crown closure increased due to reforestation of degraded forests and agricultural areas as well as the conversion of coppice forest to high forests over the 31 year period. As a result of reforestation of degraded and agricultural areas, regeneration of mature forests and conversion of coppice forests to high forests, regenerated or young forest areas increased between 1971 and 2002. These results showed that legal or illegal human based interventions played an important role on forest ecosystem structure in Sarıyer forest planning unit.

Urban settlements are among the most complex structures and important habitats created by human societies. The functioning of the urban system creates many destructive impacts on soil conservation, air and water quality, climate changes and especially biological diversity (Doygun and Alphan 2006). The factors contributing to the decline of several biological populations often cause extensive changes in plant species richness and composition that these are habitat loss and the resulting fragmentation (Hernandez-Stefanoni 2005), introduced species (Terzioğlu and Anşin 2001), over-grazing (Pykälä 2004), agriculture and livestock, mining, industry, transportation and communication and urbanization (Apan et al. 2002). Successful biological conservation efforts require ecologists and urban planners to simultaneously understand patterns and processes of landscape change, such as habitat loss and fragmentation (Collinge 2001).

Analysis of the landscape metrics revealed that landscape structure in Sarıyer forest planning unit had changed substantially over the 31-year study period, resulting in fragmentation of the landscape as indicated by the large patch numbers and the smaller mean patch sizes. Such situation would affect biodiversity in forest ecosystems and quality of landscape negatively (Dupouey *et al.* 2002, Hernandez-Stefanoni 2005, Collinge 2001). The most striking change among land use covers was detected in mixed forest class as it increased from 114 ha in 1971 to 2650 ha in 2002.

In conclusion, understanding of the factors affecting the land use and land cover is increasingly important for the design and planning of urban areas and the sustainable management of natural resources. Thus, it is extremely crucial that both composition and configuration of landscape have to be quantitatively evaluated to draw appropriate lessons for landscape management.

REFERENCES

Abdullah, M.S. and Nakagoshi, N., 2006, Changes in landscape spatial pattern in the highly developing state of Selangor, peninsular Malaysia. *Landscape and Urban Planning*, 77 (3), pp. 263-275.

Alphan, H., 2003, Land use change and urbanization of Adana, Turkey. Land Degradation and Development, 14, pp. 575-586.

Apan, A.A., Raine, S.R. and Paterson, M.S., 2002, Mapping and analysis of changes in the riparian landscape structure of the Lockyer Valley catchment, Queensland, Australia. *Landscape and Urban Planning,* 59, pp. 43–57.

Baskent, E.Z, Jordan, G.A. and Nurullah, A.M.M., 2000, Designing Forest landscape (ecosystems) management. *The Forestry Chronicle,* 76, pp. 739-742.

Baskent, E.Z. and Jordan, J.A., 1995. Designing forest management to control spatial structure of landscapes. *Landscape Urban Planning*, 34, pp. 55-74.

Chen L., Wang J., Fu B. and Qiu Y., 2001, Land use change in a small catchment of Northern Loess Plateau, China. *Agriculture, Ecosystems and Environment,* 86, pp. 163-172.

Collinge, S.K., 2001, Spatial ecology and biological conservation. *Biological conservation,* 100, pp. 1-2.

Doygun, H. and Alphan, H., 2006, Monitoring urbanization of Iskenderun, Turkey, and its negative implications. *Environmental Monitoring and Assessment*, 114, pp. 145-155.

Dupouey, J.L, Dambrine E., Laffite J.D. and Moares C., 2002, Irreversible impact of past land use on forest soils and biodiversity. *Ecology*, 83, pp. 2978–2984.

Fiorella, M. and Ripple W.J., 1993, Determining successional stage of temperate coniferous forest with Landsat satellite data. *Photogrammetric Engineering and Remote Sensing,* 59, pp. 239-246.

Gautam, A.P., Webb, E.L., Shivakoti, G. and Zoebisch, M., 2003, Land use dynamics and landscape change pattern in a mountain watershed in Nepal. *Agriculture, Ecosystems and Environment,* 99, pp. 83-96.

Hernandez-Stefanoni, J.L., 2005, Relationships between landscape patterns and species richness of trees, shrubs and vines in a tropical forest. *Plant Ecology,* 179, pp. 53–65.

Iida, S. and Nakashizuka T. 1995. Forest fragmentation and its effect on species diversity in sub-urban coppice forests in Japan. *Forest Ecology and Management*, 73, pp. 197–210.

Iverson, L.R., Graham, R.L. and Cook, E.A., 1989, Applications of satellite remote sensing to forested ecosystems. *Landscape Ecology,* 3, pp. 131-143.

Johnson, L.B, Richards, C., Host, G. and Arthur J.W., 1997, Landscape influences on water chemistry in midwestern streams. *Freshwater Biology,* 37, pp. 209–217.

Kammerbauer, J. and Ardon C., 1999, Land use dynamic and landscape change pattern in a typical watershed in the hill side region of Central Honduras. *Agriculture, Ecosystems and Environment,* 75, pp. 93-100.

Keleş, S., Sivrikaya, F., Çakir, G. and Başkent, E.Z., 2006, Incorporating water production value of forest ecosystems into forest management plans. 1th International Symposium on Non-Wood Forest Products, Trabzon – Turkey, 1–4 November.

Keleş, S., Sivrikaya, S. and Çakir, G., 2007, Temporal changes in forest landscape patterns in Artvin Forest Planning Unit, Turkey. *Environmental Monitoring and Assessment*, 129, pp. 483-490.

Keleş, S. and Başkent, E.Z., 2007. Modeling and analyzing timber production and carbon sequestration values of forest ecosystems. A case study. *Polish Journal of Environmental Studies,* 16 (3), pp. 473-479

Kennedy, R.S.H. and Spies T.A., 2004, Forest Cover Changes in the Oregon Coast Range form 1939 to 1993. *Forest Ecology and Management*, 200, pp. 129-147.

Liu, J., Liu, S., and Loveland, T. R., 2006, Temporal evolution of carbon budgets of the appalachian forests in the U.S. from 1972 to 2000. *Forest Ecology and Management,* 222, pp. 191–201.

Luque, .S., 2000, Evaluating temporal changes using multispectral scanner and thematic mapper data on the landscape of a natural reserve: The New Jersey Pine Barrens, A case study. *International Journal of Remote Sensing,* 21, pp. 2589-2611.

McGarigal, K. and Marks, B.J., 1995, Fragstats: Usda Forest Service, Pacific Northwest Research Station, Portland, OR. General Technical Report PNW 351, p. 141.

McGarigal, K., Cushman S.A., Neel M.C. and Ene E., 2002. Fragstats: Spatial Pattern Analysis Program for Categorical Maps. Computer software program produced by the authors at the University of Massachusetts, Amherst, Available at www.umass.edu/landeco/research/fragstats/fragstats.html (accessed September 2006)

Matsushita, B., Xu, M. and Fukushima, T., 2006, Characterizing the changes in landscape structure in the Lake Kasumigaura Basin, Japan using a high-quality GIS dataset. *Landscape and Urban Planning,* 78 (3), pp. 241-250.

Musaoglu, N., Coskun, M. and Kocabas, V., 2005, Land Use Change Analysis of Beykoz Istanbul means of satellite images and GIS. *Water Science&Technology,* 51 (11), pp 245-251

Musaoglu, N., Gurel, M., Ulugtekin, N, Tanik, A., and Seker, D.Z., 2006, Use of Remotely Sensed Data for Analysis of Land-Use Change in a Highly Urbanized District of Mega City, İstanbul. *Journal of Environmental Science and Health, Part A*, 41 (9), pp. 2057-2069.

Özhatay, N., Byfield, A., and Atay, S., 2003, Important plant areas of Turkey. WWF Turkey, MASS press, Istanbul.

Pykälä, J., 2004, Cattle grazing increases plant species richness of most species trait groups in mesic semi-natural grasslands. *Plant Ecology,* 175, pp. 217–226.

Rao, K.S. and Pant, R., 2001, Land use dynamics and landscape change pattern in a typical micro watershed in the mid elevation zone of central Himalaya, India. *Agriculture, Ecosystems and Environment*, 86, pp. 113-124.

Ripple, W.J, Breadshaw G.A. and Spies T.A., 1991, Measuring forest landscape patterns in the Cascade Range of Oregon, USA. *Biological Conservation,* 57, pp. 73-88.

Sivrikaya, F., Çakir, G., Kadioğullari, A.İ., Keleş, S., Başkent, E.Z., and Terzioğlu, S., 2007, Evaluating land use/land cover changes and fragmentation in the Camili Forest Planning Unit of Northeastern Turkey from 1972 to 2005. *Land Degradation and Development*, 18, pp. 383-396

Spies, T.A, Ripple, W.J. and Bradshaw, G.A., 1994, Dynamics and pattern of a managed coniferous forest landscape in Oregon. *Ecological Applications,* 4, pp. 555-568.

Terzioğlu, S., and Anşin, R., 2001, A chorological study on the taxa naturalized in the Eastern Black Sea Region. *Turkish Journal of Agriculture and Forestry,* 25, pp. 305-309.

Turner, M.G. and Ruscher C.L., 1988, Changes in landscape pattern in Georgia, USA. *Landscape Ecology,* 1, pp. 241-251.

Upadhyay, T. P., Sankhayan, P. L., and Solberg, B., 2005, A review of carbon sequestration dynamics in the Himalayan region as a function of land-use change and forest/soil degradation with special reference to Nepal. *Agriculture, Ecosystem and Environment*, 105, pp. 449–465.

Verburg, P.H, Veldkamp, A. and Bouma, J., 1999, Land-use change under conditions of high population pressure: The case of Java. *Global Environment Change,* 9, pp. 303-312.

Wakeel, A, Rao, K.S, Maikhuri, R.K. and Saxena, K.G., 2005, Forest management and land-use/cover changes in a typical micro watershed in the mid-elevation zone of Central Himalaya, India. *Forest Ecology and Management,* 213, pp. 229-242.

Wear, D.N, Turner, M.G. and Flamm, R.O., 1996, Ecosystem management with multiple owners: Landscape dynamics in a southern Appalachian watershed. *Ecological Applications,* 6, pp. 1173-1188.

In: Land Use Policy
Editors: A. C. Denman and O. M. Penrod
ISBN: 978-1-60741-435-3

Chapter 8

LAND USE CHANGE IN BANGLADESH AGRICULTURE: TRENDS IN PRODUCTIVITY, DIVERSITY AND SELF-SUFFICIENCY (1973-2006)

Sanzidur Rahman*
School of Geography, University of Plymouth, Plymouth, PL4 8AA, UK

ABSTRACT

Land is the scarcest resource in Bangladesh economy. The average land-person ratio is only 0.12 ha which is inadequate to sustain livelihood of an average farm household. The present chapter paper provides a detailed analysis of the agricultural land use changes at the national level in Bangladesh over a 34 year period (1973-2006) and examines the trends in productivity, crop diversity and its link towards achieving self-sufficiency in food production. Results revealed that agricultural land use in Bangladesh became intense reflected by an increase in cropping intensity from only 142.9% in 1973 to 176.9% in 2005 facilitated by an increased provision of irrigation infrastructure to diffuse a rice-based Green Revolution technology package throughout the country. Although total cereal production (dominated by rice) has increased substantially, productivity of crops per unit of key inputs (i.e., land area, fertilizers, and pesticides) has been declining consistently over the years, thereby, raising doubt on the sustainability of the agricultural sector. Contrary to expectation, crop diversity seems to have increased over the years. Also, Bangladesh seems to have achieved the goal of self-sufficiency in food production, mainly contributed by a boost in foodgrain production. However, concentration of energy availability from cereals as opposed to non-cereals raises concern on the dietary health of the Bangladeshi population. Bangladesh needs to widen its technology base and go beyond the diffusion of a single crop of HYV rice and should diversify its land use towards producing non-cereals, which are more profitable and could enhance farmers' earnings and livelihoods as well as generate valuable foreign exchange for the economy through exports.

---

* Address for Correspondence: Dr Sanzidur Rahman ; Senior Lecturer in Rural Development; School of Geography ; University of Plymouth; Drake Circus; Plymouth, PL4 8AA; England, UK; Phone: +44-1752-585911; Fax: +44-1752-585998 ; E-mail: srahman@plymouth.ac.uk

Keywords: Land use change, productivity, crop diversity, self-sufficiency, trend analysis, Bangladesh.

1. Introduction

Land use change is becoming important these days because of its close relationship with global climate change and global food security (Tong et al., 2003). In general, land use change can be strongly affected by socio-economic factors such as land use policies, population growth, urbanization, agricultural product prices and world trade. To a certain extent, agricultural development policy is the most important factor affecting land use change in Bangladesh, which has one of the lowest land-person ratio of only 0.12 ha (FAO, 2001). Agriculture constitutes the major source of livelihood in Bangladesh accounting for 23.5% of national income and employs 62% of the labour force (MoA, 2008). The dominant sector is the field crop agriculture accounting for more than 60% of agricultural value added. Among the field crops, rice is the major staple crop, occupying 70% of the gross cropped area (BBS, 2002). If supporting activities, such as, transport, storage and marketing of agricultural products are taken into account, then the share of agricultural sector GDP is likely to be over 60 percent of total (Alauddin and Tisdell, 1991). Historically, being a food deficit country, Bangladesh has pursued a policy of rapid technological progress in agriculture. Consequently, over the past four decades, the major thrust of national policies were directed towards transforming agriculture through rapid technological progress to keep up with the increasing population (Rahman, 2002). Development programs were undertaken to diffuse modern varieties of rice and wheat with corresponding support in the provision of modern inputs, such as, chemical fertilizers, pesticides, irrigation equipments, institutional credit, product procurement, storage and marketing facilities. As a result farmers concentrated on producing modern varieties of rice all year round covering three production seasons (*Aus* – pre-monsoon, *Aman* – monsoon, and *Boro* – dry winter seasons), particularly in areas that are endowed with supplemental irrigation facilities. This raised concern regarding the loss of crop diversity consequently leading to an unsustainable agricultural system. For example, Husain et al., (2001) noted that "the intensive monoculture of rice led to displacement of land under low productive non-rice crops such as pulses, oilseeds, spices and vegetables, leading to erosion of crop diversity, thereby, endangering sustainability of crop-based agricultural production system". Mahmud et al., (1994) noted that "area under non-cereal crops has continuously fallen since late 1970s, mainly due to the expansion of irrigation facilities, which led to fierce competition for land between modern *Boro* season rice and non-cereals". However, systematic analysis of the land use change in Bangladesh covering a longer period has not been attempted since early 1990s. The existing analyses cover until 1991 at the latest (e.g., BASR, 1989; Khalil, 1991; Alauddin and Tisdell, 1991, and Mahmud et al., 1994). Also, only one attempt has been made to link the diffusion of Green Revolution technology to food availability (i.e., Alauddin and Tisdell, 1991).

Given this backdrop, the objectives of this study are to: (a) analyze land use change and the level of crop diversity in Bangladesh covering a 34 year period (1973 – 2006); (b) examine the dynamics of crop productivity per unit of major inputs (land, fertilizers, and pesticides); and (c) examine the trends in food and energy availability per capita as a proxy measure to indicate self-sufficiency in food production.

The chapter is divided into 4 sections. Section 2 describes the methodology used including source of data. Section 3 presents the results of the exercises. The final section concludes.

2. METHODS

The principal data on Bangladesh's agricultural system is taken from the latest available issue of Agricultural Handbook of Bangladesh, 2007 (MoA, 2008), various issues of the Statistical Yearbook on Bangladesh from 1975 to 2002 published by the Bangladesh Bureau of Statistics (BBS, various issues), and Economic Trends from 1990 to 2007 published monthly by Bangladesh Bank (BB, various issues).

2.1. Derivation of Land Use Change

We have analyzed the changes in areas planted and production of eight major crop groups at the national level covering a 34 year period from 1973 to 2006. The crops included in the analyses are: (i) foodgrain which includes local varieties of rice and HYV rice grown in each of the three seasons (*Aus* = pre-monsoon; *Aman* = monsoon; and *Boro* = dry winter), wheat, maize, barley, and other minor cereals; (ii) cash crops which include jute, cotton, sugarcane, tobacco, tea and betel leaves; (iii) pulses which include gram, mungbean, lentil, khesari, blackgram, and other pulses; (iv) oilseeds which include mustard, sesame, linseed, groundnut, coconut, and other oilseeds; (v) spices which include onion, chilli, garlic, ginger, and other spices; (vi) potatoes which include potatoes and sweet potatoes; (vii) vegetables which include brinjal, tomatoes, cauliflower, cabbage, radish, and other summer and winter vegetables; and (viii) fruits which include mango, banana, pineapple, papaya, jackfruit, litchi, guava, and melon.

Average annual compound growth rates were computed in order to determine the rate of change of the variable of interest. The growth rates were computed using semi-logarithmic trend function: $lnY = \alpha + \beta T$, where Y is the target variable, T is time, ln is natural logarithm, and β is the growth rate.

2.2. Input and Output Analysis

Information was also collected on major inputs of fertilizers, pesticides, area under irrigation and distribution of HYV seeds for cereals (rice and wheat). Fertilizers are expressed in actual nutrient contents of N, P, K, S, and Zn. The types of fertilizers included are: Urea, Triple Super Phosphate, Single Super Phosphate, Muriate of Potash, Diammonium Phosphate, Sulfur and Zinc. Pesticides include information on active ingredients of insecticides, herbicides and fungicides. We analyzed partial measures of crop productivity with respect to major inputs, i.e., trends in crop yield per ha, yield per unit of fertilizer nutrients and yield per unit of active ingredients of pesticides.

2.3. Analysis of Crop Diversity

Two classes of variables can be used to represent the specialization variable. The Herfindahl index, which is based on the area allocated to a particular enterprise (Llewelyn and Williams, 1996) or the Ogive index, which is defined as a concentration of output shares of various enterprises (Coelli and Fleming, 2004). The Herfindahl index is represented as:

$$DV = \sum_{i=1}^{n} P_i^2 ,$$

where P_i is the proportion of land area involved in a particular enterprise. The value of Herfindahl index ranges between 0 and 1 with 0 denoting perfect diversification and 1 perfect specialization. In this study, we have selected the Herfindahl index of crop diversification.

2.4. Analysis of Food and Energy Availability

One of the principal objectives of Bangladeshi agricultural and/or land use policy is to attain the goal of self-sufficiency in food production. Historically, Bangladesh has been a food deficit country with 10 percent of its domestic demand being imported using valuable and scarce foreign currency (Hossain, 1989). Green Revolution was promoted in order to fulfil this goal of self-sufficiency. We utilized three proxy measures to examine the level of self-sufficiency in food production. These are: (i) foodgrain availability per capita per year, (ii) Gross Value Added (GVA) from agricultural production in USD per capita per year, and (iii) energy availability (Kcal) from various food groups per capita per day. GVA expressed in USD reflects the real prices of agricultural production[11]. In order to determine energy availability from food crops, we used the standard calorie availability per 100 gm of individual crop weighted by its share of edible portion. The information on calorie availability and the share of edible percent of each crop was taken from the Household Income and Expenditure Survey (HIES) conducted by BBS (BBS, 2006).

3. RESULTS

3.1. Trends in Land Use Change and Crop Diversity

Figure 1 presents the trends in land use change in Bangladesh over the 34 year period under consideration (1973 – 2006). The bottom panel of figure 1 also presents the growth

[11] The exchange rates were taken from Economic Trends published monthly by Bangladesh Bank (BB, various issues)

rates of selected indicators of land use change. The overall land area in Bangladesh was 14.28 million ha in 1973 which later increased by 4% to 14.84 million ha in 2006 owing to reclamation of new lands rising from the river beds (known as *char* lands). However, the share of cultivable land declined from 65% in 1973 to 57% in 2006 due to a shift in the use of land for housing, infrastructure and urban uses. As a result, the net sown area available for agriculture declined at an annual rate of -0.3% from 8.24 million ha in 1973 to 7.97 million ha in 2006. However, due to improvements in irrigation environment, the gross cropped area (GCA), which takes into account the land sown twice or three times in a year, has steadily increased at a rate of 0.4% per year from 11.6 million ha in 1973 to 13.4 million ha in 2006. In other words, land use became very intensive as reflected by the change in cropping intensity from 142.9% in 1973 to 176.9% in 2005 with an estimated growth rate of 0.7% per annum.

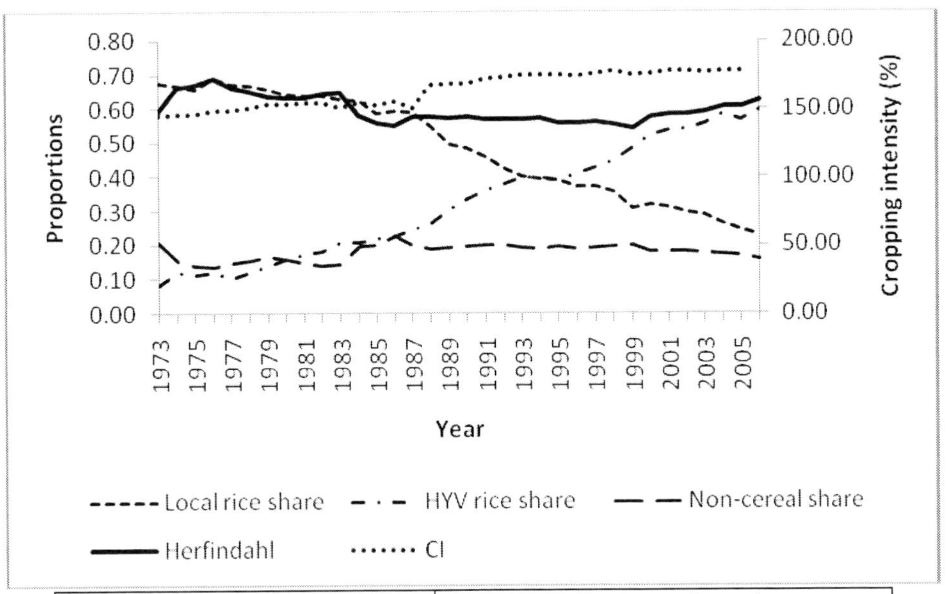

Variables	Average annual compound growth rates
Net sown area (NSA)	-0.003***
Gross cropped area (GCA)	0.004***
Cropping intensity	0.007***
Share of local rice area in GCA	-0.034***
Share of HYV rice area in GCA	0.059***
Share of total rice area in GCA	0.002***
Share of non-cereals in GCA	0.005**
Herfindahl index of crop diversity	-0.004***

Note: All growth rates (Figures 1 through 8) are computed using semi-logarithmic trend function: $lnY = \alpha + \beta T$, where Y is the target variable, T is time, ln is natural logarithm, and β is the growth rate.

*** = significant at 1 percent level ($p<0.01$)

** = significant at 5 percent level ($p<0.05$)

Source: Computed from MoA 2008.

Figure 1. Trends in land use change in Bangladesh (1973 – 2006).

An interesting feature to note in figure 1 is that the share of total rice area in GCA increased at a minimal rate of only 0.2% per annum whereas the share of non-cereals has increased at a higher rate of 0.5% per annum, which clearly contradicts with the findings of Husain et al., (2001) and Mahmud et al., (2004), who claimed that monoculture of HYV rice has been seriously hampering crop diversity. The main shift has been in the varietal composition of rice. The share of local rice area in GCA declined steadily at a rate of -3.4% per year. On the other hand, the share of HYV rice area increased steadily at a rate of 5.9% per annum. Also, the share of total rice area in GCA has been kept at bay with only 0.2% growth rate because land use under other crops has been increasing. The computed Herfindahl index provides conclusive proof. The value of the Herfindahl index declined at a rate of -0.4% per annum from 0.65 in 1973 to 0.60 in 2006 with large falls during the 1980s (as evident in figure 1), implying that crop diversity has been increasing in Bangladesh instead of falling as many suggest (e.g., Husain et al., 2001; Mahmud et al., 2004; Alauddin and Tisdell, 1991). Rahman (2008), based on an analysis of the level of crop diversification between two Agricultural Censuses of 1960 and 1996, noted that the level of crop diversity has actually increased by 4.5% over a 36 year period from 0.59 in 1960 to 0.54 in 1996.

Figure 2 presents additional information on land use change with an estimated annual growth rates of major crop groups presented at the bottom panel. It is clear from figure 2 that except jute area, all other non-cereal areas experienced positive growth rates. Among the cereals, wheat experienced an explosive growth during the 1980s and 1990s. The wheat area was only 0.13 million ha in 1973 which increased to a peak of 0.88 million ha in 1999 and then fell sharply to 0.48 million ha. Wheat area and production experienced a crisis at a global scale during 2000 and Bangladesh was not an exception. As a result, the average annual growth rate has been estimated at 3.7% only[12]. Among these non-cereals, only jute area declined annually at a rate of -2.0% mainly due to a lack of demand for fibre products owing to the availability of cheap synthetic alternatives worldwide. The jute area declined from 0.68 million ha in 1973 to 0.39 million ha in 2006. Pulses did not show any significant improvement. Vegetables and potatoes recorded impressive growth in area estimated at 2.6% and 2.1%, respectively, although they constitute less land area in absolute terms. The area under vegetables and potatoes covered only 0.19 million ha and 0.34 million ha in 2006. Bangladesh has been exporting vegetables since early 2000 and the trend is on the rise. According to the Export Promotion Bureau of Bangladesh, a total of Tk 4,232.9 million (USD 61.8 million) was earned by exporting different varieties of vegetables against the target of Tk 2,800 million (USD 40.86 million) in the year 2007-08. It was Tk 2,498.1 million (USD 36.31 million) in the year 2006-07 (New Nation, 2008).

[12] Although other minor cereals are included with wheat, their contribution to growth is negligible.

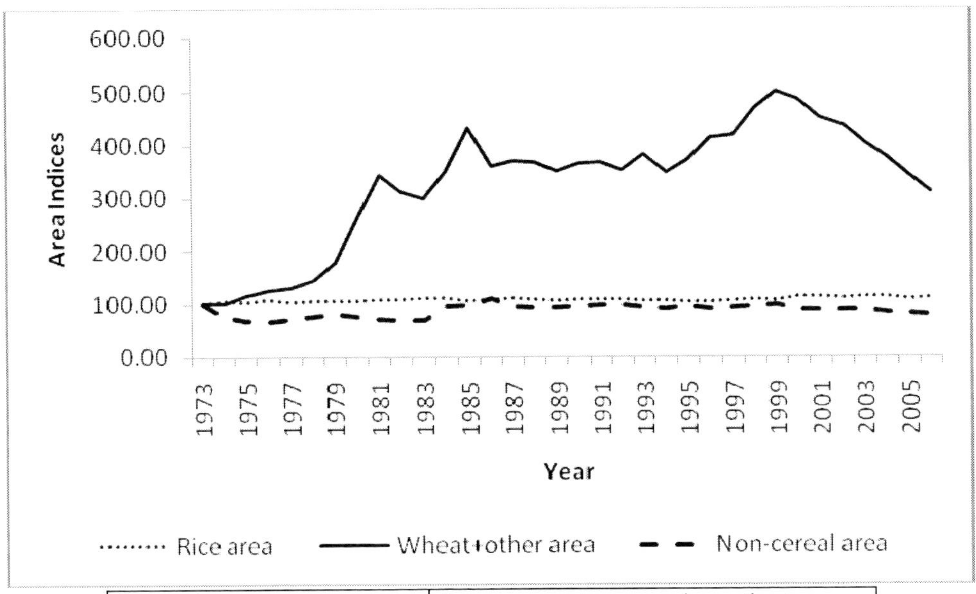

Area under crops	Average annual compound growth rates
Local rice	-0.034***
HYV rice	0.059***
Total rice	0.002***
Wheat and other cereals	0.037***
Jute	-0.020***
Pulses	0.010
Oilseeds	0.013***
Spices	0.017***
Potatoes	0.021***
Vegetables	0.026***
Fruits	0.008***

Note: *** = significant at 1 percent level ($p<0.01$)
Source: Computed from MoA 2008.

Figure 2. Trends in cropped area (1973 – 2006).

3.2. Trends in Production Growth and Productivity

Once land use change has been analyzed, we next examine the trends in output and yield levels of major crops, modern inputs, as well as overall productivity per unit of land area, fertilizers, and pesticides[13]. Figure 3 presents the trends in production growth of food crops along with the estimated growth rates of major crop groups at the bottom panel. As expected, total production from local rice declined at an annual rate of -2.1% from 7.44 million tons in 1973 to 4.32 million tons in 2006. However, total rice production has been boosted from contribution of HYV rice which steadily increased at an annual rate of 6.5% from a mere 2.45 million tons in 1973 to an impressive 22.21 million tons in 2006. Overall, rice production grew at an estimated annual rate of 2.7%. The total rice production reached 26.53 million tons

[13] Labour productivity is also an important concern. However, due to ambiguity in the number of actual labour involved in agricultural production, we did not compute this measure.

in 2006. It is interesting to note that although jute area declined at an annual rate of -2.0%, the production declined only at a rate of -0.6%, implying that yield rate of jute may have increased (discussed later in this section). The production growth of wheat and other minor cereals has been impressive as well, and are increasing at an annual rate of 6% from an initial level of 0.14 million tons in 1973 and reaching at a peak level of 2.05 million tons in 1999 and then falling sharply to 1.27 million tons in 2006. Production of all other non-cereals recorded a growth between 1.2% and 3.2% per annum, which is very encouraging.

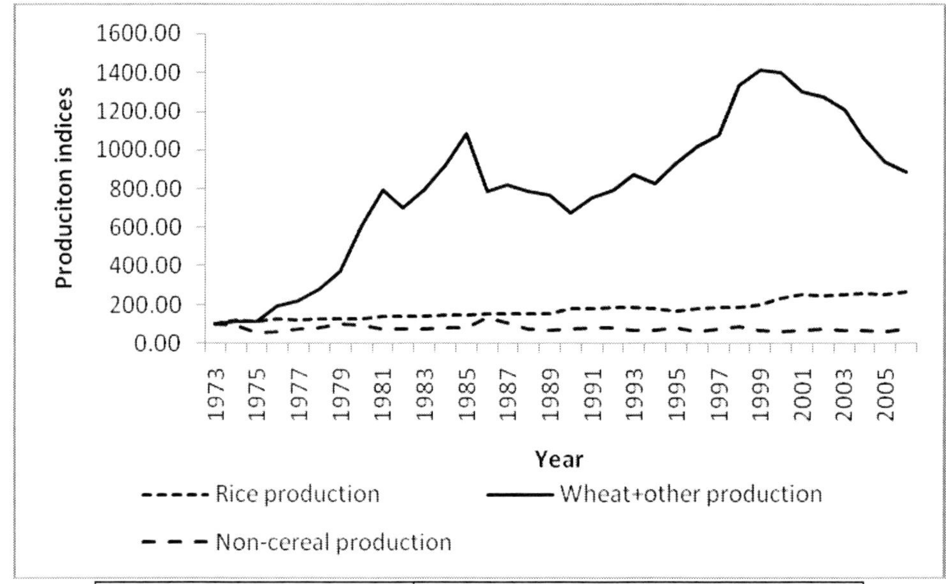

Production of crops	Average annual compound growth rates
Local rice	-0.021***
HYV rice	0.065***
Total rice	0.027***
Wheat and other cereals	0.060***
Jute	-0.006*
Pulses	0.021***
Oilseeds	0.024***
Spices	0.022***
Potatoes	0.032***
Vegetables	0.030***
Fruits	0.012***

Note: *** = significant at 1 percent level (p<0.01)
* = significant at 10 percent level (p<0.10)
Source: Computed from MoA 2008.

Figure 3. Trends in crop production (1973 – 2006).

Figure 4 presents the trends in the use of modern inputs in Bangladesh agriculture. It is clear from figure 4 that the growth in input use has been explosive, particularly fertilizers and pesticides, which became an integral part of modern day agriculture. Fertilizer consumption was only 0.18 million tons of nutrients in 1973, which increased by 11 times to 1.70 million tons of nutrients in 2006. Fertilizer use in Bangladesh is dominated by nitrogen fertilizers

(70% of total in every year), although use of zinc and sulfur started from 1981 and has been increasing gradually. Pesticide use was only 3.13 thousand tons of active ingredients in 1977 which increased 5.5 folds to 17.39 thousand tons of active ingredients in 2002. The government also provided substantial support in expanding the irrigation area which is essential for growing HYV rice in the Boro season. The proportion of irrigated area to GCA was only 10.97% in 1973 which increased to 37.51% in 2006, recording a steady increase at a rate of 4.4% per annum. Growth in the distribution HYV seeds for cereals (i.e., rice and wheat) is also impressive. The government has distributed 5.48 thousand tons of HYV cereal seeds in 1974 which increased at an annual rate of 5.9% to 45.62 thousand tons in 2006.

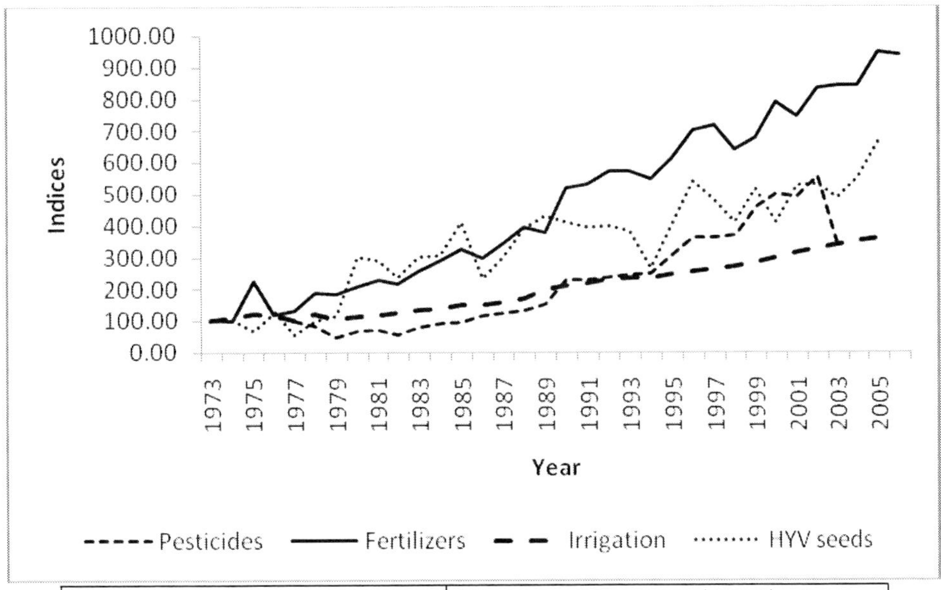

Modern inputs	Average annual compound growth rates
Fertilizer nutrients	0.067***
Pesticides (active ingredients)	0.089***
HYV seeds for cereals	0.059***
Irrigation area	0.044***

Note: Information on pesticide use is available from 1977 – 2003 only.
Information on HYV seeds distributed is available from 1974 onwards.
*** = significant at 1 percent level (p<0.01)
Source: Computed from MoA 2008.

Figre 4. Growth in input use (1973 – 2005).

Figure 5 presents the trends in yield rates of major crops as well as use rates of two major inputs, fertilizers and pesticides. The striking feature in figure 5 is the performance of HYV rice. The yield growth of HYV rice is half the rate of yield growth in local rice varieties. The overall yield level of rice increased at 2.5% per annum due to the fact that yield rate of HYV rice is still twice the yield rate of local rice. For example, yield of HYV rice was 2.31 ton/ha which was 2.7 times the local rice yield of 0.87 ton/ha in 1973. However, the yield level of HYV rice in 2006 was 2.92 ton/ha but reduced to a multiple of 1.9 times than the yield of local rice of 1.42 ton/ha. Yield rate of wheat and other minor cereals also grew at an annual rate of 2.2% per year increasing from 0.74 ton/ha in 1973 to 2.11 ton/ha in 2006. The growth in yield rates of non-cereals is lower than expected ranging from only 0.4% for fruits to 1.4% for jute. On the other hand, use rates of fertilizers and pesticides exploded over the years. Fertilizer use rate was only 14.25 kg of nutrients per ha in 1973 which increased to a staggering 127.18 kg of nutrients per ha in 2006 recording an annual growth rate of 6.3%. The growth in pesticide use is even higher. Pesticide use was only 0.26 kg of active ingredients per ha in 1977 which increased to 1.23 kg of active ingredients per ha in 2002, recording an annual growth rate of 8.5%.

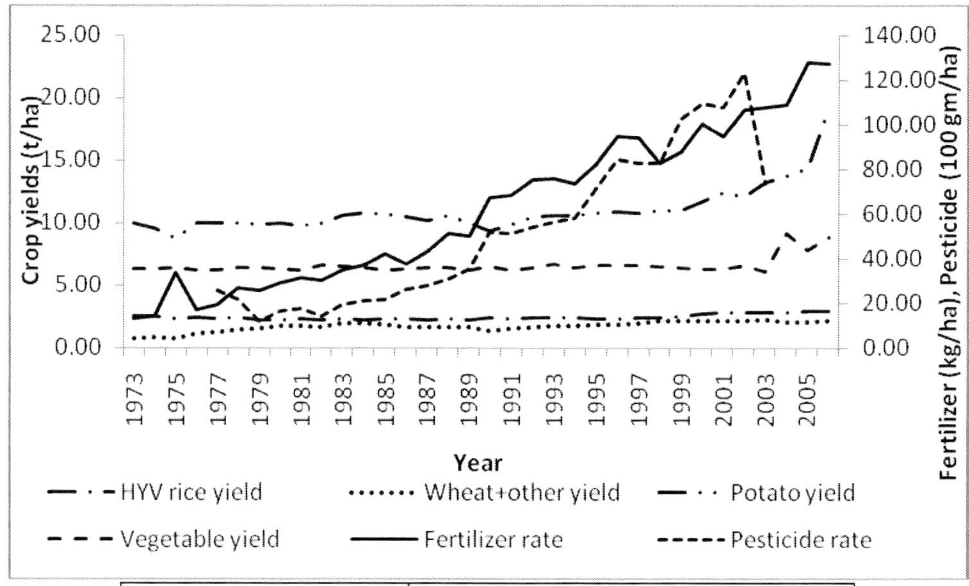

Crop yield levels	Average annual compound growth rates
Local rice	0.012***
HYV rice	0.006***
Total rice	0.025***
Wheat and other cereals	0.022***
Jute	0.014***
Pulses	0.011***
Oilseeds	0.012***
Spices	0.005*
Potatoes	0.011***
Vegetables	0.005***
Fruits	0.004
Input use rates	
Fertilizer use rates	0.063***
Pesticide use rates	0.085***

Note: Information on pesticide use is available from 1977 – 2003 only.
*** = significant at 1 percent level ($p<0.01$)
* = significant at 10 percent level ($p<0.10$)
Source: Computed from MoA 2008.

Figure 5. Trends in crop yield and input use rates (1973 – 2006).

Finally, we examine crop productivity per unit of land, fertilizers and pesticides. Since information on fertilizer and pesticide use in specific crops is not available, only a partial measure of productivity on aggregate production is computed[14]. The result of the exercise is presented in figure 6, which makes a disappointing reading. Only, land productivity showed positive small growth rate, whereas productivity from fertilizers and pesticides revealed sharp decline at an annual rate of -4.6% to -6.7%, respectively, which raise concern on the sustainability of this modern input based agricultural system.

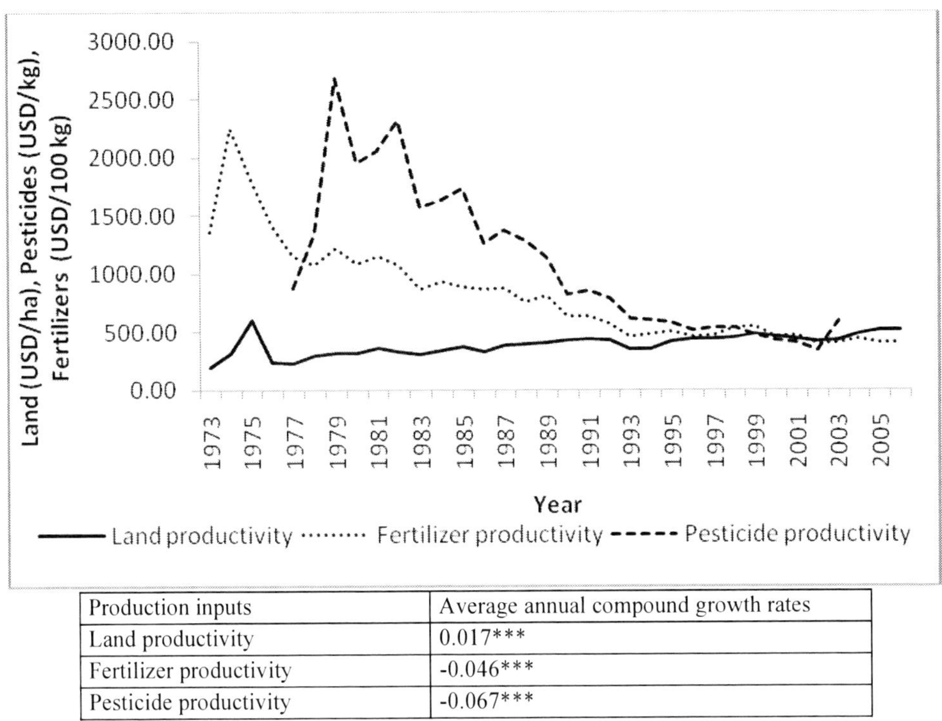

Production inputs	Average annual compound growth rates
Land productivity	0.017***
Fertilizer productivity	-0.046***
Pesticide productivity	-0.067***

Note: Land productivity = gross value added of aggregate production in USD per ha of gross cropped area;

Pesticide productivity = gross value added of aggregate production in USD per kg of active ingredients;

Fertilizer productivity = gross value added of aggregate production in USD per 100 kg of nutrients.

Information on pesticide use is available from 1977 – 2003 only.

*** = significant at 1 percent level (p<0.01)

Source: Computed from MoA 2008; BB (various issues), BBS (various issues).

Figure 6. Growth in partial measures of productivity of major inputs (1973 – 2006).

3.3. Prospects for Achieving Self-Sufficiency

The final element of analysis was to examine whether Bangladesh has succeeded in its goal towards achieving self-sufficiency in food production. Figure 7 presents the trends in population growth and per capita food availability during the period of 1973 to 2006. It is clear from figure 7 that foodgrain availability per capita grew steadily at a modest rate of 0.9% per year, although population grew at a high rate of 1.9% per year. In other words,

[14] We have used gross value added (GVA) of aggregate crop production in USD which reflects real change in output.

growth in foodgrain production was able to offset the growth in the population base, which is very encouraging indeed. The foodgrain availability per capita has increased from 135.2 kg per capita per year in 1973 to 200.3 kg per capita per year in 2006. However, when real growth in per capita contribution from agricultural production is considered, no visible growth is observed. The value added from agricultural production reached a peak in 1975 to USD 93 per capita but then remained in the region of USD 49 since 1995, thereby showing stagnancy in real growth in the value of agricultural production per capita per year. The principal reason may be due to a very high rate of population growth starting with a very high population base which tends to offset the observed growth in the real return derived from the agricultural sector although production of foodgrain has outstripped the influence of population growth and managed to show a modest growth of 0.9% per capita per year.

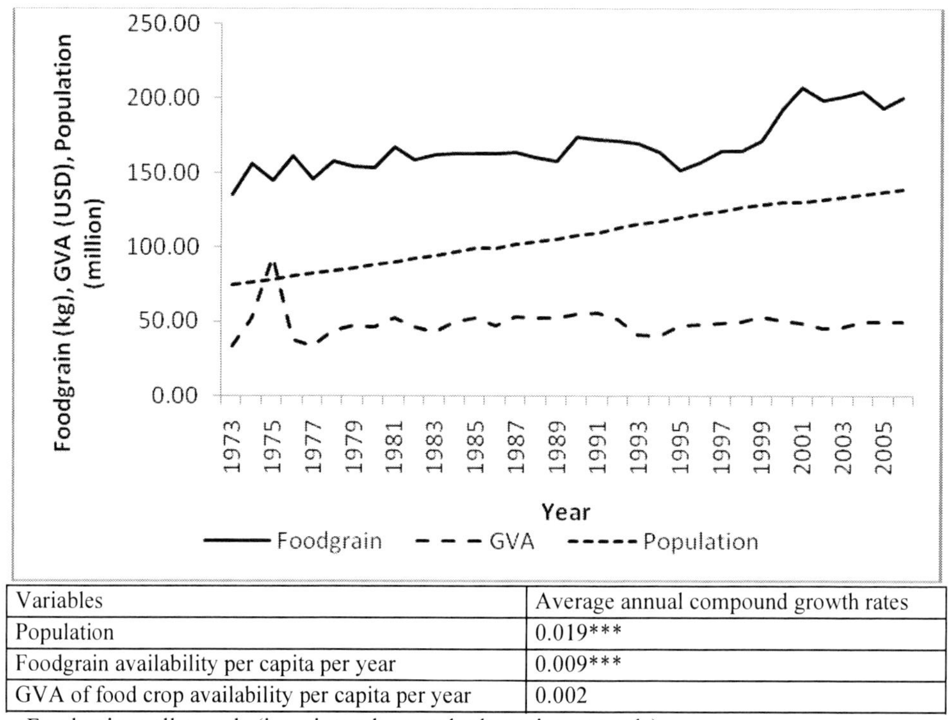

Variables	Average annual compound growth rates
Population	0.019***
Foodgrain availability per capita per year	0.009***
GVA of food crop availability per capita per year	0.002

Note: Foodgrain = all cereals (i.e., rice, wheat and other minor cereals).
*** = significant at 1 percent level (p<0.01)
Source: Computed from MoA 2008; Bangladesh Bank (various issues), BBS (various issues).

Figure 7. Trends in population growth and per capita food availability from crops (1973 – 2006).

Bangladesh is not only a food deficit country, but also deficient in nutrition. Mian (1978), based on a joint FAO recommended standard for South Asian countries, constructed a least-cost long-term diet sets with available food items that attain the recommended nutrition level of 2,112 kcal and 58 grams of protein per capita per day. Figure 8 presents the trends in energy availability per capita per day from various food crops. Although energy availability grew at a modest rate of 0.8% per year, the main contributor to this growth are the cereals dominated by rice and wheat, while the energy derived from non-cereals recorded a decline, particularly energy from fruits. The average energy availability increased from 1,752 Kcal per capita per day in 1973 to 2,451 Kcal per capita per day in 2006, which is very encouraging.

However, it should be noted that this measure is very crude and does not take into account energy derived from meat and fish products, which constitutes an important source of protein in human diet. Nevertheless, results from figures 7 and 8 together provides an indication that Bangladesh has achieved the goal of self-sufficiency in foodgrain production in recent years, which is consistent with the anecdotal claims made by all the ruling political parties since year 2000 onward.

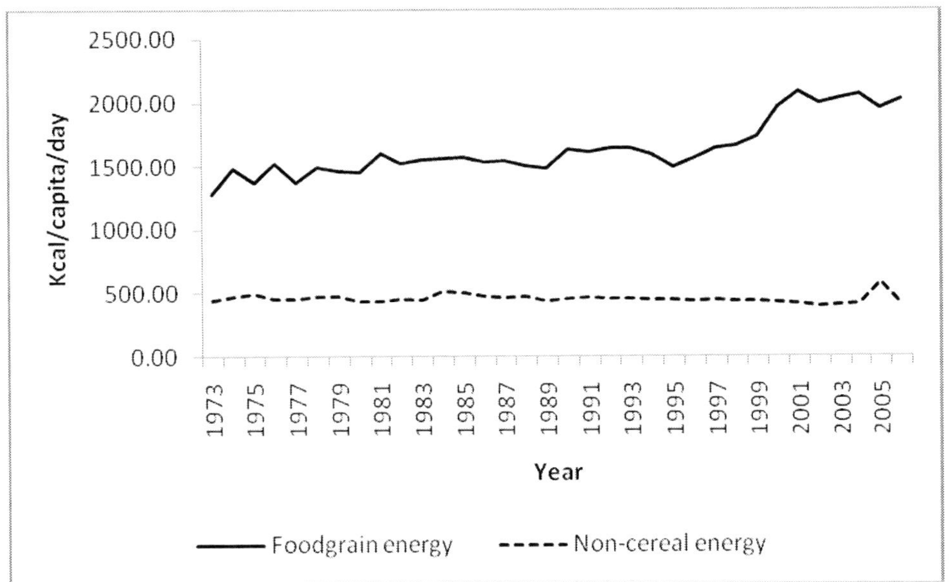

Source of energy availability	Average annual compound growth rates
Energy from foodgrain	0.011***
Energy from non-cereals	-0.003**
Cash crops	-0.015***
Pulses	0.004
Oilseeds	0.007
Spices	0.007
Potatoes	0.015***
Vegetables	0.013***
Fruits	-0.008**
All crops	0.008***

Note: Foodgrain = local rice, HYV rice, wheat, maize, barley, and other cereals; Cash crops = sugarcane and tobacco; Pulses = gram, mungbean, lentil, khesari, blackgram, and other pulses; Oilseeds = mustard, sesame, linseed, groundnut, coconut, and other oilseeds; Spices = onion, chilli, garlic, ginger, and other spices; Potatoes = potatoes and sweet potatoes; Vegetables = brinjal, tomatoes, cauliflower, cabbage, radish, and other vegetables; Fruits = mango, banana, pineapple, papaya, jackfruit, litchi, guava, and melon.

*** = significant at 1 percent level ($p<0.01$)

** = significant at 5 percent level ($p<0.05$)

Source: Computed from MoA 2008; Bangladesh Bank (various issues), BBS (various issues).

Figure 8. Trends in energy availability (Kcal) from food crops per capita per day (1973 – 2006).

4. Conclusion

The present paper attempted to provide a detailed analysis of the agricultural land use changes at the national level in Bangladesh over a 34 year period (1973-2006) and an examination of the trends in productivity, crop diversity and its link towards achieving self-sufficiency in food production. Results revealed that agricultural land use in Bangladesh became intense reflected by a sharp increase in cropping intensity from only 142.9% in 1973 to 176.9% in 2005 facilitated by increased provision of irrigation infrastructure to diffuse a rice-based Green Revolution technology package throughout the country. Although total cereal production (dominated by rice) has increased, productivity of crops per unit of key inputs (i.e., land area, fertilizers, and pesticides) has been declining consistently over the years, thereby, raising doubt on the sustainability of the agricultural sector as well as its ability to maintain and/or reach the goal of self-sufficiency in food production. However, contrary to the widespread apprehension that Bangladesh is fast losing its crop diversity owing to HYV rice monoculture spurred by the diffusion of Green Revolution technology, results showed that crop diversity has actually increased at a modest rate of 0.4% per year as indicated by the computed value of the Herfindahl index of crop diversification. It is encouraging to note that Bangladesh has shown success in raising its foodgrain availability per capita and was able to outstrip the influence of the high rate of population growth. However, the real gain in returns derived from the agricultural growth could not outstrip the influence of population growth but managed to offset it and was able to maintain a stable contribution. Although we see consistent growth in the energy derived from all food sources (excluding meat and fish products) per capita per day, the main contributor to this growth in energy availability was the foodgrain sector, as expected. However, consistent decline in energy derived from the non-cereals, particularly, fruits have important implication on dietary health of the Bangladeshi population.

Given the results from the aforementioned analyses, we can conclude that the Green Revolution technology has delivered its expected outcomes, i.e., contributing positively towards attaining the goal of self-sufficiency in food production. However, the concentration of food energy availability from the cereals as opposed to non-cereals is a source of concern for the dietary health of the Bangladeshi population. It is, however, encouraging to note rising trend in non-cereal production, which could pave the way for a diversified agricultural system that is relatively more sustainable. The declining trend in productivity from current Green Revolution technology is not going to sustain in the future. Thus, Bangladesh needs to widen its technology base and go beyond the diffusion of HYV rice and/or wheat should diversify its land use towards producing non-cereals, which are more profitable (Rahman 1998) and could enhance farmers' earnings and livelihoods as well as generate valuable foreign exchange for the economy through exports.

References

Alauddin, M., Tisdell, C. 1991. The Green Revolution and Economic Development: The Process and Its Impact in Bangladesh. Macmillan, London.

BASR, 1989. *Growth performance of cereal production since the middle 1970s and regional variations*. Bangladesh Agricultural Sector Review. Dhaka: United Nations Development Program (UNDP)/Bangladesh Agricultural Research Council (BARC). Dhaka, Bangladesh.

BB, (various issues). Economic Trends (monthly publications) from 1990 to 2007. Bangladesh Bank, Dhaka.

BBS, (various issues). Statistical Yearbook of Bangladesh, 1975, 1980, 1984/85, 1989, 1990, 1992, 1995, 1997, 1998, 2000, and 2002. Bangladesh Bureau of Statistics, Dhaka.

BBS, 2006. Household Expenditure and Income Survey, 2005. Bangladesh Bureau of Statistics, Dhaka.

Coelli, T.J., Fleming, E., 2004. Diversification economies and specialization efficiencies in a mixed food and coffee smallholder farming system in Papua New Guinea. *Agricultural Economics*. 31: 229-239.

FAO, 2001. *Supplements to the Report on the 1990 World Census of Agriculture. Statistical Department Series (9a).* Food and Agriculture Organization, Rome. http://www.fao.org/es/ess/census/wcahome.htm

Hossain, M., 1989. *Green Revolution in Bangladesh: Impact on Growth and Distribution of Income.* Dhaka: University Press Limited.

Husain, A.M.M., Hossain, M., Janaiah, A., 2001 *Hybrid Rice Adoption in Bangladesh: Socio-economic Assessment of Farmers' Experiences*. BRAC Research Monograph Series No. 18. BRAC, Dhaka.

Khalil, M.I. 1991. *The agricultural sector in Bangladesh* – A database. U.S. Agency for International Development, Dhaka, Bangladesh.

Llewelyn, R.V., Williams, J.R., 1996. Nonparametric analysis of technical, pure technical, and scale efficiencies for food crop production in East java, Indonesia. *Agricultural Economics*, 15: 113-126.

Mahmud, W., Rahman, S.H., Zohir, S., 1994. *Agricultural growth through crop diversification in Bangladesh.* Food Policy in Bangladesh Working Paper No. 7. International Food Policy Research Institute (IFPRI), Washington, D.C.

Mian, A.J., 1978. "A Least Cost Nutritional Diet for Bangladesh: An Alternative Approach to Food Supply". Ph.D. Dissertation. Ohio: The Ohio State University.

MoA, 2008. *Agricultural Handbook of Bangladesh, 2007.* Ministry of Agriculture, Government of Bangladesh, Dhaka.

Rahman, S. 2008. "Bio-physical and socio-economic determinants of adopting a diversified cropping system: a case study from Bangladesh". In Castalonge, O.W. (ed.) *Agricultural Systems: Economics, Technology and Diversity*. New York: Nova Science Publishers, Inc.

Rahman, S. 1998. Socio-economic and environmental impacts of technological change in Bangladesh agriculture. Unpublished PhD dissertation. Asian Institute of Technology, Pathumthani, Thailand.

Rahman, S. 2002. "Technological change and food production sustainability in Bangladesh agriculture". *Asian Profile.* Vol. 30 (3): 233–245.

Tong, C., Hall, C.A.S., Wang, H. 2003. Land use change in rice, wheat and maize production in China (1961 – 1998). *Agriculture, Ecosystem and the Environment*, 95: 523–536.

New nation, 2008. Vegetables exports up by Tk 173.81 crore. The New Nation, Daily Newspaper (18 August, 20080, Dhaka, Bangladesh.

In: Land Use Policy
Editors: A. C. Denman and O. M. Penrod
ISBN: 978-1-60741-435-3

Chapter 9

AGRICULTURAL COOL ISLAND (ACI)

***Rezaul Mahmood*[*1] *and Kenneth G. Hubbard*[2]**

[1] Department of Geography and Geology and Kentucky Climate Center; Western Kentucky University; Bowling Green, KY 42101

[2] High Plains Regional Climate Center; School of Natural Resource Sciences; University of Nebraska-Lincoln; Lincoln, NE 68583-0728

ABSTRACT

Land use change has been an inevitable consequence of human activities throughout the centuries. One of the most prominent impacts of human activities can be found in agricultural expansion and resultant modification of the natural landscape. Numerous observed data- and model-based studies have shown that agricultural land use change has modified meteorological, seasonal, and climate-scale root zone soil moisture distribution, energy partitioning, near surface energy balance, and temperature. The most typical spatial scales include local and regional. Studies along a similar theme even suggest that these changes affect meteorological events (e. g., convective activities). In addition, widespread adoption and application of irrigation further enhances these impacts.

Based on the results from several of our own and numerous studies completed by others, the objective of this paper is to propose the concept of '*Agricultural Cool Island' (ACI)*. It is overwhelmingly evident that agricultural land use change has lowered mean maximum and extreme maximum temperatures. This, in turn, has led to a lowering of the diurnal temperature range. This temperature decrease occurred primarily due to changes in energy partitioning which are associated with changes in bio-physical characteristics of the landscape. In many cases the changes are related to changes in root zone soil moisture and its role in energy partitioning. Since this cooling is clearly evident and the most notable of all impacts, we coined the concept ACI.

As suggested above, lowering of temperature (which is an important aspect) is not the only impact of agricultural land use change. There are many other impacts of these modifications. The changes associated with the impacts can be dynamic over time and space. We note that ACI is both a self-contained and interactive entity. The feedback loops within this entity itself are non-linear and complex like other components of the earth system. In light of these, like urban heat island (UHI), we suggest that the concept

---

* Corresponding author: e-mail: rezaul.mahmood@wku.edu; Phone: (270) 745-5979; Fax: (270) 745-6410

of ACI should allow for more focused and organized scientific investigations. Furthermore, ACI should serve as a platform for well thought-out research activities.

Keywords: Agricultural Cool Island, land use change, impacts.

INTRODUCTION

Over the last couple of centuries various regions of the world have gone through rapid changes from natural land cover to agricultural land use (Waisanen and Bliss 2002; Ramankutty and Foley 1999). The latter research developed a global land use change data set and demonstrated widespread expansion of agriculture and resultant land use change over all continents. Waisanen and Bliss (2002) reported that in the Midwest and the Great Plains changes reached close to 60% of total land area. The changes were greater than 10-fold between 1850 and 1940 and more than 1-fold between 1940 and 1997 for the Midwest and the Great Plains (Waisanen and Bliss, 2002). In some areas more than 80% of the land use has changed from non-irrigated to irrigated agriculture (total change 23-fold from the 1950s to 1990s) during the second half of the 20th century (figure 1). These land use transformations are expected to modify local and regional near surface atmospheric temperatures. In particular, due to widespread adoption of irrigated agriculture and subsequent limited sensible energy availability we expect a reduction in long-term daily maximum temperatures. Moreover, non-irrigated agriculture with greater evapotranspiration (ET) rates compared to natural grass produced similar impacts. A number of observed data-based and model-based studies provide evidence for such changes.

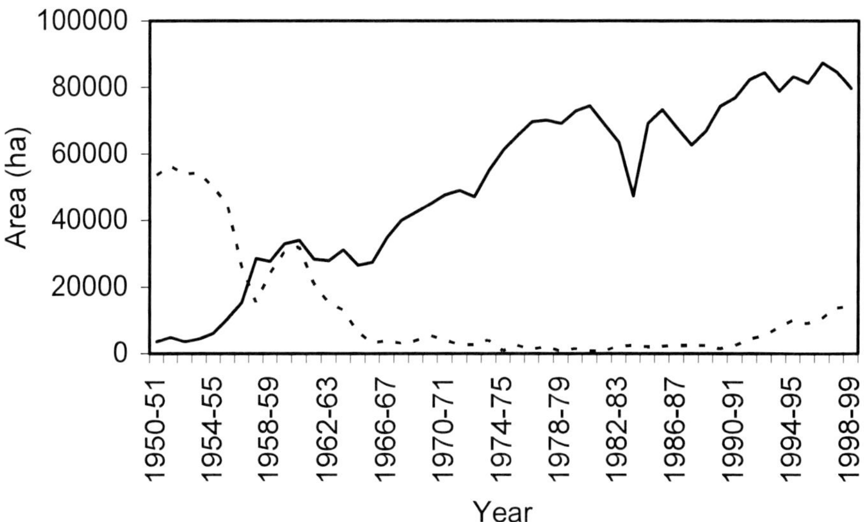

Figure 1. Changes in irrigated (unbroken line) and non-irrigated (broken line) areas York county, Nebraska, USA. (Source: Mahmood, 2002).

Marland et al. (2003) suggested that land surface change would affect regional and global climate by modifying surface albedo and energy budgets. It is argued that since it is an important component of the climate system, land surface changes and subsequent impacts should be seriously considered (Marland et al. 2003). These statements can be included for agricultural land use change. Recently, Cai et al. (2004) and Pielke et al. (2002) argued that the two most important anthropogenic impacts on climate are greenhouse gases and land use changes. However, they have also asserted that the impacts of land use changes have been treated like a noise.

In light of these developments, the objective of this paper is to formally present the concept of 'Agricultural Cool Island' (ACI) and provide the basis of its importance and formulation. This paper will show cooling of temperature is not the only impact of agricultural land use change. *The authors recognize that there are other important affects (e. g., changes in energy balance, energy partitioning, root zone soil moisture, convective activities, albedo, surface roughness) of ACI on earth system and they are complex. However, this study considers cooling of temperature as one the most notable and obvious impacts and thus concluded that the ACI would be the most appropriate way to describe and highlight the concept.* Nevertheless, it needs to be noted that this paper includes brief discussion on impact of land use change on convection initiation and their timing, soil moisture and convection, for example. We suggest that like 'urban heat island' studies the ACI needs critical focus because of its impacts on local and regional weather, climate, and hydrology.

To achieve the goal of this paper we provide examples and rely on results from previous studies. The list (and discussion) is *not intended to be comprehensive and all encompassing. Moreover, it is not a review paper* in a classical sense and does not present any new data analysis. Here we make note of some of the more widespread and well-known aspects of the impacts and the approach is to use *selected* relevant literature to support the concept.

Findings from Observed Data Based Studies

Impacts of land use change on the climate system were identified through a number of observational studies. Here we present a summary of the past investigations. A significant decrease in temperature during the period 1981-1995 was found in northeast Colorado and it was suggested that this change has occurred due to significant expansion of irrigated agriculture (Chase et al. 1999). In an earlier study Segal et al. (1989) found that the temperature difference between irrigated and adjoining non-irrigated areas eastern Colorado can be up to 10 °C. These results are physically consistent with Idso et al.'s (1981) findings. They found that the surface temperature for irrigated alfalfa could be 12 °C cooler than the surface temperature of a dry alfalfa field with severe water stress.

Radaatz (1999) noted that agricultural land use change has produced a cooling during the maximum plant growth stages (mid-summer) in the Canadian Prairies. They attributed this to a higher rate of ET, compared to prairie, at this time of the growing season. Similarly, Hogg et al. (2000) found 2 °C cooling of summer time temperature in the western Canadian interior and noted that latent heat flux dominates the energy partitioning during summer which results in cooling (Hogg et al., 2000).

Temperature trend analysis suggests a decreasing trend in growing season mean temperature and mean maximum temperature in Nebraska (Mahmood et al. 2004). Observed data-based calculations suggest that both growing season mean and mean maximum temperature can decrease at the rate of -0.01 °C yr^{-1}. It was found that the highest rate of decrease in mean maximum temperatures for all irrigated locations was observed during the months of July and August (Mahmood et al. 2004). Plant water requirement reaches to its maximum in July and August in response to enhanced physiological activities and growth. To meet this demand irrigation water application also increases. Elevated thermal and radiative condition, in combination with increased availability of water led to a higher rate of ET during these months, resulted in a greater rate of reduction of mean maximum temperatures (Mahmood et al. 2004). Extreme high temperatures also show a decreasing trend in irrigated locations with the highest rate of decrease in July and August. Conditions similar to above (land use change) caused this type of temperature modification.

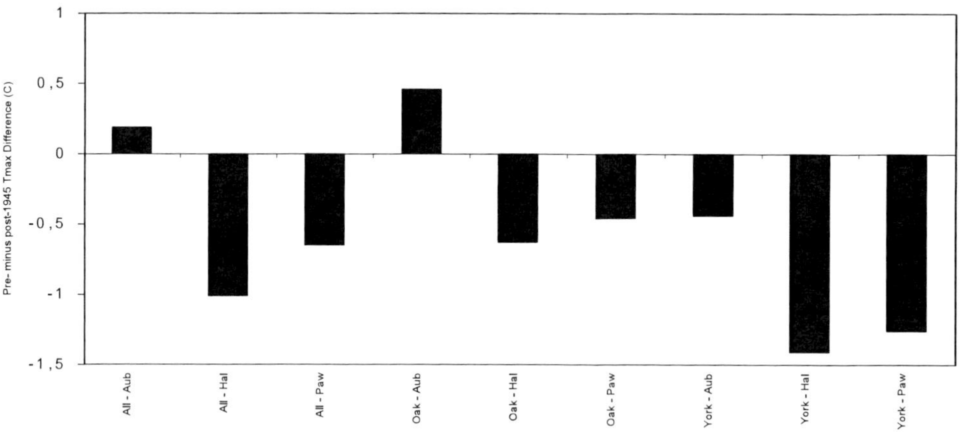

Figure 2. Cooling at irrigated locations in Nebraska, USA during post-1945 period. Negative values show cooling. Alliance (ALL), Oakland (Oak), and York are irrigated locations while Halsey (Hal), Auburn (Aub), and Pawnee City (Paw) are non-irrigated locations. (Source: Mahmood et al., 2006).

The HCN time series-based pairwise comparison of growing season temperatures for 1906-1945 and 1946-1999 for Nebraska and Ogallala aquifer region (Mahmood et al. 2006; 2008) show that mean maximum temperatures at irrigated sites were lower compared to non-irrigated sites. . For example, mean maximum growing season temperature at irrigated Alliance was 2.41 °C colder compared to non-irrigated Auburn while irrigated Oakdale was 2.18 °C colder compared to non-irrigated Pawnee City. It is also found that cooling at irrigated locations was greater during post-1945 period compared to pre-1945 years. Our calculations show that mean maximum growing season temperature at irrigated Alliance was 0.64 °C and 1.65 °C cooler compared to non-irrigated Halsey during pre-and post-1945 period, respectively. In other words, there was a 1.01 °C cooling during the post-1945 period (figure 2). A composite analysis suggests that, on average, irrigated locations in Nebraska have cooled down 0.58 °C during post-1945 (figure 3). Hence, the second half of the 20th century experienced greater cooling primarily as a result of extensive introduction of irrigation. The time series were also divided between pre- and post-1950 and 1955 to determine whether it is possible to find signals for the period of maximum land use change. It is clear from the figure 3 that second half of the 20th century experienced greater cooling.

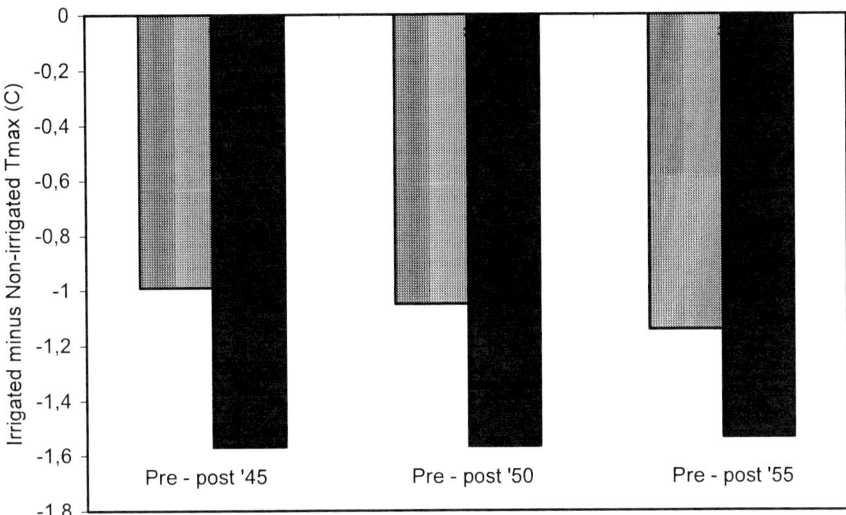

Figure 3. Composite analysis of cooling of growing season maximum temperature in Nebraska due to irrigation. (Source: Mahmood et al., 2006).

Further data analyses suggest that growing season mean temperature at irrigated locations were up to 4.11 °C cooler compared to non-irrigated areas during pre- and post-1945 years. As above, in most cases decrease in mean temperature was greater during post-1945 years compared to pre-1945s. Compared to Pawnee City, York was 0.27 and 1.04 °C cooler during pre-1945 and post-1945 years, respectively, for example. Thus, a 0.77 °C cooling of mean temperature has occurred at York.

It is expected that if ET increases notably then near surface dew point temperature would also increase reflecting higher atmospheric moisture content. Mahmood et al. (2008) analyzed dew point temperature for six non-irrigated and 11 irrigated locations in Nebraska. Compared to non-irrigated sites, significantly higher dew point temperatures were recorded for all irrigated locations. This study has found 1.56 °C higher average growing season dew point temperature over irrigated areas (figure 4). It has also reported up to 2.17 °C higher dew point temperature for peak growing season months. The results clearly show that land use change significantly modified near surface atmospheric moisture distribution and thus temperatures.

McPherson et al. (2004) investigated the impacts of the winter wheat belt on the near surface temperature. They found a cool anomaly of mean maximum temperature over the Oklahoma wheat belt during the growing season and reported higher daily maximum dew point temperature in March and April. These months coincide with the maximum growth period for the winter wheat. They have also reported increase in daily dew point temperature over the wheat growing areas compared to the surrounding landscape. A lowering of vapor pressure deficit was also found over wheat land use. Sandstrom et al. (2004) investigated changes in long-term (1949-2000) summer (June-August) extreme daily dew point temperature for the Central US. They found a consistent increase in extreme daily dew point temperature during the study period. Their study suggests that this increase is related to rapid expansion of agriculture in the Midwest region and subsequent enhancement of evapotranspiration.

Similar to the above findings, Kalnay and Cai (2003) found a cooling trend in maximum temperature during spring, summer, and fall in the Midwest for 1950-1999 time period. They have noted that increases in daytime evaporation due to land use change (introduction of agriculture) resulted in decreasing maximum temperature. Analysis of growing season (June-August) temperature data (1930-2000) from central valley of California indicates a slightly negative trend in maximum temperature and a strongly positive trend in minimum temperature (Christy et al. 2006). The authors of this study suggest increased evaporation resulted in lowering of maximum temperature while moist land surface releases previously absorbed energy during nighttime causing an increase in minimum temperature.

Bonan (1999) analyzed the impacts of land use change on temperature of the Midwest and the Northeast and noted that the decrease in DTR resulted from greater cooling of daily maximum temperature compared to daily minimum temperature. Dai et al. (1999) estimated that soil moisture and precipitation reduce DTR by 25-50%. They have found that soil moisture is negatively correlated with DTR and suggested that evaporation of soil moisture (latent energy partitioning) and subsequent cooling played the key role in lowering of DTR. The authors of this paper argue that land use change due to introduction of irrigation or any other modification would alter root zone soil moisture and near-surface temperatures (e. g. Mahmood et al. 2004). This study suggests that increase in latent energy flux due to irrigation and subsequent modification of energy partitioning results in decreasing DTR.

FINDINGS FROM MODEL BASED STUDIES

In an effort to determine the impacts of land use change on temperature, Roy et al. (2003) conducted model simulations for July of 1700, 1910, and 1990. They have found 1 °C cooling of mean July surface temperatures over a large part of the Great Plains and the Mid-West. Comparison of simulated temperatures from 1910 and 1700 suggest that most of the cooling was concentrated in the Central Great Plains of the US. In addition, a similar assessment for 1990 and 1700 identified an amazing expansion of this cooling over the southern, central and northern Great Plains (figure 6; Roy et al. 2003) and linked this change with transformation of grassland to farm lands which has potentially increased ET and reduced the Bowen ratio and temperature.

Zhao and Pitman (2002) investigated the impacts of land cover change and increasing CO_2 on maximum temperature frequency and convective precipitation. The model simulations suggested a reduction in the return value of maximum temperature in Europe. It was noted that removal of deciduous forest and introduction of croplands reduced stomatal resistance. This caused higher latent energy flux and lowering of temperatures. Zhao and Pitman (2002) also found that land cover change resulted in a 2 °C reduction of maximum temperature in Europe and the level of atmospheric CO_2 did not have any impact on this estimate. Hence, land cover change and its impact on temperature was independent of CO_2

concentration. Eastman et al. (2001) found that mean maximum temperature would be 1.2 °C cooler compared to current land uses over Central and Northern Great Plains under potentially modified future natural vegetation coverage. Narisma et al. (2003) investigated the impacts of land cover change on January temperatures in Australia and found that latent energy flux will increase and temperature will decrease over NE Australia.

Bounoua et al. (2000) used global NDVI data to create maximum and minimum vegetation scenarios. Their study reported a 1.8 K cooling during the growing season in the northern latitudes and suggested that this cooling was due to a greater amount of energy partitioned into latent heat. They have also noted that in the presence of drier soils the energy partitioning pattern will change. Bounoua et al. (2002) also found that in the temperate latitudes land use modification to crop land would lower summer temperature up to 0.7 °C. It was concluded that declining temperature was connected to morphological and physiological changes in vegetation that resulted in increased albedo and latent energy flux, respectively. In another model-based study, Bonan (1997) estimated a cooling trend in daily maximum temperatures and decrease in DTR over major agricultural areas of the United States.

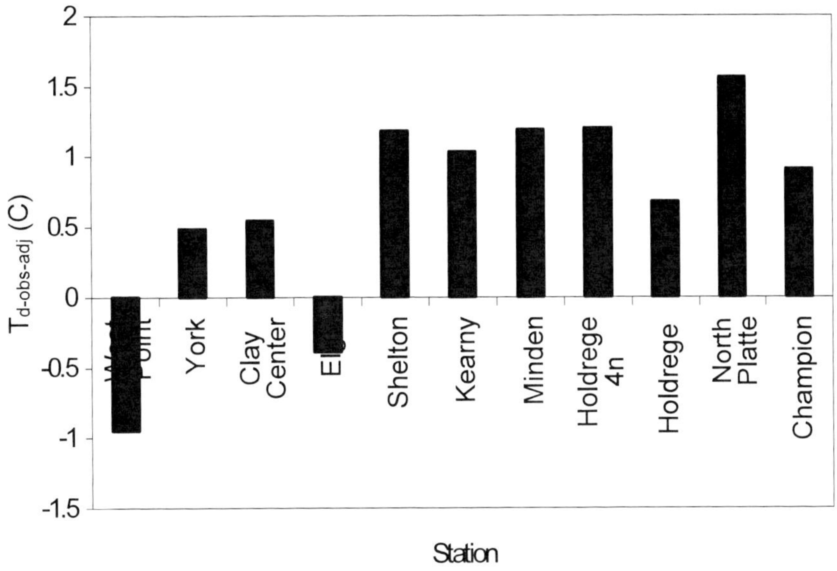

Figure 4. Increase in average growing season dew point temperature due to irrigation in Nebraska, USA. (Source: Mahmood et al., 200).

The authors of the present paper have applied a soil moisture-energy balance model for three land uses (natural grass, rainfed and irrigated corn) at three locations in Nebraska to determine land use changes and its impacts on near surface hydrologic conditions (Robinson and Hubbard 1990; Mahmood and Hubbard 2002, Mahmood and Hubbard 2003, 2004). These locations represent the east (wet) to west (dry) hydroclimatic gradient of the Great Plains. The results show that land use change has modified ET and near-surface soil moisture content (hence, energy and water balance). In some cases ET for irrigated corn is nearly 36% higher compared to natural grass (figure 5). In the past, Mahmood et al. (2001) found notable change in energy partitioning due to the ramifications of modified land use. Through applications of Regional Atmospheric Modeling System (RAMS) Adegoke et al. (2003) also found increase of near surface atmospheric moisture content due to irrigation. It was expected that a change in energy partitioning of this magnitude would modify surface temperature records which was evident from subsequent analyses of data (Mahmood et al., 2004).

These outcomes clearly point toward the fact that agricultural land use change modifies water consumption behavior of a particular landscape and subsequently water and energy balance and temperature, among others. We suspect that the effect is potentially largest on daily maximum temperature since it occurs most commonly during late afternoon which coincides with the most active transpiring phase of plants. In addition, transforming of natural landscape to irrigated agriculture would provide particularly pronounced impacts.

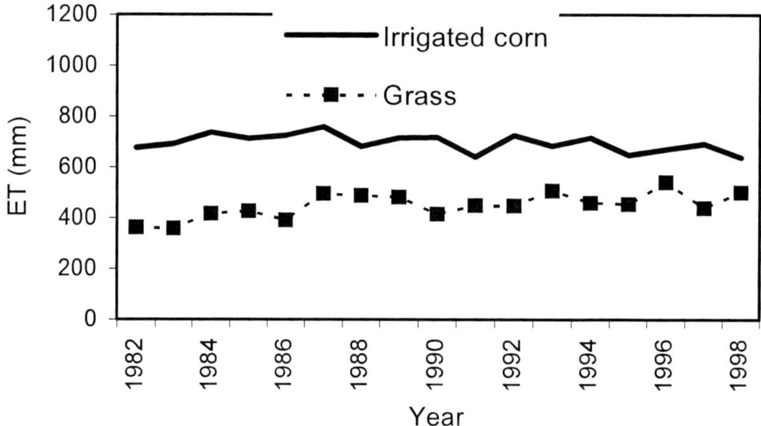

Figure 5. Evapotranspiration from irrigated corn and grass in McCook, Nebrasak, USA. (Source: Mahmood and Hubbard, 2002).

Why It Is Important to Study *ACI*

There are many facets of human impacts on climate. Agricultural land use change and its impacts on climate is one of these facets. The above discussion clearly demonstrates the significance of meso- and regional scale-agricultural land use on climate at these scales. Furthermore, introduction of this paper noted the rapid and extensive changes in land use in the 19th and 20th century. We suggest that these land use change will continue in the 21st century in many parts of the world in response to anthropogenic activities. In these contexts, we discuss justifications for focused studies of ACI.

1 Agricultural land use change affects regional and sub-continental scale energy balance. In particular, increased latent energy partitioning leads to decreases in seasonal air temperatures including mean maximum and mean temperatures.
2 Widespread adoption of irrigation increases the near surface soil moisture, forces more of the energy into latent at the expense of sensible energy and thus cools (lowers) maximum temperatures.

3 Pielke et al. (2002) suggested that energy partitioning directly influences near surface temperature and should be considered as a climate forcing. Agricultural land use also affects energy balance and thus needs to be viewed under the category of climate forcing.

4 Agricultural land use change moderates extreme temperatures. It is found that these decreases are negatively 'correlated' with the increases in ET during the maximum plant growth stages.

5 It is common knowledge that as we change types of vegetation cover, albedo also change which eventually affects energy balance and temperature. Thus, replacement of natural vegetation with croplands produces similar impacts.

6 Dew point temperature has increased over both irrigated and non-irrigated agricultural land uses. Dew point observations also show month-to-month variations over the growing season as a result of plant water consumption behavior during the plant growth cycle.

7 Increased dew point affects the living condition of surrounding localities. For example, Changon et al. (2003) noted that the cases of increased heat-stresses in Chicago were partly associated with increased dew point temperature in the agricultural mid-west and the advection of this air mass to the city. Thus, impacts of agricultural land use changes are not limited to its immediate vicinity.

8 Sudden 'dipping' of DTR and daily maximum temperature with spring-time phenological change is well documented (e.g., Schwartz 1996; Schwartz and Karl 1990; Durre and Wallace 2001). These changes are associated with increased latent energy flux which leads to lowering of daily maximum temperature and DTR. In a region of heterogeneous farming practices, the pattern of water consumption and energy balance varies by individual crop. For example, peak period of latent energy flux varies among different types of plant covers. The effects would be felt earlier for a cool season crop than for a late season crop. In other words, we would expect to see changes in timing of the dip of daily maximum temperature and DTR at local scales associated with varying agricultural practices (increased patchiness of dipping of daily maximum temperature and DTR)..

9 In addition to cooling, agricultural land use change will increase and decrease the frost-free season and freezing days, respectively. Initial results of our ongoing investigation suggest that irrigated areas experience fewer days with below freezing temperature. On the other hand, a modeling study by Marshall et al. (2004) demonstrated that land use change has modified summertime local temperature and precipitation in peninsular Florida. This study has focused on the pre-1900 natural and current land uses. They found that energy partitioning (sensible and latent) has changed notably. In addition, modifications in spatial distribution of convective rainfall have occurred and daily maximum temperature has increased. It was suggested that draining of natural wetlands to agricultural fields significantly reduced latent energy partitioning and thus increased daytime temperature. The increase in modeled temperature is consistent with observed records. In a related study, Marshall et al. (2003) argued that present day land use in the key agricultural areas of peninsular Florida has resulted in greater severity and frequency of freezing conditions. Model simulations show that for the natural land use in pre-1900 a

persistent heat flux would originate in the wetlands and force temperatures to remain above freezing level.

10 Agricultural land use change and its potential impacts may also occur at meteorological time scales. Yan and Anthes (1987) demonstrated that changes in soil moisture and the relative extent of adjacent moist and dry surface affects timing, intensity, and life-span of convection. In other words it is possible that widespread application of irrigation and resulting increases in soil moisture could affect convective development.

11 Rabin et al. (1990) demonstrated with observed data from agricultural areas of Oklahoma that land use affects convection and cloud formation. Hanesiak et al. (2004) also found that agricultural land use affects initiation and timing (daily time–scale) of deep convection in the Canadian Prairie provinces. Radaatz (2003) and Radaatz and Cummine (2003) suggested that wheat phenology and tornado days per week are linked in Canada. These studies, again, call for additional focused studies on ACI.

12 Changes in land use and plant cover, along with energy partitioning, and water consumption, also affects CO_2 balance on local and regional scales.

13 We suggest like UHI, the ACI has meteorological, monthly, seasonal, and climate scale characteristics and they vary. Therefore, it is dynamic and needs further attention.

14 ACI is both a self-contained and interactive entity. We suspect that feedback loops within this entity itself are non-linear and complex like other components of the earth system.

15 Pielke (2002) concluded that if we exclude land use changes and their impacts on the climate system, agreement between general circulation model (GCM) simulations and observations may be due to 'wrong reasons' (Pielke 2002). Although, most of our argument is based on local and regional scales assessments, we suggest that the Pielke's (2002) observation applies to ACI (at its scales) and underscores the need for special focus.

16 Pielke (2002) proposed that the following hypotheses needed to be tested. 1) Landscape directly and indirectly influences earth's radiation budget, 2) land use change affects local, regional and global climate at all time scales, and 3) forcing due to land use change is as important as radiative forcing associated with a doubling of carbon dioxide. It is clear that his suggestions are overarching and apply to all types of land use and all scales. Hence, again, based on the results from the studies above, we suggest ACI can be used to test the validity of these hypotheses.

Conclusion

A recent report, published by the U. S. Climate Change Science Program (2005) identified land use change, including agricultural, as one of the key areas of research. This provides further support for ACI and related focused studies. In our opinion a clear conceptual understanding of ACI helps to fulfill this objective. Moreover, these research activities need to encompass all aspects of ACI and the associated dynamics at meteorological and climatological time-scales. It is important that we improve our understanding of feedbacks between ACI and local and regional atmosphere and any implications for climate variability and climate change at these scales. Additionally, we recommend that the scientific community should undertake ACI related studies for various part of the world to define and characterize the behavior under different geographical and climatic regimes. The results of these studies would not only be helpful in answering basic science questions but should also reduce uncertainties in weather, climate, and hydrologic predictions at relevant scales.

REFERENCES

Adegoke, J. O.; Pielke Sr., R. A.; Eastman, J.; Mahmood, R; Hubbard, K. G. A regional atmospheric model study of the impact of irrigation on midsummer surface energy budget in the U. S. High Plains. *Mon. Wea. Rev.* 2003, 131, 556-564.

Bonan, G. Effects of land use on the climate of the United States. *Clim. Change.* 1997 37, 449-486.

Bonan, G. Observational evidence for reduction of daily maximum temperature by croplands in the Midwest United States. *J. Clim.* 1999, 14, 2430-2442.

Bounoua, L.; Collatz, G. J.; Los, S.O.; Sellers, P.J.; Dazlich, D.A.; Tucker, C.J.; Randall, D.A. Sensitivity of climate to changes in NDVI. *J. Clim.* 2000, 13, 2277-2292.

Bounoua, L.; Defries, R.; Collatz, G.J.; Sellers, P.; Khan, H. Effects of land cover conversion on surface climate. *Clim. Change* 2002, 52, 29-64.

Cai, M.; Li, H.; Kalnay, E. Impact of land use change and urbanization on climate. 2004 Proceedings of 14th Conference of Applied Climatology, Seattle, WA. (www.ametsoc.org)

Changnon, D.; Sandstrom, M.A.; Schaffer, C. Relating changes in agricultural practices to increasing dew points in extreme Chicago heat waves. *Clim. Res.* 2003, 24, 243-254.

Chase, T.N.; Kittel, T.G.F; Baron, J.S.; Stohlgren, T.J. Potential impacts on Colorado Rocky mountain weather due to land use changes on the adjacent Great Plains. *J. Geophys. Res.*1999, 104, 16, 673-16, 690.

Christy, J.R.; Norris, W. B.; Redmond, K.; Gallo, K. P. Methodology and results of calculating central california surface temperature trends: Evidence of human-induced climate change? *J. Climate*, 2006, 19, 548–563.

Dai, A.; Trenberth, K. E.; Karl, T.R. Effects of clouds, soil moisture, precipitation and water vapor on diurnal temperature range. *J. Clim.* 1999, 12, 2451-2473.

Durre, I.; Wallace, J.M. 2001. The warm season dip in diurnal temperature range over the eastern United States. *J. Clim.* 2001, 14, 354-360.

Hanesiak, J.M; Raddatz, R.L.; Lobban, S. Local initiation of deep convection on the Canadian Prairie provinces. *Boundary-Layer Meteor.* 2004, 110, 455-470.

Hogg, E.H.; Price, D.T.; Black, T.A. Postulated feedbacks of deciduous forest phenology on seasonal climate patterns in the western Canadian interior. *J. Clim.* 2000, 13, 4229-4243.

Idso, S.B.; Reginato, R.J.; Reicosky, D.C.; Hatfield, J.L. Determining soil-induced plant water potential depressions in Alfalfa by means of infrared thermometry. *Agronomy J.* 1981, 73, 826-830.

Kalnay, E; Cai, M. 2004. Impact of urbanization and land use change. *Nature* 2004, 423, 528-531.

Mahmood, R.; Hubbard, K.G. Simulating sensitivity of soil moisture and evapotranspiration under heterogeneous soils and land uses. *J. Hydrol.* 2003, 280, 72-90.

Mahmood, R.; Hubbard, K.G. An analysis of simulated long-term soil moisture data for three land uses under contrasting hydroclimatic conditions in the Northern Great Plains. *J. Hydrometeor.* 2004, 5, 160-179.

Mahmood, R.; Hubbard, K.G. Anthropogenic land use change in the North American Tall Grass-Short grass transition and modification of near surface hydrologic cycle. *Clim. Res.* 2002, 21, 83-90.

Mahmood, R; Foster, S.A.; Keeling, T.; Hubbard, K.G.; Carlson, C.; Leeper, R. Impacts of Irrigation on 20th Century Temperature in the Northern Great Plains. *Glob. Planet. Change* 2006, 54, 1-18

Mahmood, R.; Hubbard, K.G.; Carlson, C. Modification of growing-season surface temperature records in the Northern Great Plains due to land use transformation: Verification of modeling results and implications for global climate change. *Int. J. Climatol.,* 2004,24, 311-327.

Mahmood, R., Hubbard, K.G.; Hou, Q. Soil moisture monitoring and modeling in the Great Plains. In: Hubbard, KG and Sivakumar, MVK (eds.), *Automated Weather Stations for Applications in Agriculture and Water Resources Management: Current Use and Future Perspectives,* High Plains Climate Center, Lincoln, NE and World Meteorological Organization Geneva, Switzerland, 2001, pp. 163-171.

Mahmood, R.; Hubbard, K. G.; Leeper, R.; Foster, S. A. Increase in near surface atmospheric moisture content due to land use changes: Evidence from the observed dew point temperature data. *Mon. Wea. Rev.* 2008, 13, 1554-1561.

Marland, G; Pielke Sr., R.A.; Apps, M.; Avissar, R.; Betts, R.A.; Davis, K.J.; Frumhoff, P.C.; Jackson, S.T.; Joyce, L.; Kauppi, P.; Katzenberger, J.; MacDicken, K.G.; Neilson, R.; Niles, J.O.; Niyogi, D.D.S.; Norby, R.J.; Pena, N.; Sampson, N.; Xue, Y. The climatic impacts of land surface change and carbon management, and the implications for climate-change mitigation policy. *Clim. Policy.* 2003, 3, 149-157.

Marshall, C. H.; Pielke Sr., R.A.; Steyaert, LT. Crop freezes and land-use change in Florida. *Nature.* 2003, 426, 29-30.

Marshall, C.H.; Pielke Sr., R.A.; Steyaert, L.T.; Willard, D.A. The impact of anthropogenic land-cover change on the Florida Peninsula Sea Breezes and warm season sensible weather. *Mon. Wea. Rev.* 2004, 132, 28-52.

McPherson, R.A.; Stensrud, D.J.; Crawford, K.C. The impact of Oklahoma's wheat belt on the mesoscale environment. *Mon.Wea. Rev.* 2004, 132, 405-421.

Narisma, G.T.; Pitman, A.J.; Eastman, J.; Watterson, I.G.; Pielke Sr., R.; Beltran-Przekurat, A. The role of biospheric feedbacks in the simulations of the impact of historical land cover change on the Australian January Climate. *Geophys. Res. Lett.* 2003, 30, 2168 doi:10.1029/2003GL018261.

Pielke Sr., R.A. Overlooked issues in the U. S. National Climate and IPCC assessments: an editorial essay. *Clim. Change* 2002, 52, 1-11.

Pielke Sr., R.A.; Marland, G.; Betts, R.A.; Chase, T.N.; Eastman, J.L.; Niles, J.O.; Niyogi, D.D.S. and Running, S.W. The influence of land-use change and landscape dynamics on the climate system: relevance to climate-change policy beyond the radiative effect of greenhouse gases. *Phil. Trans. Royal Soc. London A,* 2002, 360, 1705-1719.

Rabin, R.M.; Stadler, S.; Wetzel, P.J.; Stensrud, D.J.; Gregory, M. Observed effects of landscape variability on convective clouds. *Bull. Amer. Meteor. Soc.*1990, 71, 122-130.

Radaatz, R.L. Anthropogenic vegetation transformation and maximum temperatures on the Canadian Prairies. *CMOS Bulletin SCMO,* 1999, 27,167-173.

Radaatz, R.L. Agriculture and tornadoes on the Canadian Prairies: potential impact of increasing atmospheric CO2 on summer severe weather. *Nat. Hazard* 2003, 290, 113-122.

Raddatz, R.L.; Cummine, J.D. 2003. Inter-annual variability of moisture flux from the prairie agro-ecosystem: impact of crop phenology on the seasonal pattern of tornado days. *Boundary-Layer Meteor.* 2003, 106, 283-295.

Ramankutty, N; Foley, J. Estimating historical changes in global land cover: Croplands from 1700 to 1992. *Glob. Biogeochem.l Cyc.* 1999, 13, 997-1027.

Robinson, J.M.; Hubbard, K.G. Soil water assessment model for several crops in The high plains. *Agronomy J.* 1990, 82, 1141-1148.

Roy, S.B.; Hurtt, G.C.; Weaver, C.P.; Pacala, S.W. 2003. Impact of historical land cover change on the July climate of the United States. *J. Geophys. Res.* 2003, 108, doi: 10.1029/2003JD003565

Sandstrom, M.A.; Lauritsen, R.G.; Changnon, D. A central U. S. summer extreme dew-point climatology (1949-2000). *Phys. Geogr.* 2004, 25, 191-207.

Schwartz, M.D. Examining the spring discontinuity in daily temperature ranges. *J. Clim.* 1996, 9, 803-808.

Schwartz, M.D.; Karl, T.R. Spring phenology: nature's experiment to detect the effect of green-up on surface maximum temperatures. *Mon.Wea.Rev.* 1990, 118, 883-890.

Segal, M.; Schreiber, W.E.; Kallos, G.; Garratt, G.R.; Rodi, A.; Weaver, J.; Pielke, R.A. The impact of crop areas in northeastern Colorado on midsummer mesoscale thermal circulations. *Mon. Wea. Rev.* 1989, 117, 809-825.

U. S. Climate Change Science Program and the Subcommittee on Global Change Research. Our Changing Planet: The U.S. Climate Change Science Program for Fiscal Years 2004 and 2005. 2005, Washington. D.C: U. S. Climate Change Science Program.

Waisenan, P.J.; Bliss, N.B. Changes in population and agricultural land in conterminous United States, 1790 to 1997. *Glob. Biogeochem.Cycl.* 2002, 16, 1137, doi: 10.1029/2001GB001843.

Yan, H.; Anthes, R.A. The effect of variations in surface moisture on mesoscale circulations. *Mon. Wea. Rev.* 1988, 116, 132-148.

Zhao, M.; Pitman, A.J. The impact of land cover change and increasing carbon dioxide on the extreme and frequency of maximum temperature and convective precipitation. *Geophys. Res. Lett.* 2002, 29, 10.1029/2001GL013476.

In: Land Use Policy
Editors: A. C. Denman and O. M. Penrod
ISBN: 978-1-60741-435-3

Chapter 10

A FRAMEWORK FOR THE ECONOMIC VALUATION OF LAND USE CHANGE*

Lars Hein[15] **and Rudolf S. de Groot***
Environmental Systems Analysis Group, Wageningen University
P.O. Box 47, 6700 AA Wageningen , the Netherlands

ABSTRACT

There is a broad recognition that sustainable land management (SLM) is crucial for ensuring an adequate, long-term supply of food, raw materials and other services provided by the natural environment to the human society. However, to date, SLM practices are the exception rather than the rule in many parts of the world. Among the causes for unsustainable land management is a general lack of understanding of the economic costs of land degradation and the benefits of sustainable land management. This paper presents a methodological framework for analyzing the benefits of sustainable land management. The framework comprises three complementary types of assessment: partial valuation, total valuation and impact analysis. The first two allow for static assessment of selected respectively all economic benefits from a certain land use. The third approach is dynamic, and allows for analyzing the costs and benefits related to changes in land use. Each approach requires the application of a number of sequential methodological steps, including (i) ecosystem function and services identification; (ii) bio-physical assessment of ecosystem services; (iii) economic valuation; and (iv) ecological-economic modeling. The framework is demonstrated by means of a simple case study in the Guadalentin catchment, SE Spain.

---

* A version of this chapter was also published in *Ecological Economics Research Trends*, edited by Carolyn C. Pertsova published by Nova Science Publishers, Inc. It was submitted for appropriate modifications in an effort to encourage wider dissemination of research.

[15] Correspondence to: , Wageningen University P.O. Box 47, 6700 AA Wageningen , the NetherlandsPhone: + 31-317-482993, Fax+31-317-484839 Email: lars.hein@wur.nl; dolf.degroot@wur.nl

1. Introduction

There is a broad recognition that sustainable land management (SLM) is crucial for ensuring an adequate, long-term supply of food, raw materials and other services provided by the natural environment to the human society. SLM involves both the long-term maintenance of the productive capacity of agricultural lands, and the sustainable use of natural and semi-natural ecosystems, such as semi-arid rangelands or forests. Nevertheless, SLM practices are the exception rather than the rule in many parts of the world. A whole range of social, institutional and economic factors play a role with regards to the lack of sustainability in the management of natural resources. For instance, farmers and local ecosystem users may be driven by immediate food and income requirements and may have limited possibilities to adjust harvest levels to the carrying capacity of the ecosystem.

One of the factors that is often identified as being critically important is that the various economic benefits that are provided by multifunctional agricultural landscapes and natural ecosystems tend to be underestimated in decision making. Agricultural and natural ecosystems provide a whole range of valuable goods and services, ranging from the supply of food or medicinal plants, to the regulation of water flows and biochemical cycles, to the provision of sites for recreation or cultural events. Many of these services directly or indirectly contribute to human welfare and, as such, have economic value.

The general lack of recognition of these values in decision making is caused by a range of factors. First, these benefits are often difficult to specify, as they are widely varying in terms of the type of benefit supplied, and as they operate over a range of spatial and temporal scales. Second, several of these benefits have a public goods character and/or are not traded in a market. In spite of their welfare implications, they therefore do not show up in economic statistics. Third, there is often a mismatch between the stakeholders that pay the (opportunity) costs of maintaining an environmental benefit (e.g. by not converting a forest to cropland) and the beneficiaries of that benefit (e.g. downstream water users benefiting from the regulation of water flows).

Through assessment of the economic value of the multiple benefits provided by land and ecosystems, it is possible to increase the awareness of stakeholders and decision makers of the economic benefits resulting from sustainable land management. Since economic considerations generally play a key role in decision making, it is anticipated that economic valuation of environmental benefits can contribute to a more sustainable and a more efficient decision making. Analysis and valuation of ecosystem services can also guide the setting up of mechanisms to compensate the suppliers of ecosystem services for the costs related to providing those benefits in a Payment for Ecosystem Services (PES) mechanism.

To date, a wide range of assessments of the costs of land degradation and the benefits of sustainable land management have been carried out (e.g. Lal and Stewart, 1990; Pimentel et al., 1995). In addition, a number of conceptual frameworks have been proposed for analyzing the economic aspects of environmental change. The Millennium Ecosystem Assessment (2003) has provided a general framework for ecosystem services assessment, and, for instance, Barbier et al., 1997 presents a framework for the economic valuation of wetlands. However, to date, to the best knowledge of the authors, a comprehensive and systematic framework for analyzing the economic consequences of changes in land management is still lacking.

This study presents a conceptual framework for analyzing the costs of land degradation and the benefits of SLM. The framework supports three main approaches (partial valuation, total valuation and impact assessment), each of them is illustrated with a case study. Note that these case studies are based on limited data and simplified methodologies, and their only purpose is to illustrate the application of the framework.

2. A Framework for Analyzing the Economic Impacts of Land Use Change

A general framework for analyzing the economic impacts of land use change is presented in Figure 1. The framework can be used for three distinct approaches to analyzing the economic benefits of SLM: (i) Partial Valuation; (ii) Total Valuation; and (iii) Impact Assessment.

i Partial valuation. Partial valuation involves the economic valuation of only one or a limited set of environmental benefits. It can be used where only few environmental benefits supply the large majority of benefits to society, and where appraisal of only few benefits is required to support decision making. This approach can be applied, for instance, in case the impact of SLM on food security needs to be assessed.

ii Total valuation. The second approach is 'Total valuation'. This approach is appropriate where a full accounting of the benefits provided by an area under a certain management system is required. In this case, all services need to be identified and valued. For instance, in case a decision needs to be taken involving the selection of one of two land use conversion options, it may be important to analyze all benefits provided in the two options. Note that, in specific cases, it may be clear that some services only generate a very minor part of the total benefits, as in the case of carbon sequestration in a system that absorbs only minimal amounts of carbon over time. In this case, it may be decided to skip these minor services and include them only as a pro memory post.

iii Impact assessment. The third approach is 'Impact assessment'. It involves analyzing the impacts of changes in environment and land management on the supply of benefits to society. This approach needs to be applied in case of a change in the management of an area (e.g. through the adoption of various SLM practices). In this case, it is necessary to analyze both the economic value of the benefits generated by the system under consideration, *and* how the supply of these benefits will change following a change in management practices. This approach is also relevant for the prediction of the impact of environmental pressures, e.g. pollution, that may cause a change in the state of the environmental system. Hence, compared to the two previous approaches, this approach requires an additional step, dealing with how the impact of the change in management or pressures can be analyzed or modeled.

The framework comprises five complementary steps: (i) Problem definition and selection of the assessment approach; (ii) Identification of ecosystem functions and services; (iii) Biophysical assessment of ecosystem services; (iv) Economic valuation of ecosystem services; and (v) Ecological-economic modeling. These steps are described below.

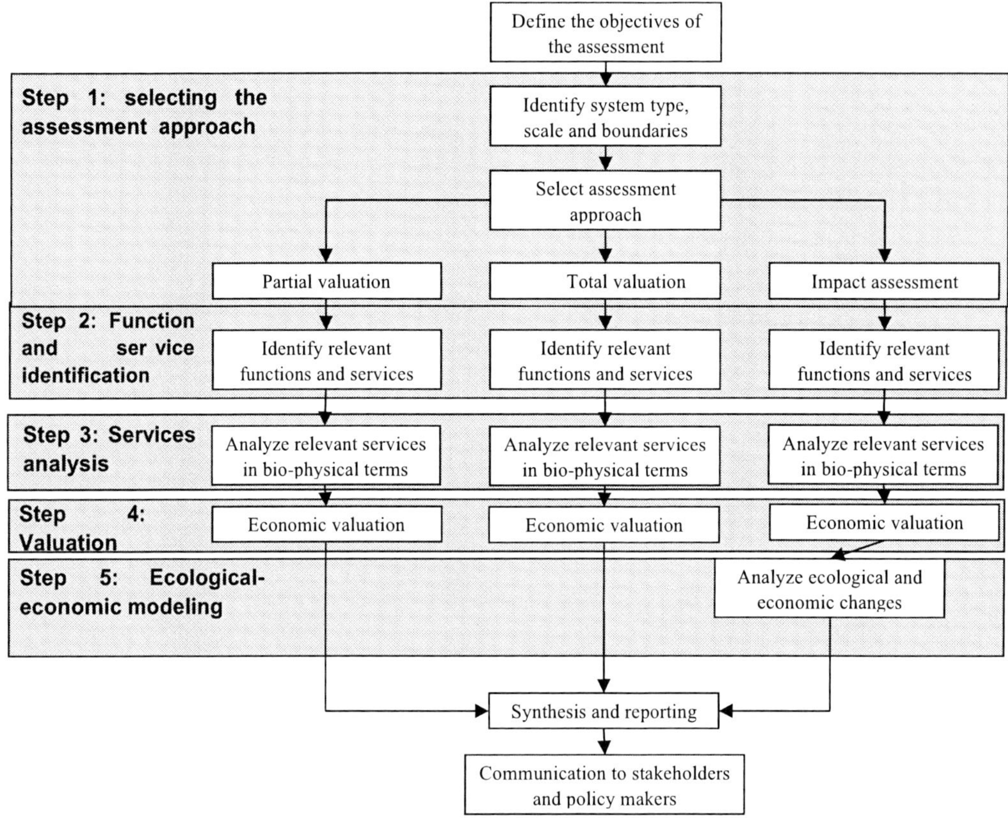

Figure 1. Framework for analyzing the costs of and degradation and the benefits of sustainable land management.

2.1 Problem Definition and Selection of the Assessment Approach

Economic valuation of land use changes (as any other analysis) requires that the object of the valuation is clearly defined. Hence, it is necessary to define the system to be analyzed, in terms of its spatial and temporal boundaries. The ecosystem is the entry point often used for valuation of ecosystem services and environmental benefits. Following Likens (1992), ecosystems are defined as: 'the individuals, species and populations in a *spatially defined area*, the interactions among them, and those between the organisms and the abiotic environment'. This spatial approach makes it easier to define the physical boundaries of the area to be analyzed. Following the Millennium Ecosystem Assessment, ecosystems may comprise both natural and/or strongly man influenced systems such as agricultural fields.

As ecological and institutional boundaries seldom coincide, stakeholders in ecosystem services often cut across a range of institutional zones and scales. Whereas for the analysis of land degradation processes, ecosystem services and ecosystem dynamics the ecosystem is the appropriate unit of analysis, in the identification of policy measures the administrative and institutional contexts need to be explicitly considered. This incongruence between ecological and political boundaries is very common in environmental management, and flexible solutions need to be identified on a case-by-case basis.

Following the definition of the system boundaries, the appropriate valuation approach needs to be selected. As explained in the Introduction section, the user may be interested in (i) Partial valuation; (ii) Total valuation; or (iii) Impact assessment. Table 1 provides some examples of analyses that can be carried out with these three approaches.

Table 1. Examples of the Potential Applications of the Three Main Valuation Approaches

Valuation approach	Examples
Partial valuation	Valuation of the production of non-timber forest products by a forest. Valuation of the hydrological service of an upland forest in order to define a payment vehicle from downstream users to upland managers to maintain this service.
Total valuation	Valuation of the ecosystem services supplied by a forest in order to compare the benefits of timber logging with those of sustainable management Valuation of the services provided by a natural area in order to identify which stakeholders benefits from the area and which stakeholders may be expected to contribute to financing the preservation of the area.
Impact assessment	Analyzing the impacts of pollution control measures in a wetland on water quality and ecosystem services supply in order to compare the costs and benefits of pollution control measures Analysis of the impact of disturbances (e.g. road construction, or desertification) on the supply of ecosystem services

2.2 Ecosystem Function and Services Identification

In the early 1970s, the concept of ecosystem function was proposed to facilitate the analysis of the benefits that ecosystems provide to society. An ecosystem function can be defined as "the capacity of the ecosystem to provide goods and services that satisfy human needs, directly or indirectly". Ecosystem functions depend upon the state and the functioning of the ecosystem. For instance, the function 'production of firewood' is based on a range of ecological processes involving the growth of plants and trees that use solar energy to convert water, plant nutrients and CO2 to biomass.

A function may result in the supply of ecosystem services, depending on the demand for the good or service involved. Ecosystem services are the goods or services provided by the ecosystem to society (following the definition of the Millennium Ecosystem Assessment, 2003). The supply of ecosystem services will often be variable over time, and both actual and potential future supplies of services should be included in the assessment.

Ecosystem functions, and the services attached to these functions, vary widely as a function of the type of ecosystem and the socio-economic setting involved. For example, the capacity of the ecosystem to provide firewood depends on the forest cover and the amount of woody plant biomass contained in the system, as well as, in the longer term, on the primary productivity of the forest. However, the actual supply of firewood also depends on the *demand* of different stakeholders for firewood. This demand is determined by the need for wood energy as well as the availability of other sources to satisfy household energy needs.

Table 2 provides a comprehensive list of ecosystem services, containing 24 different types of services. By and large, the list follows the MEA (2003). Compared to MEA (2003) some minor adjustments have been made in order to ensure consistency in its application to SLM. The list contains three types of ecosystem services, which are based on a different type of interaction between people and ecosystems: Provisioning services, Regulation services and Cultural services. Contrary to Millennium Ecosystem Assessment (2003), but analogous to Costanza et al. (1997) and Hein et al. (2006), there is no category 'supporting services'. Supporting services represent the ecological processes that underlie the functioning of the ecosystem. Their inclusion in valuation may lead to double counting as their value is reflected in the other three types of services. In addition, there are a very large number of ecological processes that underlie the functioning of ecosystems, and it is unclear on which basis supporting services should be included in, or excluded from a valuation study.

Table 2. List of Ecosystem Services (based on Ehrlich and Ehrlich, 1981; Costanza et al., 1997; DeGroot et al., 2002; Millennium Ecosystem Assessment, 2003; Hein et al., 2006)

Category	Definition	Ecosystem services
Provisioning services	Provisioning services reflect goods and services extracted from the ecosystem	- Food - Fodder (including grass from pastures) - Fuel (including wood and dung) - Timber, fibers and other raw materials - Biochemical and medicinal resources - Genetic resources - Ornamentals
Regulation services	Regulation services result from the capacity of ecosystems to regulate climate, hydrological and bio-chemical cycles, earth surface processes, and a variety of biological processes.	- Carbon sequestration - Climate regulation through control of albedo, temperature and rainfall patterns - Hydrological service: regulation of the timing and volume of river flows - Protection against floods by coastal or riparian systems - Control of erosion and sedimentation - Nursery service: regulation of species reproduction - Breakdown of excess nutrients and pollution - Pollination - Regulation of pests and pathogens - Protection against storms - Protection against noise and dust - Biological nitrogen fixation (BNF)
Cultural services	Cultural services relate to the benefits people obtain from ecosystems through recreation, cognitive development, relaxation, and spiritual reflection.	Provision of cultural, historical and religious heritage (e.g. a historical landscape or a sacred forests) - Scientific and educational information - Opportunities for recreation and tourism Amenity service: provision of attractive housing and living conditions Habitat service: provision of a habitat for wild plant and animal species

Note that, in principle, the user has the choice of valuing services or functions; both express the benefits supplied by the natural environment to society. The main difference is that valuation of services is based on valuation of the flow of benefits, and valuation of functions is based on the environment's capacity to supply benefits. The first expresses clearly the current benefits received, but additional analyses are required if the flow of ecosystem services is likely to change in the short or medium term (e.g. if current extraction rates are above the regenerative capacity of the ecosystem). In this case, calculation of the NPV requires that assumptions are made on the future flows of services.

Functions better indicate the value that can be extracted in the long-term, and their value is not biased by temporary overexploitation. However, it is often much more difficult to assess the capacity to supply a service than to assess the supply of the service itself. For instance, for the function 'supply of fish', this requires analysis of the sustainable harvest levels of the fish stocks involved which needs to be based on a population model including reproduction, feed availability and predation levels. Hence, in most valuation studies, it is chosen to value services rather than functions, and to account for potential changes in services supply in the assessment.

An important issue in the valuation of ecosystem services is the *double counting of services* (Millennium Ecosystem Assessment, 2003; Turner et al., 2003). Specifically, there is a risk of double counting in relation to the regulation services that support the supply of other services from an ecosystem. In general, regulation services should only be included in the valuation if (i) they have an impact outside the ecosystem to be valued; and/or (ii) if they provide a *direct* benefit to people living in the area (*i.e.* not through sustaining or improving another service) (see Hein et al., 2006, for more information on double counting). A prerequisite for applying this approach to the valuation of regulation services is that the ecosystem is defined in terms of it's spatial boundaries – otherwise the external impacts of the regulation services can not be precisely defined.

2.3. Ecosystem Services Assessment

The next step in the economic assessment is the quantification, in bio-physical units, of the relevant ecosystem services identified in the previous step. For *production* services, this involves the quantification of the flows of goods harvested in the ecosystem, in a physical unit. For most *regulation* services, quantification requires spatially explicit analysis of the bio-physical impact of the service on the environment in or surrounding the ecosystem. For example, valuation of the hydrological service of a forest first requires an assessment of the precise impact of the forest on the water flow downstream, including such aspects as the reduction of peak flows, and the increase in dry season water supply (Bosch and Hewitt, 1982). The reduction of peak flows and flood risks is only relevant in a specific zone around the river bed, which needs to be (spatially) defined before the service can be valued. An example of a regulation service that does usually not require spatially explicit assessment prior to valuation is the carbon sequestration service – the value of the carbon storage does not depend upon where it is sequestered. *Cultural* services depend upon a human interpretation of the ecosystem, or of specific characteristics of the ecosystem. The benefits people obtain from cultural services depend upon experiences during actual visits to the area, indirect experiences derived from an ecosystem (e.g. through nature movies), and more abstract cultural and moral considerations (see e.g. Aldred, 1994; Posey, 1999). Assessment of cultural services requires assessment of the numbers of people benefiting from the service, and the type of interaction they have with the ecosystem involved. Table 3 presents potential indicators for the biophysical assessment of ecosystem services.

Table 3. Potential Indicators for the Biophysical Assessment of Ecosystem Services

Category	Key goods and services provided	Potential indicators
Provisioning services	- Food - Fuel (including wood and dung) - Timber, fibers and other raw materials - Biochemical and medicinal resources - Genetic resources	- For all provisioning services: amount of product harvested per year; Inputs required for harvesting (time, equipment, etc.); Total inputs and outputs in case the good is used as input in a production process
Regulation services	- Carbon sequestration - Climate regulation through control of temperature and rainfall patterns	- Amount of C sequestered - Differences in average and extreme rainfall and temperature.
	- Hydrological service - Protection against floods by coastal or riparian systems	- Impact of vegetation on water flow, - Height and effectiveness of coastal belt
	- Control of erosion and sedimentation	- Amount of sediments generated or erosion avoided
	- Nursery service: regulation of species reproduction - Breakdown of excess nutrients and pollution	- Numbers of juveniles produced per area unit. - Difference in pollutant concentrations between water flowing in, and water flowing out of the system
	- Pollination	- Crop yields in areas with adequate pollination compared areas with pollination deficit.
	- Regulation of pests and pathogens	- Crop yields in areas with and without such control, or health impacts in areas with an without such control.
	- Protection against noise and dust	- Noise levels, particulate matter levels, and concentrations of specific pollutants on either side of the vegetation belt
	- Biological nitrogen fixation (BNF)	- Amounts of N fixed.
Cultural services	Provision of cultural, historical and religious heritage - Scientific and educational information - Recreation and tourism - Amenity service: provision of attractive housing and living conditions - Habitat service: provision of a habitat for wild plant and animal species	For all services: amount of people benefiting from the service; type of benefits people obtain. For the habitat service: number of species; number of red list species; hectares of ecosystem, ecosystem quality versus ecosystem in natural state, biodiversity indices.

2.4. Economic Valuation

Following welfare economics, the economic value of a resource can be determined via individual preferences as expressed by willingness to pay (WTP) or willingness to accept (WTA) for a change in the supply of that resource (Hanemann, 1991). Aggregation of individual welfare impacts is required to obtain the welfare impact on society. Where relevant, this aggregation needs to consider equity issues, for instance where the interests of one stakeholder group (e.g. traditional ecosystem users), are considered to be more important than those of other stakeholder groups.

The appropriate measure of economic value is determined by the specific context of the resources being managed. Care needs to be taken that the valuation method gives a proper indication of the value of the service involved, reflecting a true WTP or WTA, and avoiding the double counting of services or values. It is also important that the user is aware of the concepts of marginal and total value, where marginal value reflects the value of an incremental change in the supply of a resource, and total value the overall value of a resource.

There are several types of economic value. Following the Millennium Ecosystem Assessment (2003), the framework distinguishes the following four types: (i) direct use value; (ii) indirect use value; (iii) option value; and (iv) non-use value. They are elaborated in Table 4. The aggregated economic value of an area, combining these four value types, is often referred to as Total Economic Value (TEV). Note that other authors have proposed different classifications of economic value types, see for example Hanley and Spash (1993) and Kolstad (2000).

Table 4. Types of Economic Value

Value Type	Description
Direct use value	This value arises from the direct utilization of ecosystems, for example through the sale or consumption of a piece of fruit. All production services, and some cultural services (such as recreation) have direct use value.
Indirect use value	This value stems from the indirect contribution of ecosystems to human welfare. Indirect use value reflects, in particular, the type of benefits that regulation services provide to society.
Option value	Because people are unsure about their future demand for a service, they are normally willing to pay to keep the option of using a resource in the future – insofar as they are, to some extent, risk averse. Option values may be attributed to all services supplied by an ecosystem.
None-use value	Non-use value is derived from knowing that an ecosystem or species is preserved without having the intention of using it in any way. Kolstad (2000) distinguishes three types of non-use value: existence value (based on utility derived from knowing that something exists), altruistic value (based on utility derived from knowing that somebody else benefits) and bequest value (based on utility gained from future improvements in the well-being of one's descendants).

These different values may or may not be reflected in a market value. In most cases, a significant part of the Direct Use Value will be reflected in market transactions, but most of the other value types will not. This is because, for instance, the services have a public goods character, or because a market has not (yet) been established for the service. However, it is clear that, because of the economic benefits they provide, the non-market economic values need to be included in economic cost-benefit analysis.

Two types of approaches have been developed to obtain information about the value of non-market ecosystem services: expressed and revealed preference methods (Pearce and

Pearce, 2001). These methods have also been called direct and indirect valuation methods, respectively. With *expressed valuation methods,* either market prices or various types of questionnaires are used to reveal the willingness-to-pay of consumers for a certain ecosystem service. The most important direct approaches are the Contingent Valuation Method (CVM) and related methods. The *revealed preference methods* use a link with a marketed good or service to indicate the willingness-to-pay for the service. They use either physical or behavioral linkages to a marketed good. With physical linkages, estimates of the values of ecosystem services are obtained by determining a physical relationship between the service and something that can be measured in the market place. For instance, with the damage-function (or dose-response) approach, the damages resulting from the reduced availability of an ecosystem service are used as an indication of the value of the service (Johanson, 1999). In the case of behavioral linkages, the value of an ecosystem service is derived from linking the service to human behavior – in particular expenditures to offset the lack of a service, or to obtain a service. Table 5 presents an overview of the various valuation approaches, detailed descriptions of the various valuation methods can be found in Pearce and Turner (1990, Hanley and Spash, (1993), Munasinghe (1993) and Cummings and Harrison (1995).

Table 5. Valuation Methods and their Applicability to Different Value Types

Valuation method	Suitable for	Value category			
		direct use value	indirect use value	option value	non-use value
Indirect methods:					
1) averting behavior method	Applicable to services that relate to the purification services of some ecosystems.	x	x		
2) travel cost method	Can be used to value the recreation service.	x			
3) production factor approach	Applicable where ecosystem services are an input into a production process	x		x	
4) hedonic pricing	Applicable where environmental amenities are reflected in the prices of specific goods, in particular property.	x		x	
Direct methods:					
5) CVM	The use of CVM is limited to goods and services that are easily to comprehend for respondents – excluding most regulation services	x		x	x
6) market valuation	Ecosystem goods and services traded on the market	x	x	x	

If the value of ecosystem services is expressed as NPV (instead of as an annual flow), the discount rate is a crucial factor. Discounting is used to compare present and future flows of costs and benefits derived from the ecosystem. The discount rate to be used in environmental cost-benefit analysis is still subject to debate (e.g. Howarth and Norgaard, 1993; Norgaard, 1996; Hanley, 1999). For instance, Freeman (1993) indicates that the discount rate, based upon the after- tax, real interest rate, should be in the order of 2 to 3% provided that the streams of benefits and costs accrue to the same generation, whereas Nordhaus (1994) argued that a 6% discount rate is most consistent with historical savings data. In general, the use of a high discount rate will favor ecosystem management options that lead to relatively fast depletion of resources, whereas a low discount rate will stress the economic benefits of more sustainable management options (Pearce and Turner, 1990; Tietenberg, 2000).

2.5 Ecological-Economic Modeling

The fifth step involves a dynamic assessment of the impact of land use changes on the supply of ecosystem services, and the resulting economic impacts. It comprises a quantitative analysis of the relation between drivers, ecosystem state and ecosystem services supply, as elaborated below.

(i) Modeling of drivers and management options. This first steps involves the modeling, in physical terms, of the impacts of a driver or management options on the ecosystem. This requires the modeling of the main ecosystem components, the feedback mechanisms between them, and their relation to drivers and management options. Following a systems modeling approach, ecosystem components can be interpreted as sets of connected state (level) variables, and the drivers and interactions as flow (rate) variables interacting with the components. The model should capture the relevant inputs, throughputs and outputs over time. This may comprise a range of theoretical, statistical or methodological constructs, dependent upon the requirements and limitations of the model.

For systems subject to complex dynamics, it is important that these dynamics are reflected in the model. In spite of the large number of ecological processes regulating the functioning of ecosystems, recent insights suggest that the main ecological structures are often primarily regulated by a small set of processes (Harris, 1999; Holling et al., 2002). This indicates that inclusion of a relatively small set of key components and processes in the model may be sufficient to accurately represent the (complex) dynamics of the system.

(ii) Linking ecosystem state to the supply of ecosystem services. In the second step, changes in ecosystem state have to be connected to changes in the supply of ecosystem services. This relation is strongly dependent on the type of ecosystem service. For provisioning services, relevant state indicators include the stock of the harvested produce (e.g. forest standing biomass). Changes in state are directly reflected in the capacity to provide the product. However, in many cases, the dynamics of the system can not be effectively captured with only one state variable, as in the case where forest growth is a function of both standing biomass and soil quality (see for instance Hein and Van Ierland, 2006 for an example). For regulation service, there will often be a range of state variables required to analyze changes in the supply of the service. For instance, the effectiveness of the pollination service depends on the amount of healthy pollinators available. Often, only one or few species of pollinators pollinate the large majority of the crop, but these pollinators depend on the availability of suitable habitat, and the absence of disturbances such as high concentrations of pesticides. For cultural services (the habitat service excluded), it is often not the ecological complexity that maintains the service, but rather specific aspects of it. For instance, the majority of Dutch recreationists values birdlife in a recreational site, but is rather indifferent regarding which species or how much variety of birds is encountered on the site. In view of the large variety among ecosystem services, suitable indicators and relevant processes need to be identified on a case-by-case basis.

(iii) Analysis of the impacts of ecosystem change and of the management options. Once the ecological-economic model has been constructed, it can be used to assess the impacts of the ecosystem change on the supply of ecosystem services, as well as of the efficiency and sustainability of different ecosystem management options. The efficiency of ecosystem management can be revealed through comparison of the net welfare generated by the ecosystem and the costs involved in maintaining and managing the ecosystem (e.g. Pearce and Turner, 1990). Through a simulation or an algebraic optimization approach, efficient management options, *i.e.* management options that provide maximum utility given a certain utility function, can be identified. See for instance Chang (1992) for a theoretical construct of optimization procedures, Hein (2006) for an example of a simulation approach to optimization, and Hein and Weikard (2006) for an example of algebraic optimization. The sustainability of management options can be examined by analyzing their long-term consequences for the state of the ecosystem including its capacity to supply ecosystem services (Pearce et al., 1989; Barbier and Markandya, 1990).

3. Case Study: Costs of Erosion in the Guadalentin, SE Spain

The framework is applied to the Puentes Catchment in the Guadalentin Basin in South-eastern Spain. The Guadalentin Basin extends over some 3300 km^2, covering the southern half of the province of Murcia and the eastern tip of the province of Andalucia. It is among the driest areas in Europe, with an average annual rainfall of around 300 to 400mm. The case study area covers the catchment of the Puentes reservoir in the region of Lorca (see figure 2). The study area covers in total around 16,000 ha and has a total population of only 1740 people. Besides arable land, the area consists of a mix of shrublands, stipa lands, Mediterranean deciduous forest lands, *Pinus halepensis* afforestations and, locally, badlands. An overview of the land use in the study area is presented in Table 2.

Table 2. Land Use in the Study Area (2003)

Category	Case study area (ha)
Irrigated cropland, of which	1100
- irrigated horticulture	*350*
- irrigated tree crops	*750*
Dryland cropland; of which	10750
- almonds	*4250*
- olives	*900*
- barley	*4500*
- wheat	*1100*
Category	*Case study area (ha)*
Shrublands	2840
Forests	450
Pine afforestations	450
Villages	50
Total	15640

Source: Comarcal, 2003.

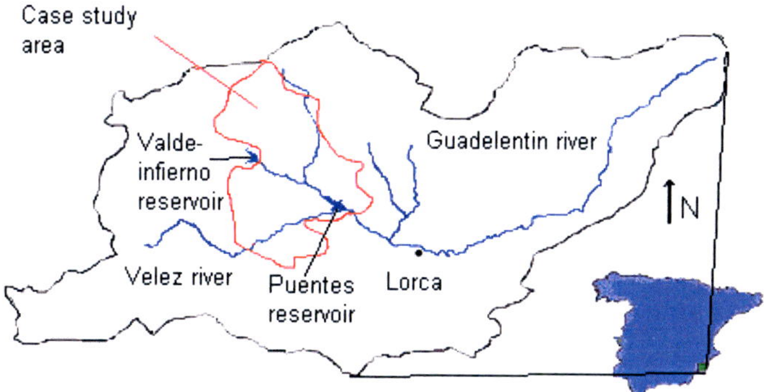

Figure 2. Map of the Puentes Catchment in the Guadalentin Basin, Spain.

(i) Problem definition and selection of the assessment approach. In the case study, the framework is used to assess the costs of erosion in the Puentes catchment. For the assessment, the Impact Assessment approach is selected. The study focuses on erosion in dryland cropland, as erosion rates are highest in this land use unit (Wesemael et al., 2003).

(ii) Identification of ecosystem functions and services. Traditionally, the Guadalentin Basin has been used for dryland agriculture (mainly cereals and tree crops) and grazing (mainly sheep and goats). Since the 1970s, there has been a strong increase in irrigated agriculture, partly driven by subsidies and increased export opportunities provided by the EU. In the Puentes Catchment, the following environmental functions can be distinguished: (1) irrigated agriculture; (2) dryland agriculture; (3) grazing; (4) hunting; and (5) nature conservation. They are strongly linked to the land use units, as described below.

1. *Irrigated agriculture.* As water is the most limiting natural resource for agricultural production, the best, and hence usually the flattest lands, are used for irrigated agriculture. Irrigated agriculture includes a variety of crops including artichokes, broccoli, tomatoes, peppers, melons, grapes, etc. Olives and almonds are the most important irrigated tree crops of the area (they are also grown, in much larger areas, as a dryland crop). In the last five years, the area of irrigated agriculture declined considerably in the case study area because many borewells have dried up or have become saline.
2. *Dryland agriculture.* Barley and wheat are the main dryland crops in the area. The large majority of the barley and wheat (durum) grown is cultivated under rainfed conditions. Usually, a piece of land is cultivated only once in two years, with the fallow year used for the build up of soil moisture. In addition, dryland agriculture includes substantial areas of tree crops, in particular almonds and olives. The area under almond cultivation has increased substantially in the last decade as a result of EU agricultural subsidies.
3. *Grazing.* Grazing, mainly by sheep and goats, is practised on fallow land, shrub land and in the forests. The number of sheep and goats has

somewhat decreased in the last decades, as a result of low wool prices, but a more marked difference is the strong growth of the size of the herds, now commonly including several hundreds of animals.

4. *Hunting*. Hunting is practised by locals, but many of the lands are also leased out as hunting lands to hunting clubs from outside the area. Game includes wild boar and deer. Hunting is practised in the forests, shrublands, pine afforestations and the dryland agricultural areas.
5. *Nature conservation*. Nature conservation is another important function. As the area is among the driest parts of Europe, it's flora is particularly interesting, with a large number of drought adapted species. However, the intrinsic value of the nature in the area is difficult to translate into a monetary value – the implementation of a Contingency Valuation Study to determine this value is outside the scope of the study. The nature conservation function is highest for the natural forests occurring in the area, with additional value confined to the extensively used agricultural areas and the pine afforestations.

(iii) Bio-physical assessment of ecosystem services. The agricultural production function has been analyzed by means of the yields of the various crops. The grazing service has been quantified by analyzing the amount of offspring produced per herd, assuming that revenues from wool production are zero because the current very low wool prices. Hunting has been analyzed through assessment of land leased out to hunting organizations, and the nature conservation service through a survey of species diversity based on literature (Consejería de Agricultura, Agua y Medio Ambiente, 2002).

(iv) Economic valuation of ecosystem services. In order to assess the production value of the *agricultural functions*, the net results obtained per hectare have been calculated for each crop. This has been done by first estimating the average production per hectare multiplied with the crop value, to get the gross benefits of the functions. The net benefits have been calculated by subtracting the fixed and the variable production costs from these gross benefits. Fixed costs include the costs of stables, machinery, etc.; variable costs include the costs of agricultural inputs and labour. Labour is valued at the average labour costs for the region (from Comarcal, 2003). Subsidies have not been included in the analysis (which causes the net value of the cereals to be negative). For the irrigated crops, the costs of water have been included at the price farmers pay for it. For the *grazing function*, the same approach has been followed with the added note that the yields relate only to the production of meat (prices of wool are very low and do not justify livestock keeping in the area). *Hunting* is valued by means of the willingness-to-pay of hunters for land leases, as revealed through interviews with farmers and the local hunters' association. The *nature conservation* function is not valued in monetary terms in this study, but table 3 accounts for the non-use value of this function, in a qualitative manner, through a ranking. Based upon the occurrence and diversity of species in different land-use units, the nature conservation function receives the highest score in relation to its non-use value. A non-use value is also attributed to two other functions that contribute to the landscape of the region: grazing and dryland agriculture. An overview of the environmental functions, including an estimate of their relative values, is presented in Table 3.

(v) Ecological-economic modeling. Erosion occurs in all upland areas, with highly varying erosion rates. The most sensitive areas are the steep uplands, with marl baserock, and without vegetation cover, the least sensitive area are the flat or well protected sites. Erosion rates are lowest under natural forest and well-established pine afforestations (0.5 to 2 ton/ha/year), intermediate on the dryland agricultural fields (5- 100 ton/ha/year), high in shrublands (10 – 150 ton/ha/year) and highest on the badlands (100-1000 ton/ha/year) (Kosmas et al., 1997; Hein, 1997). A main difference between the shrublands and the upland agricultural fields is that the shrublands tend to have developed crusts that reduce infiltration rates and increase erosion. In agricultural fields, these crusts are broken through ploughing. This case study considers the costs of erosion in dryland herbaceous and dryland tree crops. It is assumed that the erosion rates under barley are representative for the dryland herbaceous crops, and the erosion rates under almond trees are representative for the dryland treecrops. For these two crops, the erosion rates on different slopes are shown in table 4.

Assessment of the average nutrient content removed through erosion. The Cartographía Ambiental (2000) presents the average nutrient contents of the soils that are used for agriculture in the study area – including calcaric xerosols, calcaric regosols and lithosols – based on five profiles that represent average values for specific soil types. Each profile is based on around 20 to 25 different samples of the soils in each unit. For the current study, it is not known how the different soil types are distributed over the different crops, as the location of dryland and irrigated horticultural crops is often rotated and, hence, differs each year. Therefore, for this study, the average of these soil profiles has been taken – considering the first 22 centimetres of the profile. This depth relates to the depth analysed in the available data set, and takes into account that erosion in the area is a combination of overland flow, rill and gulley erosion. These analyses show that the nutrient contents of the soil are: 0.12 kg N/ton soil, 0.02 kg P/ton soil; and 0.18 kg K/ton soil.

Table 3. Environmental Functions and Approximate Values of the Puentes Catchment

Environmental function	Specification	Economic Value (euro/ha/year)	Non-use Value	Comments
Irrigated agriculture	Horticulture (e.g. broccoli, artichokes, olives)	1348 281		Approximation of net value added
Dryland agriculture	Almonds, olives, cereals	175 136 -30	+	Approximation of net value added
Grazing	Sheep and goats grazing shrubland + crop residues	16	+	Approximation of net value added
Hunting	Fees paid to land owner + local government	14		Willingness to pay for hunting licenses
Nature conservation			+++	No monetary indicator available.

Source: see Annex 1 for details on the economic valuation of the functions 'agricultural' and 'grazing'. The valuation of the function 'hunting' is based upon the average annual rent received by interviewed farmers from hunting associations (n = 15 farmers). The non-use value of the different functions is based upon a relative classification by the author, based upon species diversity from Consejería de Agricultura, Agua y Medio Ambiente (2002). More information on the functions and valuation can be obtained from the author. Only the costs of erosion through its impact on dryland agriculture are calculated. These costs are assessed using a simple replacement costs analysis. It is analysed how much plant nutrients are removed from the soil on an annual basis, and what expenditure the farmer has to make to overcome this loss of nutrients, through the increased use of fertilisers. This analysis requires the assessment of (i) the total soil loss through erosion; (ii) the removal of nutrients; and (iii) the replacement costs for the farmer on the basis of the prices of fertilisers. Step (i) has been discussed above (table 4), and the other two steps are discussed below:

Table 4. Mean Values for Soil Loss (Ton·Ha^{-1}·Year^{-1}) for Dry Herbaceous Crops and Almond Trees in the Region of Murcia. It is Assumed that these Rates are Representative for the Study Area

Dry crops	Slope (%)	Mean value for soil loss (ton·ha^{-1}·year^{-1})
Herbaceous crops	<5	7.1
	5-10	22.7
	10-20	92.0
	20-30	166.8
	30-50	206.9
Almond trees	<5	8.3
	5-10	17.2
	10-20	73.7
	20-30	98.2
	30-50	121.5

Source: Ministerio del Medio Ambiente (2002).

Estimation of the costs of erosion by consideration of the price of fertilisers. In order to translate these physical data into an economic indicator, the replacement costs of the nutrients removed through erosion have been assessed, based on the prices that farmers pay for inorganic fertilisers in the area. Only the most commonly applied types of inorganic fertilisers are considered, i.e. 'triple 15' for the almond orchards, and a mix of 'triple 15', 'ammonium sulphate' and 'superphosphate' for barley. The replacement costs per unit of nutrients are presented in table 5.

Table 5. Replacement Costs per Unit of Plant Nutrient

Nutrient	Barley (€/kg compound)	Almonds (€/kg compound)
N	0.51	1.33
P	0.67	1.33
K	0.53	1.33

The overall calculations of the per-hectare costs of erosion are summarised in table 6. The loss of nutrients is calculated by multiplying the erosion rates with the nutrient contents of the soil, i.e. 0.12 kg N/ton soil, 0.02 kg P/ton soil; and 0.18 kg K/ton soil. The costs of erosion are calculated by multiplying the loss of nutrients with the costs of each nutrient and, subsequently, summing the costs of the loss of the three types of nutrients.

In order to calculate the total costs of erosion for the two crops, the slope distribution of the crops has to be considered (table 4). This slope distribution is derived through superimposing a slope map (from Ministerio de Medio Ambiente, 2002) with the land-use map of the case study area (Lopez-Bermudez et al., 2002), and calculation of the area of each slope category for the two types of land-use.

Table 6. Calculation of the Per-Hectare Costs of Erosion

Crop	Slope (%)	Erosion (ton/ha/year)	Loss of nutrients (kg N, P, K/ha/year)			Costs of erosion (€/ha/year)
			N	P	K	
Dry herb crops	< 5	7.1	0.85	0.14	1.28	1.2
	5-10	22.7	2.72	0.45	4.09	3.9
	10-20	92.0	11.04	1.84	16.56	15.6
	20-30	166.8	20.02	3.34	30.02	28.3
	30-50	206.9	24.83	4.14	37.24	35.2
Dry tree crops (almond trees)	<5	8.3	1.00	0.17	1.49	3.5
	5-10	17.2	2.07	0.34	3.10	7.4
	10-20	73.7	8.85	1.47	13.27	31.4
	20-30	98.2	11.79	1.96	17.68	41.8
	30-50	121.5	14.58	2.43	21.87	51.7

Source: For the erosion rates, see table 4; for the calculations of the costs of erosion: see text for explanation.

In terms of the costs and benefits of erosion control measures, the measures currently applied by farmers are relatively cheap. Questionnaires showed that farmers apply only three erosion control techniques (i) contour ploughing; (ii) gulley control; and (iii) maintenance of terraces (Oñate et al., 2003). Contour ploughing, maintaining terraces, and the construction of small bunds to ensure that water is diverted from the gullies require a limited amount of extra time for the farmer. Interviewed farmers mention these costs to be less than 20 euro/ha/year – hence in the same order of magnitude as the costs of erosion. In particular, these measures are profitable for slopes exceeding around 10%. Hence, the generally low costs of erosion explain the modest interests of farmers in applying erosion control techniques in the area.

Table 7. Calculation of the Costs of Erosion Through its Impact on Dryland Agriculture

Crop	Slope (%)	Costs of erosion (€/ha/year)	Percentage of the total area (%)	Costs of erosion (euro/year)
Dryland herbaceous crops (in total 5600 ha)	< 5	1.2	46	3,078
	5-10	3.9	37	7,993
	10-20	15.6	15	13,541
	20-30	28.3	2	3,328
	30-50	35.2	0	0
Dryland tree crops (in total 5150 ha)	<5	3.5	30	5,444
	5-10	7.4	35	13,377
	10-20	31.4	26	41,398
	20-30	41.8	7	14,208
	30-50	51.7	2	6,390
				Total: 109,000

4. Conclusions and Recommendations

This paper presents three approaches that can be followed to analyze and value the economic costs of land degradation and the benefits of sustainable land management: (i) partial valuation; (ii) total valuation; and (iii) impact assessment. Partial valuation can be used to analyze the importance of ecosystems, or the benefits of sustainable management, in relation to the provision of a limited set of ecosystem services. Total valuation involves valuing all services provided by an ecosystem, and can be used, for instance, to compare the costs and benefits of different types of land cover options. It can be used to analyze the benefits provided by an ecosystem under sustainable land management with the benefits of an ecosystem under 'regular' management. Impact assessment is a more dynamic approach to ecosystem services valuation, which allows analyzing the economic impacts of changes in land management, for instance to assess the economic impacts resulting from the degradation of a specific ecosystem.

A number of general recommendations can be provided for the economic analysis of land degradation and SLM. First, the objective of the study needs to be clear, as the objective determines the scale and the system boundaries, the appropriate valuation methods, and the data requirements. Second, in the implementation of the study, care needs to be taken to analyze both the ecological and the economic aspects of the ecosystem services involved. In particular for the regulation services, it is often as time-consuming to quantify the service in ecological or biophysical terms (Step 3) as it is to conduct the actual valuation itself (Step 4). Third, the uncertainties in the analysis need to be discussed, the impact of the study will depend on the amount of credit it will obtain and it is important to communicate how reliable the study's outcomes are. Fourth, valuation studies require an interdisciplinary approach involving economists, ecologists, hydrologist, sociologists, etc., depending on the functions and environmental setting to be studied.

References

Aldred, J. 1994. Existence value, welfare and altruism. *Environmental Values* 3 : 381-402.

Barbier, E.B., M. Acreman and D. Knowler, 1997. *Economic valuation of wetlands; a guide for policy makers and planners.* Ramsar Convention Bureau, Gland, Switzerland.

Cash, D.W. and S.C. Moser, 1998: Cross-scale interactions in assessments, information systems, and decision-making. In: Critical Evaluation of Global Environmental Assessments, *Global Environmental Assessment Project*, Harvard University, Cambridge, MA.

Chiang, A.C., 1992. *Elements of dynamic optimization.* McGraw-Hill Inc., Singapore.

Comarcal, 2003. Oficina Comercial Agricultura Alto Gadelentin, Lorca. Regional Agricultural Statistics.

Consejería de Agricultura, Agua y Medio Ambiente, 2002. La Estrategia Forestal de la Región de Murcia.

Costanza, R., R. d'Arge, R.S. de Groot, S. Farber, M. Grasso, B. Hannon, K. Limburg, S. Naeem, R.V. O'Neill, J. Paruelo, R.G. Raskin, P. Sutton and M. van den Belt, 1997a: The value of the world's ecosystem services and natural capital. *Nature* 387: 253-260.

Cummings, R.G. and G.W. Harrison, 1995. The measurement and decomposition of nonuse values: a critical review. *Environmental and Resource Economics* 5: 225-47.

De Groot, R.S., M. A. Wilson and R.M.J. Bouman, 2002: A typology for the classification, description and valuation of ecosystem functions, goods and services. *Ecological Economics*: 393-408.

Diamond, P.A., and J.A. Hausman, 1994. Contingent valuation: is some number better than no number? *Journal of Economic Perspectives* 8: 45-66

Ehrlich, P. and A. Ehrlich, 1981. Extinction: the causes and consequences of the disappearance of species. Random House, New York.

Freeman, A. M., 1993. *The measurement of environmental values and resources: theory and methods.* Resources for the Future, Washington D.C.

Hanemann, W.M., 1995. Contingent valuation and economics. In: K. Willis and J. Corkindale (eds.). *Environmental valuation: new perspectives.* CAB International, Wallingford, UK. pp. 79-117.

Hanley, N., and Spash, C.L., 1993. *Cost-Benefit Analysis and the Environment.* Edward Elgar, Vermont, USA.

Hanley, P., 1999. Cost-benefit analysis of environmental policy and management. In: J.C.J.M. van de Bergh (ed.), 1999: *Handbook of Environmental Resource Economics.* Edward Elgar, Cheltenham, UK, pp. 824-836.

Harris, G., 1999. This is not the end of limnology (or of science): the world may be a lot simpler than we think. *Freshwater Biology* 42: 689-706.

Hein, L., K. van Koppen, R.S. de Groot and E.C. van Ierland, 2006. Spatial scales, stakeholders and the valuation of ecosystem services. *Ecological Economics* 57, 209-228.

Hein, L., Assessing the costs of eutrophication control in a shallow lake ecosystem subject to two steady states. *Ecological Economics* 59, 429-439.

Hein, L. and E.C. van Ierland, 2006. Efficient and sustainable management of complex forest ecosystems. *Ecological Modelling* 190: 351-366.

Hein, L., 1997. The socio-economic impact of erosion in the Guadalentin Basin, Spain. Report 9705, Foundation for Sustainable Development, Wageningen, the Netherlands.

Holling, C.S., 1992. Cross-scale morphology, geometry and dynamics of ecosystems. *Ecological Monographs* 62: 447-502.

Howarth, R.B and R.B. Norgaard, 1993. 'Intergenerational transfers and the social discount rate'. Environmental and Natural Resource Economics 3: 337-358

Howarth, R.B., 1996. Discount rates and sustainable development. *Ecological Modeling* 92: 263-270.

Hufschmidt, M.M, James, D.E., Meister, A.D., Bower, B.T. and Dixon, J.A., 1983. *Environment, natural systems and development, an economic valuation guide.* The John Hopkins University Press, London.

Johansson, P., 1999. Theory of economic valuation of environmental goods and services. In: *Handbook of Environmental Resource Economics.* J.C.J.M. van de Bergh (ed), 1999. Edward Elgar, Cheltenham, UK, pp. 747-754.

Kolstad, C.D., 2000. *Environmental Economics.* Oxford University Press, New York, Oxford.

Kosmas, C., Danalatos, N., Cammeraat, L.H., Chabart, M., Diamantopoulos, J., Farand, R., 1997: *The effect of land-use on runoff and soil erosion rates under Mediterranean conditions.* Catena 29, 45-59.

Lal R, Stewart BA. 1990. *Soil Degradation.* Springer Verlag: New York.

Levin, S.A., 1992. The problem of pattern and scale in ecology. *Ecology* 73: 1943-1967.

Mäler, K.G. and Jeffrey R. Vincent Handbook of Environmental Economics, Volume 2 : Valuing Environmental Changes (*Handbooks in Economics*). North Holland, Amsterdam.

Martinez-Alier, J., G. Munda and J. O'Neill. 1998. Weak comparability of values as a foundation for ecological economics. *Ecological Economics*, 26(3): 277-286.

Millennium Ecosystem Assessment, 2003. Ecosystems and human well-being: a framework for assessment. *Report of the conceptual framework working group of the Millennium Ecosystem Assessment*. Island Press, Washington, DC.

Ministerio del Medio Ambiente, 2002. Inventario nacional de eosion de suelos 2002-2003. Ministerio del Medio Ambiente, Madrid.

Munasinghe, M. and A. Schwab, 1993. *Environmental economics and natural resource management in developing countries*. World Bank, Washington, DC.

Munda, G. 2004. Social multi-criteria evaluation (SMCE): methodological foundations and operational consequences. *European Journal of Operational Research*. 158 (3): 662-677.

Nordhaus, W.D., 1994. *Managing the global commons: the economics of climate change*. MIT Press, Cambridge, USA.

OECD, 1995. *The economic appraisal of environmental projects and policies, a practical guide*. OECD, Paris.

Oñate, J.J., Peco, B., Sánchez, A. and Sumpsi, J.M. 2003. Report on the results of the farm questionnaire survey in the Guadalentín target area. Deliverable 20. Medaction: *Policies for land use to combat desertification*. Madrid.

O'Neill, R.V. and A.W. King, 1998. *Hommage to St Michael: or why are there so many books on scale?* In: D.L. Peterson and V.T. Parker (editors) Ecological scale: theory and applications. Columbia University Press, New York, pp 3-15.

O'Neill, J. 2001. 'Representing People, Representing Nature, Representing the World', *Environment and Planning C: Government and Policy*, 19: 483-500.

O'Riordan, T., C. Cooper, A. Jordan, S. Rayner, K Richards, P. Runci and S. Yoffe, 1998. *Institutional frameworks for political action*. In: Human choice and climate change, Vol. 1: The societal framework. Battelle Press, Columbus, OH, pp. 345-439.

Pagiola, S. and G. Platais. 2002. *Market-based Mechanisms for Conservation and Development:* The Simple Logic of Payments for Environmental Services. In Environmental Matters–Annual Review, July 2001–June 2002 (FY 2002). Washington, DC: World Bank's Environment Department.

Pearce, D.W., A. Markandya, and E.B. Barbier, 1989. *Blueprint for a green economy*. Earthscan, London.

Pearce, D.W., and R.K. Turner, 1990. *Economics of natural resources and the environment*. Harvester Wheatsheaf, Herfordshire, UK.

Pearce, D.W. and C.G.T. Pearce, 2001. *The value of forest ecosystems. A report to the Secretariat of the Convention on Biological Diversity*, Montreal, Canada

Pimentel D, Harvey C, Resosudarmo P, Sinclair K, Kunz D, McNair M, Crist S, Shpritz L, Fitton L, Saouri R, Blair R. 1995. Environmental and economic costs of soil erosion and conservation benefits. Science 267: 1117–1123.

Posey, D.A., 1999. Cultural and spiritual values of biodiversity. *A complementary contribution to the Global Biodiversity Assessment*. Intermediate Technology Publications, London.

Tietenberg, T.H., 2000. *Environmental and Natural Resource Economics (5th edition).* Addison Wesley Longman, Inc., Reading, Massachusetts, USA.

Turner, R.K., C.J.M. van den Bergh, T. Soderqvist, A. Barendregt, J. van der Straaten, E. Maltby, E.C. van Ierland, 2000: Ecological-economic analysis of wetlands: scientific integration for management and policy. *Ecological Economics* 35: 7-23.

Wathern, P., S.N. Young, I.W. Brown and D.A. Roberts, 1986. *Ecological evaluation tecniques. Landscape Planning* 12: 403-420.

Wesemael, B., Cammeraat, E.H., Mulligan, M., Burke, S., 2003. The impact of soil properties and topography on drought vulnerability of rainfed cropping systems in southern Spain. Agric., *Ecosyst. Environ.* 94: 1-15.

ANNEX 1. ECONOMIC VALUATION OF SELECTED ENVIRONMENTAL FUNCTIONS IN THE PUENTES CATCHMENT, SPAIN

Table A.1.1. Agriculture[1]

Function	Average revenue[2] (€/ha/y)	Production costs[3] (€/ha/y)	Economic value generated (€/ha/y)
Irrigated agriculture			
- broccoli, artichoke	7525	6177	1348
- olives	3544	3263	281
Dryland agriculture			
- almonds	404	429	175
- olives	945	809	136
- wheat and barley	131	161	-30

Key:

1. In order to calculate the economic value, subsidies have been excluded from the calculations (which causes the economic value of cereal production to be negative).
2. Market revenues. These are obtained by multiplying average production (kg/ha/year) with the average prices for the crops (euro/kg). Production and price data are from Comarcal (2003) and Lopez Bermudez (1999).
3. Production costs. These include both variable costs (seeds, fertilisers, pesticides, water, labour) and fixed costs (depreciation, at 10% per year, of machinery and the irrigation system). The costs of labour are from Comarcal (2003). The other cost figures have been obtained through interviews with 40 farmers in the study area.

Table A2.2. Grazing

	Sheep	Goats	Total	Source
1. Total number of animals	12,811	3,724		Comarcal, 2003
2. Birth rate	1.3	1.3		Interviews pastoralists
3. Number of animals born	13,879	4,034		Row 1 x row 2
4. Required for replacement (20%)	2,562	745		Interviews pastoralists
5. Animals sold per year	11,317	3,289		Row 3 – row 4
6. Price per animal (euro)	50	60		Interviews pastoralists
7. Total revenues (euro/year)	565,840	197,352	763,192	Row 5 x row 6

Table A2.2. (Continued)

	Sheep	Goats	Total	Source
8. Revenues supplied through grazing (75%)			572,394	Interviews of the pastoralists showed that 75% of the feed is from grazing, 25% is supplementary feed
9. Labour costs (24 pastoralists)			360,000	Shadow costs of labour per person (Comarcal, 2003)
10. Total (€/year)			212,394	Row 8 – row 9
11. Total (€/ha/year)			15.6 €/ha/year	Divided by 13590 (total area dryland agriculture + shrubland, see table 2)

INDEX

A

B

C

D

G

H

I

J

K

L

M

N

O

P

Q

R

S

T

U

V

W

Y

Z